A FAR PLACE

Historical Novel

2nd Edition

1894 - 1965

JOHN and MARY WESTERHOFF WAMHOFF

JUNE 22, 1894 – FORT WAYNE, INDIANA

Author's paternal grandparents

Scripture quotations are taken from the King James Version of the HOLY BIBLE. Permission, all rights reserved to utilize unrestricted internet photos issued under the expiration of the statute of limitations except where protected.

The opinions expressed by the author are not necessarily those of Green Spring Publishing, Windsor, Colorado.

The depiction of actual people was derived from family letters, stories, official documents, and writings of the era. Most of the events in this book are centered around actual events. Where ever there were conflicting versions, the author relied upon imagination and personal interpretation or motives.

ISBN for printed material: 978-0-9904096-5-6

ISBN for e-book version: 978-0-9904096-6-3

Author's photograph: Clayton Jenkins Photography.
Fort Collins, Colorado

Cover Photo used with permission from Jerry Ewen,
Shell, Wyoming

Cover Design: Karen Schutte

Interior Layout Design: Elizabeth Klenda, Frontier Printing.
Fort Collins, Colorado

Interior photos are the personal property of the author unless otherwise stated and used with the permission of the original owner.

About the Cover

Talented photographer, Jerry Ewen was born in Greybull, Wyoming, and grew up on a ranch near Shell, Wyoming. He graduated from Greybull High School and attended North Western Community college in Powell, Wyoming. In 1967 he enlisted in the Army, graduating from Army Helicopter Flight School in 1968. Jerry served one year in Vietnam as an evacuation helicopter pilot where he completed 1,121 combat missions flying a UH-1H "Huey". He received 21 awards, including the Air Medal, Army Commendation Medal, and Purple Heart.

After his discharge in 1970, Jerry worked in civilian aviation as a helicopter pilot. Changing professions, he spent the next twenty years as a self-employed home contractor. He is also a published author---*Chicken Soup for the Veteran's Soul.*

Jerry and his wife Kathy have been married for 53 years and live at the foot of the Bighorn Mountains in Shell, Wyoming on the ranch where he grew up. They are the parents of three children and seven grandchildren. Jerry has avidly pursued amateur photography as a lifelong hobby. He admits he loves to photograph anything and everything; he has an endearing love of all things Wyoming.

NOTE: When I saw this photograph which Jerry Ewen had taken, I knew in an instant that this, was the cover I wanted for my book---- A FAR PLACE. It spoke to me as I am sure it speaks to you. I thank Jerry Ewen for his service to this country and for the permission to use this beautiful photograph.

Novels by Karen Schutte

Historical Fiction

<u>Maternal Family Saga:</u>

THE TICKET – 2010
Awarded 1st in Historical Fiction
Wyoming Historical Society

SEED OF THE VOLGA – 2013
Finalist – Pen/Faulkner Award for Fiction
One of 7 Finalists – National Indie Excellence Awards

FLESH ON THE BONE – 2014
Awarded 1st in Historical Fiction,
Wyoming Historical Society;
USA Book Awards – Finalist;
Top four Nationally Cover design
& Top seven Historical Fiction.

TANK COMMANDER – 2016
Best Book Awards – Finalist
Top 3 Nationally for Cover Design
Top 6 for Historical Fiction

<u>Paternal Family Saga:</u>

GERMAN YANKEE – 2018

*A FAR PLACE – 2020

To the Reader

As the sequel to GERMAN YANKEE, this book will be the final addition to my paternal family saga series, a direct circumstance of literally running out of family stories.

So many people have contributed to the writing of this book, especially my husband Mike and our Shih Tzu, Sofie, who allowed me time away from them and other duties, to write. In my research, I uncovered more information about my grandfather, John Wamhoff, than I believe my father, Arnold Wamhoff, was ever aware of or shared with us. He admired his father greatly but knew little about his background or his childhood except for the fact that John grew up with several stepmothers. John Wamhoff left a fractured home at an early age to pursue a life of his own making, to fulfill his dreams. He was a man of many hats, characters, and ambitions.

Mary Wamhoff was without a doubt the sweetest most genteel woman I have ever known. Against her desire, she left an established home/life in Germantown\Garland, NE., where she grew up. It wasn't her dream—to follow her husband to the wilds of rural Wyoming and to endure the hardships of establishing a new life there, away from everything and everyone she loved.

We read about my grandmother, Mary (Mazzie) Westerhoff Wamhoff in GERMAN YANKEE. We take up the story of John and Mary Wamhoff shortly after their elopement to Fort Wayne, Indiana, on June 23, 1894. I chose not to change the names of the characters in my last two novels. Eternal thanks to my mother, Beata Wamhoff who gave me the precious gift of the family photo album. Also, for the priceless interview with my father, Arnold Wamhoff, before he died in 2003.

The first step was to sort through and chronologically arrange the daunting stacks of historical information/files. I was fortunate to have access to several extensive reference/historical books about Emblem, WY. Two of them were written by Emblem authors—Jeannie Edwards Cook – **Wiley's Dream of an Empire,** and Tom Davis - **They Called it Germania**.

As I began writing this sixth book, I contemplated the length of time it would take to write. As it turned out, COVID 19 hit, and

I had plenty of time on my hands. Writing is truly a journey of discovery, a leap of faith, devotion, and persistence. As I have discovered while writing my other novels, at a certain point the story takes hold of the reins. The story develops a pulse---it has a specific rhythm, its own pace. I was excited as the familiar rhythm of organization and writing consumed me. A page at a time, a day at a time, a month at a time. In the end, as I wrote the final page, I continued to be filled with wonder as to how each of my books was 'born'.

To my village of exceptional technical readers and historical editors, and those who helped me along the way---I owe my deepest gratitude. I pay tribute to my grandparents for embracing the venture of leaving a comfortable life in Nebraska to homestead in the wilds of Wyoming. Finally, to all of you who enjoy my books---you have made my dream come true by liking what I do and by telling me in so many ways. As movie star Sally Field declared as she accepted her Oscar, "You like me----You really like me!"   Thank you!

NOTE: The accepted spelling of the proper name Big Horn RE: mountains, river, county, has been changed to Bighorn.

<u>WAMHOFF</u> – Family Name History

The German surname Wamhoff is of local German origin, belonging to the category of surnames derived from a particular geographical feature, either man-made or natural, near which the original bearer once lived or held land. In this case, this surname derived from the Old High German "wame, wane" meaning swampy, marshy, and "hof" which originally denoted a yard or enclosure, and also farm. Thus the name indicates "one who dwelled on a farm situated on the marshy ground. In some instances, the name is derived from the first name of the father of the initial bearer. Here the name denotes "son of Wamhoff", a corruption of the ancient personal name Wanulf, composed of the Old High German words 'man' meaning 'hope, expectation' and 'wulf', meaning wolf. In time, this given name became corrupted to Wannlof, Wanhoff, Wemhoff, and Wamhoff.

Today this surname is more common in the United States than it is in the land of its origin, Germany.

~~~~~~~~

Great-grandfather, Wilhelm Wamhoff:

Historical Information on Wilhelm Wamhoff*: Given Name: Heinrich Diederich Wilhelm Christian Wimhoff; May 28, 1817; Birth Place: Aplerbeck, Westfalen, Preussen, Germany. Father's name: Heinrich Wilhelm Wimhoff; Mother's name: Maria Christina Knippenberg.*

Death Date: September 22, 1897, in Dorr, Allegan, Michigan. He was 80 years old, occupation—farmer and businessman.

NOTE: Passenger lists show that on October 15, 1853, Wilhelm Wimhoff (spelling may have been changed at Castle Gardens Emigrant Center)--- a 36-year old farmer from Hannover, Germany, wife Julia 28, and infant Elise, arrived on the ship, 'Orphan' which sailed from Bremerhaven to New York. Records indicate his birthdate as 1818; literacy – unknown; he traveled in steerage under affiliate manifest ID – 00007646 and affiliate ARC identifier 1746067.

~~~~~~~

1870 U.S. Census: Fort Wayne, Indiana: William Wamhoff, age 52; laborer of a harness and fur shop, the value of said real estate $2000; the reported value of personal property $600; living with daughter Mary (1856), age 14 keeping house; son 'John Henry' (1866), age 4; and Jim Klang, age 74, a friend from Hannover.

Note: Mary and **John Henry** were both born in the United States.

There is no indication of what happened to William Wamhoff's wife Julia and infant daughter Elise, neither are mentioned in the 1970 Census. William married shortly after Julia died, perhaps after she gave birth to John. Official records in the Fort Wayne, Indiana Registrar's office, show the official marriage document for William Wamhoff and Sophia Dasler in 1880. One daughter was born to this union and Sophia later died; there is no note as to divorce. William married again in 1884 to Ernestine Brandt and there were three daughters born to this union (I have found no further reference to them). **John Henry Wamhoff** would have been eighteen years old at that time, about the age when he left the family home.

A prior U.S. Census indicates that William Wamhoff remained as the proprietor of a fur/harness store in Fort Wayne. The Nebraska Census of 1885 for Precinct H, Seward, Nebraska indicates the following: William Wamhoff, 67, farmer, Ernestine Wamhoff, 51; Sophia Wamhoff, 15; John Wamhoff, 19; Mary Bultemeier, 29; Clara Bultemeier, 3; Emma Bultemeier, 1.

A FAR PLACE

Prologue

1894: Each time Mazzie stole a glance at the dashing young man standing across the dance hall, his brazen stare, unsettled her. Mazzie whispered discreetly to her younger sister, "Emma, that, that dark-haired fellow standing next to brother Willie---he, he continues to look this way. Do you know who he is?"

Emma looked across the crowded floor and her eyes twinkled with amusement. "I certainly do. He has quite a reputation with the ladies in the county. You don't know who he is? For heaven's sake, Mazzie, you need to get out more! You are such an innocent!"

Mazzie felt a warm flush spreading over her as she fidgeted in her pale blue silk dress. "Land sakes Emma, you say the most outlandish things, ever. What in the world would someone like him, see in me? He's obviously much older than I and quite the dandy. I'm just a plain farm girl from Garland."

Emma turned and looked at her older sister in dismay. "Plain, farm girl?" Have you taken a good look in the mirror lately? You are a stunningly beautiful girl, Mazzie. I notice all the boys' heads turn when you walk by and you are simply oblivious!"

~~~~~~~~

Emma poked Mazzie in the ribs, "Well, don't look now, but brother Willie is bringing that handsome devil this way. Press your lips tightly to get more color in them and for pity's sake, pinch your cheeks. You look positively pale!"

Catching his sister's eye, Willie Westerhoff and his friend pushed through the crowd until they stood in front of the young women. The well-dressed man beside Willie reeked of confidence and attitude. His liquid blue eyes sparkled as he nonchalantly flicked the ash from his cigar. Mazzie felt her insides tingle and she feared she might even swoon.

Touching her on the elbow, Willie nodded to Mazzie and winked. "Miss Mary Elizabeth Westerhoff, I would like you to meet a friend of mine who has taken great interest in making your acquaintance. May I present, the honorable John Henry Wamhoff?"

~~~~~~~

John's blue eyes sparkled brightly with mirth as he bowed deeply. Without hesitation or permission, he took Mazzie's hand in his and very slowly, put his lips to her soft skin—lingering a moment longer than was proper. Mazzie felt her insides quiver with excitement. Her full pink lips curled ever so slightly in a demure smile and her soft blue eyes twinkled with amusement. She managed to reply coyly, "I am most pleased to meet you, Mr. Wamhoff. Do you live here in Seward or are you passing through?"

John cocked his head, his eyes questioned her intent. "Why of course, I live here, and please call me John. I own a small business in Garland as well as farming in Precinct H. We moved here from Fort Wayne, Indiana several years ago. We find the region quite promising and it is hard to believe you and I have not met before this evening."

Without further chitchat, John made his move. Taking Mary by the elbow, he propelled her to the porch. "Miss Mary, would you care to take in a bit of air? You look somewhat pale?"

Once outside, John wasted no time, "Ahhh, the cool breeze is most welcome. It was becoming quite stuffy inside the dance hall. If, I may be so blunt----I---."

Mazzie took two steps backward and lifting her defiant chin, her eyes narrowed and shot fire. "Mr. Wamhoff, let me make something clear, something you have gravely misconstrued. I most definitely am not the swooning female you perceive me to be. I have five brothers and I am quite familiar with the ways of men. Do not make the mistake of thinking you can 'sweet talk' me. I guarantee I have a much stronger will and intellect and am not easily swayed. On the other hand, I find you quite interesting." She turned to depart, then swirled unexpectedly to face him. "I would caution you to take your time. You move much too fast."

John Wamhoff's expression appeared as though she had slapped him, then his lips curled in slight amusement and stirred intrigue. "Miss Mary Elizabeth, I apologize most sincerely if I came across as being---well bold and presumptuous. I promise I will try my best to proceed with caution if that is what you expect."

Mary smiled sweetly and touch his cheek with her finger. "That is, precisely, what I expect Mr. Wamhoff, precisely. I bid you a good evening, I am sure you have other conquests awaiting."

~~~~~~~~~

Several days later, Elizabeth asked Mary to walk with her into the village to pick up a few things. They stopped at the grocer's and Mary spied some fresh spinach which she put into the basket for dinner. Elizabeth paid for the food and as they strolled down the boardwalk, they came to the new furniture store. "Oh mercy, look at that small chair in the window! I haven't been inside this store. Let's go in and see how much that chair is. I've been wanting just the thing to put in the corner of my bedroom!"

Mary held the door open for her mother as they strolled into the dimly lit store. Elizabeth headed directly toward the window where the chair was displayed; while Mary turned the other way and walked down the aisle, taking in the clever manner in which the owner displayed groupings of complementary furniture. Sensing someone behind her, Mary whirled and came face to face with John Wamhoff. "Wha—what are you doing in this furniture store?"

John smiled proudly as he said, "I own this furniture store, Miss Mary. I told you the other night, I had business interests in Garland besides farming with my father. I also provide another service for the community in that I am the mortician when needed."

Mary's hand flew to cover her mouth. Her blue eyes opened wide with amazement and shock as she managed somehow to stammer, "You---You own, this store and, ---? How—why, would you want to be a mortician? I can't imagine doing that."

John smiled as Mary struggled to regain her composure, "Yes, well, Miss Mary, I must excuse myself as I think I have a customer upfront---who is your mother, is she not?"

Mary followed at a discreet distance as John approached her mother, allowing her to examine the chair. "Good day, Mrs. Westerhoff, I see you have exceedingly good taste. That particular chair is quite a favorite of mine as well. If you would like, I would be most happy to deliver it to your home tomorrow morning. You can observe how it looks in your room; and if it meets your approval, then we can discuss the price."

On their walk home, Elizabeth turned to Mary who was walking beside her in an obvious daze. "Mary, what has come over you? You are simply all aflutter. Is it that young man in the furniture store? I must admit he is quite the charmer and a very good salesman. It didn't go unnoticed that he watched every move you made. I assume you have met him before?"

Mary tried to laugh gaily, "Oh Mama, for pity's sake. He's just a fellow I met at the dance a week or so ago. There is nothing shy about him, is there? I have concluded he's quite full of himself." Elizabeth couldn't help but smile and speculate that her daughter may have met her match.

~~~~~~~~

The next morning Mary took more time with dressing and her hairstyle than normal; which did not go unnoticed as sister Emma watched her. "Oh Mary, my word—there are two, no wait---three hairs out of place! I know, why you are taking so much time with yourself today, your beau is delivering a chair for Mama!"

Emma watched as Mary perfected her appearance and then blurted out, "Mary, I know it's none of my business, but what is it that infatuates you so with this John Wamhoff? If I were you, I would watch my step with him."

Mary blushed as she turned and said, "Oh Emma, it's his city manners. He doesn't wipe his nose on his sleeve or his pants. He doesn't have to be told to wipe his feet at the door; he doesn't spit that dreadful tobacco juice and---" Mary began to giggle--- "he doesn't break wind in the presence of a lady!"

The two sisters hugged and headed for the stairs. Mary gave Emma a playful pinch as she skipped gaily down the stairs, just in time to see John walk through the door carrying her mother's new chair. Mary stood to the side as John positioned the chair and explained its construction. As he was getting ready to leave, he pulled her aside and said, "Miss Mary, would you like to go on a picnic with me tomorrow? It's my day off and it looks to be a beautiful day."

In the months ahead, the two of them were inseparable - going to dances, horseback riding, long walks, picnics, and family gatherings. She tried to hold John off but found herself looking forward to spending more and more time with him.

~~~~~~~~~

One evening after the supper dishes were washed and put away, Mary sat on the front porch with her mother, helping her roll yarn into balls. Elizabeth said, "Mary, I can't help but notice how much time you are spending with John Wamhoff. What do you know about him except that he is Lutheran and seems to be a hard worker? His people don't come from around here and he, uhhh, seems rather aggressive in his manner."

Mary stopped rolling the yarn and put her head down as if to think. She raised her head slowly, her face was flushed and her blue eyes were moist with tears. "Mama, I have never felt like this about a boy, a man---before. I don't know if I am in love with John, but Mama---I don't want to be away from him. There is, like---almost an electric current between us. He is so clever, such a hard worker, he has so many ambitions, dreams of things he wants to do, and what he wants in life. I----I think Mama, that I might be in love? Is this what being in love feels like?"

Elizabeth took Mary's hand in hers and said, "Mary, dear girl, you are only seventeen. You won't be eighteen until March. You haven't dated many boys. You really should 'smell a few flowers' before you pick one!"

Mary thought for a moment then said, "When you and Pap were married, you were only eighteen as well and he is ten years older than you, just like John is ten years older than I am."

"I urge you to make sure, to take your time, Mary. Marriage is wonderful, but it is hard. It takes a lot out of a woman---bearing and caring for children, the endless work, being a wife. But, if and when you find the right man, you will know---yes, you will know! Take your time, girl promise me that. If you do decide to marry him, your life won't be easy because he is an ambitious man and I for one know about living with an ambitious man. They are driven, and as the years go by you sometimes feel like an afterthought."

~~~~~~~~

Three weeks after Mary turned eighteen on the 5th of March, John invited her for a buggy ride into Seward. A sleek roan horse pulled the black, 2-seated buggy over the dirt road, up and down the rolling hills of Nebraska. Mary decided this was the perfect opportunity to ask John about his family. "John, why don't you ever talk about your family, like I do?"

John pulled the buggy off into a grove of eastern cottonwood trees where the tiny spring green leaves twinkled with the breeze and sprouts of new grass pushed up through the soil. He wrapped the reins around the brake post, then turned to Mary. He took her small hand in his. "Mary, my dear, It is quite simple. I didn't have an idyllic childhood like the one you have had. My mother died after I was born. My father remarried shortly after my mother died. He worked long hours in his fur shop and expected my ten-year old sister, Mary, to care for me. She is the one who raised me. She was the only one who gave me any sort of love. As soon as she became of age, she ran off and married, and I never saw her again. I never experienced a parent's love or tenderness. My father was hard, cold, and not interested in a sniveling child. He kept trying marriage; when I was, oh, about five, he married again. I took it for a while - the beatings, the exclusion---and my father never said a word in my favor. My stepmother was the meanest, nastiest woman there ever was and she made my life miserable. Sophia, died in childbirth when I was sixteen and I wasn't sorry---I know that might shock you Mary, but it was an abrupt and welcome end to my torment."

John ran his fingers through his thick head of hair. "After Sophia, my father married Ernestine. I was eighteen and that's when I left home and struck out on my own to make my own way. I guess he had a good enough marriage with her and over time they had three little girls. I'm not sure what went on or didn't, but pretty soon there was a woman by the name of Bultimier and she came with a couple of little ones as well. I don't know, I can't tell you who was who and what the circumstances of his life were after I left home. My father is ---- well, he's a complicated man who takes what he wants and he moves through life like a bull in a china shop, not caring who or what he hurts."

John paused to clear his head. "Mary, I'm not like my father. I care about people and about what people think of me. I greatly admire your father, John Westerhoff and I guess one might say he is someone I would wish to pattern my life after. I don't want you to be afraid of getting close to me because of my family. I don't want anything to do with them. All I know is that I want to marry you in the worst way. I also want to be able to give you a good life. I tell you this now---I will be a good husband to you if you will have me. Mary, I love you---I think I have loved you from the first moment I set eyes on you. You complete me, Mary, in every way. I know you just turned eighteen and some may think that it is too young, but I would like for us to marry as soon as you are ready. We could live above the furniture store. I make a very good living and can provide for your every want."

"I don't want my family involved in our lives; so, perhaps that means eventually we may move away from here. Say yes, my beautiful Mary! Say you will marry me!"

"Oh John, my John---yes, yes, yes---I will marry you. You tell me the time and the place---perhaps we should elope? That way, it will be 'our' day only."

~~~~~~~

Fort Wayne, Indiana---June 23, 1894: Mary's long silky burnt gold hair tumbled in soft waves over the pillow as she wiped the sleep from her eyes and stretched her slender arms over her head. Slowly, she brought her hand down and gazed at the gold ring on her left finger. One long shapely leg stuck out from the rumpled bedsheets, as she lay back watching her husband light his cigar. "How am I going to explain this to my parents?"

John Wamhoff moved to the edge of the bed and wrapping his fingers in her thick hair, he pulled Mary to him. "I can't believe we are husband and wife. I am sure some members of our families will be disappointed, perhaps even angry that we have gone off by ourselves to marry. But my love, it is the way we wanted to start our life together---just the two of us. I have our return tickets on the train. We leave in the morning for Germantown."

Chapter One

NEW BEGINNINGS

The new Mrs.Wamhoff's hands shook as she nervously fidgeted with her gloves. She dreaded facing her parents with the news that she and John had married without their presence. Mary hoped the letter she had sent ahead had accomplished its intended task and softened the shock of their elopement. She caressed the carved gold band on her left finger, gazing at it and daydreaming about how different her life would be now that she was married. She turned her head ever so slightly and out of the corner of her eye, watched her husband, John. *Oh my, he is so handsome, so dear. I will go to my grave trying to understand why he chose me for his wife.*

They disembarked from the train. John picked up their suitcases and together they strolled down the street toward his store. He led her inside and they walked through the aisles, directly towards the stairs in the back which led up to his apartment. At the top of the stairs, John sat the suitcases down and before Mary could respond, he swooped her off her feet and carried her through the doorway into what would be their first home. With her arms tightly around his neck, Mary laughed gaily and buried her face in his coat, then kissed him tenderly as he lowered her to the floor.

"Dear wife, at your convenience, you may go downstairs and choose the furniture you want, to make this apartment comfortable. However, remember we are on a budget, so you must not get carried away just yet. Please leave some of the furniture to sell." John walked to the front window and looked out onto the street below. "As soon as possible, I plan to buy a small house; but for now this will have to do."

Mary was all smiles as she peeked into the small rooms of their apartment. "Oh, John, this is perfect for now, just perfect. I can hardly contain myself---to think I can choose a few pieces of furniture for our home right away. I am so happy John, so very happy!"

~~~~~~~

Early the next morning, after enjoying a leisurely breakfast, and discussed how they should tell her parents. Mary felt it was up to her to break the news.

The dew-filled morning air was filled with twittering birds as Mary walked purposely along the boardwalk. As she turned the corner and crossed the main road, she looked ahead into the Westerhoff barnyard where chickens were busy, clucking, and scratching for their breakfast. Mary swallowed twice before she pushed open the white picket gate and walked to the back door where she paused, steeling herself for the anticipated confrontation. Quietly she pushed it open and stepped onto the back porch. She paused and watched her mother as she stood at the sink, singing softly as she washed the breakfast dishes. Mary stepped into the room and paused, watching her mother perform a task she must have done thousands of times over the years.

"Mama---Mama, it's me!"

Startled, Elizabeth dropped a dish into the dishwater. She turned slowly as she and her daughter locked eyes. Mary felt a huge lump in her throat and her heart was beating out of her chest. "Mama, I hope you can forgive me. I love him, Mama I love him so very very much! I'm sorry you had to find out by letter. I had to let you know before we came back."

Elizabeth smiled and opened her arms as her middle child filled them and wept on her shoulder. Elizabeth settled Mary at the kitchen table and filled a cup of hot coffee for her. "Sit, Mazzie, and we will talk." Elizabeth gave Mary a moment and then she said, "So, you are a married woman. I hope with all my heart that you are happy and you never have any regrets about the way you and John married. You realize your life will never be the same again. You have new responsibilities now that you have somebody else to look after, to cook and wash for, to comfort, to have children with. Your life will never be your own again, Mazzie---you will have moments of solace, but they will be very few. Marriage is hard work, it is wonderful, it is fulfilling---the children are blessings. If he is as honorable a man as your father, then you will have a good life and you will be able to work through the hard times. You have grown up around your father so you know how difficult an ambitious man can be at times. You will have your challenges but if the Lord smiles down on you, you will also have great rewards. Patience and trust, Mazzie---those are two things you must have and they are also two things which don't come easy for you." She smiled as she said, "Your husband doesn't know what challenges he faces with you as his wife either. Try to remember that he is the head of your household—not your boss, but your partner!"

Elizabeth smiled and said, "Now, tell me about your wedding."

Mary looked at her mother and beamed with newly-wedded bliss. "Eloping seemed the best way to marry. Of course, we both wanted you there on our wedding day, but John didn't want his family---it's a complicated matter. It made sense to do it our way and we had a wonderful, exciting trip to Fort Wayne. I got to see where he grew up and lived when he was young. He had such a difficult childhood—never knowing the love you and Pap gave me. I want to make the rest of our life together, better for him. I love him more than I ever knew I could love somebody. If anyone is to understand that, I know it will be you."

Mary and her mother chatted for a few more minutes and then Mary asked, "Where is Pap?"

Elizabeth rose from the table and pointed to the barn. "He's feeding the cows out in his barn." She paused then added, "He took the news harder than I did. You know you were always his favorite little girl. He is trying hard to accept it---I just want you to understand that." She started to turn to go back to her dishes and then said, "Why don't you and John come for supper tonight---fried chicken and new potatoes!"

Mary kissed her mother, then pushing the screen door open, she started toward the big red horse barn. Standing in the doorway to the horse barn, she closed her eyes, breathing in the familiar smells of the barn and the corrals. She stepped cautiously onto the well-worn path down the center between the stalls. Mary heard him talking to the horses before she saw him. She moved past the horse stalls until she came to the one where he worked. She paused, "Pap---Pap, it's me---Mazzie."

The silence was deafening as Mary waited for her father to turn and acknowledge her. "Pap, please talk to me—I didn't mean to disappoint you. I love John and---eloping---eloping was the only way for us to be together. Mama was the same age when she fell in love with you, Pap. Surely you remember those days and those feelings. Give us your blessing Pap, it's important to both of us. John admires you so very much—he never had a father like you— he was never loved by a parent like I was. He's ambitious and a hard worker, just like you, Pap. Maybe that's part of why I love him so— because he is somewhat familiar. He works hard and has dreams of having his own place, his own life, of being important in the community--just like you."

John Westerhoff stabbed the pitchfork into the hay. He turned and held his arms out to his middle daughter. Mary saw the tears in his blue eyes and his weathered face grimace with emotion as she moved into the familiar fold of her father's arms.

They stood like that for a while, each trying to gain control over their emotions before speaking. Finally, John pushed Mazzie back and looked at her tear-stained face. "Mazzie, Mazzie, my girl. Now, you are a woman, a wife---not my little girl anymore. I wasn't ready to give you up—not yet. But you've always had a mind of your own and what you did was not unexpected. You always see and do things differently, according to what is in your heart and head; this was no different." John led her over to a bench where they sat.

"Mazzie, I don't know your husband, pure and simple. I am holding my opinion until I get to know him. I do see he is already prosperous and ambitious---farming, running that store, and taking on mortician duties when called upon. I hearsay he is also Lutheran, so that is a plus for you. At least you will go to the same church."

John reached down and took her left hand, touching the gold ring. "You are still my girl, but now, another man's wife. I'll always remember our good times and the bad ones too, like that blizzard when by God's grace, we found you, your brother and sister."

Mazzie reached up and laid her hand against her father's whiskery cheek. "Pap, you've always been there for me, my hero---you have been my rock and you always made me feel loved and special. I am and always will be so very proud to be your daughter. Just because I went and got married, that won't change, Pap, you are my father. I'll always love you and Mama."

Mary dabbed at the tears on her cheeks and said, "Mama invited us to supper tonight. That will give you all a chance to get to know John a little better. I've got to run now, have shopping to do before John is through working for the day. I love you Pap!"

Mary hurried through the open barn door as her emotions began to rise in her throat. After a bit, she stepped off the road, and in the seclusion of the lilac bushes, she fell to her knees as great wrenching sobs erupted from deep within. When she had released the pent-up emotion, she rose and stepped back out onto the road, back to town. Quickly wiping the tears from her face, Mary headed for the furniture store. She pushed open the door and listened to the familiar tinkle of the bell which announced the arrival of a customer. John looked up from where he was working on his books. He stood as Mary rushed into his arms. Neither spoke until Mary said, "They were wonderful John, so caring—we even have an invitation to a fried chicken supper at six if that works for you?"

The days and weeks seemed to fly by. Mary helped John in the furniture store when he needed her. She caught on fast and was as good a salesperson as was he. She enjoyed unpacking new pieces and helping John arrange groupings of furniture so the customers could imagine how they would look in their own homes. Mary took on a second job at the post office, helping to sort and place mail. She liked to keep busy and her savings jar was beginning to fill.

~~~~~~~~

August: John rose early and went down to the store to work on his books and orders, leaving Mary to sleep in. She woke around 7:30 feeling guilty for having slept so late. Mary climbed out of bed, threw on her robe, and headed for the kitchen to fix their breakfast. It wasn't until she cracked the second egg into the frying pan that a flood of nausea hit her and she barely made it to the slop bucket. Mary curled up on their bed as tears rolled down her cheeks. She knew what was wrong. She knew she wasn't 'coming down with something'. No, 'this' was something that normally lasted nine months. *I had so hoped that we wouldn't have children right away, but if I figure correctly, I must have gotten pregnant on our wedding trip. Well, it is what it is and I must make the best out of it now.*

~~~~~~~~

In late August, John and Mary were invited to the Westerhoff home for another Sunday dinner. Mary had recovered from her 'morning ailments' and was feeling wonderful. Before they sat down to eat, John Westerhoff gave a moving prayer of thanksgiving for the blessings of the past year. Mary and her husband looked at each other and smiled---as they had agreed to wait until after dinner to share their news.

After dessert, John Westerhoff made a motion to move his chair back. John Wamhoff stood quickly and cleared his throat. "Uhh, before everyone leaves the table, Mary and I have an announcement to make for which we are most thankful." He held out his hand for her to stand beside him. "We expect our first child in March."

Mary's pregnancy went as smooth as syrup. After the initial morning sickness, she felt fine and the doctor said she was quite healthy. She and John were amazed at how her stomach grew and when the baby began to move, they would lay in bed and watch an elbow, a tiny foot, or whatever it was move inside of her. Mary sewed and learned to knit clothes for her baby. She didn't care if it was a boy or a girl, she only prayed for a healthy baby and an easy delivery.

Mary spent the morning working on baby clothes. After a light lunch, she laid down for a nap. When she woke, she began to stand up when she felt an odd tightness in her stomach. It passed and so she didn't give it any more thought. *I have felt different lately, I can't put my finger on it, but just not right? Now that I think of it, the baby hasn't been moving as much as it did for a while, but then I don't know if that is normal or not? Maybe when the area gets a bit cramped it can't move as much.*

Mary did some laundry, then arranged a chest filled with clothes and nappies for the new baby. The birth was almost five weeks off, but Mary noticed she had been spotting blood for a week or two---*it's probably normal. I'll ask Mama when I see her tomorrow.* Mary bent over to pick up a tea towel --- from under her dress a gush of water ran down her legs. She immediately knew what had happened. She dropped the towel and doubled over with a contraction. "No, oh---NO---it's too soon----I know it's too soon!"

John wasn't working down in the furniture store like he usually did---he had gone out to the farm to help his father with a few things and wasn't due back until supper time. Mary knew this was not a false alarm---this baby was not waiting. She gathered her things together and prepared to walk to her parent's home where her mother would know what to do. Mary moved to the top of the stairs and looked down to see if she could see the new store clerk. "Homer, Homer---can you ---arrgh---can you come up here and help me down the stairs?"

Mary heard Homer take the stairs, two at a time. "What is it, Miss Mary?" The words were no sooner out of his mouth when she doubled over with another contraction. Mary's face was ashen as she managed to stammer, "Oh, Homer---Hom-mer—it's the baby! It's too soon, Homer. I need to walk over to my parent's house—I need my mother."

Homer's eyes opened wide, then his mouth--but nothing came out. Suddenly he got his wits about him and he stammered, "Ohhh, Mrs.---What do you want me to do?"

Mary handed him her valise and said, "Let me take your arm to steady myself. You must help me down the stairs and over to my parent's house if you would be so kind." Homer held tightly onto Mary's arm as they descended the stairs and made their way through to the front door. Before they went out he hung a 'Closed' sign in the door, then they proceeded slowly down the boardwalk and across the street. When they reached the other side, Mary grabbed onto a tree as another pain ripped through her.

"Oh, Homer, is it too late to change my mind about having a baby?"

Homer stifled a giggle as he said, "Well now, Mrs.----I don't recall ever hearing of this sort of thing being reversed or stopped! Just hang on, we are almost to the house. Your mother will know what to do, she's birthed many babies."

Three hours later, John Wamhoff was pacing back and forth in the Westerhoff's kitchen. He knew the doctor and Mary's mother were both tending to her, but just hearing her scream and cry out made him crazy with worry.

John remembered when the doctor walked into the house, he had heard Mary cry out, "It's too soon, ---nothing feels right? Help me, please help me, doctor."

Mary was in and out of consciousness as the pain intensified. She was aware of the terrible pressure to 'push', and gladly took the spoonful of laudanum the doctor gave her. "It will help take the edge off the pain. I know you feel like pushing but try your best not to until I tell you." Mary could hear her mother and the doctor talking, but it sounded muffled as if they were in a tunnel. It was all about the pain, the unbearable all-consuming pain, worse than anything she had ever known.

"I can't Mama, I can't do it!"

Elizabeth said, "Take a deep breath and wait for the next contraction, and then Mazzie—you show em' what gumption you have and you push with the pain!"

Mary heard the doctor say, "Okay, it's almost over now, Mary—the head is right here. No, Mary, don't push now. Let your womb and the contractions push the baby out gently."

Elizabeth said, "Mary, Mary—listen to me—pant, Mary; pant and exhale in long 'whooshes'. The shoulders are out - now give us an easy little push." Mary tried but she slipped into unconsciousness, her last thought was---none of this delivery is right—all w-rongggg—my ba--by."

The doctor passed the newborn baby to Elizabeth who looked into the face of her granddaughter. The baby was so very tiny and limp--lifeless. She had a blueish color, not red like newborns usually are. Tears rolled down Elizabeth's face as she recalled how it felt to lose a baby, a child. *Oh Mary, my girl---this is going to be so hard for you, but it is what it is. This tiny soul was never meant to be---your first baby.*

Slowly, Mary regained consciousness and recognized the doctor, her parents, and John standing close to the bed. Not one person was smiling. She tried to sit up but collapsed back onto the pillow.

Then it occurred to her---*the delivery, the pain—baby---where is my baby? Why is everyone looking like this? Why don't I hear my baby crying?*

The doctor bent forward and took Mary's hand. "Mary, you've had a very difficult delivery. The baby was turned wrong. She was born with the cord wrapped around her neck. She wasn't ready to come into this world yet. Sometimes things go wrong inside. There was----nothing you did or could have done and nothing I could do for her. I am very sorry Mary. Very sorry, but your baby daughter didn't live."

Screaming, screaming---the room, her world was filled with screaming. Mary felt a cold cloth on her face and firm hands on her shoulders. She opened her eyes to see John. His face was pale and tear-stained. "Mary, Mary---oh my love, my precious. Our daughter was so tiny. She was perfectly formed but she couldn't survive everything that happened. I won't leave your side, Mary, I am here."

Then it was her mother, her father, Emma, the doctor---everyone was sorry! But nobody could give her back her baby girl. Mary said, "I want to see her, I want to hold her---NOW!"

The doctor left the room and came back in with a tiny body wrapped in a blanket. He placed the lifeless baby in Mary's arms. "Mary, I would caution you to let your body rest. To not have another baby for at least a year or two."

John sat on the edge of the bed and held her hand, "Mary, I believe we should give a name to our baby."

Mary looked down at the tiny perfect face of her daughter. "Amanda Jane---it is the name I had thought of if we had a daughter---Amanda. I want her to be buried in the Germantown Cemetery close to the plots my parents have chosen."

~~~~~~~~

Against her doctor's recommendations, eleven months later, Mary delivered her second child - a beautiful, robust son. Elizabeth hurried from the room and into the kitchen where the new father and grandfather were sitting at the table drinking coffee. She cupped her son-in-law's face in her hands and smiling, said, "You have a perfect, new son. He was a pretty big boy and Mary will need a good bit of time to recover. However, both are fine. Come with me and meet your first-born son----and grandson!"

John Wamhoff rushed to the bed where Mary sat propped up with pillows, holding their newborn son. He bent and kissed her pale, tear-stained face, and reached for their perfect baby cradled in her arms. "Ahhh Mary, he is wonderful. How much did he weigh?" Cradling the infant in his arms, John exclaimed, "He looks half 'growed' to me."

Mary smiled weakly, "The doctor thinks he is probably around eight pounds plus a bit more. I would have preferred a smaller baby, but he is so healthy and it's over now. Would you like to tell my parents what our new son is to be named?"

John beamed as he announced, "He is to be named William John after our fathers."

~~~~~~~~~

John worked every minute of every day to support his new family. He bought a small two-bedroom house on Black Street in Germantown. Mary delighted in choosing furniture for her home, and she hung lace and red velvet drapes at the windows. The floor in the front room was covered with a fine carpet that John had purchased just for her. She spent her time tending to the house and their son. Baby Bill was so healthy and growing like a weed—it was a busy but happy time for them. The next few years flew by and the little family flourished.

In April 1899, Mary knew she was pregnant again. Based on her calculations, the baby was due after the first of the year.

~~~~~~~~~

January 23, 1900: Ruth Elizabeth Wamhoff was born on a Tuesday after an easy pregnancy and birth. She was a beautiful baby with a head of blond hair and the sweetest little face. Five-year-old Brother Bill couldn't keep his hands off his baby sister. "I wanna hold baby sister."

Mary recovered quickly and her days were consumed caring for her two small children. By April, curly-headed Ruth weighed twelve pounds. Bill was growing like a weed, and he was tall for his age, like the Westerhoffs. He had his father's broad shoulders and was as stubborn as the day was long.

Life was good as John seemed to succeed at everything he put his mind to. He was highly respected in Germantown—but, not as respected and beloved as his father-in-law, John Westerhoff.

Chapter Two

WE WALK BY FAITH, NOT BY SIGHT
2 Corinthians 5:7

April 1900: The westbound loop of the B&M train pulled into the station at Germantown, Nebraska. This loop was connected to the extensive Nebraska line of the [1]Union Pacific Railroad which ran the east-west route from Omaha to Cheyenne, Wyoming. As the steam belched from beneath the black smoking iron beast, a dapper John Wamhoff disembarked, carrying his valise. He momentarily surveyed Germantown, then headed over to his store on Main Street.

Whistling as he walked, John moved in long confident strides past the collection of stores on Germantown's Main Street. He turned the doorknob and entered the front door of his furniture/mercantile store. The bell over the doorway tinkled familiarly as he firmly closed the door and scanned the store to see who was about.

Store assistant, George Wildorf, was writing up an order for a client as John waved to him and walked to the desk where the books were kept. He quickly scanned the sales of the past week.

John's mind raced ahead as he speculated whether or not George might be interested in buying the store. Leaning back in his chair, John let his thoughts take over. *I must speak to Mary as soon as possible. We have some decisions to make. This is what I have been waiting for, the chance to be my own man, to have what I've always dreamed of---to be like my father-in-law without walking in his shadow.* A wide smile crossed his face as he thought. *I feel it in my bones--THIS is my destiny---the opportunity I've waited for, and it's within my reach. Now I play my cards!*

~~~~~~~~~

At five o'clock sharp, John closed the door of the store, bid good evening to Geroge, and headed east toward his house on Black Street. Walking like a man with a purpose, it didn't take him long before he was on his front porch. He paused a moment, *I must get this right and present this timely prospect to Mary so she visualizes the possibilities of this opportunity as I do. She must agree with the timeliness; agree that this is the chance to grab hold of the future which awaits us.*

~~~~~~~~

"Mary, Mary my dear, where are you?" John raced through the small immaculate house looking for his wife, finally spotting her and their two children out in the backyard. Their baby daughter was only three months old and playing with a cloth doll as she sat on a blanket on a small patch of grass, while five-year-old Bill was busy helping Mary pull debris from around the bushes.

Mary stood when she saw John and rushed into his arms. "Oh my, you have been gone so long, I thought perhaps you had run off with some young thing!" Bill attached himself to his father's leg and wasn't about to let go. John picked up Bill, throwing him up into the air. He put him down and kissing him, said, "I have to talk to, little Mother. Bill, you are doing a good job cleaning out the bushes, so let's see if you can finish by yourself!"

Mary laughed as John kissed her soundly and took her by the hand. "Come, Mary, sit down on the step here. I have something very exciting to share with you, very exciting indeed."

Mary's blue eyes were wide with curiosity as John guided her to the back steps where they sat. "Mary, when I tell you of my encounter on the train and what a difference it could make in our future, you will be as astonished as was I. It seems remarkable—destiny—my chance meeting with this Lutheran missionary, [2]Pastor August Wunderlich from Omaha. His missionary travels take him through Nebraska, up into South Dakota, Montana, and now the Bighorn Basin of Wyoming."

John stood, nervously pacing as he continued speaking rapidly, "Pastor Wunderlich told me about a tantalizing meeting he had a few months ago with a well-known land developer by the name of Solon Wiley, who discovered this fertile, sage-covered benchland in the Bighorn Basin of Wyoming which has recently been opened for settlement. Numerous Mormon families have already moved into lower portions of it and settled areas around the Shoshone River basin and along the Greybull River. However, there is this particular area of flat benchland just to the north of

Burlington. As an ancient river bottom, it has very fertile soil which holds great opportunity, especially with the irrigation project which the Mormons have begun. Mr. Wiley is deeply involved in working with them as well as other investors to build canals, dams, and headgates to control and utilize the river water coming from the high mountains to the west. "

John didn't give Mary a chance to speak as he continued, "Mary, oh Mary—there is all this land, land to be had, to homestead under the Homestead Act which is almost extinct. Pastor Wunderlich has already started a German Lutheran colony in this particular area. Last spring he took the first group of about thirty Lutherans from Hemingford and Rushville, Nebraska, and also from Ardmore, South Dakota. They moved their families, farming machinery, livestock, and household goods---they have built adobe and dugout houses and have plans for a wood church. Most traveled by train to Billings, Montana, then overland south, crossing the Montana/Wyoming border---down into this formerly remote Wyoming valley known as the Bighorn Basin. He tells me it is a beautiful and fertile country with high blue, snow-covered mountains surrounding it."

Reverend Wunderlich and family. *Edna Guebert*

"Pastor Wunderlich told me there is another route which may be better for us---to travel by train from here to Cheyenne, where we could buy wagons, livestock, and whatever we need for the journey at a most reasonable price. We would then follow the road along the railroad tracks north to Douglas and then west through Casper, Wyoming. From there we simply follow the stage route northwest which is built over the Old Jim Bridger Trail. This trail/road would take us up and over the Bighorn Mountains into --- the Bighorn Basin. Once we ferry across the Bighorn River, it's only a matter of a few days before arriving at the Benchland. The railroad is already building track into the Basin from the north, which in time, would be another asset for us."

John paused long enough to look at Mary's face. It was not what he had hoped for, not at all. Her face was pale and her eyes glistened like blue steel. She stood motionless, her jaw clenched tightly with her hands clasped together in a prayerful knot. Aghast, Mary stammered, "John--John Wamhoff—I--I am in shock that you are even considering this---this wild story. It all sounds like a great needless risk, involving years of struggle in a wild remote place. We have two small children to consider and you are talking about selling your prosperous business. You expect me to give up my comfortable home with carpets, velvet drapery, and lovely Victorian furniture---to---to travel by wagon over the prairie, perhaps fighting off Indians, to a place you have only been told about? You would have me give up a life that I've grown to love so that you might—and I do emphasize 'might'--- realize a new opportunity for yourself? You can't be serious. John, I can't believe you don't realize what you are asking me to give up---to leave everything and everyone I have ever known? Just so you,---you can go off on this wild goose chase and live some dream of yours, which I might add could very well be nothing but folly! It sounds quite foolhardy to me."

Mary stood, picked up the baby and grabbing Bill by the hand, turned, and went into the house to prepare the evening meal. She settled the children, then began to peel potatoes. Her hands were shaking so badly, she had to stop and calm herself. Her fingers gripped the edge of the table until they were white. Tears ran down her face at the thought and enormity of John's proposal.

~~~~~~~~~

Mary fed the children and put them to bed. She put John's supper on the table as she sat across from him, her plate empty. Mary's face was etched with fear as worry and alarm filled her eyes. She was tied in knots, far too upset to eat.

John asked, "What? You aren't eating? Come on, Mary, I have spoken to you before of looking for an opportunity to better myself, to become my own man and not live under the giant shadow of your father's prosperity or the ill reputation of my father."

Mary raised her face and boldly looked John straight in the eye. "You--you, are the only one who thinks you live under my father's reputation here in Germantown. He is a highly respected man who has done a great deal for this community and you begrudge him that. You are jealous John, that is your problem. You want what my father has, don't you---and you know that will never happen here in Germantown, admit it! Furthermore, why do you have to choose a place as far away as this, which you have never even seen?"

John slapped the table with the palms of his hands and shoved back his chair. "Listen to yourself, Mary! I am your husband and it's my job to give you and our children a better life. I admire John Westerhoff. I have always said openly that someday I hoped for an opportunity to build a life fashioned after what he has done here in Germantown. He had the opportunity right here, to build something new for himself and his family which he didn't have in Illinois. I might add, he never laid eyes on this property either—only the opportunity." John added, "Your mother came with him with two small children, didn't she? She left their comfortable home in Illinois to travel by wagon and live in an adobe house until your father built up the farm. She had faith in him."

Before Mary could reply, John said, "But you, Mary, are you telling me that you won't do the same for me as your mother did for your father? That you would deny me the opportunity to build something to be proud of, to build a new life of our very own, because you don't want to leave your comfortable house and nice furniture? You are a grown woman with the capacity to see the opportunity this would provide for our family."

John paced back and forth across the kitchen floor. Mary sat stone-faced, glued to the kitchen chair, with trepidation eating holes in her. She saw the writing on the wall and there was no doubt about what was going to happen whether or not she agreed.

John paced the floor, "We will have the same opportunity to build a close-knit Christian community there in Wyoming, why don't—why won't you see this? This particular part of Wyoming is not easy to get to. That's exactly why it hasn't been settled or homesteaded to the extent the rest of the west has been. I've figured it all out, how we would sell out here, giving us a sufficient startup fund, and how we would travel there. Don't disappoint me, Mary— you are made of stronger discipline and conviction, I know you are.

I need you and our children with me, I need my family to support this new life I want for all of us. If any woman can do this, it's you— I have no doubt."

~~~~~~~~

The next morning, John rose early and went to the store without speaking of Pastor Wunderlich again. After a sleepless night and still distraught, Mary moved stoically through her morning routine. Standing at the kitchen sink, washing the breakfast dishes, she knew she had to confide in her mother. Pushing Ruth in a pram with Brother Bill holding onto the side, she walked quickly down the boardwalk to her parent's home at the edge of town. Mary drew in a deep, relaxing breath as she walked under the cool shade of the lovely trees her father had planted during those first years in Nebraska. Her Mother's spring flower garden was glorious with color and fragrance. It was hard for her to imagine this land any other way than what it was on this day.

Mary lifted Ruth from the pram and pushed open the door to the back porch. Her mother was sitting in the front room working on her mending. "Oh my, Mary—what a nice surprise. Come here my little Bill and give your grandma a big hug."

Mary sat in the chair, across from her mother. After a few moments, Elizabeth looked up. Tilting her head she said, "So, something tells me this isn't just a friendly visit on this beautiful morning. What's on my girl's mind?"

Mary laid the baby on her tummy on a blanket, then looked up at her mother, with tears in her eyes.

Elizabeth sensed this wasn't going to be good as she busied little Bill with a ginger snap cookie. "Okay, Mary, what is the matter? Are you pregnant again?"

Mary tilted her head back and looked at the ceiling, smiling ever so slightly as tears ran down the back of her throat. "Oh Mama, no, it isn't that, thank heaven. It's just that---." Mary attempted to stifle a sob that escaped her throat. "It's just that John wants to move away—to leave Germantown."

Elizabeth smiled and said, "Well my dear, there are lots of nice farms or towns nearby—or does he want to move into Seward where he could have a larger store?"

Mary gritted her jaw, "No, Mama---not Seward, not Nebraska---to Wyoming. Oh, Mama ---- this, Wyoming is such a far place. He met a Lutheran missionary on the train from Omaha who has convinced him this particular unsettled area of the Bighorn Basin of Wyoming, would be a wonderful opportunity to start a new German Lutheran colony. There is already a handful of people living there. They are working on getting water to the farms which need to be irrigated; not dryland farming like here in Nebraska. John said there are Mormons already living there who have built canals and have plans for a vast dam." Mary hesitated just a moment, as her emotions threatened to get the better of her, she swallowed hard then added, "And, and that we would live in an *adobe house* for a few years until he can get a farm going. It would be the place he has dreamt of m-making a life similar to what Pap built here. "

Mary covered her face with her hands as heartwrenching sobs came from deep inside her. Elizabeth rose, moved across the room, and stood in front of her daughter. Reaching down she pulled her to her feet, "Well, Mary, I can't say this comes as a surprise. I've always felt that John Wamhoff has had an eye on your father's success from day one. This town is too small for the two of them as I see it. This place in Wyoming sounds like just the ticket for him----for him to fashion his life after your father's, but all on his own. It offers him a clean slate on which to build the life he envisions, a place to be his own man."

Mary cried even harder, "Yes, that's it exactly, but what about the life I want, that I dreamed of? I have it now, right here in Germantown, with my family close by. I have everything I want and he expects me to throw my dreams away, just so he can have his!"

"Mary Elizabeth, I will tell you this. When you are married to an ambitious man, you have to prepare yourself to do many things that you aren't particularly eager about. I know you don't want to move away from here, from Nebraska to this far place in Wyoming, but it is what your husband thinks is best for you and your children. It's where and how he believes he can build a good life for your family. I know you have it in you, Mary, to make a home there. It will be hard at first, like nothing you have ever known, but you are a fighter--- determined to have it your way, you always have been. However, you are also a smart woman, you are no shrinking violet, no Mary, not you! You will dig deep and you will make a good home there; and in the end, it will be something you too will be proud of."

Elizabeth smiled reassuringly at her middle daughter and continued, "Mary, nothing ever---ever stays the same no matter if it's something good or bad. I am confident you will be able to do this thing. Make up your mind, and just like I did, you will make a home for your husband and children wherever you live. Adobe houses aren't all that bad—they are very warm in the winter and cool in the summer. I wouldn't take your velvet curtains with you though. You can pack them away and when the day comes when you have a proper house again, you can hang them in the windows. Your lovely lace curtains would give the windows a nice civilization, paired with a heavier material to keep out the cold."

Mary stood and slowly walked across the kitchen to the sink where she had washed many a dish while growing up. She turned and looked at her mother through puffy, teary eyes. "Mama, I don't know how to keep an adobe house clean. I have so many questions and fears. Where we will sleep, how will I cook and care for my babies? Who will be with me when I have another baby?"

Elizabeth warmly embraced her middle daughter as she spoke. "Mazzie, there will be other women there who will know how to do things and know where to get things you don't. I want to give you this here booklet in which I have written down some of the old-time remedies for when your babies or you are ailin', and there isn't a doctor close by. Most of them work real well and you can mix them right at home. This all brings back so many memories of when your Pap and me moved here from Illinois. The years ahead won't be easy, but nothing worthwhile ever is---you remember that and you do the best you can do---always do the best you can.

Remember what our Lord says in the Bible, Philippians, chapter 4 verse 11 which has given me comfort many a night. *"For I have learned, in whatsoever state I am---therewith to be content."* Those words have given me the strength to go on, to do what I had to do---so many times in my life. You are going to find out for yourself the depth of your inner strength as a strong woman, wife, and mother---you will do what you have to do, I have no need to worry about that. Just you pray that the Lord keeps you all safe on your journey and that you remain close to him and stay in his ways over the years." Elizabeth patted Mazzie's back and said, "You make up your mind now, that you are going to march out there and bend your back to the task—as you did in that terrible blizzard. You were only eight or nine years old but you did what you had to do even if you didn't want to, even if you were scared!" Elizabeth wrapped her arms around her daughter, then cupped her face in her hands as she said, "My Mazzie---you were always the adventuresome one, the one with gumption! This may test all you have to offer!"

~~~~~~~~

John Wamhoff had no problem selling his mercantile store at a fine profit. His father sold their joint farming venture and moved back to Indiana. By the first of May, John and Mary had sold everything they owned or couldn't take with them to Wyoming. It was devastating for Mary to part with her charming little yellow clapboard home, decorated with Victorian furniture, carpets, and velvet drapes. She knew it would be a long time, if ever, that she would have a life or things this nice again.

~~~~~~~~

Elizabeth helped Mary pack several trunks with the essential things she would need on the trail, as well as when they first arrived in Wyoming.

Mary's father said, "Mazzie, it sounds like John has a solid plan to travel across Nebraska by train to the Wyoming border, and then on to Cheyenne. It's where he can get the best deal on quality wagons, horses, and the necessities you will need. You could take the train to Casper City, but Cheyenne is the best place to buy everything you will need for the trip and to set up once you arrive in the Bighorn Basin. John has thought this through.

John has talked to the right people and has maps of the roads and trails you will travel, following the new roads along the railroad tracks and over the North Platte River to Casper. I would say the man has done his homework and he is pulling at the bit to get on the road. I can't say I blame him---brings back memories of when we struck out from Illinois to make a new life here in Nebraska. It's an exciting opportunity and a great time in your life. Trust and pray,

Mazzie. I know you are a strong woman, a good woman---you can do anything you set your mind to!"

Mary stopped packing and gazed out the window. "John is making arrangements for some of our furniture and larger things we will, to be shipped on an emigrant car for a reasonable fee. It takes quite a spell for them to travel that way. We will already be in the Bighorn Basin before they arrive in Billings, Montana, and then will be taken by freighters down to Wyoming where we will pick them up. At least I will have our beds, table, and chairs to begin with--- and a few things I am partial to."

"You know, Pap, the good thing is that the [3]Homestead Law is still in effect so once we get to the benchland, we can choose our parcel, live on it for five years, build a house, and then with a small payment the land will be ours."

Mary looked up at her father, "Pap, what if we get there and we or I can't make a go of it—what if I hate it?"

John looked her straight in the eye, "Mazzie—if that be the case, then you must reach deeper until you find what you need to persevere and get through it. I have faith in John, and I have no doubt whatsoever that you will---will do what you have to do! If I know anything, I know you, my girl, my marvelous Mazzie!"

~~~~~~

June, 1901: The crowd that gathered at the train depot in Germantown was both sad and happy to see the ambitious young couple leave for their great adventure.

Elizabeth had packed a basket of food for them to eat on the train ride to Cheyenne. But not until the train pulled away, did she let go of her own emotions. "Oh John, it's like watching us all over again—leaving Illinois to come out here to start a new life. I suppose it's the way of the Lord, for young families to leave their homes to strike out on their own. I just hope God gives our Mazzie the strength she will need. She isn't as excited about moving as I was."

~~~~~~

John Wamhoff watched closely as Mary stared out the grimy window of the train. He knew well enough to leave her to her thoughts and in time she would regain her temperament. She occupied herself with feeding little Bill and Ruth a light lunch and then got them settled down for naptime. They were all becoming accustomed to the rocking of the train car every time the great iron wheels slid over a rough seam in the rails. She closed the window, not because she didn't want fresh air, but because the air coming in was filled with coal smoke from the locomotive along with insects and dust.

Mary straightened her skirt, tidied their seats, and then---she was ready—ready to be the woman John needed her to be. "John, once we arrive in Cheyenne, do you have any idea where to go to pick up our wagons and everything we will need? How do you know WHAT we will need on this trip to the Bighorn Basin? Do you even know how long we will be in the covered wagons on the road? Also, how do you know these other people from Colorado and Kansas who will be traveling with us?"

John blinked once, licked his lips, glancing out the window. "Mary, Mary—so many questions, I'm not sure I'll have time before we get to Cheyenne to answer all of them! My dear, you know me better than to ask questions like that. Of course, I have already made arrangements by post to purchase everything we will need in Cheyenne. There is an outfitter in Cheyenne by the name of Nicolalsen & Stuht, who has been in the business for a good length of time and has a stellar reputation. I've bought and paid for everything which will be stocked in our two wagons. I was given solid connections to these reputable outfitters and merchants; I didn't just pick them out of a book. The wagons will be ready to go once we arrive in Cheyenne. I thought it might please you to spend one night in the highly recommended new Plains Hotel in downtown Cheyenne. We may all benefit from a good night's sleep on real beds before living out of a covered wagon for several weeks. And finally---no, I have not met these folks who will join our group, but I expect they will be much like us, looking for a new life."

Mary closed her eyes, then looked at John, " I hope it all goes as smoothly as you expect. What is done is done, so now I must rise to the occasion and do my part, whatever that may be."

John reached across space and took her hands in his own. He lifted them to his lips and gently kissed them. "Mary, my dear. You know I am making this move because I believe in this new life for us. I love you and our children with all my being. You have birthed three children in our five years—we have been through a lot, including the loss of our first child, Amanda. I know it was hard for you to leave our comfortable life and your family in Germantown---but Mary, we can do this. With you by my side----we WILL carve a successful new life in a new land. Thank you, my dear. Thank you for putting your trust in me." John gazed out the window of the train as the rolling green hills of Nebraska slipped away. "One more thing Mary. I hope in time your dream will join mine and together we will build this new life with optimism."

John's words struck Mary deeply and she looked out the window, trying to find the words to respond. "John, I thank you— that, that you realize what I am giving up. I also hope we can work together to build a good life in Wyoming. I am going to try my best and that's all I can say for now." Mary paused as another question popped into her head. "John, I understand you have maps of the roads which we are to travel on? How long John---how long is this going to take, and how far?"

John opened his valise and pulled out a map. 'We are traveling on graded county roads and later, crossing the Bighorn Mountains, on current stagecoach roads. It will save us 200 miles by not going around the eastern side of the Bighorn Mountains and up to Montana, then backtrack down into the Bighorn Basin. They tell me if the weather is good; if we don't have any problems crossing/fording the rivers in the Bighorn Basin, or if we don't experience any serious break downs, the trip should take about four to six weeks. Most folks traveling by wagon call it a good day if they make twenty miles a day. If everything works as we hope, the weather holds, and we are lucky, it'll take us over a month to get to the Bighorn Basin and the benchland claims."

John laid the map out on Mary's lap. He pointed to Cheyenne. "Here is where we will begin our journey in the covered wagons. By the way, I chose the wagons which are eleven feet long, four feet wide, and over two feet deep. The curved upper bows rise another five feet above the wagon bed, so we'll have pretty decent headroom when standing. Some people might take herds of cattle and sheep along as well. I'm not going to do that. It would only slow us up. Each wagon will have three or four teams of Percheron workhorses pulling it, so we have plenty of horsepower to pull the wagons over the distance. We'll buy the rest of our livestock after we are settled and have barns and sheds for them."

John thought for a moment then added, "I also chose this style of covered wagon because once we reach our claim, I can use the wagon bed to farm with---to haul merchandise or supplies, and for general transportation as well."

"Now, to answer your question about the other parties which are joining us in Cheyenne. I know they are not going to the Bighorn Basin with us. We will part company just west of Douglas, Wyoming after we cross the bridge over the North Platte River. The junction is near where the historic remains of Fort Fetterman stand. They plan to head north to start a ranch in Montana.

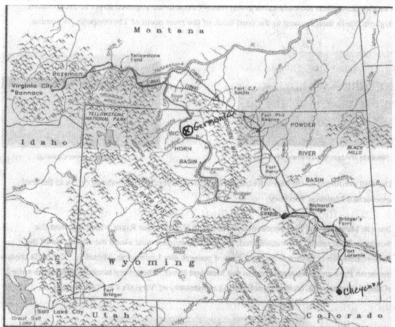

John smoothed out the map. "See here, Mary, we will travel northward across this open land; we may or may not have to ford a couple of seasonal creeks. There are plenty of small towns along the way where we can restock our supplies. We will cross the Laramie River and the [4]North Platte River on the railroad built bridges."

"We may see a few signs of the once-famous Oregon Trail along the way. However, Mary, I read where travel on that famous trail almost completely stopped around 1869, after the Union Pacific Railroad was completed to the West Coast. Folks could travel in the comfort of the train, rather than drive a team of horses and wagons across the country! It now takes days – weeks to do what used to take months."

"Before the Wyoming Central, Union Pacific, and Cheyenne Northern railroads came in and built bridges across the North Plate at Douglas and Casper, the travelers took what is called Child's Crossing just north and west of Douglas. It avoided the river crossings and high ferry fees, which saved them time and money. The ferries back then charged an arm and a leg to take the pioneers across the rivers. The 'Crossing' stayed on the north side of the North Platte River until they came to what they called the Upper Crossing Ferry near Casper. This was an excellent route as long as they stayed near the river for water and grass for the horses. We'll gladly cross the rivers on bridges when we have to."

"As I mentioned, from Cheyenne to Casper, we will have good roads to travel on, not some rough and ready stagecoach roads. They are well-maintained and have bridges over the larger rivers and creeks. Our road parallels the Cheyenne Northern railroad which Bill will enjoy---getting to see the trains come by and all. I read where it took that railroad a year and a half to build their tracks from Cheyenne to Wendover, Wyoming, then on to Douglas which was a central city of that time. Casper later became the target railroad city--it's in the center of the state and an ideal spot for shipping out local wool and oil.

It was after this railroad was built that Laramie County put in a new county road—parallel to the railroad. That's when the old road from Cheyenne to Ft. Laramie was abandoned and the fort closed, around 1890. Most military forts in Wyoming like, Fort Laramie, Fetterman, and Casper closed around that time, after treaties with the waring Indians came into being. "

"We won't switch to the stage route, which frequently crosses what was the Old Jim Bridger Trail until we are on the other side of Casper. We'll stay right on that stage road which will take us over the very southern end of the Bighorn Mountains where the trapper Jim Bridger discovered the passage in 1850. This short cut saved pioneers fifty miles. There will be some freighter and stagecoach traffic on the road so if we have a breakdown we've got company. I was counting on the stagecoach stations along the way for water and food, especially out in the Rattlesnake Hills west of

Casper. But as fate and time have it, most of them are out of commission—no longer needed as the U.S. Mail has made better accommodations to get mail to folks out in that country. From what I can tell, it started back in the day when the settlers, Pony Express, and stagecoaches were having numerous vicious Indian attacks along the northern route. They changed their route to a safer area-- through Laramie, Rawlins---staying in the southern end of the state. I was told some of the stage stops may still be open for business."

Courtesy: Tom Davis, historian

John leaned back in the seat and stretched his limbs. "Not to worry Mary, we will come upon several small towns with access to fresh water and food staples all the way to Casper City. According to this here map that takes up from Cheyenne, we travel through Wheatland, Wendover, Douglas, then Casper."

"We've got us several good reference maps." John could see more questions building in Mary's head. She tilted her head to the side and asked, "John, I'm just curious. I remember hearing you mention that several of those families who are already living in the Bighorn Basin, traveled by train to Billings, Montana. Why didn't we go that way? It sounds a bit easier."

John replied, "That might be true my dear, but there are numerous small train connections which aren't reliable and the passengers are responsible for transferring all of their luggage, their heavy trunks, and animals from train to train. Sometimes there is a considerable wait at the depots until their next connecting train comes along, if at all that day. Then, when they finally reach Billings, Montana—they still have to buy wagons, outfits, animals, and supplies to make the trip south into Wyoming and the Bighorn Basin. Both routes are hard going, but by my calculations, this southern route is less risky, though a bit longer, but more comfortable for you and the children. We have made our decision and I am sure we'll make the best of it. I just pray the Lord gives us good weather."

Mary said, "All these unknown parts frighten me, but I am prepared to take it a day at a time. I'm trying to consider it all as a great adventure, but I do worry about how the children will tolerate everything. I can assure you I will boil all the water we drink. I have read the literature you gave me about Cholera from unsanitary water. One thing it did say is that once we're past Laramie Peak, chances of getting Cholera are less prevalent because of the higher elevations."

~~~~~~~~~~

Looking out the grimy window of the train, Mary turned to John and asked, "Are there Indians living in the Bighorn Basin?"

John smiled as he replied, "I understand there are only a few peaceful Crow, Shoshone, and Arapaho Indians but the government is trying to settle them on a reservation."

Mary said, "All of this information helps me rest easier, John. Just to know what is going to happen—what to expect and where we are going gives me confidence. I am feeling weary. I think I will try to close my eyes while the children are sleeping." She leaned across the seat and kissed him gently on the cheek. "John, one more question. Do you expect me to drive one of those wagons?"

John said, "I have high hopes of hiring a driver in Cheyenne. No, Mary, I wouldn't expect you to handle four teams of horses and two babies." Mary turned her face toward the window so John wouldn't see the tracks of the tears which ran down her ivory cheeks.

Chapter Three

"ON THE TRAIL"

June, 1901:It was late in the afternoon as toward the west, the sun slid from a bird-egg blue sky through a scattering of puffy white clouds to disappear behind high mountains. The Union Pacific

train began to reduce speed as it approached the thriving frontier town of Cheyenne, Wyoming. Mary looked out the window and caught just a brief glimpse of a haphazard array of simple white, tan, and unpainted shiplap board homes. There were very few trees, yards, or lawns.

The train engineer slowly applied the brakes causing the train to buck and shake as it neared the bustling station. The screech of metal on metal along with the startling hiss of the steam woke Ruth, who immediately began to cry. Five-year-old Bill's face was pasted to the glass, gazing out the train's window. He was mesmerized by the seething array of cowboys, horses, and of course, the collection of black steam trains in the busy railyard.

Mary glanced out of the window at the imposing Cheyenne depot. *Oh my goodness, this may be my final glimpse of large buildings and civilization for a good while. I love the unique fashion of it all as well as the unorderly charm. It's perfect pandemonium— all those freight wagons, teamed with mules, oxen, or horses—*

everyone and everything jockeying for position in the dusty streets which are filled with piles of animal droppings and puddles of this and that. This is certainly the wild west.

Mary's hands shook as she reached to tidy her hair. *I must not let John or the children see my apprehension.* She busied herself with making sure both children were orderly as she gathered their belongings, making ready to disembark once the train came to a halt.

After a few minutes, John returned from speaking to the conductor and arranging for their trunks to be transferred to the holding station. They would retrieve them the next day when they were ready to load their wagons.

John smiled at Mary as he enthusiastically commented, "Well, we have made it to Cheyenne. We'll take a breather and then we'll be ready for the second leg of our journey. Are you as excited as I am, my dear? I hope our traveling companions from south of the border have left word for us at the hotel and that they are here, ready to travel north."

Mary was having a difficult time hiding her concern. "John, are you sure our things will be okay, left at the station? Is it a secure room where they hold our trunks? I do look forward to staying at the Plains Hotel. At least it won't be moving."

John glanced outside the train window as he replied to his wife, "Mary, you do worry about too many things. I have it all handled. Cheyenne sits at the edge of eastern civilization as we know it and the untamed west. On July 10, 1890, the Wyoming territory became a state and we are quite fortunate to be able to take advantage of the opportunities it holds for pioneers and homesteaders such as ourselves." John reached for her hand and helped her from the train.

Mary carried Ruth and a satchel of personal items as John had a firm grip on Bill's hand and a suitcase. As they disembarked from the train, a gust of blustery Wyoming wind greeted them; an element which they would soon become quite familiar with. John showed Mary to an empty metal bench and said, "You and the children wait here, Mary, and I will find us a hack or some sort of buggy to take us and our overnight luggage to the hotel."

Seated on the train station's large wooden platform, Mary was mesmerized by the two-story sandstone station with the bold signage---UNION PACIFIC RAILROAD-- hanging over the heavy, wooden, double doors. It was bedlam—floods of people moved from every direction, trying to get as close to the incoming train as possible. Mary suddenly felt as if she were in a bad dream. People were charging here and there, yelling orders, cursing anything and everything as they pushed and shoved their way through the train station. Trepidation coursed through her veins and she was on the verge of tears when through the din of noise and confusion, she heard John call her name.

"This way my dear. I'll take Bill and you carry Ruth. Our ride is waiting for us at the edge of the boardwalk. I am sure you will feel better once we are in the hotel." With her free hand, she lifted her long skirt as John led her across long unstable twin planks which acted as a bridge across the mucky mire in the street, to where their ride awaited them.

Looking up and down the streets of the frontier town, Mary noticed most of the buildings had false fronts, some newly built with fresh boards and clean windows, while others were older with peeling paint, grimy windows, and disgusting stains running down the sides of the walls. She gazed down the street to the east where she saw several rows of modest homes sitting on the edge of what was considered the town. To the east, to where Nebraska and home was; she felt the sudden pang of homesickness.

At the door of the hotel, the driver unloaded their overnight valises and took them inside, while John helped Mary and the children from the hack. They walked into the lobby where Mary had an excellent view of the saloon. She was shocked to see actual gun-toting, swearing gamblers throwing dice and playing games of cards. She put her hand over her nose to avoid the heavy stench of tobacco, alcohol, and unwashed men that drifted from the saloon.

~~~~~~~~~

Once upstairs, Mary stood in the middle of the hotel room John had rented for them. Gold striped wallpaper covered the walls—a ghastly bedcover of red-orange cabbage roses covered the iron bed. Unsavory images of the gamblers and others in the lobby lying on this very bed filled her head and shivers skittered down her spine. *I suppose I must get used to this sort of thing as we head farther into the wilds of Wyoming.*

The next morning John rose before dawn and after grabbing a quick breakfast, hurried off to see about their wagons and provisions. He was anxious to make contact with their traveling companions before the noon hour.

Mary was left to luxuriate in the warm feather bed as long as her two small children would allow. Reluctantly, she slid from beneath what she knew would be the best night sleep she would have in a month of Sundays. She fed Ruth and changed her nappy, then attended to Bill. "You are getting to be a big boy now, dressing all by yourself. When sister Ruth gets older, you can teach her how. Well now, how would you two like to go down to the hotel restaurant and have a nice breakfast---maybe flapjacks and orange juice? I would love a cup of hot coffee with cream!"

~~~~~~~~~

John shook hands with Jim Klane, a fellow traveler who was looking to hire on as a driver with one of the wagons, heading north. John said, "By golly Jim, I was hoping like the devil to meet up with a fellow just like you, who would be willing to drive one of my wagons. My wife will tell you that we are headed to the end of the earth, but in reality, it's the Bighorn Basin of Wyoming where I hope to homestead with a group of Lutheran colonists."

Jim Klane replied, "Well, I'll tell you this John, that's exactly why I was hanging around the area where the wagons meet up and all. I was hoping to hire on and eventually make my way further north to the Montana country. It looks to me like this Bighorn Basin is right on the border, so it's my lucky day!"

The two men climbed the wooden steps of the general store which had come highly recommended as the place to buy last-minute provisions and equipment for the journey. With his final list in hand, John twisted the doorknob and pushed the wooden door open. Jim caught the eye of the proprietor and nodded, "Good morning to you sir. My name is Jim Klane; this here is John Wamhoff." John shook hands with the proprietor and said, "We are heading up north to Casper. Here is a list of extra things we will be needing. You might add another sack of flour, and maybe some rock candy. I think that will do it!"

The two men loaded up their purchases from the store and John said, "Jim, I didn't expect you to pay half of that bill. I say this is our lucky day. It was supposed to be like this—I needed you and you needed me. Come along over to the hotel and meet my wife and our two children; I'll buy you breakfast."

The two men made their way through the throngs of people crowding the boardwalk in Cheyenne's downtown. They pushed open the door to the hotel and threaded their way through the appropriately attired lobby toward the bustling dining room.

Tending to two children in a public restaurant was a bit of a challenge, but Mary handled it with calm and confidence. Holding Ruth on her lap, she and Bill ate a hearty breakfast of eggs and flapjacks. Mary finished her coffee and called for the bill just as Bill said, "Oh look, Papa is coming through the door. He has another man with him too!"

~~~~~~~~~

Mary's heart skipped a beat as she watched her handsome, confident husband make his way through the tables to where they sat. John bent over and kissed her on the cheek. "Mary, I would like you to meet Jim Klane, our new friend, and driver!"

Jim leaned forward and gently taking her hand in his, said, "It's a pleasure to meet you, mam. John didn't tell me you were such a looker!

Mary blushed as she replied, "Why I thank you, Mr. Klane, do sit down. Have you eaten breakfast?"

Jim and John both took a seat. Addressing Mary, Jim said, "And, please call me Jim. Folks call my father, Mr. Klane!" John ordered up breakfast and another pot of hot coffee, then said, "Mary, I know you have been wonderin' just how we would handle two wagons. Well, we will drive the wagon filled with our trunks, food, and things we will need on the way to the Bighorn Basin. Jim will drive the other wagon that is filled with seed, farm tools, building tools, and some of your smaller furniture. I was most fortunate in that I ran into Jim and we hit it off right away. He's eager to join us on our trip into the Bighorn Basin ---a new adventure and he comes highly recommended as a driver with good knowledge of wagons, horses, and sheep. He has graciously agreed to come with us and help out as a means of getting to the Bighorn Basin. He has plans of going on to the north, to the Montana country, but perhaps we might persuade him to stay over the winter with us.

John said, "Jim was a great help to me in the final selection of our teams of massive Percheron and sturdy workhorses this morning-- I must add, he did an excellent job!" Jim replied, "I think it's a good idea to have four teams of horses, per wagon. You never know when one might go lame or something. Insurance, that's what it is!"

They finished their coffee and paid the bill, then John said to Mary, "I think it's time we depart. We are supposed to meet our group from the south, around ten o'clock by the wagon maker's barn."

As they walked out of the dining room, Mary couldn't help but notice the group of young maids gathered at the clothesline, beating carpets. Mary remembered when her mother would hand her and Emma each a carpet whip and send them out to the clothesline where their carpets were hung. "Now, beat them until they cry, UNCLE!" Mary smiled at the tender memory of home and her childhood.

~~~~~~~~~

June 4, 1901: At dawn on Tuesday morning, the small caravan of four, heavily-loaded covered wagons were prepared to head north toward Douglas, Wyoming, where they would follow the new and improved wagon road to Casper. The Miller and Rohrhoff families were still at the wagon maker's when John and Jim arrived with their wagons. John helped Mary down from the wagon. He took Bill firmly by the hand as Mary carried Ruth in her arms. "Mary, I would like you to meet Matthew and Laura Miller; as well as Herb and Ida Mae Rohrhoff, all from lower Missouri."

John turned to where Jim was standing and said, "Folks, I'd also like you to meet our friend and the driver of our second wagon, Jim Klane".

Mary gave them her brightest smile and extended her hand in friendship. "It's so nice to finally meet all of you. We are glad to have the company, very glad indeed; although John tells me we will part company west of Casper where you plan to continue to Montana country."

Ida Mae stepped forward and wrapped her ample arms around Mary. "We are mighty happy to join you as well. Herb and I have three boys and who knows where they are, probably hanging from some tree limb!" A deep hearty laugh rolled out of her stout body. "They are all boy, just plain ornery, and constantly on the move. We plan on lettin 'em walk most of the way, just to tire them out!"

Laura Miller smiled sweetly at Mary and added, "Mathew and I don't have any children just yet. As you can see, we expect our first baby very soon and I am countin' on you and Ida Mae to help me with the birthin', if'n you don't mind. I see you have two of your own, Mary, and I am sure you can imagine that I am a bit concerned to have to go through birthin' clear out here in the wilderness."

Mary said, "I'm sure Ida Mae and I will do our best for you when your time comes Laura. It's best not to worry yourself, the Lord will be with you I am most confident."

John, Jim, Herb, and Matt walked toward their wagons and climbed up on the seat as Matt circled his hat above his head in the cool Wyoming morning. "Okay, we're all ready when you are. Wagons rrr-oll!"

The four heavily-loaded covered wagons lumbered through Cheyenne. Once out of the frontier town, they found themselves on a graded road. In single file, they headed north over the gently rolling hills. Riding on the wagon seat beside John, Mary sat up straight and tall so she could see ahead. All she saw was one rolling grassy hill after another. To the west, the range of blue mountains rose from the prairie floor. "John, I am beginning to think Wyoming doesn't have any trees to speak of. Rather like Nebraska was in the beginning, according to Pap. However, they do have real mountains, and I never realized how huge they were."

John laughed and replied, "Oh, Wyoming has trees, down in the gullies, along the rivers, and in the mountains where there is water---any place where there is water, there will be trees, especially on the mountains."

John and the others learned quickly how to take a steep hill at a slight angle. Thankfully the road builders had removed the worst of the steep hills—there was just one rolling hill after the other. Mary soon learned that after they crested one hill, there was another one to take its place. Every once in a while the road skirted a steep-sided ragged gulch which appeared as though a deranged snake cut through the prairie. In reality, it had been carved out by centuries of rushing stormwater. Thankfully, there were narrow, one-way bridges over the deepest gullies and creeks.

Mary rode in silence, thinking about the wagons and what they carried. They had everything they needed to survive—a good iron sheet stove, pans, food, trunks packed with one change of clothes along with their precious winter clothes, medicines, etc. Mary had placed the extra blankets and goose down quilts on the floor of their wagon for their bed. Ruth slept with them, while Bill slept at the foot of the bed. She gazed at the endless sky and prairie. *What a big beautiful sky this is, looks like it goes on forever.*

Bill and little Ruth were sound asleep in the nest of blankets Mary had made for them behind the seat. "Land sakes---John, just look at that view from

this hill, we can see for a fifty miles or more—to the end of the world. It is a most beautiful sight, isn't it? We certainly don't have mountains in Nebraska, at least what they call a mountain here. Nothing I have seen can compare to these Wyoming mountains. They look worrisome. John, we won't have to go over them, will we?"

John turned and patted Mary's arm, "No my dear, we won't have to cross any of 'these' mountains, but there will be some pretty steep hills to go over on this trail. There have been many before us who have done it, we just have to follow their lead. Not to worry Mary, not to worry. They tell me the large mountain over there to the west is called Laramie Peak and it towers over the Black Hill range. Many of the early pioneers used it as a guide mark. It is a grand sight, is it not?"

Mary sat straighter on the seat and stretched her neck to see it all. "Oh John, the grass is so tall here, practically up to the horses' bellies in some places. Tallgrass like that---that means it's good land, right John? Why don't we stop here and see about a farm?"

John turned his head briefly and said impatiently, "We can't afford this land and it isn't farmland, Mary. We are going up into the [5]Bighorn Basin because we have the opportunity to homestead it. I've told you that!"

~~~~~~~~

John looked ahead at the road that seemed to stretch to infinity in front of them and thought to himself. *Not to worry, Mary, until we get ready to cross those Bighorn Mountains; that is going to be a test for us all. Sure am glad I hired Jim, it's good to have an able-bodied man along. He can certainly handle himself and those four teams of horses---- I've seen it first hand.*

Mary was quiet for a while, a thousand questions and thoughts racing through her head. "John, how far is it to this Douglas?

John looked straight ahead as a smile broke across his face. "Well, now--it's around one hundred and twenty miles to Douglas, as the crow flies. So, factoring in bad weather and other sorts of things, it will most probably take us just over a week, maybe more, to make it to that area." He was silent for a moment, then added, "I expect once we get halfway, to Douglas or Casper--we will take a day to rest, check the wagons, and refresh our food stock; especially the staples like flour, beans, rice, cornmeal, sugar bacon, salt, dried fruit, coffee, and of course, tobacco. You'll be wanting to wash some clothes and I'm countin' on you baking extra loaves of your good bread."

Mary laughed, "Well, that doesn't sound like much of a rest for me, now does it? Maybe I will teach you how to wash clothes in the river, John Wamhoff. Seriously, John---it's something you should learn!" Much to her amusement, Mary didn't miss the concerned sideways glance John gave her.

~~~~~~~~~~

The first night they camped near a shallow muddy creek called Lodgepole. The men led the horses downstream to drink their fill while the three women left their large iron pots on the campfires, and taking up their 'water skins', headed for the creek. The women carried the heavy skins, filled to the brim with creek water, back to camp, and poured them into the iron pots. They brought the water to a boil, letting the mud and other foreign objects settle to the bottom of the pots. In the morning, they carefully poured the good 'top' water from the pots into other containers to drink and cook with. They knew they must be very careful to boil the creek and river water to prevent Cholera.

The next morning, after a hearty breakfast of hot biscuits, ham and eggs, applesauce, and plenty of hot coffee, the men hitched up the horses while the women chatted and washed the breakfast dishes. The first light of the new day was just breaking over the horizon when they hit the road. The fresh morning air was pleasantly cool as the long warming rays of daylight spilled over the rolling hills of spring grass. Mary held little Ruth in her arms while Bill sat between them. Bill was so excited, he loved being up in the seat beside his father, "Dad, can I drive the horses, can I? When will we see the trains come by on the track?"

John looked down at his first-born son and said, "You need to sit nice and tall so when the train does come, you won't miss it. Now, when you are a little bit bigger my boy, you can drive the horses. It's very hard to drive four teams of horses pulling this big wagon. We wouldn't want to tip it over now, would we? Mama would be very upset, and you know what that is like! I will teach you how to drive the horses and lots of other things once we are settled on our new farm." John put his arm around his son and added, "Yes, sir, you are going to be a big help to your Papa someday, in the meantime you can hold the ends of the reins, that would be a big help!"

Bill looked up at his father, his eyes large with excitement, "Are we going to live on a farm like GranPap's? We aren't going to live in a town like before? I sure will like to live on a farm with cows and horses and chickens. I'll like that a lot! When will we be there? Huh?"

Bill stood up with one hand clutching his father's shirt and pointed off into the distance. "I see one, I see a big black train coming down the tracks! The lad began waving his arm."

~~~~~~~~

The small group of wagons had their travel routine down to a working system. After traveling all the next day, they found water at Horse Creek. The men took the animals down to the creek edge and the women tagged along with their water skins to fill before starting a campfire and the evening meal. The children lagged behind, picking up a few sticks and small logs to start the campfires.

Mary looked up at Laura and said, "I've got all the water I can carry. Are you and Ida Mae about ready to get back to camp and start the fires?"

Ida Mae replied, "I'm ready. Now, let's hope the kids found enough sticks and wood to get us a good fire ago'n."

Mary turned and was heading back to camp when little Bill burst from the brush. "Mama, that--that little Miller boy is afraid to move cause there's a big snake with a rattle on its tail and it looks like it's gonna eat him! He is real scared!"

Laura screamed as Ida Mae and Mary began running up the trail. Bill led them to where he left the Miller boy and the snake. "Right over there mama, see Jack standing there. I told him not to move, to stay real quiet like---just like GrandPap told me."

The women were quick to spot the rattler--- partially hidden under a rock, coiled uptight with his tail rattling back and forth, ready to strike!

Ida Mae grabbed a large branch and said, "Now Jack, when I hit the snake with this here branch, I want you to run back up the hill, hear me?" Jack nodded his head, his eyes wide with fright and tears. Ida Mae began to lift the branch very slowly as she inched toward the snake who was concentrating on Jack. When she was just near enough to reach the snake, she screamed, "NOW---NOW Jack, RUN!" Ida Mae brought the branch down on the snake again and again as it flopped and flipped trying to escape. When she stopped, Jack was gone and the snake was dead.

Ida Mae sat down on the ground and began to cry. "I never did anything like that in my whole life, but my brother saved my life from a rattler in just the same way. I thank God I membered how to do it." She tried to stand but was shaking so hard that Mary took her by the arm and helped her back up the hill to camp.

After supper was over, dishes were washed and children tucked safely in bed, the men sat on one side of the fire and the women on the other. Mary cradled her cup of coffee in her hands, "How do women do it, living way out here in this wilderness?"

Ida Mae slapped her knee and said, "Why Mary, I've driven mules, chopped wood, dressed out a kill, walked behind a plow, and I'm still a woman---and today I killed a snake! I suppose - women are tough out here because we have to be. We can drive that team, plow and harvest crops, birth a baby, all of those things, and then get supper on! We endure roaring blizzards, the blistering sun and wind that weathers our skin to leather, and loneliness that has driven some insane. You will find, you might think you can't do something, then it's left up to you and you just do it, pure and simple. One thing you can't do is get down and start feelin' sorry for yourself— remember—this too shall pass! Tomorrow is a new day!"

~~~~~~~~

June 6, 1901: At first light, the men rose from their warm beds and led the horses and the one cow and her calf down to the creek to drink their fill before it was time to harness them back to the wagons. John said, "I've been looking at the map---we've got Bear Creek coming up and then Chugwater Creek after that. I'm hoping there is a bridge across both of them creeks, with all this high spring runoff from the Laramie Mountains to the west there. I guess we wait until we get to the creeks to find out."

In the meantime, Mary and the other women cooked up a big breakfast of ham, flapjacks, syrup, eggs, and black coffee. They took the boiled creek water and carefully poured it into clean containers—they were getting their routine down. Before they knew it, it was time to load up and head out. John and Jim inspected the wheels and gave them a healthy dose of tar oil to keep them turning smoothly. Every member of the wagon train had a job to do.

Jim led off this morning, followed by John, Matthew, and Herb brought up the rear. Mary adjusted her sunbonnet, "It's right humid and warm already this morning. As Pap used to say, it feels like a good day for a storm."

John just grunted in reply. He was trying his best to forget John Westerhoff and all of his innate wisdom. Mary pointed to the east and north, "Look over there John, look at those thunderheads building. There's just the hint of a breeze coming from the northeast too. Feels like a storm to me, for sure."

John replied, "Well, we'd better keep moving as long as we can and not stop for the dinner meal today. We can just eat on the run. We gotta be makin' better time than we have or it'll take us another week before we get to where we're going!"

Mary thought for a moment then asked, "John, I don't understand why you bought four teams of horses for each wagon. Seems to me that two teams of horses could do the job!"

John turned to his wife, smiled, and then replied, "Insurance Mary. Insurance in case something happens to a horse or two. Besides, there may be a few hills later on where we will need all four teams to pull these heavy wagons up and keep them steady going back down. Besides that, I will be able to use all the horsepower to farm with, once we get to our new place."

After a bit, John said, "Just look at this country, Mary. I wouldn't have wanted to be with those early pioneers who had to fight Indians as they traveled through this land. The other thing I think is interesting is that the Oregon Trail is never clearly defined on the maps I've studied. In some of the larger trains, several wagons traveled in columns of perhaps a hundred, two hundred yards apart depending on weather and the shape of the trail. It cut down on the dust they had to eat as well."

"We aren't even to the where the Oregon Trail crossed, but plenty of pioneers came this way—you can see their wagon ruts even now. In the mid to late '80s when most of 'em came across Wyoming; there were plenty of Indians, buffalo, and all sorts of animals. Now, there aren't Indians or buffalo; most of the deer and such have been taken by the settlers who live along this trail. I did hear that we might get lucky and shoot us an antelope. I don't have any druthers about some fresh meat, whatever it is. I've noticed that every now and then we come across a ranch with barbed wire fences blocking the original trail. Not a very hospitable gesture if you ask me, but then if I were the landowner, I surely wouldn't want a bunch of wagons making roads across my fields. Times, they are a 'changin'."

The storm clouds continued to build to the west and looked like huge cauliflowers all piled together. Mary said, "John, when you were little, did you like to lay in the grass and look up at the clouds and try to pick out a figure or a form of an animal or person?" John turned to his wife and dryly replied, "I was never little, Mary, nor did I ever have time to lay and look at clouds!"

Mary chuckled and said, "I almost believe that John!"

They had no trouble crossing the shallow Little Bear Creek, but then when they came to North Bear Creek they were certainly relieved to see another one-way bridge.

Jim pulled up beside the other wagons, "I suggest we camp here tonight before heading north to Chugwater station tomorrow. I think we are in for a pretty good storm, I feel it in my bones. Best be we are hunkered down when one of these Wyoming summer storms hit. In a day or two, we will come to the Laramie River, on the other side of a town called Wheatland, where we might want to stop for a few supplies."

Not long after they were bedded down for the night, the storm rolled in. The thunder rumbled across the vast prairie. It was so loud that it woke the two little ones. Mary held them close as the lightning split open the night sky with massive zigzags tearing through the thick black clouds that hid the moon behind their veil. Soon, Mary heard the sound of large drops of rain collide with the taunt tarp covering the wagon top. Splat, splat---followed by another volley of lightning and thunder. Suddenly the splat turned into a thud as hail began to fall—it was only pea-sized hail, but it sounded so much bigger when hitting the canvas. John whispered, "I hope those balls of hail don't get as big as I have heard they can. These prairies have a reputation for producing some humdinger hail storms!

~~~~~~~~~

June 12, 1901: It took the small wagon train another day to reach Wheatland, what with two broken wheels, a lame horse, a broken harness---and, a false alarm with Laura Miller's advanced pregnancy.

They stopped briefly in the small Wyoming town and stocked up on a few essential food stores, horseshoes, and a new leather bridle for one of the teams. They moved off the main road and drove the wagons across the prairie, to camp beside the Laramie River before dark set in. The men had decided to take a day off and camp next to the river. Mary rose early the next morning and headed to the river to wash a few clothes before setting her batch of sourdough to rise. She picked her way down the rocky path to the shade of low hanging trees. The early morning sunlight flickered through the tiny green leaves sending rays of light to dance on the shallow water near the shore. Mary was mesmerized as she dropped to her knees, to take it all in---the peace, the solace, the beauty. She breathed deeply and felt the tranquility flow through her body and mind. *To my way of thinking, there is no more beautiful time of day. The sun warms the earth, sending its golden rays across the great blue sky. Just listen to the birds. I hear a robin, a meadowlark, and—oh, the morning doves---such peaceful sounds—their soft cooing echos through the early morning just like on the farm in Nebraska. But as John keeps reminding me, there are always things to miss no matter where you go. Memories are for taking with us.*

~~~~~~~~~

After Mary washed the basket of dirty clothes, she spread them on the bushes to dry in the heat of the sun. Then, she turned reluctantly and headed back to camp. This time alone had been what she needed—a break from the rigors of the trail—eating dust all day and tending to two little ones. Back at camp, Mary and John put together a quick lunch.

As they ate, John said, "Mary, the other men, and I are planning on going over our wagons and livestock today. This might be the opportunity for you to check your food stock and see if there is anything else you need for the rest of the trip. We won't see another opportunity to stock up until we get to Douglas."

Mary grabbed John by the arm before he could walk away. "John, I've been thinking. I surely appreciate the Miller's sharing their cow's milk. It's not that Ruth needs it, I can still nurse her, but Bill needs milk too. Also, you saw how they took the cream and put it in the butter churn then fixed it to the back of the wagon. It bounces around all day, and by nightfall, they have the best butter one ever tasted." Mary fidgeted a bit then raised her chin, "John, I would like for us to buy a cow, maybe when we get to Douglas or sooner if the opportunity arises. We will need our own when we leave the Miller's outside of Douglas. Besides, we'll need one on the farm! It won't slow us up any more than it has."

John said, "I was hoping not to have to drag a cow behind the wagon, but I can see your point; so, I guess we might see if there is one for sale on down the road."

~~~~~~~

Around midday, Ida said, "Mary, would you check Laura. I think she is about ready to birth her baby, but far as I can tell, the head ain't down yet. I sure hope this little gal ain't gonna try and have that baby butt end first!"

Mary smiled calmly at Laura and replied, "I'll take a look at her, and between the three of us, I am sure we can do what needs to be done."

Mary laid her hands gently on Laura Miller's stomach. She moved them this way and that, trying to feel the position of the baby.

"Laura, is there any blood or tightening of your belly?"

Mary said, "I don't feel the feet up at the top where you can usually feel them kicking when the head is down in the birth position, but I wouldn't worry none—they can move overnight and get into the position. I think it will be very soon." Mary wrapped her arms around Laura as she and Ida Mae exchanged looks of concern.

Mary returned to her wagon, pulled out her birthing box, she examined the contents to make sure she had everything she needed. A square piece of canvas waterproofed with beeswax, towels and washcloths, a pair of scissors, string, and a small tincture of Laudanum. Mary repacked the box and stashed it back under the blankets until it was needed. She closed her eyes and bowed her head, saying a quick prayer. *Dear Lord God, please be with Laura and deliver her safely with her first child. Be at my side as I try to help her do this thing. Give me wisdom and help me make the right decisions. This I ask. Amen.*

~~~~~~~

June 15, 1901: They traveled all the next day, following the railroad lines. Bill got all excited every time he spotted a train. It occupied his time, just watching for a train. Herb found a nice grove of cottonwood trees off the road, near the river---a spot which other travelers hadn't spoiled yet. They pulled the wagons up and the men unharnessed their teams and led them down to the water's edge, taking the three older boys and Bill with them.

Ida Mae and Mary went to the river later to collect water for the next day. Ida May said, "I brought along Laura's skin. I have me a feeling she might be in labor. She told me she was not feeling well, cramping and the like!"

Mary said, "Ida, I don't have a good feeling about this birth. I've had three-- lost my first baby after the birth---she had the cord around her neck. With all three, at this stage of the pregnancy, I always felt the head down—I think Laura's baby is breech. We both know that isn't good, especially with the first baby. She is going to have a tough time!"

~~~~~~~~

It was sometime after midnight that Matt Miller knocked on the side of John and Mary Wamhoff's wagon. "Mary, Mary," he whispered, "Mary, I think it's Laura's time. She is in a bad way and calling for you. I can't take it---I can't stand to see her hurtin' like that and there's nothing I can do. Will you come, now?"

Mary threw a dress over her petticoat and chemise. As she climbed down from their wagon, she smoothed back her hair and carried her birthing bag in her left hand. She could hear Laura moaning before she even got to the wagon.

"Laura, Laura---it's Mary, I'm here to help you now. I want you to take a deep breath, relax let nature do the work. Listen to what I tell you. Matt is right outside, pacing as he ought to do." Laura managed a smile at the image of her husband pacing.

"When did you first notice the pains and how far apart are they now?"Laura's face contorted with the force of another contraction. "I've been feeling right poorly since after supper time. I just stayed in the back of the wagon and tried to work through each pain myself. But now---now—they are getting closer, and so hard. It hurts so bad, Mary. I don't know if I can do this!"

With the next pain, Laura's head came up and a low guttural growl came out of her mouth followed by a scream. "Breathe, breathe, Laura—like a puppy dog---try to work with the pain and contractions not against it.!"

Laura's screams filled the night air with each contraction. Ida Mae crawled into the wagon to try and help Mary with Laura. When the next pain came, Mary looked under the sheet. The baby was pushing through and it wasn't the head that was coming---it was breech--just as Mary and Ida Mae feared.

Another hour passed when finally, Mary said, "Okay Laura, you can push now. Give me a good strong push. I'm going to take hold of the baby and gently pull as you push."

Laura gave another long screeching push and the baby was out. She tried to sit up to see it as Mary said, "Laura, don't move—I need you to hold very still. I have to untangle the cord which is wrapped around his leg."

Laura smiled weakly, "A boy?"

Mary worked feverishly with the tiny bluish baby. When the cord stopped pulsing, she cut and tied it; then wiped the birth from the baby's face and blew into his tiny mouth. She worked on him for what seemed an hour, but he was beyond saving. Laura weakly managed to lift her head in an attempt to see her son. "I don't hear him crying—is he alright?" Mother and baby died within minutes.

Mary put her face into her hands and cried like she hadn't cried in ages. It was over---all over. Mary couldn't get it out of her head---*I didn't save Laura or her baby—I failed.*

~~~~~~~

The small wagon train took another half-day off as they dug a grave for Laura and her son. Matthew was going through the motions as complete numbing shock dulled his unbelievable grief. Matthew buried his wife and son---then, he went down to the river's edge to work it out with the Lord. They made twelve miles that afternoon. They noticed where the old road was blocked because of a sheepman's fence. There were some areas in Wyoming where the ranchers ran cattle---they didn't fence the land. They hated fences and sheepmen.

The next morning Matt came over to Mary's wagon and said, "I want to thank you for being there for Laura. I know you and Ida Mae done all you were capable of doing. The baby, the way like---he was born---was too much for both of them. I don't know if this is proper, but I, and----I think Laura would want you to take the baby's clothes and this here cradle that I made. If'n you have room in your wagon, it would please me, Mary. For sure, it would make me glad if you would accept them for your next baby." With that, he turned and stumbled away as undeniable sobs choked him up.

~~~~~~~~~

Mary couldn't get enough of the beautiful blue mountains that seemed to rise abruptly out of the flat Wyoming prairie. They tended to console her with their majesty and grandeur. Mary had no idea how people crossed them; she was just glad they were going around them and not over them, or at least that's what John had told her.

Sitting around the campfire that evening, Mary overheard the menfolk talking about crossing the river on a ferry[6]. Herb said, "I heard that those early emigrants crossed at any number of places from the mouth of Deer Creek all along to Casper—wherever the water depth looked best."

Jim took a swallow from the mysterious liquid in his jug, "That's right! Sure am glad we don't have to cross the Platte this time of year. Those there bridges are a God's send!" He took another pull at the jug.

Matt looked across the campfire, "John and Jim, it's been a pleasure traveling with the two of you and we wish you the best, especially getting over those Bighorn Mountains. I guess we'll have our share of mountains in the Montana country."

John rose, threw what was left of his cigar onto the campfire, and said, "It's been our pleasure to travel with you too. We regret what happened to Laura and your baby, Matt, as we know what it's like to lose a child. I admire your decision to continue to Montana and build a new life. Best of luck to you gents and good night!" Mary noticed that Jim just stayed by the wagon, he didn't say anything to Matt. *I feel he's got his reasons, he's hurting, I can* see.

~~~~~~~~~

It had rained during the night and the morning air smelled of wildflowers and sage. The next day was clear and sunny as the four wagons approached the junction to Montana. John and Jim waited and watched as the Miller and Rohrhoff wagons headed north. John waved at Jim then they flicked the reins over the backs of their teams and headed west. Now, it was just them, just two wagons—heading for Casper, then, the Bighorn Mountains.

As they drove towards Casper, John turned to Mary and said, "I.ve talked it over with Jim and we think you and the little ones deserve another night in a fine hotel to rest and soak in a hot soapy tub. What do you think about us stopping at the Natrona Hotel in Casper? Jim said he wouldn't mind staying with the wagons and teams, allowing us to spend the night at a hotel. After Casper, it's 140 miles of badlands, then hills, mountains, streams, and steep roads down into the Lucerne Valley and the Bighorn River." You think on it and let me know."

John decided against sharing the worst stories he'd heard, the difficulties and unpleasant situations folks had experienced while crossing the vast arid prairie and the looming Bighorn Mountains. Some things were best left, unsaid!

~~~~~~

As they neared Casper, Mary turned to John, "I think the children and I would greatly benefit from staying at that three-story Natrona Hotel in Casper. Did you say it was on the corner of South Center and Midwest Avenue? I assume the stables where Jim will stay with the wagons is nearby? A bed and a bath sound like just what the doctor ordered. The children and I thank you!"

Mary spotted the restored hotel immediately when John turned their wagon onto Center Street. "Oh Mercy me, there it is, isn't it just the prettiest building ever? I love the soft beige with olive green trim, it's so restful and it makes the building stand out. I simply can't wait to sink into that tub of hot water and wash my hair! You could do with a bath yourself if you know what I mean."

Chapter Four

RATTLESNAKE HILLS

June 21, 1901: Refreshed from their one night at the newly refurbished Natrona Hotel and the time spent basking in the tub of hot soapy water, Mary sat beside John on the wagon seat with Bill between them. Jim was driving the lead wagon today.

"John, do you expect we will see any stagecoaches along the way? Do you know how long it takes them to make the same trip we are taking? What did you say these hills were called? Something terrible as I remember!"

John smiled wickedly as he looked off in the distance, "These, are the Rattlesnake Hills---arid prairie land. Well now, back to those stagecoaches--they get down to business—they drive day and night. They drive those horses at a fast trot and even a gallop when the weather is good and the road is flat. They exchange teams and even drivers at various stage stops along the way. It takes them just over two nights and a day to reach Thermopolis and the other way to Riverton and Lander. It's going to take us seven days of driving only in the daytime and resting our horses and bodies at night. We certainly won't push our teams as the stages do. Nice and steady we go! I 'spect it will take us four days to reach Wolton, then another three to cross the mountains—if we don't have any breakdowns and the weather cooperates. As I mentioned before, we'd like to make twenty miles a day if we can. We'll see what cards we are dealt with!"

~~~~~~~~~

"Oh, my heavens! John—this land looks completely different compared to what we've been through so far. It was so green along the river with a few hills, trees, and ravines, but this-this is barren with hardly anything growing at all. It's—it's so rocky with deep gullies and ravines, and—and the soil looks almost yellow. At least we have this stagecoach road to follow. I can't imagine heading out into that vast stretch of nothingness without some sort of trail!"

After a moment or two, she sneezed, then added, "And John, all I smell is dust, dryness, and heat!" A shiver ran up Mary's back as a rivulet of sweat trickled down it.

~~~~~~~~~

That next morning they rode past a stagecoach stop where a coffin-like coach appeared loaded and ready to head back toward Casper. The windows were shut tight, against the insufferable dust that boiled up from the road. Mary stared at the driver and felt sorry for the people inside the coach. "John it must be like a sweatbox in there. How in the world do they even breathe?"About an hour later, John

stood up in the wagon bed to take another look at the road ahead. "Well if that doesn't beat all. Now it looks like we've got a road grader coming down the road—we've got all sorts of traffic today! I wonder how often them fellas have to grade this road. Guess we should try and find a spot to pull over to let them by." John followed Jim's lead as they pulled off the road to make way for the grader.

As the men on the grader drove past, they waved their appreciation that the two wagons pulled over. Sarcastically, Jim speculated, "I spect they put that beefy guy on the back to give the blade some extra weight!"

For two days and into the third, they crossed the most desolate stretch of land they had ever set eyes on. It was a good day when they could find decent drinking water at the few ranches and stagecoach stops. Mary was beginning to wilt in the heat and the children were restless and cranky from being tossed about and being hot. Mary began wiping the children's faces and even her own with a damp rag, just to get the dust off. It was worse than miserable.

NOTE: *They turned north about where present-day 'Moneta' is located.*

John said, "We should come to the town of [7]Wolton in about another five miles where we will spend the night. Supposedly they have a hotel. Perhaps, a soft bed and a hot bath would make us all feel better?" Tomorrow we start the slow climb up the foothills and head for Lost Cabin in the Bridger Mountains. As far as I can tell, after Lost Cabin we turn due west and follow Bridger Creek--- staying in the valley it has cut through the Bighorn Mountains."

Mary dabbed at the grit in her eye and tried to cool Bill and Ruth's faces with a bit more water on a cloth. "I've been thinkin' on what you said about that hotel in Wolton. Sounds pretty good to me, John, I can't wait!" She gazed off in the distance and whispered, "A bath and a bed---for all of us, should help our dispositions!"

Mary said, "There is something special about the sky out here—it's---it's so big and such a beautiful color of blue. Just look at those huge white puffs of clouds floating across the sky towards the mountains. It's like the sky goes on forever but oh, John, I've never in my day, set eyes on anything like this barren land! I hope with all my heart that our land isn't anything like this. I'd want no part of that and I hope you realize that. I have this terrible foreboding that I am getting myself into something I am not going to like one bit!"

John wasn't oblivious to his wife, but he was beginning to tire of explaining every detail to her. What she didn't know, wouldn't hurt her. It is, what it is and they were committed. He kept a sharp eye on her expression, her face — but he knew, oh, he knew! She was working up for a good cry—sooner or later!

~~~~~~~~~

John watched Jim drive the wagon ahead of theirs and thought to himself, *It was a blessing that I ran into Jim there in Cheyenne. I've offered him a job once we get to The Bench. I am going to need someone like him especially if we take on the sheep business along with farming. I haven't said a word to Mary yet, but I want to take a good look at the [8]sheep operations in Wolton. I've been thinking that might be a good cash business to get into as insurance, in case the crops don't come in. If they come in, then, we are rolling in the gravy!"*

As they were talking, John noted how the barren land was gradually, discreetly changing—the sagebrush was taller and there was more of it, which indicated better soil and more rain. John's breath caught in his throat as he glimpsed a snow-covered peak of the Bighorn Mountains off in the distance.

John noticed Mary looking with disdain at the surrounding desolation. "Mary, have you decided---is it Wolton at the hotel tonight or camp out again? I think it would do us all good to have a

nice hot bath and sleep in a real bed. We'll rest up, clean up, have us a good meal, then we'll hit the trail tomorrow." John hesitated then thought—'*Oh, what the heck'*. "Mary, while we are in Wolton, Jim and I have a mind to speak to some of the sheep operations there. We want to find out if there is money to be had in running a few hundred sheep once we get settled in Germania! He is thinking of staying on with us and helping with the sheep and crops."

John pulled a piece of paper from his pocket. "Here, Mary---here is the map of where we are going. I know I showed it to you before but you might be comforted by looking at it again. We've crossed the worse of it!" He pointed to the position where they were.

Mary silently studied the map which John had handed her. It didn't help much! "John, I still have this awful feeling in the pit of my stomach. I won't lie to you and tell you I think this is a good idea. Just looking at this barren, god-forsaken country doesn't help and the thought of going over those mountains in the distance is worrisome. I've never---I ---didn't know mountains were THAT big! And now, you are thinking of sheep are you? Well, I guess there's no harm in asking about them."

She paused and then added, "I don't mean to complain John, but I never realized how riding in a wagon for more than a couple of days can become quite tiresome. I fear my backside will never recover!"

John reached over, put his arm around Mary, and pulled her close to him, "Well now, just be content that you can ride and don't have to push or pull a wagon or pushcart like those Mormon folks we saw a ways back." John looked off in the distance, " Mary, I want you to understand that we have this same road, a good stagecoach road, on which we are going to cross over those mountains. It's not some narrow old cow trail."

June 25, 1901: Their two wagons crested a gentle hill, and holding onto the reins, John stood up in the wagon. "There she is--- there is Wolton!" It was about two o'clock when they finally arrived in Wolton which wasn't much more than a meager collection of log cabins and hastily erected shacks, except for the hotel which appeared, rather substantial. Numerous bands of sheep and their incessant bleating echoed through the streets. Jim pulled up in front of the hotel. "John, why don't you go ahead. Take Mary and the

Courtesy: Tom Davis/Western History Center/Casper, Wy.

children to the hotel and check-in. I can see to the horses and wagons for the night.

John helped Mary and the children from the wagon and they entered the hotel. John secured rooms for fifty cents a night and ten cents extra for the bath. They climbed the carpeted stairs to the second floor. As soon as Mary and the children were settled, John said, "Jim and I are going to take a look at the sheep operation while you and the children rest a bit. The more I think about it and the country we are going to settle in---running sheep, as well as farming, makes good sense. But I have to get more information about the sheep business before I make that decision. We'll be back to wash up for supper at about six."

Mary settled the children in what the locals called a hotel room. She took one look at the grimy windows and thought—*now there is something a little elbow grease, vinegar, and water would take care of. If I had to live here, I'd be putting some cayenne pepper in the scrub water to discourage the mice and whatever else occupies this room!*

It was exactly six p.m. when Jim, John, Mary, and the children were shown to a table in the Wolton hotel dining room. John held the chair out for Mary as she took Ruth on her lap. Self-conscious of her appearance, Mary tidied her hair and drew an audible deep breath then looked around the nicely attired dining room—nicely, for a hotel at the end of the earth!

After a hot dinner of tasty lamb chops, mashed potatoes, and gravy, Mary took the children up to their room. Over another mug or two of beer, John and Jim stayed behind to discuss business.

John watched Mary and the children exit the dining room, then leaned back and lit a cigar. "Well Jim, my man---we certainly learned a good deal of important information regarding the sheep business today. That Oliver Johnson runs about everything in this town and was an open book regarding the operations here. The Cooper Dipping Plant was more than interesting and I can see where it is advantageous to run the sheep through that bathing solution before they are shorn. Dipping cleans the wool up right nice and gets rid of any scab they might have before they are shorn."

Jim took a long slow drink of his beer then added, "It looks to me like they have it down to a science alright. We got some names of sheep ranchers in the Bighorn Basin, as well as the procedure of leasing and getting permits to use rangeland for grazing. We will have to keep our ears and eyes open to find where the best grazing land is."

Jim sat his beer down and said, "There is one other thing I've been thinking about John—I don't need much—room and board and a few dollars a month for necessities will get me by. I realize money is going to be tight until we get things going. After we get on our feet and sell some sheep or the crops--- then, if you see your way clear to pay me a little, I'd be grateful. I know it's your land and your farm, and I appreciate the opportunity to work with you. I don't have much of a life but I know farming and raising sheep. I'll work wherever you need me. Think on it and we can talk later. Well, John, I think I am going to turn in. Tomorrow we start the climb!"

~~~~~~~~

The first thing Mary had noticed earlier when she opened the door to their room was the large metal bathtub in the center of the floor. There was a note nearby instructing her to pull the bell when she was ready for hot water. Mary sat her baby down on the floor and without hesitation, pulled the bell! While waiting for the man to bring the hot water, she inspected the mattress for bedbugs. *We can't be too careful, those things are such pests, and their bite itches for days. I know they like to hitch a ride with anyone and that's the last thing we need in the wagon with us.* Just to be on the safe side she dipped a cloth in the kerosene lamp oil and wiped down the bedstead, legs, and laid the saturated cloth under the mattress. *That should deter any bedbugs at least for the night.*

After bathing Bill and Ruth and putting them to bed, Mary pulled the bell again for more hot water and soap. She could barely contain herself until the boy left with the buckets. Quickly, Mary stripped down and dipped her toe into the sudsy water. That's all it took before she was neck-deep in the hot bath!

Mary released a long breath as the hot water covered her dreary, dust-covered body, letting the heat of the water seep into her bones and her mind. *Ohhhh mercy me-- AHHH, I never in all my days thought a bath could feel so good—almost heavenly! I want to wait up for John and find out what he and Jim discussed after dinner.* After washing the dust from her long hair, she felt her eyelids grow heavy as her body and mind gave in to the delicious warmth of the bath. She stayed in until the water began to cool, then climbed out, toweled herself off, and slipped her gauzy white nightgown over her head. Mary towel dried her hair, then slid beneath the cool clean sheets and in an instant fell into a sound sleep.

~~~~~~~~

John unlocked the door to their darkened room and quietly stepped in so as not to wake his wife and children. He saw the bath still sitting in the middle of the floor and hesitated only a moment before stripping off his clothes and sliding beneath the tepid soapy water. It wasn't exactly the relaxing bath he had hoped for himself but he was glad Mary and the children had partaken of it when it had been warmer.

John washed quickly and climbed out of the tub with other things on his mind as he dried off and crossed the room where his sleeping wife occupied the bed. He slipped between the sheets and reached for Mary.

~~~~~~~~~

June 26, 1901: The small wagon train left the 'luxuries' of Wolton behind as they began crossing the four miles of 'white death'—an alkali flat which lay at the foot of the Bighorn Mountains. Mary looked out over the dismal land. "Oh John, I thought we were through with this sort of land!"

John patted her hand and said, "I imagine this was probably a large lake at one time—took all the runoff from those mountains. Sheep and cattlemen know to keep their stock away from that water, that is, if they want to keep them alive.

Look to the mountains Mary, we will begin our climb in no time at all. I am thinking we won't bother stopping in Lost Cabin, but keep moving while we have daylight and decent weather. By the way, we just learned that J. B. Okie founded that small town—they tell me that he is known as the Sheep King of Johnson County to the north. which includes Sheridan and Buffalo, Wyoming." John chuckled, "Someday I'm going to be known as the Sheep King of the Bighorn Basin!"

～～～～～～

After leaving Lost Cabin, they began the most daunting part of their journey yet, the ascent over the Bighorn Mountains. Mary looked in disbelief at the steep hill ahead. She stood up in the seat and said, "Oh John, there is no way the horses can pull this heavy wagon UP that hill. But, up the hill, they went---with the four teams of horses pulling the wagons. THEN, they came to the top and the earth appeared to fall from beneath them! Both John and Jim pulled their wagons to a stop, climbed down, and began to prepare for the perilous descent. They rough-locked all of the wheels then walked around both wagons making sure all the harnesses and wheels were up to what lay ahead. John said to Mary, "Just keep your eyes on that ranch at the foot of the hill. Don't look up, don't look to the side---look straight ahead at the blue sky and keep the children in the back! And Mary—above all, do not scream!"

Mary grabbed onto John's shirt, "But-but John, what is to stop the wagons from going end over end or fish-tailing around? I heard you tell Jim that at the top, some of these mountain passes drop four hundred feet and more. I'd like to meet the fellow who measured them!"

John turned and looked at her with his steely grey eyes. "Jim and I will stop the wagons from going end over end. You just hang on and be still!"

Against all odds, Mary did what John told her to do. Her fingers gripped the sides of the wagon seat until they were numb. Her back arched stiff and she bit her lower lip until she tasted blood. Her eyes squeezed shut, then opened wide in terror as she felt the wheels of the wagon skid and the forward momentum of the wagon push against the horses causing the brakes to grind, squeal, and smoke. She was beyond terrified but kept her eyes on the Moore Ranch, and she prayed, then prayed harder.

Once they reached the bottom of the hill, Mary turned and with absolute authority, said to John, "If we come to any more hills like that, I am taking the children out of the wagon and we will walk!"

Grinning ear to ear, John wiped the sweat from his forehead and said, "I just might join you!"

John and Jim jumped from their wagons to release the brakes and then they proceeded on down the road. Everyone was relieved and thankful for a safe climb and descent. John would be the last to admit that even his legs were a bit wobbly. And, he knew, this wasn't the only steep grade they would face.

~~~~~~~~~

The elevation of the land began a more gentle swell as they traveled along the valley near the bubbling Bridger Creek. Mary looked with wonder at the seemingly prosperous ranches that dotted the beautiful valley. Peace and relief flooded through her as the hills now became greener, the sagebrush larger, and the air cooler. She lifted her head to breathe in the pungent sage and the smell of cool, running water. It was such a gift; a welcome relief after crossing the endless bone-dry prairie and suffering heat that they had endured over the past week.

Mary looked up the far rise of mountains to where sheer solid cliffs of granite rose from the earth. Then, she looked behind them at the desolation of the vast arid Wyoming prairie. At that moment she wasn't sure which she preferred. *I know it wasn't easy crossing that God-forsaken land behind us, but then I look ahead and wonder---wonder how in heavens name will we ever get over these mountains. I had no idea mountains could or would be this huge.*

Five-year-old Bill's eyes were wide with wonder as he gazed at the cloud-covered blue mountains ahead. "Dad, will we drive the wagons through the clouds? Can I touch the clouds? Can I Dad, can I?"

~~~~~~~~~

Mary also continued to wonder about just how they were going to get over the mountains. "John, does this road go 'over' the mountains? How in the world will the horses pull these heavy wagons—how will they manage?"

John Wamhoff turned his head and smiled at his wife. "Mary, the road we are on does not go 'over' the mountains so to speak, but winds through the valleys alongside Bridger Creek. For thousands of years, the creek gradually cut us a pathway between those high peaks and through the gentle rises; clear up to the pass where we will begin our descent into the Bighorn Basin. Now, it's freshwater and all the trout---breakfast, dinner, and supper--whenever we want it. You can't beat that now, can you?"

Mary hooked her slender arm through the crook in her husband's muscular arm and snuggled closer to him. "I shall just have to trust that you and Jim know what you are doing. I figure we should be just fine since this road is traveled often by the stagecoach and the freight wagons." Mary paused and then added, "John, last night—when you came back to the room. It was---" she blushed as she struggled with the words, "Well, it has been a spell since we've been 'together'. Being on the road in this wagon doesn't give us much privacy."

John reached over and kissed her rosy cheek. "Don't you go worrying none about us being together. We'll make up for it when we get settled, you can count on that!"

~~~~~~~

June 27, 1901: On the second day out of Wolton, the trail crossed Badwater Creek near present-day Lysite, Wyoming, and came to where the road began to follow Bridger Creek and the valley it had carved through the mountains.

Mary was excited, "Oh, John, is that Bridger Creek with the wonderful fresh clear water you've been talking about?"

John smiled and replied, "You are right my dear. I wouldn't think we will have to worry about any dead critters floating down that creek. That water is 'snow-melt', straight from high on the Bighorns. I guarantee it is the best tasting water you have ever had—at least in the last month!"

Bill piped up and asked, "Dad, when we camp tonight, can I wade in it?"

John put his arm around his son and replied, "Well now then, if the water isn't running too fast, I spect you can -- just at the edge now. Don't you go any further out because there are deep holes; and besides, you have to watch out not to slip on the rocks? I also might warn you that it's probably very, very cold."

Mary sat on the seat with little Ruth in her lap. "Oh John, I can't get enough of just looking at how that creek winds its way along, like a writhing snake. I can see what you meant now, that our climb over the mountains will be gradual-like----along the side of this creek." Mary thought of something else, then added, "John, what happens when there is no room for our wagon alongside the creek?"

John smiled and reminded her, "We aren't on a trail, Mary; it's a stagecoach and freighter wagon road---they made it wide enough and filled in spots so we can get by. Now, when them folks are dealing with the spring runoff and that water is running fast, then I 'spect there are some banks that give away into the water." John looked up the trail for a bit, deep in thought, and then continued, "I read in some pamphlet that in the early days, when this road was just a trail, some spots were so steep that they had to lower wagons, horses, and cows by ropes. How'd you like that?"

Mary's eyes opened wide as she replied, "OH, mercy me— that sounds terrifying. I can't imagine doing something like that."

They could have made another five miles, but John and Jim decided to call it a day. Jim pulled his wagon into a gentle mountain meadow with grass up to the horse's belly—the babbling brook just a stone's throw away. John pulled on the reins, fixed the brake then jumped down. He reached for Mary and the children, helping them off the wagon and down into the lush grassy meadow.

John and Jim removed the cumbersome heavy harnesses then curried their horses down. Mary secured Ruth in a sling on her back and walked slowly, reverently through the meadow covered with splashes of mountain flowers---honeysuckle, columbine, larkspur, lupine, and others she couldn't even name. She felt Bill tug on her skirt and when she turned around he had a small bouquet in his pudgy little hands. "For you Mama. I picked them for you!"

Mary bent down and scooped him up in her arms. "Oh sweetheart, they are so very pretty. Thank you!" Mary put him down and took his face in her hands. "Bill, I want to tell you that this is a very pretty country, but there are some bad things which we can't see all the time. Big animals like mountain lions and bears---and that is why you must always stay close to me or Dad. Oh, Mercy, I need to rub some ointment on you and your sister. The mosquitoes are just something fierce out here and they might eat you up!"

After rubbing Bill and the baby's skin with the ointment Mary released her son to his father and Jim, who were taking the horses to the creek to drink their fill of the clear, clean water. Jim said, "I think this will be a mighty nice place to spend the night. I can't wait to fall asleep listening to the sound of the water rushing over those rocks on its way down the mountain. We can all get a good night's rest before we face the next day's climb over this mountain. Dark is going to come early on this side of the mountain, once the sun slips behind those hills."

Jim held the horses while John carried cooking water back to the wagons so Mary could start dinner. She kept Ruth strapped to her back, which pleased the baby while giving Mary two hands to work with. Mary said, "John if you'll chop a little wood and then lift that sheet-iron stove off the back of the wagon for me, I'll have supper ready in no time. I'll fry up all of those fish you and Jim are going to catch and we can eat them for supper tonight as well as breakfast." She paused and with a wicked smile added, "that is--- after you gut them!"

Mary sorted through her pots and pans, then called after John, "Thanks for getting that stove down for me. You keep a good eye on Bill. See to it that he doesn't get too far out in the stream now."

When the stovetop was good and hot, Mary put her cast iron fry pan on it and began to slice the potatoes along with a hand full of wild onions. She threw in a dollop of lard and a couple of pieces of bacon for flavor; then she fished around in the wagon for her other good fry pan.

~~~~~~~~~

John and Jim were deep in conversation as little Bill rolled his pants legs up and ventured a short way into the fast-running icy water. He was having a time of it playing in the shallows of Bridger Creek; picking pretty stones from the water and stuffing them in his pocket, first one then another--inching a little further out until he lost his footing and landed on his butt with cold water up to his waist. Bill lct out a holler as the shock of the icy mountain runoff saturated his clothes. The swift current began to pull him out into the deeper channel—even with all the rocks in his pockets.

John raised his head when he heard Bill yell. Throwing the horses' reins to Jim, John splashed through the shallows into the deeper area of the creek. John reached down through the water, grabbed his bawling son by the belt, and hauled him out of the stream. On the way to the bank, Bill received a good sound whack on his wet behind which only increased the volume of his wailing!

John said, "Dang it, Bill, I told you to stay in the shallow water. Now see what happens when you don't listen. For that, you will go to bed without supper tonight!" John handed his son off to his mother who stripped the cold, wet clothes from his little body and rubbed him down with a dry towel.

Mary said, "John, I think Bill learned his lesson about not going too far out in the water without making him miss supper. Jim promised to catch some trout out of the creek and that will be a real treat. You and Jim go on now and catch those fish. I've got some biscuits raising and a hot pan waiting for those fish."

~~~~~~~~~

Later after supper was over, the dishes had been washed in
the creek, and the children were bedded down for the night, Mary
joined John and Jim by the fire. John was smoking a cigar and Jim
had lit his pipe. Mary stretched her arms high and wide, then rubbed
her lower back as she eased herself down onto a blanket next to the
smoldering fire. She curled her legs underneath her then reached up
and pulled the pins from her top knot, letting her hair cascade over
her shoulders. She slowly ran her fingers through her hair,
luxuriating in the release of tension. She began brushing her long
brown hair in slow fluid strokes; oblivious that Jim was watching
her. After a few minutes, Mary laid the brush down and lifted her
head to watch the fluttering aspen leaves on the trees that bordered
their campsite.

Turning back to both men, she exclaimed, "Land sakes, that
was a tasty supper. Thank you for the fresh trout! Although the food
in Wolton was fine enough, there's nothing like fresh trout and fried
potatoes." Mary sipped some creek water and added, "We'll have a
fine breakfast with some of the leftover fish, potatoes, and a few
eggs mixed in! I always like it when I can put together a breakfast
out of whatever we had leftover from supper." She paused, then
asked, "John, how many days do you figure it'll take us to cross the
mountains down into the Bighorn Basin?"

John rubbed his whiskers, then said, "Well now, Jim and I
were just discussing that very matter. We think if we don't have any
trouble, it might take us two more days to cross the mountains if
luck is on our side. We might run into some snow lingering in the
high valleys. It's still early in the summer, so that's a real
possibility."

John reached into his pocket and pulled out a map. He
carefully unfolded it and replied, "I figure we are about two-thirds
of the way to the Bench!"

John traced the route they planned to take after leaving Lost
Cabin--- following Bridger Creek over the Bighorn Mountains then
down across the badlands until they came to Kirby Creek. From
there, they would follow the gentle downslope of the creek valley to
where NoWood Creek flowed into the notorious Bighorn River.
They planned to follow just to the east of the river until they arrived
at the ferry crossing, at Alamo (present-day Manderson)—then

through more badlands until they crossed the Greybull River, and then up onto the benchland.

John's face broke into a wide grin as he showed Mary their destination---the Bench! "There it is, Mary, right in the upper corner of the map,---our new home!"

Mary studied the squiggles and marks on the well-worn map. Jim stood up, stretched, and said, "Well now, I'll let you two daydream over that map. I'm going to grab some shut-eye. We got us a big day tomorrow!"

Mary looked up at him and said, "Have a good night's sleep, Jim." She gazed at the moonlit starry sky and said to John. "Oh my word, isn't that sky magnificent—I feel so close to the stars—they're so much bigger way up here on this mountain top."

Somewhere up on the ridge above their camp, a pack of coyotes began to yip and howl back and forth. Chills ran down Mary's back. "John, I do think it's time we go to the safety of our wagon. They won't come down for the calf, will they? They sound too close for comfort. That yowl of theirs—makes fear chills run all through me."

John said, "Now don't you worry yourself. Jim is sleeping near our pretty little calf. No coyotes or wolves are going to feast on her! He's got that shotgun right handy, I'm sure of it."

Mary looked wide-eyed. "Wolves? I had no idea there might be wolves up here too. I don't think I want to have a run-in with either of them!"

~~~~~~~~

The next morning they were up before the sun. John and Jim unhobbled the horses and led them down to the creek to drink their fill. Mary followed along with the cooking pot to make the morning coffee. She sat on the bank of the creek as the first rays of the sun caught the shimmering leaves of the aspen trees. "Oh John, just look how the leaves look like little mirrors as they twinkle with the morning light. Did you ever see such a sight in your life? I barely slept last night, what for the howling of those dang coyotes. How close do you think they were? I noticed after Jim gave them a blast from the shotgun, they seemed to reconsider and went on into the night."

After the group started back up the trail to camp, the horses lifted their heads and looked upstream as a doe and her two fawns stepped out of the willows. Cautiously she led her babies to the edge of the water, keeping her distance and an eye on the men and horses. Jim commented, "We could use some fresh venison, but I couldn't take the mama from those little tikes."

Mary laughed and said, "Well now, if you had bought those beefsteaks they had for sale at fifty cents a pound in Wolton, we could have been eating them. Not to mention the potatoes at twenty-five cents a pound. Pretty pricey eating if you ask me? There are probably folks who would pay that much in Wolton, just to avoid eating lamb again!"

Mary climbed up to where she had spotted several currant bushes with green berries. *I certainly wish it was later in the month—I could have made a nice cobbler with those currants. Oh well, we need to get on the road anyway!*

Before long, the two wagons were loaded up and continued on their trek up the east side of the Bighorn Mountains. Men and horses were cool and comfortable in the mountain air.

Mary couldn't get enough of the landscape. How the creek ran lazily, gurgling and bubbling through an open meadow; and in the next instant, it was raging through a narrow gorge where quaking aspen and evergreens fought for a foothold. Then, just as suddenly the landscape changed as they came out into an open area where there were vast fields of glacial moraine, rock, gravel, and house-sized boulders. Mary looked high on the mountainside and saw where the field of rock had broken away over the decades and where lingering drifts of last winter's snow remained.

~~~~~~~~~

It took the two wagons another day to make their way up the meandering road along Bridger Creek. John said, "This road is in fair shape if we can stay out of the deep ruts that other wagons have made in bad weather. It's just the steep grade of some of the hills that make it slow going! We aren't in any hurry to get across these mountains—Jim and I are going to let the horses pick their way."

Mary said, "John, why don't you and Jim switch the horses around and let another team lead now and then?"

John said, "Well now, your Pap told me this— there are some teams, some horses, who are best left in the lead and others who prefer to follow. They have personalities much like us. So, we found those who like to be in the lead and that's where they stay!"

Mary smiled and replied, "I think I do recall Pap saying something like that." She paused then added, "John, I think this is the best part of the trip. It is so beautiful up here and the water is so fresh." She laughed, recalling Bill's experience in the creek. "I don't think Bill will venture out in the creek again after the scare he had. He's been mind'n me right well!"

John patted her hand, "If that is the worst he ever does, we'll be lucky. It all comes with raising kids I suppose. Little Ruth is a good traveler—she hardly ever makes a fuss, but then most of that is because when she isn't sleeping, you have her tucked in that wrap around your chest or on your back. She likes that well enough!"

~~~~~~~

They made camp early that night because of the dark clouds gathering to the northwest. Mary said, "I feel rain in the air, don't you John?"

John replied, "I do and besides, there is a particular calm— no wind—like everything is getting ready for a storm. So we will take heed and make our camp early today. Better safe than sorry. I'd suggest a cold supper too. I don't want to make a fire in case the wind starts up.

After securing the horses, they ate cold biscuits with cheese and ham along with yesterday's applesauce and called it good. They crawled into the safety of their wagons just as the first rumble of thunder rolled across the mountains. Jim could see flashes of lightning as the storm approached their camp. In the other wagon, Mary cuddled the children next to her and John as the rain began to fall. She laid in the dark, wrapped in John's arms, and listened to the sound of the raindrops battering the taut wagon canvas.

As usual, they rose with the sun and ate a quick breakfast, then broke camp. John said, "We need to make up some time today and get down this mountain."

Jim replied, "You got that right, but I don't want to drive these wagons on mucky roads along a steep drop off either. That rain didn't amount to very much so by the time we get to the narrow one-way road it should be dried out fine and dandy!"

~~~~~~~~

June 29, 1901: They crested the summit of the Bighorns and began their cautious descent down the western side, into the basin area. The open meadows were a sight to behold. The storm had moved on and had left them with a bird-egg blue sky. The mountainside was a vast carpet of every kind of flower that would bloom at that altitude. Mary was beside herself. "John, oh John—I have never in my life seen such a sight. What kind of place is this Wyoming? Parts of it look like God forgot all about it and other parts, like these mountains---well, it looks like he lives right here!"

Shortly before the noon hour, John stood up in the wagon and waved to Jim. "Let's stop here and let the livestock have a good feed on this grass. Mary wants to lay in the meadow and look up at the sky. Won't hurt us to have another look at our wagons before we start down the mountain either, give those axels an extra dose of tar and such!"

Mary pointed to the sheer rock mountain that loomed to the north of their road. "Over there John, there's still snow on that mountain! I'm so glad we don't have to go over that. This road has been a godsend. Soon we shall be down in the Bighorn Basin. I must admit that I am getting excited to see our new home."

John smiled at her, "Mary, now remember that where we are going to farm isn't in the mountains. It will be out on a prairie without many trees, just like Nebraska was when your parents homesteaded. But, as I have promised you--we will plant trees, lots and lots of trees. I want to put in rows of those fast-growing Western Cottonwoods. Also, we must have us an orchard of apple, cherry, and plums once we are settled on a spot. I've got a mind to plant me some hops for my beer as well!"

Mary looked at John with grave concern, "Well John, what a surprise that is---hops! I know this isn't where we will live. I just hope our new home is not as ugly and barren as the badlands between Casper and Wolton!"

Luckily, she didn't catch Jim glancing at John, as the two exchanged unspoken knowledge.

That evening, Mary went to bed early with the children. John and Jim sat around the fire talking and sharing a pint of hooch. Jim said, "John, I'm somewhat concerned about that road we'll be taking tomorrow. There was talk in Wolton that near the summit there is

room for one wagon to pass on the road. There's no way two wagons can pass. I heard that there usually is a stage official who leads the wagons one way, then turns around and takes the waiting wagons the other way. I hear it's a hair-raising road; narrow, with no place to go but over the edge, hundreds of feet to the bottom of the canyon. They tried to build a fence of sorts but as I hear it, a horse and wagon could easily go through it. It's more than likely just to give a person some visual sense of safety."

"Its also got a pretty steep grade in places and we got us some heavy wagons. I know the stagecoaches get through, but they are lighter and they have two teams of horses pulling them as well. Our four teams are going to come in right handy, Im'a thinkin'."

John replied, "I wouldn't worry none on it, Jim. After all, you can just close your eyes and let the horses find the road!" John slapped Jim on the back and laughed until his sides hurt. He could feel Jim's eyes bore into his back as he walked to his wagon, and it only made him laugh harder.

~~~~~~~

The sun slowly presented itself, like a glowing disc burning through the clouds until it melted them away. Shots of melon, gold, red, and orange ran through the morning sky, with the promise of another beautiful day. Mary was up before the others to washup in the creek before she started breakfast. She stood for a bit and gazed at the narrow gap between the rugged mountains that lay ahead of them; then turned back to the east and looked at the steep road they had passed the day before. It was obvious they were climbing at a sharp rate.

This was the day Mary had been dreading. John had explained how they would make their way over the treacherous, narrow canyon pass. Mary simply couldn't get it out of her head— terrifying images of their team and wagon plunging off the narrow road and into the raging creek below.

~~~~~~~

Later that morning they arrived at the spot where the narrow, one-way road began; they got in line and waited until the official stage man on horseback came to lead them through. Mary dared, only once, to peer over the edge of the road down to the rampant creek waters below. It was terrifying! After cresting the summit without incident, the road angled down along the Kirby Creek drainage. Everyone let out one big sigh of relief, as the stage man

turned around to lead the waiting group of wagons back the other
way.

~~~~~~~~~

The rains came again, sometime in the night. Mary lay
awake on her bed in the wagon and listened to the soft patter of
raindrops on the wagon cover. She pulled the blanket up under her
chin and snuggled down as the sound of the rain lulled her to sleep.
As the storm built and spread across the mountains, deafening
cracks of lightning lit up the black night like the Fourth of July,
followed by a volley of thunder that rolled up the valley floor.
Frightened, Bill joined his sister and their parents in bed, as nobody
could sleep through all that commotion.

Come morning, there was a dusting of snow on the grass
and trees, but higher up on the mountain a significant amount of
snow glittered in the morning sunlight. It was downright chilly
outside, with no sign of it letting up. They ate a cold breakfast and
hitched the horses to the wagons. The road was miserable, muddy,
and slippery--it was slow going. It was close to the noon hour when
the clouds finally began to move out and patches of clear blue sky
broke through. Before long, the grade of the land began to even out
as well. That afternoon they crossed the beginning of Nowood
Creek. They continued along Kirby Creek as it spread out through
the mile-wide valley it had cut as it flowed from the mountains. The
beautiful, lush valley spilled into the arid hills of the Bighorn Basin.

~~~~~~~~~

That night they made camp near the foot of the Bighorn
Mountains in a beautiful wooded glade near the rushing creek. The
sound of fast-running water and the evening breeze brushing
through the leaves of the trees was intoxicating. After another
supper of fried potatoes and fresh trout, Mary put the children to bed
and then joined Jim and John as they sat around the campfire. The
men smoked and Mary leaned back on a log, stretched out, and
listened to them talk as she took the pins from her hair.

Jim caught himself staring at how the flames of the fire shimmered in her long auburn hair. He found it hard to pull his eyes away from her.

To break his mood, Jim pulled out a bottle and poured whiskey into three cups. Mary put up her hand. "Oh, thank you; Jim, but I don't drink strong spirits!"

Jim threw back his head and laughed. "Now then, I think I might have to introduce you to 'Doc--- Al K. Hall'---guaranteed to take care of what ails you!

Mary elbowed Jim in the ribs. "Well, okay, just a spot to help me sleep!" Jim had a wide grin on his face as he poured Mary, 'just a spot'.

John leaned back against a log and decided to give Mary a little ribbing. "Now, Mary, you know you have tasted liquor now and then. This is a special occasion---our last night on the mountain. Tomorrow, we head into the badlands at the foot. Just keep remembering that there wasn't a thing growing on those Nebraska hills when your folks homesteaded their place, and now it's a beautiful farm."

An hour later, Mary excused herself and climbed into the wagon to prepare for bed. She had to admit she felt a little woozy after drinking that 'spot' Jim had poured for her, or maybe it was the refill? John and Jim were having a lively conversation around the campfire and it became louder the more whiskey they drank. Mary couldn't help but eavesdrop on what they were saying.

Jim lit his pipe, inhaled, and then said, "John, that conversation we had with them herders in Wolton was right interesting. The more I see and hear about this country, the more I am thinking that sheep would be a smart cash investment."

John emptied his cup, as Jim quickly refilled it. "We might as well kill this bottle—it would lighten the load just a tad now!"

John inhaled the smoke from his cigar, and said, "I'm thinking the same as you, Jim. I'd be right beholden' to you if'n you'd hire on with me. We make a good team. It's good land in the 'basin'---folks call it red gypsum and it's said to be strong in lime and potash which is what we need to grow wheat and barley. We have a lot to learn about raising sheep in the 'basin'. I'd like to talk with some sheep ranchers who have been in the business down there though before I dive headlong into it! Wouldn't you agree?"

Jim lifted his cup to his mouth, drank the rest down then wiped it clean with his shirttail. "I certainly do agree that we have some homework to do on them sheep. Jim lit his pipe and inhaled deeply, "Now about tomorrow. I spect it will take us about another day or two, to get downriver to that ferry crossing at ---what was the name of that place?"

John looked at the map and replied, "Well now, we already crossed that Nowood River or Creek whatever they want to call it---we follow the trail down alongside the Bighorn River—let's see—oh, right there—Alamo!" (Manderson) There's supposed to be a ferry there to take us across. I sure wouldn't want to try and ford that rouge river especially if it's running high and fast. Chances are that this time of year with the spring runoff ---it is!"

Jim added, "And, you can usually tell it's plenty deep just by how smooth the water flows! I hear say it's got a pretty bad reputation—they call it the 'killer river' 'cause of all the whirlpools, sandbars, and the brutal undercurrent!"

John said, "Right you are, right you are! We should stock up on our water after we cross the river because there's going to be another dry stretch for a couple of days until we reach the Greybull River."

John looked off into the distance. "You know, Jim, Reverend Wunderlich told me of two German Lutheran families--- Bosch and Goss, or something like that; sheep ranchers who have large spreads around these parts. They are parishioners of his and he said they would most likely be right hospitable."

~~~~~~~~~~

The next day was bittersweet. Nobody was eager to leave the cool beauty of the mountains. After their descent, they came to several ponds of alkali which were a strangely beautiful sight. What water was left in the ponds was as white as milk. There were wire reeds along with an odd type of grass surrounding the pond, and Mary noticed there were no animal footprints. *They obviously know it's bad to drink!*

Chapter Five

BIGHORN BASIN

Old Chinese Proverb: *If your vision is for a year, plant wheat. If your vision is for ten years, plant trees. If your vision is for a lifetime, plant people.*

     July 2, 1901: That next morning, Mary rose before John and the children. She took her small water pot and pushed her way through the brush, picking her way over the rocky path down to the Bighorn River. She found a perfect spot where the river water lapped lazily at the banks. Mary filled her water skin then rested it on a flat spot on the sandy river bank. She paused in thought for only a moment before taking her shoes off then wading out to where the cold water splashed against her calves. Feeling the current pull at her legs, Mary inched her toes forward until she felt the river bottom drop sharply. She backed up from the dangerous edge and stood there, basking in the coolness of the water as the first light filtered through the cottonwood trees and sparkled on the water. Without warning, uncontrolled tears ran down her cheeks as her mind went ahead to what she feared the next days would disclose; and more than anything---of what she left behind. *Oh dear Lord, I know we are getting close – close to where we will live. I don't see anything to encourage me---everything is dry dirt hills and sagebrush, except close to the rivers. It's so far from my home, from my family and I miss them to my very core. I have a terrible foreboding that I might never see my parents again—it won't leave me. Help me, Lord. Help me to do my best, to accept my task, and my destination.*

     Mary snapped out of her melancholy mood as she started back up the steep bank towards their camp, intent on getting breakfast ready.

     John stood in her path.

     They stared at each other for what seemed like minutes before John stepped forward and took her into his arms. "Oh my, Mary; my Mary. What are those tears on your cheeks? I know how worried you are and where your imagination is going. I feel you are going to be deeply disappointed with the land where we are going to homestead. It's raw land without trees, boardwalks, and nice houses. We can do this—you and me. Together we can build something to hand down to our children—and to their children----something to be proud of. But I can't do it alone, nor do I have any heart to do it alone. I need you by my side, Mary."

Mary pushed John back so she could look into his eyes. "Yes, John, of course, I am worried about what I can only imagine lays ahead. I know it's probably going to be the hardest thing I've ever done besides losing our Amanda. But, John, I gave you my vow on our wedding day. I will stay by your side, I will do my best and I will try to have a cheerful heart---that's all I can promise. I will try it!" She looked off into the distance with a giant lump in her chest and tears in her eyes. "We left what would have been a good life, an easy life, a civilized life to come out here! This is going to be a hard life, John; hard for all of us! I only hope that in the end, it's worth it."

~~~~~~~

They stayed on the eastern side of the fast running Bighorn River[8] for the rest of that day. The green beauty and coolness of the mountains to the east flaunted their memory. Yet as Mary found herself looking to the east, she was comforted by the beauty of those mountains. All that lay ahead to the west was the river and a horizon of barren, sagebrush-covered hills. As they rode in the wagon, she thought to herself---*I overheard John say last night that we would stay on this side of the [9]Bighorn River for two days as it cuts through the low lands flowing north. I'm relieved we will take a ferry across rather than try and ford that river. It looks treacherous to me.*

On the other side of a tent settlement known as, Worland, they passed several prosperous-looking sheep ranches nestled in the rolling sage hills. As they neared the river, there were more small farms, pulling water from the river to irrigate their fields. Mary said, "John, look across the river on the west bank. I see some farms that look to be doing quite well. Maybe we could stop here?"

John replied, "Mary, we've discussed this before--this land cost too much money"

As luck would have it, as they crested the next hill, they saw a tidy sheep ranch spread out through the sage-covered hills with a comfortable-looking ranch house. John waved to Jim to pull into the ranch, hoping it might be one of the sheep ranches Pastor Wunderlich told them about. As luck had it, Wilhelm Goss, was out in his sheep corrals as the unexpected wagons pulled into his yard. John and Jim braked and jumped down. Curiosity, getting the better of them, they walked over to the vast assortment of corrals where Mr. Goss was working. John tipped his cap and said, "Good day! We are part of the German Lutherans on our way to the Bench, north of Burlington, and the Greybull River. Reverend Wunderlich told us about two German sheep ranchers in these parts—Goss and Bosch. Might you be either?"

Wilhelm Goss smiled and extended his hand. "Yah, Yah, I am Vilhelm Goss. You are velcome to vater your horses and if you need fresh vater, ve have a good vell over dere by the house. Mama is inside, busy vith the little ones, but you are velcome to help yourselves."

John smiled and replied, "We are grateful for the water. We are running short of good drinking water. We'll ferry across the Bighorn River tomorrow if it doesn't rain. Say, once we get settled and build us a house and barns, we've been thinking of starting a sheep operation. Do you sell your lambs to folks around here or take them all to Wolton?"

Mr. Goss said eagerly, "Oh nein---I vould sell you some of my lambs. That vould be a gute thing for both of us, and I vould give you best price because I vould not have to ship dem. I vould be glad to help you get started in the business and tell you vhat I have learned! You get settled on your land first, then you come back and ve talk. Oh, by the vay---the good Pastor has given a new name to your Lutheran settlement---it is now called, Germania!"

John and Jim gave their thanks, waved goodbye to Mr. Goss, then headed for the ferry crossing which was still a good half-day away. About an hour later they all had a refreshing spit-bath from a brief shower that rolled through the area. Mary laughed, "Mercy, that felt good! At least we didn't get drenched and it didn't turn the roads into a muddy mess. It just cooled us off and settled the dust.

John watched the storm move to the south and said, "I'm a bit relieved that the storm didn't do more. Those clouds looked right ugly. I've heard talk about some of the storms that brew upon these plains---wind that can knock you to the ground and torrents of rain that'll wash the whiskers off your face!"

Mary put her hand over her mouth and giggled, "Now then, John, you are exaggerating just a tad there, I'm sure."

John turned and smiled wickedly, "Think what you want, little mother, think what you want!"

~~~~~~~

That next morning, as they prepared to make their way to the ferry crossing, John and Jim discussed the chance meeting with Wilhelm Goss and the possibility of starting their sheep business.

John said, "Jim, that meeting didn't 'just' happen—it was meant to be. I know God is with us and is opening doors for us. It was neighborly of Mr. Goss to offer to help us, and I am quite certain he is the man I will eventually speak with about sheep!"

Later that afternoon, Jim pulled alongside John's wagon and pointed to the huge thunderheads building over the Bighorn Mountains. "I'd say we would be smart to find a spot to hunker down in. Looks like a pretty good one coming right at us. I can hear thunder and see some lightning already."

As Jim and John looked for a good place to stop, the advancing storm rolled in like beer barrels down a stairway. A bolt of lightning struck not two miles away, followed by booming thunder. Mary held her hands over her ears as Bill climbed on top of her and Ruth began to scream at the top of her lungs. Another bolt of lightning was so close it seemed to rock the wagon and the horses nervously danced to the side. Jim and John had all they could do to hold the four teams from bolting. Large drops began to fall as another lightning strike hit a tree not far off. John followed Jim to the side of a cliff facing away from the direction the storm was taking. They knew better than to head for a clump of trees even though it was tempting. Mary said, "Oh my word John---I swear I felt the hair on my head stand up with that last strike!"

~~~~~~~

On the morning before Independence Day, they waited in line while the Alamo ferry took a wagon ahead of them across the river. John and Jim paid 75 cents per wagon to the ferryman—a Mr. Nordstrom and waited their turn.

As they were busy getting the horses and wagons ready for the crossing. Jim said in a low voice, "John. I've been thinking about tomorrow----I have this feelin' Mary isn't going to like that last stretch before we get to Germania. On that map, it looks like darn rough and desolate country---all dirt hills and sagebrush. I don't envy you none, John—you've got your work cut out for you convincing your little woman to settle in this raw country."

John smiled nervously at Jim and said, "Well now, Jim, you know what the good book says about 'worrying about tomorrow'. Besides, I got her to come this far. I don't think she'll be real eager to go back over that mountain!"

Mary watched with wavering skepticism how the ferry was controlled with strong ropes, tied securely around sturdy trees on the river bank. She noticed how the man beside the tree gradually loosened the ropes letting the boat float with the current, while at the same time controlling how far it went. The ferry floated across

Courtesy: *Wyoming at 125: Our Place in the West* – **Bill**

and downstream, instead of trying to fight the current and go straight across the strong river. Suddenly, it was their turn as the ferryman motioned for them to come on board. There was only room for one wagon and two teams on the flatboat ferry. John led the other two teams of horses into the river and loosely roped them to the side of the crudely-built ferry and prepared to let them swim across.

Mary held Ruth on her lap and Bill insisted on standing up in the driver's seat with his little hand grasping his mother's blouse, so he wouldn't miss a thing. John stood on the ferry, near their horses. Peering over the edge, Mary saw how the ravenous river caused the ferry to buck and sway. She could feel the strong pull of the current and how it pushed the ferry downstream. Mary gritted her teeth and gripped the wagon seat until her fingers were numb.

John saw that Mary was concerned. "It'll be fine my dear. Have a little faith!"

Mary glared at him and replied, "I DO have a little faith. But, very little at this point, John!"

July 5, 1901:They began to lose light on the eve of the next day as they neared the banks of the shallow Greybull River. There were no ferries here, as it was normally a shallow, slow-running river. They camped on the south bank that night (no trout only catfish). After supper, John and Jim walked along the brush-covered bank to find a good place to ford the shallow stream the next morning. It didn't take long to find tracks in the grass where other wagons had recently crossed.

They were walking back to camp when they heard Bill screaming his head off. John took off at a run! Mary was holding her squirming son tightly as she pulled a burning stick from the fire. Out of breath, John and Jim thundered into camp. "What is going on here? What are you doing to the boy?"

Not releasing her grip on the wriggling child, Mary looked up and said nonchalantly. "Well, this boy done got himself a fat tick here on his neck. I am heating the stick to hold to its backside so it will let go of him, and Bill thinks I am going to burn him. Can you help me with him, John?"

~~~~~~~

That night after prayers, Mary tucked the children into bed. Little Bill looked up at his mother. "Mama, I am sorry that I cried when you was trying to get that tick off me. Thanks, Mama." He put his little arms around her neck and hugged her tightly.

Mary smiled as she joined John and Jim near the campfire. John inhaled his cigar and said, "Well, Mary, we are almost there. If all goes right, I think we should see our benchland tomorrow afternoon. I suppose you have an idea of what it is going to look like. There are no trees, Mary. It's up on a flat bench, which sits next to another flat hill they call Table Mountain. To the north of Germania,' the land drops down to Dry Creek where we'll get our water until we can dig ourselves a well." John laughed and said, "I don't know why they'd name a creek 'dry creek' when there is plenty of water in it?"

John glanced at Mary, who sat still as stone with her hands folded tightly in her lap as she stared into the fire. "Mary, think on it---we will plant trees, orchards, gardens, and build a fine white house just like you grew up in; but it's going to take time. As I explained before, we will have to live in a soddy the first year or two. Jim here said he wants to stay on and help us get settled---maybe go in with us."

Then---John played his ace card or what he thought was his ace card.

"Mary, remember the bible verse: *"For I know the plans I have for you,"* declares the Lord. *Plans to prosper you and not to harm you. Plans to give you hope and a future."* **Jeremiah 29:11**

Both John and Jim held their breath as Mary's head snapped up and her eyes blazed with anger.

"Soddy?--You mean a dirt house; an adobe like Mama and Pap lived in before I was born? Don't waste your time sugar-coating it for my account." Mary lowered her head, took a deep breath, and chose her words, "Well, I suppose if Mama could do it then I 'spect I can too. It will be an experience, and Pap said they were real warm in the winter and cool in the heat of the summer months." She paused, then with a twinkle in her eye, she added, "And, John, I do remember the verse. There's no need to quote the Bible to me! That was overdoing it just a tad!"

John chose silence for a short time then said, "It's high time you know just what is involved in getting this place of ours built up and what it's going to cost. We need a house, fences, a well, a barn; feed for the stock, and provisions for our family for one year. I have brought enough capital with us to cover the first year expenses until I can secure credit at the local bank. The local stores will probably want cash until they feel they can start a credit tab for us. We might be getting frcc land, but even that will cost us money for taxes and building the canal to get water. Nothing is free."

John had gone too far and realized it too late.

Mary's eyes flashed as she shot back, "John Wamhoff, I am not an imbecile. I do know what it is going to take in time, effort, and money to get this place of ours going. I would appreciate it if you would give me some credit. That would obviously, help your cause, a great deal!"

Jim put his head down and turned away from Mary's line of vision as he began to laugh and said under his breath---*Well, John, you had that coming to you; in spades if you ask me?*

~~~~~~~~

The next morning, John forded the shallow Greybull River first, with Jim's wagon bringing up the rear. They didn't have any trouble crossing the river and were up on the other bank before nine o'clock. Not wasting any time they followed the rut-filled road northwest towards Stringtown and Otto where several Mormon farmers had already built farms and were attempting to irrigate their

fields with water from the Greybull River, using a crude, but
effective irrigation system.

John and Jim took a good look at how the Mormons got their
water up from the river and made their mental notes. Moving on,
they followed the road to the far west end of Table Mountain. The
Mormon town of Burlington was a cluster of maybe 8-10 dwellings.
It had the only post office in the area; which wasn't much, but it
served the purpose.

Courtesy: Jeannie Edwards Cook --- Burlington Post

While John stopped to water the horses and register with the
local post office for mail, Mary stuck her head in the door. It had
rough plank floors instead of dirt, but it was uneven and full of
splinters. There was a crude, homemade table with two fruit boxes
for chairs, a wood-burning stove, and over in the corner was a
sagging metal-framed bed. She approached the woman sitting at the
table. "I beg your pardon, might I be able to mail a letter to Nebraska
from here?"

The woman smiled and extended her hand. "I am Mrs. Riley,
the postmistress, and you most certainly can mail your letter. Let me
see it and I'll tell you how much that will be."

Mary smiled and said, "I'm Mary Wamhoff and we are
going to homestead on the Bench. We came from Nebraska—it was
certainly a long ways!"

The postmistress said, "You got to ride in a wagon—if you'd
walked and pulled a Mormon cart like some of us did---then you
could say it was a long way!" She laughed and continued, "I know

it don't look like much here now, but we are all working on making it a fine place to live. Anyways—welcome, and you owe me two cents for the letter. I think that Wegner's store up on Road 10, near where you are headed, has a new post office so you don't have to come so far to mail your letters. Have a good day."

Mary smiled sweetly and replied, "Thank you, it was very nice to meet you, Mrs. Riley—be seeing you."

Just to the north of Burlington, they climbed up a gentle hill, out of the ancient river channel. John's wagons crested a hill and were immediately buffeted by a strong wind from the north. Mary held onto her bonnet as the wind tore at her clothes--- great clouds of dust boiled up into their faces as large tumbleweeds rolled across the road. Bill and Ruth dove under the blankets in the back of the wagon. Without acknowledging the nasty hot wind, John looked around and said, "This looks to be a right nice piece of ground, nice and flat, and you can tell it is fertile. No telling what all this fine land would grow with some water. According to the map, the Bench is just to the east *of* us now, back toward the Bighorns."

Mary simply turned and without words, gave him 'one of her looks' that expressed everything she had to say. Then she had second thoughts---"If this wind doesn't let up, you won't have much of that nice piece of ground left!"

They drove past several small, struggling farms. John saw a man out in a field and stopped to talk to him. "Good morning! My name is John Wamhoff and this is my wife Mary, and friend Jim Klane. We are heading to Germania--- you know the group of Lutherans who are settling up there with that—that [10] Wiley Project! Going to claim us some land there and give it a try. What's your name?

"I'm Ivan Preator. Most of us Mormon folks been livin' around these parts for, oh, around three on to five years. We're working on bringing water up from the river down there to irrigate these farms. It's good land but it'd be better with some water. We got us a plan to build a dam up in those mountains to the west, but it all takes time and money"

"I take it you are with them Lutherans who built that adobe church up by Wiley's place. That bunch thinks they are going to get water up from Dry Creek there like we are here. It's not an easy thing to do, let me tell you that. But I think between blended manpower, us folks, no matter what religion, can get water up here for the good of us all, out of this Greybull River."

"Now, about Dry Creek—that is where you'll more than likely get your water until you dig a well at your place. Has some good firewood---cottonwood, down there too if you get tired of burning sagebrush. After a spell, you will be wantn' to go to Garland for supplies. You follow that road by the roadhouse, down and cross Dry Creek. You head north on the road over what we call the Divide---then you come to Coon Creek, and after a spell, you cross Whistle Creek before you get to Garland. The Shoshone River is the big river on over to the North---the Indians called it Stinking Water--- because it does have a peculiar odor!" Ivan laughed and continued, "If you need anything, just give me a holler! Good luck to you folks now, be seeing you!"

~~~~~~~

They waved goodbye to the farmer and continued north on the road. Mary looked at the arid land that lay around them. "OH Mercy me, John, I can't even see a single tree anywheres up here. There's only sagebrush and some scrubby grass, but no trees---no trees for as far as I can see! But I can see those beautiful blue mountains to the east over there. Those are the same mountains that we just crossed over, aren't they John?"

As far as Mary could see, the mountains were the only beautiful thing in this God-forsaken land! She held her head high and swallowed several times, choking back the tears. She would not cry—no---she would not cry as disappointment and doubt gnawed at her. Mary knew with every fiber of her being—that this---was where she would spend the rest of her life. Every river they forded, and every hill they crossed over, brought them closer to the future John dreamed of; and farther from the wonderful life that she had left behind, had given up. As if cold water were thrown in her face, she realized that it was all ---for him; what he wanted; what he dreamed of.

Courtesy: *They Called It Germania*
– Tom Davis

Eagerly, John cracked the reins over the backs of the horse team. He could smell the finish line--excitement blinded his concern for what Mary may be feeling, while it fueled his eagerness.

John said, "Mary, I haven't seen any sign of the Wiley Project ditches or dams. The first thing on the agenda is to secure a current map of which sections are available and decide where we want to live in Germania! As we discovered, Burlington and Otto are mostly Mormon. They are good folks, but we want to live with our kind. Pastor Wunderlicht's vision was to establish a Lutheran settlement, like Germantown. Once I see the plot of land I want, I'll apply for it – homestead it, then Jim and I can start on our sod house and some sort of shelter for the horses before winter sets in."

Mary's silence did not go unnoticed. John hoped that eventually, Mary would come to see what he saw in this land, this opportunity.

What Mary saw was a lifetime of hard work, going without most of the nice things life had to offer back in Germantown. She knew she was being forced to live her life where she didn't want to live it. She saw through it all--- John's eagerness, his excitement, his vision of building something of his own, of being an important part of something. She also saw herself as a necessary part of his vision of raising a family, making a home, and creating his dream of an honorable life.

  John stopped the wagon on a high rise and stood up. "Look there, way off to the East. Those are the same Bighorn Mountains we crossed to the south. To the north of them is Pryor Mountain, then swing around westward and you see the Beartooth Mountains, and the big one sticking up by itself is called Heart Mountain. Those mountains to the west are part of the great Rocky Mountains where Yellowstone National Park lies. We are surrounded by mountains---everywhere you look. Someday, Mary, across this bare land, we will live to see tall groves of green trees, fenced fields of grain, with cattle, and sheep in the pastures—and Mary---fine, white frame houses. Now, all we can see are sagebrush-covered hills and flat barren lands! Mark my words, Mrs. Wamhoff—we shall see a new Germania! We are going to build us a fine community here, I feel it in my bones!"

  John waved for Jim to pull up beside them. He pushed the brake forward, wound the reins around the brake, and jumped from the wagon. Mary watched him intently as he squatted down and dug his finger through the exposed dirt and putting it to his mouth, tasted it.

  "John, for heaven's sake! What in the world are you doing?"

  John was grinning ear to ear. "Your Pap told me that if it's bad soil, it'll taste salty---if it's good soil, it'll taste like blood. This, this is blood! It's good soil---we've got us good soil, Mary!"

John was silent for a few moments just taking in the lay of the land. He remembered John Westerhoff telling him to beware of land that was too flat. *'You'll have to deal with marshes and sloughs and it is always slow to drain'*. John thought to himself—*It might be called a bench but for sure, as far as I can see, it is a bumpy bench—there are many hills and low places spread throughout!*

Before long, they came to a sign that read, 'Road Ten'. John waved for Jim to follow as he turned north on the road, "Well, now, it looks like Wiley's roadhouse should be a couple of miles up this road here. The map indicates we are to turn due north and follow it to where the church, roadhouse, store, and post office are located--- at the townsite of Germania. I was told we can camp there for a few days until we choose our land. It should be right handy for you, Mary, to be close to the store and post office. You might even meet a few people.

Mary looked out over the dry desolate land. "John, as soon as we are settled, I'd like it greatly if you would buy some chickens; lots of chickens, a couple of goats and pigs, about five turkeys, and maybe another good milk cow. I know until then, you can shoot sage chickens, rabbits, and wild turkeys for meat if they live around here. And, next spring, I want to plant a big garden too, so I can put up a large portion of our food for the winter."

John replied, "That sounds like a plan but before I go and get them things I have to build us a good house, some sheds, barns, and coops for the animals. They tell me it will cost about $2.50 an acre to clear the land. Wood is $3 a ton and when we hire help— they are paid $1 day plus board. It'll take time Mary, but having Jim as part of our operation will certainly help us finish all we need to do before the snow flies. He's God's gift to us, Mary---it's a good omen that he wishes to stay and work with us to build this dream. He's a good man, that Jim is!"

Mary's thoughts turned to Jim. *We don't know for certain who he is or where he came from, just that he wants to work with us. All I can say is that I trust him, but I also feel that something bad has happened to him. I see it in his eyes, the man has been deeply hurt. Someday, maybe he will tell us and let us help him. I know in my heart that Jim is a good man who is haunted by his past, whatever that may be.*

Chapter Six

GERMANIA

July 6, 1901: The Wamhoff's turned north on Road Ten and went about two miles before coming to a scattering of buildings—the proposed townsite of Germania. Jim and Herman Wegner's store/post office was their first stop. It sported a false front façade with six by six-foot paned windows and double doors---and it was whitewashed too. The store was well stocked and it housed the post office along with a central telephone. The telephone's main

Courtesy: Jeannie Cook --- Wegner's Store

switchboard was to the north in Red Lodge, Montana. They built a line that extended from Red Lodge through Garland, Wyoming to Germania, and Burlington. Just to the east of Wegner's store, across the road, was the adobe Missouri Synod Lutheran Church and Si Pierce's blacksmith shop.

Due north on the 'main street', John spotted a fairly large building. "By George, that has to be Solon Wiley's two-story roadhouse, complete with a second blacksmith shop and barns for stagecoach horses and the freight wagons that stopped there. "That man doesn't miss a lick, now does he? They tell me that he paid to have the first phone line ran to his roadhouse, but later put it in Wegner's store."

John headed straight for Wiley's. He didn't waste any time getting his hands on a map of the available land in Germainia so he might file a claim as soon as possible! John's hands shook as he unfolded the topographical map of Germania.

John climbed back up onto the wagon seat with the map clenched tightly in his hands. He sat down and turned to Mary, "Here it is—our opportunity to choose where we are to live in Germania! We'll camp here tonight, giving us a chance to look this map over carefully. Then tomorrow, Jim and I can ride out and take a look at the lay of the land. Mary, I'm sure you and the children are tired of riding in this wagon and it might feel good to stretch your legs a bit; maybe walk over to the church and stock up on supplies at the store."

~~~~~~~~~

Mary spent the better part of the day, washing clothes and baking bread; then she and the children walked over to the store where she bought them each a lollipop while stocking up on a few necessities. After re-organizing their wagon, she and the children took a short walk over to the Lutheran church to get acquainted.

~~~~~~~~~

Later that afternoon, John and Jim rode up to the wagon after having been gone most of the day, looking over the available sections of land. Mary said, "The children and I walked over to the church today and met some folks. Did you know that they already have your name on a list of first members? They were so nice to me, I also learned that our church is the ---the second established Lutheran church in the state of Wyoming---and—and they are planning to build a wood-framed schoolhouse next year."

Mary handed John the list of members of the Lutheran church. *Christian Ahlgrimm, J. Adam Preis, Friedrich Mayland, John D. Kathmann, Friedrich Moeller, P. S. Wunderlich, Herman Ahlgrimm, William Pepper, Otto Goedicke, Dietrick Moeller,*

Herman Werbelow, Mathin Bosh, Herman Teyler, and the latest member to join--John Wamhoff!"

They had found a decent spot to pitch a temporary camp, nestled in a small clump of trees. After supper, Mary put the children down to bed in the wagon then joined John and Jim by the campfire. She sat down, drawing her knees up to her chin, and wrapping her arms around them. Mary waited for an opportunity to speak and

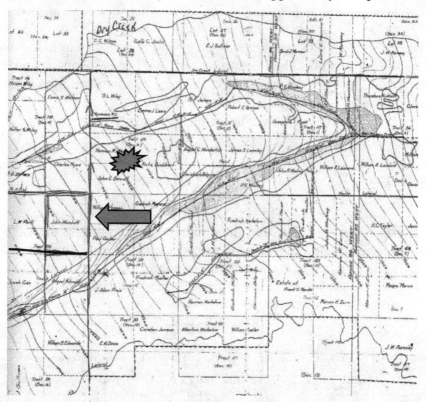

lifting her head, she said, "John, do you have an idea what plot of land you are wanting? I've noticed you and Jim pouring over that there map." John smiled, "Yes, as a matter of fact, there is a particular 160 acres that I have my eye on; near the corner of that main Road 10. You can see it here on the map. We walked it today. No large boggy places, no alkali; and by the way, it has some fairly tall black sagebrush which is a good sign of fertile ground." John pointed to the far left corner of the Bench Canal Drainage District map. "I like this other 160 acres across the road that belongs to

Pastor Wunderlich. Someday if the Pastor moves on or wants to sell, I might snag that as well."

John looked off into the distance, "I know better than to take on too much at first. If I were by myself, 160 acres would be about all I could handle. If we decide to run sheep, we'll need more land to graze them on. Jim and I were talking about adding that 160 acres across from Aggards on the upper end of the Bench---tract # 95---if we decide to run sheep too. We wouldn't live on it but we would need it for the sheep. But, first things first---file the claim and then start building our home. We won't have a moment's rest as we need shelter for the stock, and to dig a well before the snow flies. There's plenty of sagebrushes to grub out—we'll use that for firewood; put up fences, then plot out a garden in the spring. I was going to ask you, Mary, if you would mind if Jim slept at the house with us until we can get a separate bunkhouse built for him?"

Mary laughed, "Oh for lands' sake John. Jim has practically lived with us for the past two months—he's like a brother! Of course, he can sleep at the house."

John suddenly turned serious, "Mary, this is very serious now—you and the children have to be on constant watch for rattlesnakes out here. They tend to want to go where it is shady—out of the sun. Also, when we get the chickens and stock, I'm going to show you how to shoot cause we'll have coyotes, you can bet on that!"

Mary's eyes opened wide, she tipped her head back and she began to laugh, "You---you, are going to show me how to shoot a gun? You don't know anything about me, do you, John Wamhoff? Do you seriously think Pap didn't teach us, girls, how to shoot? I'm probably a better shot than you are! However, I must admit I'm not a fan of rattlesnakes and I also know how to take a shovel to them!"

~~~~~~~~~

After visiting Wiley's store the next morning, John said, "I just received some interesting information. "Walter Wiley, Solon Wiley's brother, runs the store and the post office. He said they get mail delivery on Tuesdays and Fridays. According to him, Road Ten is the 'main street' of Germania. It is 'the' road that the stage and freighters take north to Garland and beyond. Walter told me that

Solon laid the townsite out right here, where the freight road comes up out of Dry Creek because there's a lot of traffic on this road." John bent forward and got serious. "Walter also told me to remember--- that if Solon Wiley ever says 'frog'—he expects us to jump!" John put his head back and laughed until tears rolled down his cheeks. "That tells us something about the man, doesn't it now?"

John said, "Okay, Mary, here is what I found out. Because of the Carey Desert Land Act of 1894, which provided segregated lands to be reclaimed by irrigation; we can take up a 160-acre homestead when I can present our water rights purchase agreement from the Wiley Canal Company. I have to come up with 25 cents per acre—which adds up to $40. That goes to the state, with another 25 cents per acre to be paid in four years. To obtain a deed for our land, we'll have to prove the land is irrigated, cultivated, and that we live on the land.

John pushed his hat back on his head in frustration. "Above THAT, I have to pay Solon Wiley's, Bighorn Basin Development Company, for our 'water right purchase'; and it has to be paid before we can settle on the land we want. Wiley is willing to allow settlers to 'work out' what they owe him by working on the canal he's building. That's right big of him I'm thinking!"

John tightened his jaw and narrowed his eyes, "I am going to pay him outright, Mary, and be done with it. We have the money and I do not want to be held accountable for any debt while I am concentrating on getting settled"

Mary smiled and said, "You have it all figured out, don't you. I think I'll take the children and walk over to the post office. I want to send another letter to my folks and let them know we have arrived in Germania. I saw the red mailbox outside there where I can just drop a letter to be mailed."

Sitting around the fire, John and Jim talked long into the night. John said, "We need to build adobe brick forms. I think we'll mix up the clay with straw in the back of your wagon. We'll fill the brick forms and let them dry. While they are drying, we can mark out where the walls will be for our two-story adobe house. Look here at the plans I've drawn up for the house. The lower walls will be double-wide to hold the weight of the second story."

Jim rubbed his beard, "We've got us so much to get done. We just have to make our plans and then work like honey bees. I think we both want to get a house and outbuildings built before winter sets in. There are plenty of stories about how bad the winters can get this far north!"

Jim added, "It'd be a good idea to get stocked up on food for the winter as well. I can work on the house and barn if 'n you want to take the wagon over to Garland and get a load of food staples and materials for the house, like nails and such."

John said, "You know Jim, I've been thinking I'd like to pick up some lumber in Garland and build two or three wagon boxes without the bottoms, just the sides--to extend the depth of our wagons. That would be right handy to haul more straw, grain, and hay until we get hay racks." Jim replied, "That very thought occurred to me the other day. We will see about it in Garland!"

~~~~~~~~~

Even before they officially filed a claim on the land, John and Jim paced out the locations for the barn and the house; and staked out the plot for the garden just to the south of the house. After a few days, they broke camp at the roadhouse and headed south on Road 10 to the land John had filed on, where they set camp again— this time on their own land. On the NE4 of Section 9 T52R96, they didn't waste any time in starting the adobe house. They were surprised on the second day to see a wagon load of local men arrive to help them make and stack the dried adobe bricks.

One man commented to Jim, "It makes short work when a lot of us pitch in. This is going to be some house---two-story!" They stacked the bricks until the walls were between eight and nine feet high. As soon as they could get in, Mary and some of the women sealed the cracks with mud mixed with straw and old newspaper.

While the house was being built, the Wamhoffs continued to live out of the covered wagon. Mary pitched in making the adobe bricks and even Bill proved to be a good helper. Jim and John made numerous trips down to Dry Creek to cut timber for the supports and wood floors in the house. Another neighbor brought his grasshopper plow over, with which to cut rectangles of sod for the barn walls. With the help of numerous neighbors, the Wamhoffs had the first floor of their two-floor adobe house up and ready by September 23rd.

On one of their trips across the hills to Garland, they managed to secure a large cedar ridgepole and sturdy side timbers to hold the second story sod roof.

Jim and John laid thick cottonwood poles crosswise for the first-floor ceiling and rough-cut planks over that for the floors. Some folks lived in adobe homes and some lived in dug-out houses cut into the hillside, throughout the Bench like the Preis's down the road.

NOTE: *John Wamhoff was the only settler on the Bench to build a two-story adobe house. It was located along the highway, just to the east of where the Ted Wamhoff/Sue Coguill home is now located.*

~~~~~~~

John and Mary's closest neighbors were the Peppers and Gerbers to the east, Bennett and Wegner to the Northeast, Charles Meyer to the North, and August Rejwaldt to the south. They met other settlers with names like---Hodson, Griffin, Grabbert,

Ahlgrimm, Jensen, Moeller; and in later years more folks moved onto the Bench-- Edwards, Peterson, Gernant, Menzel, Lorenz, Fink, and Davis.

Wamhoffs didn't bother to plaster the inside walls this first winter as they were more intent on getting a shelter over their heads. John surmised, "We can whitewash the inside next spring if that's what you prefer Mary." Mary said, "I rather like the newspapers we are using to cover the walls. It's colorful and interesting at the same time!" She was just thankful she didn't have to live in a dugout. She liked the look of the two-story sod house that had actual windows to let the light in.

After another week or so, they moved into their new, two-story adobe home. The rest of their furniture hadn't arrived from Nebraska on the emigrant train, which had a reputation of being like the 'slow boat to China'! The freighters at Garland kept telling them "any day now, your beds and tables and chairs should get here!" They all knew winter was coming—the mornings were cooler and the smell of autumn was in the air. This increased the urgency of getting the outer buildings finished before the first snow flew.

Mary missed watching the leaves of the trees turning, as there were very few trees in Germania at this time; so she had to make do with watching the trees down by Dry Creek. Before the ground froze, Jim was able to dig an outhouse hole as well as a small root cellar for Mary to store a few vegetables, which the neighbors had given them along with some they had bought in Garland. Mary had to laugh when one of the neighbor women handed her an old Montgomery Wards catalog. "Just a house or I should say an 'outhouse' warming present!" It was true--they needed the soft pages of the expired catalogs to use in the outhouse, and they never used more than they needed.

Mary gazed at the house. "Oh John, it's much more than I expected. Thanks to our neighbors for pitching in and helping us get it built, now we will be warm and cozy when winter comes. We have a kitchen and living room on the lower floor and all of our bedrooms are upstairs; even Jim has his room in the north wing upstairs. We have real glass in the windows and I greatly admire that store-bought front door you purchased in Garland. I am very pleased John! The wood stoves that you put in each end should keep us toasty warm; and what with heat rising, the upstairs should be passable. Do you think it would be possible to dig a water well near the house before winter? That would benefit us as well as the stock- -not having to haul water from Dry Creek." Mary gazed over at the corrals where three milk cows stood. "Oh John, I am so grateful the Werbelows sold you those milk cows and for only $13 per head. As long as we let her calf have part of her milk, our cow will give us her fresh milk and cream.

　　　　John said, "Mr. Gifford, Mr. Pepper, Jim, and I are going to take the wagons to Garland tomorrow to get our beds and some other furniture that has finally arrived on an emigrant car from our house in Nebraska. We'll be gone four days—takes us two days to get over there and two back, unless it rains—then we'll have to deal with Coon Creek and slippery muddy roads!"

　　　　John and Jim were up before dawn on the day they were to leave for Garland. The sun rose red over the Bighorn Mountains, the

Courtesy: Garland --- from Powell Valley

promise of a clear day. John cupped his mug of black coffee in his hands and listened to the call of the turtledoves somewhere nearby. He sipped his coffee as he patterned out their day. John inhaled deeply, eager to get on the road as Jim climbed onto the wagon and they were off to Garland.

~~~~~~~~~~

Mary felt a certain peace now that some of her former furniture was situated in the new adobe home. Familiar pieces like their bed, kitchen table, chairs—Ruth's cradle, and their throw rugs made it feel like her home again. There was more to come.

The house, a well, and outbuildings were finished to house the stock in and the weather was holding. John and Jim lost no time in clearing the land with the teams of Percheron horses they had bought in Cheyenne.

Two horses were harnessed to the log-leveler which was dragged across the sage-covered land, ripping sagebrush and stubborn stumps from the ground. Homesteaders learned to drive the horses in a criss-cross fashion across the fields to tear every bit of the sagebrush from the ground.

John told Jim, "Folks say if black sage grows on your land it's a good indication that its fertile soil. We got us lots of that short salt sage as well---that comes out with a plow and a good harrow--- a lot easier than the black sage. By the way, Jim, I think we might do what Grabberts did with their sage and use it to build up the corrals and barns!" NOTE: *Black sage can grow between three to five feet tall, with trunks that are between 6 to 10 inches in diameter. It was often preferred by homesteaders over real wood for their stoves.*

Wash day was a task that none of them looked forward to; but with the water well next to the back door, the task was easier than hauling water from Dry Creek. First thing, John got the two fires going outside and hung Mary's large cast iron pots over the fire then filled them with water. She had two going at once—one was for washing and the other for rinsing. Mary checked the clothing first and used the scrub board on stubborn stains, then she threw them into the first pot of boiling water with her special lye soap—stirring it every once in a while with a large paddle. When she thought they'd 'cooked' long enough, she fished the clothes out with a wooden pitchfork and let them cool enough so she could wring them out by hand before throwing them into the rinse pot. Mary would swish the clothes around until the suds were gone, then she'd fish them out and let them cool before wringing each piece by hand again. Then she hung them up to dry on the crude clothesline. While she was doing this she also had two little ones to watch and meals to prepare! After the first wash day, Jim saw that Mary needed a decent clothesline to hang the wet clothes on. He took a half-day to cut and set the 'T'-shaped poles in the yard and string five lines of smooth wire between them.

That next week, just as Mary finished hanging the last of the washed clothes on the clothesline, Jim rode into the farmyard driving a wagon. She pushed back a few strands of damp hair, wiped her forehead, and walked over to greet him. "I want to thank you again for that clothesline, it's a fine thing."

Jim pointed to the wagon bed, "You're welcome for the clothesline—it weren't anything. Got a few sticks of wood down by Dry Creek, but also looky here what else I done got down there!"

Mary peered into the box of the wagon and there lay a deer. Without thinking she gave a 'whoop' and hugged Jim around his neck. "And Jim, you dear man, you even skinned and gutted the thing out. Slice us off some of that and I'll throw it in a pot with some taters, onions, and carrots. We'll have us a good meal tonight." She started to walk away and turned, "Oh, and Jim---would you cure that hide—it would make such a nice rug in front of the stove!"

That evening they feasted on fresh-roasted venison, warmed-over beans, carrots, and a tasty dried-fruit custard. Mary reminded John, "I used the last of the eggs in that custard and they are out of them at Wiley's store. Walter said he hopes that some come in on the next freighter from Garland. It's rather difficult to cook without eggs. Did you say you were going to buy a few chickens from some of our neighbors? The more the merrier, I say---we need eggs and I like having chickens in the yard, scratching around."

After asking around, Jim bought two dozen chickens from Wiley and that took care of that problem!

~~~~~~

Folks were generally helpful and encouraging to new settlers who were putting down roots in Germania. John learned that it hadn't taken long for several of the original people to pick up and move back to Nebraska or wherever they came from. According to them, settling in Germania was not worth the effort it was going to take to work and build the land. That night at supper John remarked, "I've been told that when them people gave up and were headed back to Billings to catch the train, they were heard to say—'*In God we trust—On the Bench we bust!*'" The Wamhoffs were finding out that Wyoming was not for the weak of heart---it was demanding and rough, but with so much beauty, reward, and promise.

~~~~~~

At breakfast that next morning, Jim said, "That darn fox got another chicken last night. I see how he gets in, then I fix that and he figures out another way to get his chicken dinner."

Mary said, "We can't afford to put out poison because of the children, but think on it Jim and maybe you could build a trap of some sort that wouldn't be of harm to the little ones." Jim replied, "Not to worry, I've got some ideas."

After breakfast was over, the men were out of the house, and the breakfast dishes were washed and put away, Mary began to prepare the bread 'sponge' for the weekly session of baking the next morning. She pulled out her jar of 'yeast foam' which she used in her recipe. It called for lard, white sugar, baking soda, flour, yeast, and warm water. After mixing it up and putting it into two large pans, she covered them and placed them close to the woodstove where they would stay warm overnight. Bill was watching her work and when she covered the bread dough and set it aside, he asked, "Mama what are you doing? Why do you cover the dough like that?"

Mary bent over and kissed his ruddy cheek, "Well now, I'll tell you. I mixed up that dough just right, and now it needs a good long nap; then tomorrow, it will be ready to shape into the bread pans. If I don't let it sleep overnight, it won't get nice and fluffy--- just like you like it. If you are a good boy, I might even fry some of the dough and you can have it with maple syrup for breakfast!"

~~~~~~~~

The next morning Mary was up early, kneading the bread dough, dividing it up, and putting it into the pans to bake. "Do you think there will be any bread left for Jim and me by the time we get back from Garland? That son of ours can eat a loaf all by himself!" John laughed and looked at the list of things Mary wanted him to buy at the store in Garland. "Remember, we need more eggs—those chicken don't lay enough to keep this family in eggs. We are running short on flour, sugar, and"—she paused, "John---I am so hungry for lemon pie. If they have any lemons, please buy them!" Mary knew John—he would come back with way more than what was on that list. John Wamhoff loved to shop and buy things for her and the children.

After filling their tummies with fried bread dough and syrup, Bill and Ruth went out in the yard to play while Mary tended to the bread, "Now, don't you two go far. There are wild animals out here and you don't want to get ate up, so stay close to the house and don't go poking around where you can get into trouble!" Bill's eyes opened wide with the understanding of what his mother said.

That evening after dinner, Jim said, " I rigged up a wooden pole, trap box that will hold that fox once he gets inside. I'd like to use some of those chicken guts you took from the chicken we had for supper. By morning I expect we'll have us that fox!"

True to his word, the next morning a mangy looking fox was indeed inside the pole trap and none too happy about it either. Jim took his gun out when the children were down for their nap and shot the critter through the head, then disposed of the body. It wasn't a week later that Bill came running into the house, fit to be tied!

"Mama, Mama---Ruth is stuck inside the fox trap and she can't get out. Come quick!"

Wiping her hands on her every present apron, Mary hurried out to the chicken coop where Ruth was indeed inside the pole trap, the door shut tight. She was bawling her eyes out and Bill was near to tears. "Is Jim going to shoot Ruth like he did the fox?"

Mary rubbed his curly head of hair and laughing said, "Oh for pity's sake Bill, Jim isn't going to shoot Ruth, but he will have to get her out, I don't know how that trap door works. You run out to the field and flag him down, tell him to come back to the farm right away!"

Minutes later, Jim rode in on a workhorse with Bill on the back, holding on for dear life. Jim jumped off then handed Bill down as they hurried to the chicken coop. Jim stood with his hands on his hips and looked at Ruth stuck inside the trap. "Well now, I never thought we'd catch such a pretty little fox as this!"

Bill pulled on Jim's shirt and said, "Come on Jim, get her out of that thing before she wets her pants!"

Jim laughed and bent to release the door to the trap, then pulled Ruth out and picking her up, he hugged her to him. "Now then little girl, I want you to promise me not to mess around any traps that I might set. You get into big trouble that way, okay?"

The next day, Jim came up with a new and better way to keep the foxes and/or coyotes out of the chicken coop at night. He built an eight-foot-high wire run around to the chicken yard. At night he put one of his border collies inside the run and 'bingo'---no more trouble with foxes or any other critters.

~~~~~~~~

John and the other men arrived back from Garland with their wagons heaped with boxes of food and other household goods. Bill ran out to the wagon and was pulling on John's leg. "What did you bring me, Dad, what? A surprise?"

John laughed and said, "Well now, I bought some '*moo juice*', some '*cackleberries*', and some '*long-tailed sugar*'. Is that what you wanted?"

Bill's expression and excitement disappeared immediately, "I didn't ask for anything like that, what is that stuff?"

John carried a box into the house, "Well Bill, those are just funny words for--- MILK, EGGS, and MOLASSES!"

Bill laughed and said, "Those sure are silly names for milk, eggs, and molasses. WHAT did you bring for ME?"

John whipped out two lollipops--one for Bill and one for Ruth. He smiled as Bill ran to the living room chair, sat back, and began working on his lollipop with gusto.

~~~~~~~~

Mary was busy as a bee getting settled into her new house before the first snow. It lacked storage, so Jim built her some cabinets with doors for her dishes and kitchenware. *It's certainly a far cry from the lovely Victorian home I had in Germantown; but it is a sound, solid house which I'm determined to make into a home. Having all of the things here, in this house that we shipped from Nebraska makes it so nice--nice to have familiar things around me again, especially in my kitchen. I think those lace curtains hanging in the windows are just lovely. I love how the light filters through the flower pattern.*

Come next spring, I will plant a big garden where Jim has already plowed the prairie; and then, I'll fill that cellar to the brim with canned goods and root crops. While Bill and Ruth were napping, Mary took a break and walked out to the edge of the field. After a bit, she turned and stood looking back at their house. *It's definitely turning colder. I can smell winter coming. I love this time of year and how the sun picks up the different colors of the land from the slant of the sun. It's a special time of year when the earth is getting ready to rest, to sleep. The sun is setting earlier now and the air seems to cool quickly when it sets. Winter isn't far off and I figure we are ready. We've gotten into a daily routine already, and I like the feel of knowing what to expect. The men chopped a ton of firewood and stacked it against the barn, and there's a nice pile just outside the kitchen door for me; it's handy that way.*

John leaves our bed around five in the morning to do chores, he usually stops to fire up the cookstove for me before he goes out. I get up not long after and dress, then start breakfast. Breakfast is on when he and Jim return and that's about the time when Bill and

Ruth awaken as well. By then I have the kitchen all nice and toasty warm with a hot breakfast waiting. I dread doing the laundry in the cold months. We wear the same clothes all week, changing on Saturday night. I won't be able to hang clothes outside—they'll freeze stiff on the line. We'll have wet clothes hanging from the rafters, dripping onto the floors. John will have to break the ice off the stock water troughs and travel will likely become almost impossible at times. We'll see how these Wyoming winters measure up to the Nebraska ones we are used to.

All the settlers who were German Lutheran, religiously attended services held in the adobe church every Sunday. The interior was whitewashed to make it as nice as possible. The Pastor built the altar of painted wood planks with the gold cross and candlesticks on it. It was covered with a gold, velvet altar cloth. A beautiful two-foot cross was carved by hand out of cedar and hung

above the altar. Rough-hewn building planks were laid across blocks—to form rough pews. The church was located on Road Ten, near the Wiley Roadhouse, stage stop, post office, a temporary adobe school, and the blacksmith shop.

Mary laughed to herself thinking about what happened the first Sunday they attended services. *The children and I followed John into the church and suddenly he stopped short. He paused only a moment, then turned to me and said. "I want you and the children to follow me and sit where I sit!" John marched right down the aisle to one bench from the front and walked into the row and sat down. I paused, seeing that the women were all sitting on one side and the men on the other. I looked at John with a question in my eyes, and he motioned for us to come on and sit beside him! Boy, did that get tongues to wagging. Separation of our family wasn't what we were used to in Nebraska and neither of us thought it was right. Families should sit together and that's just what we did. It took a while for that to catch on in Germania, but pretty soon, all the men were sitting with their families!*

On the way home from church, John said, "I hear that the church board has settled on a location for the Lutheran cemetery. They are putting it way to the south on Road Ten near Table Mountain and Dooley Gulch---and they are fencing it. These folks aren't letting any grass grow under their feet for sure!"

John added, "At the meeting the other night there was voiced great concern that our school and church are located on land owned by Mr. Wiley, who isn't a Lutheran. It's probably a matter of time before he charges us rent! The vote was to find or receive the gift of land on which to build the school, parsonage, and church---which the church will then own. I donated the southeast corner of our filing for the school because it's nearer the main road. When the time comes to build, others have vowed to donate land for the church and parsonage."

John paused and then said, "The church board voted that each member is responsible to supply a certain amount of fuel to heat the school and church with. And----guess what? When the time comes, a few church members are going to the mountains and chop down a proper Christmas tree for the church services. The ladies will be in charge of candles and treats for the children!" John paused and then added, "I think this is a good group of folks and I think our life here is going to be everything we ever wanted."

Mary's eyes opened wide and she paused a moment as a smile crossed her face. "Oh, John, I almost forgot to tell you that the ladies asked me to join their homemaker's club. We'll get together once every six weeks or so and discuss local issues, homemaking problems, and solutions. I am quite pleased---I feel like I have so many new friends."

~~~~~~

That evening, the temperature dropped to the point that John fired up the woodstove until it glowed, spilling heat throughout the adobe house. Jim retired early to his room as he usually did and John sat smoking a cigar while Mary did her mending. Mary stopped sewing, and leaned forward, gently laying her work-worn hand on her husband's arm. "John, there is--is something I have been wanting to say to you. I've been wrong and downright stubborn about us moving to Wyoming, fretting about leaving behind a life I loved. During the church service, I saw how devoted and faithful these people are. They show their faith and hope in the future--- where all I have done is complain. I want you to know-- I am deeply sorry, John. All I was thinking about was myself and what I had to give up. I know that if we are going to make this work, we both have to make the effort for our family's future. I know it now."

John looked as if someone had poured cold water over his head. He had not been expecting this from Mary. Before he could respond she added, "John, can you forgive me—give me another chance to stand at your side and build this new life? It's what our Lord wants I am most assured."

John stood and gathered Mary into his arms, he kissed her quite soundly, "I thank you, Mary. I need you as much as you need me. Together we make a good team—we will build a good life here. I love you, my dear!"

That night after putting the children to bed, John and Mary snuggled under their fluffy down quilt. They laid there, talking about the day and what tomorrow would bring. John said, "I think I am going to grow wheat on that twenty acres near the road and barley on the west forty." Mary reached over and took John's hand and laid it on her stomach. "I am going to be growing something else over the winter. We'll have to wait until June, but I'm quite sure we are going to be adding to our family!" John sat straight up in bed and wrapped his arms around Mary. "Oh, our child will be one of the first to be baptized in our newly formed congregation."

~~~~~~

Around of first of November, John was called upon to administer his profession as a mortician. He sat up a table and took his instruments to where the body was laid out in the barn and where a wood coffin was waiting. The family had supplied him with clothing for the deceased body. John was almost finished with his duties when he heard horses in the yard. He opened the door to the barn and stepped out. "Good morning to you gents, what can I do for you? I thought you were supposed to be digging the grave today."

Mr. Jensen said, "Yah, that is right John, and we got us a pretty good start on it until we hit frozen ground and the digging done stopped right there. We had to build a fire down in the hole and keep it going to melt that ground. We'll get that hole nice and deep—it'll just take a day longer than expected."

John nodded and replied, "I was thinkin' you might have a problem. Don't have to worry about the body---it's cold enough in the barn. He will be all ready for the services on Friday. You better go tend to that fire now. Thanks for lettin' me know!"

~~~~~~~

Early December 1901. John was shoeing a saddle horse in the barn when he heard Henry Wegner gallop into their yard. John stopped what he was doing and walked out to meet his visitor. Before John could say anything, Henry gently pushed John back into the barn and closed the door. "John, I think I have some bad news for your wife. There was an emergency letter they brought up from the main post office in Burlington last night. It's from Mrs. John Westerhoff to Mrs. Mary Wamhoff; marked urgent!"

John stared at the letter that Henry was holding. With shaking hands, John reached for it. He was tempted to tear it open and read it before Mary, but on second thought that wouldn't be respectful. He looked up at Henry and said, "Thank you so much for riding over here with the letter---I agree that it might be bad news."

John waved goodbye to Wegner and turned toward the adobe house where Mary was busy with the children and preparation of their supper. John pushed open the door and Mary looked up. "Wasn't that Henry Wegner out in the yard? What did he want?" Without a word, John held out the letter to her. Mary froze as she saw the letter and the expression on John's face. He crossed the room toward Mary and handed her the letter, "It's from your mother, Mary, Henry thought you would want it right away."

Mary's hands shook as she sat, and hesitated, before opening the envelope. She took a deep breath, straightened her shoulders, and tore the envelope open.

My Dear Daughter Mary,

What sadness we must share with you at this time. Your father and sister Hilda were riding to Seward in the buggy. It must have hit a rut as it overturned. They are both gone, killed in the accident. There was nothing anyone could do for them—it was almost instant death. By the time you read this, we will have had their funerals. I am so sorry, Mary. We understand that you live too far and it is difficult to travel from Wyoming, especially this time of year. We all realize you are just getting settled in your home and with Christmas coming, travel is almost impossible for many.

The funerals were very nice. Your Pap and Hilda are laid to rest in the Germantown cemetery under the pine trees. I know you was always special to your Pap. We all will miss him. Please go on with your Christmas—for the children. Robert is moving into the house with me. He will be fine company and someone for me to fuss over. Your family sends its love. Mama

John watched as Mary clenched the letter in her hand. She looked up at John with disbelief and tears in her eyes. "It's Pap AND Hilda---they were—they were both killed in a buggy accident on the road to Seward. They've already had the funerals. Mama said they all knew it was too far and difficult for us to travel all the way back to Nebraska."

Mary rose on unsteady legs and walked to the front window, she parted the lace curtains, and for the children's sake, pretended to look outside. John saw her head go down and her shoulders shook with her sobs. He moved in behind her and wrapped his arms around her thin shoulders. "Ahhh Mary, Mary. What terrible news—and so unexpected. They will both be sorely missed by so many. John Westerhoff was a great man—a fine man and little Hildy was the light of their lives. I know what he meant to you, Mary. As Christians, we know we will see him and Hildy again. Why don't you go lay down in the bedroom? Jim and I will get supper on for the children." With tears streaming down her face, Mary turned and walked towards their bedroom. Jim had heard everything and reached out to touch her shoulder as she left the room. Little Bill watched his mother. He knew she was crying but he didn't know why.

~~~~~~~

Christmas was a solemn time. Even though Mary and John tried their best to make it happy for the children. John and several of the men from the area drove to Cody and cut Christmas trees for the church and some of their homes. Their tree wasn't a big one, but Mary helped Bill and Ruth make cutout snowflakes and chains from paper to hang on it. She put the pierced tin star on the top—the one she had brought from Germantown. She thought of all the times Pap had cut their Christmas tree and they all had such fun decorating it---all the things Pap had done for his family, and now he was gone. It was odd how out of the blue she would find herself thinking about something Pap had done and the sadness would come again. Mary knew in time the memories would make her smile.

While the children were enjoying their few toys after Christmas, Mary was finally able to sit down and write to her mother. She pulled her tablet from the drawer along with a pencil. Using John's knife, she sharpened it to a fine point. Bill saw what she was doing and asked, "Mama, why don't you use a pen and that ink to write with?"

Mary kissed him on the cheek and replied, "Because it's faster to write with a pencil. With a pen, I have to dip it in the ink too often and ink costs more money as well." Satisfied with the answer, Bill turned and resumed playing with his toys. Mary paused a moment to gather her thoughts before writing-----

Dear Mama and family,

We continue to be deeply saddened by your news of the death of Pap and Hilda. It was the most terrible news one could receive. We are also saddened by the fact we were unable to attend the services. I remember the last time I saw them both, standing in the yard, waving goodbye to us. Pap was very special to me—always my champion. How are you doing by now, Mama? I am so very glad that Robert has moved in with you to take care of things around the farm and he will be good company for you. I must tell you that we are expecting another baby in the summer. I am feeling well and our new two-story adobe home is quite grand compared to some dugout homes in the area. We have made many new friends here and the church is strong. John is thinking of going into the sheep business as well as farming. I must close for now. Please write when you have time. Love and prayers from all of us----Mary

At three months, Mary was over the worst of the morning sickness and she had that 'pregnant glow'—she looked beautiful and was feeling fine. She stood at the window and watched as John and the children played in the fresh snow. Mary's hands went down to cradle her growing stomach. *Please, dear God—give us a healthy child. I can't help but wonder what our Amanda would have been like---I'll never forget our baby girl, never.*

~~~~~~~~

June 1902: It had been a wet, cold spring and all of the farmers were late getting their crops in the ground. After a long day in the fields, John and Jim were putting the horses in their stalls when John began to laugh. Jim was mystified, "What's so funny, huh?"

John slapped Jim on the back and said, "You know, Jim, if you are lookin to find you a woman, I'd suggest you be careful when you've been chewing that tobacco. You got a mighty fine piece of leaf stuck between your two front teeth! I wouldn't even want to kiss you!"

John noticed a dark expression crossed Jim's face, but he didn't respond to John's kidding. John continued, "I've been thinking strongly about farming and how we are going to proceed---when we are farming. The weather is the greatest factor we have to deal with, it rules us with a fickle hand. We might have ideas but the weather is the decider when it comes down to it. That's why I'm going to make a trip down to Worland after Mary has the baby and talk to them, sheepmen. I think sheep are the answer to us making some money without depending on the dang weather and a row crop! Since you know sheep and I don't---maybe you would be in charge of them while I try and run the farm?"

Self-consciously, Jim picked at his teeth. "Well now, John, sheep are damn hardy, but frankly, I've never seen a more stupid living thing in my life. That's why they need a herder---to keep them out of trouble and show them where to go and when! They will eat anything and that can be a problem too. The wool and lambs are money makers for sure. The trick is to keep those four-legged suckers alive, keepin' the scab off of 'em, and the coyotes away from them!"

Not to change the subject, but I am thinking we need to level out a garden plot for Mary. I realize she can't do much of anything right now, but come fall she will want to be canning up food for the winter. I can ask her what she wants in this first garden. It won't be everything she wants, but it'll be a start. I can get it planted in a day with potatoes, tomatoes, onions, cabbage, lettuce, squash, pumpkins, peas, beans, and whatever else she wants in it."

John looked surprised by Jim's eagerness to plant Mary's garden. "I am sure she will appreciate that Jim—that's darn thoughtful of you to do that!"

~~~~~~~~

It was several weeks before Mary was due to have her baby --- they had just finished supper. John leaned back on his chair and lit a cigar, inhaling, and blowing smoke rings into the air. "Well now, I do have some great news—just heard about it today. I know I've mentioned that several members of the church were concerned because Solon Wiley owns the land on which our church is currently built on. Well now, I'll be danged if Fred Mayland and Christ Ahlgrim didn't step up and offer two acres from each of their farms on the corner of Road Eleven; and Grabberts gave three acres of their farm on the other side of the road. So now we have a central spot along the main road on which to build our new church as well as the parsonage."

Mary smiled as she began to clear the dishes from the table. "John, when will they build the new church? Will it be another adobe?"

John stood up and slapped the tabletop. "No siree---the new church will be built from lumber. It will be a couple of years before we can afford to build it the right way—but we are starting with the plans now. Also, school begins on the first of September. Maybe by the time our kids start, we will have us a frame schoolhouse and it will be on our land. Each of us men also has to furnish a percentage of the fuel---sage, and firewood—to the church and parsonage. Jim and I are going to get our portion cut and stacked next week."

That evening as they were sitting around the stove, Mary said, "John, my time is near and I was wondering if we could afford to have the Grabberts daughter, Marie, come over for a few weeks or so, and take care of the house, cooking, and the children while I am recovering? Mrs. Grabbert has experience as a midwife too, so I have asked her to tend to me, when this baby comes, then Marie can stay afterward."

~~~~~~~~~

On the 5th of July, John and Jim finished digging a second well on the homeplace. John said "By darn, we hit pay dirt, Jim— look here, we barely dug down six feet and the water is starting to seep up. I think if we put a pipe down right here, we'll have us a well. It will be right handy to have that well between Mary's garden and the barn. We have another well outside the kitchen, we are in the money."

With the help of Mrs. Grabbert, Esther Emma Ernestine Wamhoff was born on July 10, 1902, and baptized in September--- the sixth baptismal entry on the Germania Zion Lutheran registry of baptisms.

In 1902, the Pastor began teaching parochial and public school classes in the small adobe school building which sat on the Edwards property. It was proving difficult to teach German-speaking children in English which was now expected in public schools. Little Bill was eager to go to school with the other children. Mary said, "Maybe next fall Bill, you need to be a little older and practice your English words too, then you can go to school!"

Chapter Seven

DAYS ARE LONG — YEARS ARE SHORT!

August 1903: Jim and John had been working all morning, clearing sage from the south side of the last field. Pushing his hat back on his head and wiping the sweat from his brow, Jim said. "Say, John, you know what I heard in Basin City the other day? Why, they say that over between Lovell and Garland, out in them barren hills, oil seeps right out of the ground like it was normal and all. Local folks who know about it go there to grease their wagon wheels, oil their boots, take some for their lamps and wipe the rest on their hands. Next time we have to go to Garland, we might just take us a look-see!"

John shook his head in wonder then said, "Jim, remember a while back when I talked about going to Worland to find out about them sheep? Well, I'm going to leave tomorrow, probably be gone for a couple of days!" John kicked at the dry dirt, "We don't have much water but I think if we use ridges about every 20 feet or so before you plant the grain, it will guide what water we have down this field, cutting down on the waste. We could use the leveler to make the ridges. Do you think you can handle those two fields of grain while I'm gone?"

Jim replied, "Sure 'nough, I can see how getting those ridges laid out would help use every drop of water we get, to irrigate the grain. I guess we try it and see how that works for now. While you're gone, I'll do the milking and gather the eggs for Mary. I'll hold down things around here---watch out for your family."

Jim said, "I've been thinkin' I'll make a couple of traps and set them up in the hills south of the cemetery--where I've seen some animal dens. Don't know if it'll work or not, but there might be a few takers! Whatever I catch will take them out of your yard and away from your animals."

Jim had more than a few takers as he built up a good pile of coyote, bobcat, fox, and raccoon pelts. He cured them and sold them to a fur trader in Cody. All except for that big bobcat---which he made into a soft rug for Mary.

~~~~~~~~

John walked into the kitchen where Mary was baking bread. "Mary, I've decided to ride to Worland and talk to them sheepmen down there. I need to get educated about those critters and decide if they are worth the risk and time. Jim will hold down the fort here and start irrigating the grain and alfalfa. You go to him if you need anything. He said he'd milk the cows and take care of the chickens, also take in the eggs and cream to the store. I feel it in my bones that I need to make an educated decision about the sheep business."

The next day, John threw a few things over the back of his Morgan horse, Trotter, and headed cross-country for Worland. He could travel faster by not sticking to the roads all the time. Over the past winter, John had read everything he could get his hands on regarding the raising of 12sheep. At least he was familiar with most of the procedures and terms like 'dipping' the sheep to rid them of parasites and the dipping pens needed to hold them. Then there was the lambing and a lambing teepee to shelter the ewe and newborn lamb. Scab was a serious skin condition caused by lice or mites that got in the wool. It was highly contagious and buyers didn't want wool that was full of Scab.

~~~~~~~~

The Boush and Goss sheep ranches were on the east side of the Bighorn River, about a half-mile apart. John imagined they used the sage and grass-covered hills to the east—toward the Bighorn Mountains as grazing land, but lived relatively close for protection from irate cattlemen who didn't want sheep overgrazing the free grassland. On the other side of the mountains, in Johnson County, they had one hell of a range war in which a large number of cattlemen and sheepmen were killed and it wasn't over yet. It wasn't any secret on this side of the mountain that trouble was brewing between the two factions. Tempers were high!

John rode up to the impressive sheep ranch which had a huge number of holding pens and three-sided sheep sheds for protection from the weather. He stood and watched with awe as a mangy, multi-colored herding dog moved some rather large sheep out of a nearby field.

Wiping his hands on his canvas apron, Wilhelm Goss walked out of the sheep shed toward John. Smiling, he said, "I remember you---it was Vamhoff—am I correct?"

John shook hands with the sheepman and replied, "You have a good memory, as that was last summer. I've been busy getting my place set up—house, barns, corrals, irrigated fields---well, you know! I came back over because I want to know more about raising sheep in these parts, and from talking to you last summer—you sound like you know a little about raising sheep."

Mr. Goss replied, "Yah, Yah, sure—I know about raising dem sheep. You better tink twice bout getting into dat business because it be plenty dangerous if you get on the vrong side of a das cattleman. Only a few years back dere was an incident down by Thermopolis—vhen several thousand sheep vere slaughtered and dem herders murdered. Dere's no need for violence, dere's plenty land for us all!"

~~~~~~~

John and Wilhelm Goss sat at the scrubbed kitchen table while he told John everything he would ever want to know about the sheep business. "I come to this country several years ago—me and

Bosch. It's good for raising sheep better den cattle because de sheep are not so picky about vhat dey eat. Dey not so much troubles except during lambing in the spring, den shearing follows dat. Dem sheeps are pretty darn onery to herd. Dey like to hang together and follow das leader vhich might be off a cliff or into das river. Vhat you do about dis is to have yourself good dogs dat keeps dem vhere dey should be."

Now, vith dem lambs, you got to cut deir tails off—dat keeps deir keister cleaner and avoids vorms. Den comes the fun part— if you don't vant to keep dem for breeding, you must cut deir 'man' parts off. You get a good sheep herder—he just bites dem off! But dem little lambs are no troubles, dey feed demselves and grow fat for you. You must remember to put out de salt blocks vith a vormiside in dem."

Mr. Goss had himself a good laugh with that one. "I tink God forgot to give dos sheep a brain or any sense. All you got to do is to get good dogs to tink for dem sheep." He laughed at his joke, then continued. "It pays to take gute care of dem sheepdogs because dey are the ones who tinks for dem sheeps."

"First ting-you got to get yourself is a good banker because you vill need to take out loans during das lambing season, shearing season, and---vell, you vill learn vhen you need more money to operate on." He leaned forward, "You vill not like dis part of the business---to borrow money—but it is da biggest and most important part of dis business and I vould tell you to learn it vell!"

Goss took a sip of his buttermilk, " Da price of the vool goes up and down like the sun and people around here don't like to eat the mutton or lamb too much. Ve don't sell the lamb around here, dat market is in de East so dat means you have to ship dem. I like to eat the lamb the vay Mama fixes it, but not the mutton, it is too strong a taste!"

"Sheep have de problem vith parasites like de Scab—you vant to keep your sheep away from dat business. And den—dere are always volves, coyotes, fox and vild dogs dat get into da sheep and cause you more troubles! Dat dipping is messy business but you vant to keep da vool clean from da parasites, you have to use good dip vaters like 'Black Leaf or Scabcura" in it!"

John was mesmerized as Goss rattled on, " Now den, Mr. Vamhoff, der are much good about das sheep. Dey are good grazers—better den das cow, and dey are better at finding food. The lambs grow like veeds if you have a good summer and forage for dem; and den dey give you deir vool vhich you sell at market. But you must be careful vhich market you take dem too. Volton, vhere you came through on the other side of the mountains----is a good place, vith the honest buyers. I vait for the railroad---dat will make this business much better in de Basin here!"

John was making notes in a notebook. "Mr. Goss, please call me John. Now, what is a good price for wool at the market? Or if I sell the lambs or ewes—what price is good?"

Goss scratched his head and thought for a moment, "Yah vell, dose questions are like the change of das day—hard to say. I vould say da vool holds up in price pretty good—about ten cents a pound. Now, it is a different story vhen it comes to da price you get for da animals. Da lambs—if dey veigh over 60 pounds, might get you $2.80 to $3 a head. For da old ewes, maybe $2.50—dey look at da condition of dem ewes, vhat dey vorth. Also, vhat da market needs—more sheep—not more sheep! It is good dat da lambs are born in da spring and by autumn dey are ready for market and you get rid of dem before vinter comes. Some sheepmen like to buy da lambs in September and fatten dem up all vinter, den dey are ready to sell by spring. Dat ist gute business, but a crazy business, never know vhat it vants to pay! It better to have less sheep in das vinter!"

John leaned forward in his chair, "Now, about in the winter, do I need to keep them in corrals and out of the snow?"

Goss laughed and said, "Yah, Yah Yohn and you may call me Vill. The sheep---dey do not need shelters at all times—but in hard vinters, best to give dem some if you vant to keep most of them." Haha "Most times, the sheeps can make do after heavy snows; dey can find something to eat under it if it isn't too deep. It's a good idea to have corrals—vith good drainage and simple three-sided sheds—open to the south for da sun. Dey need clean bedding like straw, grass, corn husks etc. and extra feed like hay, dry grass and some corn if you have it. If it's a mild vinter, I take my sheep out to da badlands and dey find da food. BUT---dey need vater. Dat is most important—dey must be close to good vater or a snowbank, always! If you are farmer too, den you can raise dryland crop of millet or cane –corn or vheat for fodder—anything you can cut and take to dem to eat—dey are not too particular"

Goss moved his chair closer to John, "Now I tell you someting serious—during lambing, da ewes must be kept dry and in good pens. Da veather vill have much to do vith if the lamb lives. If lambing is in da blizzard, you must have big barn vith lambing pens, with vater, feeders, and a stove to keep them varm. You might even have to bring a lamb in da house after birth. I make many small, portable tents for da birthing if the weather is not so good. Mama makes soft beds for da sickly lambs in the kitchen too." Goss smiled as he added, "Now after all dat bad news, are you still interested in the sheep, Mr. Vamhoff?"

John nodded his head, "Yes, yes I am. I think it is the way to go to have a cash crop—sheep followed up with row crops. Then, if one goes bad you have the other to fall back on. But it does sound like the sheep business is more complicated and in need of a larger amount of capital than I first thought."

Goss leaned back on his chair, "Yah—yah, it is vhat dey say---a risky business. But dis is good country for da sheep. The banker tells me dat Vyoming has five million sheep! So, you aren't the first vith the big idea. "Hahahah. "Oh Yohn---you must know so you don't become afraid—vhen the sheep---dey eat mostly of sagebrush, dey will leave a trail of blood instead of urine on da ground. It's not

a problem—just something vich happens, okay?"

"You need to know vhat you are doing.----Now, it is good for da sheep to be outdoors and to have da exercise---to move around. I am a great believer in moving da sheep every day to new grazing land if you can. This vay their vool stays cleaner and not matted. As soon as you can afford—build da big shed for da sheep.

This vill also make for coyote and volf harder to eat your sheep. If you use a fence—da best kind is the voven vire—vith many small squares. Da sheep cannot get out of dese fences."

John said, "I need a list of equipment to get started; what do you recommend?"

Goss leaned forward, "I vill write it down for you. I have a good herder's vagon vhich I vill sell to you for $50. I vas going to ask $60, but I like you and you need some help to get started in the sheep business. I also have some lambs and pretty good ewes to sell if interested. Of course you vill need a couple of young bucks to service the ewes. I make you good deal, under market price for you, Yohn—good German neighbor!!" Goss turned around smiling, "but I must make a little profit—for vhich you understand!"

John finished his buttermilk and said, " Now Will, what kind of sheep do you prefer in this country?"

Goss scratched his beard and then said, " I run da Merino sheeps—dey are best foragers and get along vherever I herd them. Mostly I like da Rambouillet sheep---dey have da best vool! Oh yes—to keep count of da sheep, ve put ten blackface sheep to every one thousand---or one blackface to one hundred. Dat is easy vay to count your sheeps den!"

He began to laugh, slapped his leg and said, "I almost forget to tell you how ve know da ewe, she is pregnant. Ve vant to control vhen the ewe vill have da lamb, yah? Da spring is da best time so da lamb--it can grow up in da good summer. Lambing time is hard vork, somebody needs to be vith the sheep all da time. Sometimes a lamb gets stuck and you need to help it be born or you lose mama and baby."

"Now, to control da breeding, ve tie a vest vith da red chalk on it around da neck of da ram, so ve can tell if he done his business yust by looking at da backend of da ewe. Yah, dat vorks good!" He took a sip of the buttermilk. "If da ram has a busy day, you vill have to keep fresh chalk on him!"

"It is important to find good herders. Dey vill know how to shear da sheep vhen da time comes. I give you hint---ve never vash our sheep before ve shear, only da rear end vhich is stained yellow. Buyers like da vool to have the lanolin in it, you get better price. The vool vill be a yellow-gray color instead of vhite. It is up to you vhat you vant to do."

"If I vere you, I vould decide how many sheep you vant, and I can help you make a deal vith da ferry to get dem across the river. Pretty soon we vill have a bridge and den it vill be better. Across the river dere is good grazing all summer. I know a place vith a good solid log cabin vhere you can stay until da lambs are big enough to travel farther to Germania. You vould be close to here and I could help you vith any questions or troubles you have over da first summer. Who knows, you might like dis country better dan Germania, and vant to stay down here!"

"Like I said, Vamhoff, dem sheeps not too smart. If you can get one to go through da eye of a needle, da others vill follow!" He laughed until he coughed, then spit on the ground.

Goss pushed the glasses to the other side of the table. "So now, you tink about it and talk to a banker den we do da business, agreed?"

The two men shook on the deal. John crossed over the river on the ferry and because it was getting late in the day, he spent the night on the river bank. He looked up and down the river for any sign of Indians, because he remembered when they first came here, Bill and Ruth had been afraid of the lone Indian sitting on the bank cooking a prairie dog over a fire. The next day he rode back to Germania. John's mind was on fire with everything he had learned from Mr. Goss and by the time he rode into his yard, he knew what he wanted to do first.

~~~~~~~~~~

John wrote to his bankers in Garland and told them of his plan. He had plenty of money on deposit in the bank, but he decided to take operating loans instead of using his cash. During the last two years, his cash reserves had dwindled because of the cost of getting set up on the homestead, paying the Bench Canal, and a hundred other expenses.

The bankers in Garland wrote back telling John he was good for the loans he needed. Sheep loans were normally due in the spring and fall, but the fact of the matter was—they were never fully paid off—it was a revolving wheel. The western banks took risks with farmers, sheepmen, and cattlemen that they didn't take with other businesses. They knew the sheepman would pay what he could when he could, and that's how it was.

John had decided to begin with twenty-five lambs and fifty young ewes---Goss had thrown in another fifteen old ewes and a few bum lambs adding up to ninety-five sheep to get started. "I don't get a gute price from dem old girls at sheep market if dey vould even make da trip. You might get one – two years out of dem before dey go down."

~~~~~~~

The next day when John and Jim finished with the day's labors, John stood at the dry sink, washing up for supper. Mary, who was busy preparing their supper of fried chicken, potato salad, and sauerkraut, said, "Oh, we had some excitement around here today, remind me to tell you about it after supper."

After they ate, John said, "So what was the big excitement?"

"Well, you know that field of young alfalfa you have in the back there? Well, wouldn't you know that our best milk cow, Brownie, got through the fence and ate her share of it before Bill spotted her walking funny like."

John sat up straight—now she had his attention. "What happened? All three cows were in the barn when I was just out there."

Mary said, "Well, Brownie's belly bloated up something fierce, and I've seen Pap take care of a bloated cow. Jim and you were too far away to help, so I took matters into my own hands. I put her in the milking stall to hold her tight and got my sharpest, thinnest butcher knife out of the drawer; then I took a real deep breath and stabbed upwards through her tough hide, just far enough, until I heard and smelled that foul air coming out. Glory be—just like that, Brownie backed out of the stall and she walked off without saying thank you!"

John laughed, "I'm sure glad you knew what to do Mary. I'll check on her later to make sure there isn't any bleeding or infection."

Then he leaned forward, "Well now, Mary---I have made a decision of which I assume you will approve. I am going to go into the sheep business—it's all set with the bank in Garland and Mr. Goss is going to sell me some lambs and ewes---around ninety-five head, give or take a few, plus a sheep wagon and a couple of sheepdogs. The one dog he gave me has two puppies and Mr. Goss wants me to give them to the children. We will need all the sheepdogs we can get. In the meantime, Bill and Ruth will have fun with the dogs—they can even name them."

Mary lifted her head from her sewing and said, "When does all this happen?"

John said, "Well, I figure we will harvest the wheat and barley, get the ground ready for next spring, then move down to Worland for the spring and summer, maybe into the fall. That way I'll be set up down there for our first lambing and shearing season. Mr. Goss said it would not be good to take the new lambs on a long journey and there is a small log house down there that we can use until Fall. There is good grazing land in those hills and they just finished the Hanover Canal, so there is ample water. We'll be on this side of the river---about two miles off the road, to the south on the ridge."

After watching the expression on Mary's face, John held his hands up in a gesture of surrender ---"I know, I know Mary—you probably aren't happy about uprooting the household and children again, but it will only be over the spring and summer. Jim will stay here and watch the place, the animals, and make sure water gets on the fields of wheat. I am thinking I might hire another herder when we are down in Worland. That way I will be freed up to ride herd over all of the operations."

Mary leaned back in her chair and lifting her face to his, said, "Well now John, it sounds like you've got it all planned out. Did you think about talking to me first or just assume I would go along with what you want to do?"

John slapped his knee, "Now Mary, don't start a fuss about me talking to you every time I make a decision. I have lots of decisions to make and there are going to be a lot more with the sheep business and the farm. I've got to depend on you, that you will hold up your end of the bargain!"

Mary felt blindsided as she stared at the woodstove. "John, I didn't realize 'this' was a bargain, I thought, it was a marriage, a two-way relationship and I might be respected for my input and my convenience!"

John sat stone-faced as he realized how he had treated his wife in the whole thing. He stood and blocked her way, then pulled her into his arms. "Mary, I am sorry if I seemed abrupt---you and our children are everything to me. That is why I am working hard at making a go of this place, and now with the sheep--I have a lot on my mind. I guess I do expect you to do what I need you to do, without my asking, and I am sorry. I love you—you are my life and I'll try harder not to take you for granted!"

As it turned out, Mary and the children stayed in Germania in the comforts and convenience of their home. She had a garden to raise and animals to tend to and it was the best decision for her and the little ones, not to uproot them to live in a one-room cabin. John wasn't happy about the arrangement, but he loaded up a wagon and moved to the Worland area to get started in the sheep business. John arrived at the Goss ranch around the middle of February so he could watch and learn first hand about the lambing and shearing operation. The Goss family was happy to put him up in a spare room for a month while he learned what he had to learn.

After lambing and shearing were over at the Goss ranch, John moved into the little log house, which would later become Worland's  pioneer schoolhouse. John ferried his new ewes and their lambs along with a few young ram and old ewes across the river, to the land he had rented for the summer. He also hired a couple of herders to help him—they lived in the sheep wagon. John expected he would spend the summer until the lambs were ready to travel to Germania.

John had to purchase most of his food. He hired a local girl to take care of the cooking and wash his clothes, once a week. He paid her fifty cents a day.

~~~~~~~~

Early Spring, 1904: The evening before, Mary and Jim sat at the kitchen table and talked about the layout for the massive garden and even a few fruit trees. Jim had traveled to Garland the week before and returned with a wagonload of tree starts, seeds, and everything they needed to start the garden. It took Jim three days to ditch out the garden and then all Mary had to do was plant her vegetables! As she bent over putting the tiny seeds into the open troughs, Mary thought about seeing all of the cottonwood trees and orchards which folks had planted on their farms, taking root and growing. *Maybe, in time we can turn this God-forsaken benchland into something close to Germantown, Nebraska---just maybe!*

Mary laid out a place at the supper table for Jim that night. When it was close to supper time she rang the bell and it wasn't two minutes when Jim burst through the front door with a big smile on his face. Without thinking he grabbed Mary around the waist, picked her up, and swung her around. "I can't believe you planted that entire garden in one day woman and now, have a hot meal on the table. You are a wonder for sure!" I was thinking about it today out in the field. I am so glad to see you and the little ones decided not to go to Worland, that would have been hard on you all. And, I would have missed you all greatly, especially your cooking!"

Mary said, "I have to agree with you Jim, I just didn't make any sense. Well now, I have to thank you for plowing, leveling, and ditching out the garden for me, don't I? You did all the hard work for me! You keep that up and you will spoil me."

Jim smiled widely and replied, "You were meant to be spoiled. What's for supper?"

~~~~~~~~

By the end of June, Mary's garden of potatoes, carrots, peppers, tomatoes, cabbage, onions, beets, pumpkins, turnips, along with a row of herbs was doing so well, she could hardly believe it, and the sapling fruit trees were thriving. She smiled as she thought, *the garden is doing so well, it must have been all that manure Jim spread over the ground before he tilled it.* Mary gazed at the spindly trees and dreamed of a large orchard of cherry, apple, pear trees; and maybe even some chokecherry bushes, someday. She knew Herman Werbelow had planted rows of cottonwoods and a large orchard on his farm---so she was quite certain they could manage it as well.

~~~~~~

August: Around the middle of the month, John had enough of life without his wife. The lambs were big enough now, and he was ready to head back home. He and his herder, Herbie rounded up the sheep and they began their slow drive back to Germania. As John drove the wagon, he thought about everything he had learned over the past months. They had an excellent first lambing season and now his flock numbered around 180 sheep. They had lost a few, which Mr. Goss had predicted and so John had purchased another dozen sheep along with a few bum lambs from Mr. Goss. All in all, John was learning fast about the sheep business and he had a good feeling. Taking their time, letting the sheep graze and the lambs frolic, it took a good three days to drive the herd from Worland to Germania--- even with the help of four border collies and Australian sheepdogs. In Germania, Jim had the sheep pens up and ready.

~~~~~~

Mary had been expecting John any day, but it was Bill who spotted the herd of sheep and wagons coming down the road to their homestead. Bill sat on the corral fence and watched it all with great delight. It was like a three-ring circus with all those sheep going this way and that, dogs barking and herding sheep, followed by a sheep wagon and finally, John's wagon. Mary met John at the door with a big hug and an official-looking document in her hand. "OH—look here, John---the contract came. It's the contract to purchase four shares of the Bighorn Basin Development Co.for $1600 to be paid in installments." Mary went on, "Does this mean we will have first water rights and water in the ditches for next year's crops?"

NOTE:

The first water rights were sold for $10 an acre which provided a half-foot of water for forty acres for that season.

John smiled shrewdly at her and commented, "Well now, that's what they tell us! We shall have to wait and see. I see that Jim dug a reinforced cistern to collect rain and any clean water that might come down the ditch. Glad to see that he put a heavy cover on it so the children won't get into it! And—you--you got your garden in and it all looks mighty good to me."

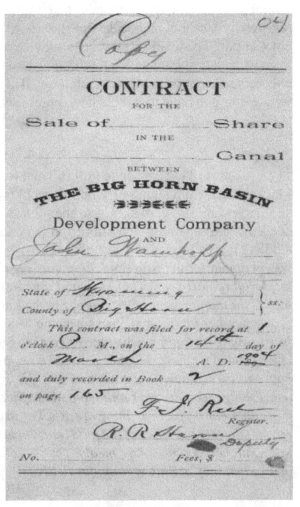

Courtesy:
Arnold Wamhoff

Mary was full of news but she waited until the children had been put to bed that evening. "Oh John, it's so exciting. While you were gone the folks here built a nice little frame school on the northeast corner of Edwards farm to the south of us, on Road Ten. I heard that the teacher Maude Blakesly, died suddenly, maybe appendicitis, and---and her father came in to finish her term." Mary stopped to catch her breath. "They have hired May Schenck to teach this fall when Bill and Ruth go to school. I signed them up at the school the other day, they said that there are twenty children registered for school in the fall, and classes will be taught in English, not German. I saw all of the books they have now---it's a far cry from what they started with. I don't know how long that little school will be sufficient to hold all the children. The day is coming when we are going to have to build a new, bigger school."

It proved to be a hectic fall. Bill and Ruth started school and Mary worked from sunup to sundown, cooking, washing, canning, and harvesting her garden, not to mention the endless care of the chickens and separating the milk from the cream, plus caring for a toddler! It was toward the end of August when Mary realized she was pregnant for the fifth time. *I am thinking this baby will be born in March of next year. That's a good time to have a baby---not so busy with the garden and canning.* She had noticed that with each pregnancy her morning sickness became less bothersome. *It might be as simple as I don't have time to be sick.* She reached down and laid her hand tenderly over her belly. *I know John could use another boy, and I could always use another girl! He's talking about buying a threshing machine and renting out his services. When he mentions that, all I can think of is the work it takes to feed those threshing crews-- the meals and all of the food that will take--- more time spent in the kitchen and planning meals! I'm grateful I only have to feed them when they are harvesting our fields.*

After a hardy breakfast of flapjacks, eggs, biscuits, and coffee, Jim harnessed the team of horses to the hay wagon and headed for the alfalfa field for the final cutting of hay. The crew he had hired to help was already out in the field to the south, getting set up. This was one task that Jim truly liked---cutting and stacking hay.

Later that morning John rode out to see how it was going. "Looks like you might get it done today, Jim---good work. I see that Herbie took the sheep wagon and the sheep and are headed out to the hills just north of Dry Creek to graze for a few days or weeks depending on what they find to eat or not. He's a good herder

Jim said, "It amazes me how much those lambs are growing. It was right smart of you to take a few of the Goss bum lambs in the bargain. We got them little buggers for pennies on the head and then sell them for dollars---I like that!" He laughed and slapped his leg.

Jim was about to leave when he thought of something else. "Oh John, I rode up the ditch the other day to see how them fellows was coming on that canal up on the line. It's a mighty big undertaking for sure and they had themselves more men working than they knew what to do with. If these farmers from around here don't have fieldwork, they are working on the canal to help pay for their shares. That ditch is coming right along---gonna bring us lots of water when they get it done too. That canal is going to take some work. I'd be happy to go up and work on it for you if you think it's necessary."

Jim pushed his hat back on his head and continued, "John, did you know that it's going to be eight miles long and twenty-eight feet across. At the bottom, it'll be darn near twenty-feet wide. Them fellows said that it will run about four feet of water. The thing that gets me is that thar ditch has a rising grade of 5.2 feet per mile---to get the water up from the river to our 22,000 acres of higher benchland---it's uphill all the way! Now, ain't that something! It's going to be the Garden of Eden around here, right soon!"

~~~~~~~~

That evening John took the lantern and milk buckets down from the hook on the back porch. "Say, Bill---I think it's about time you learn to milk the cows. I've got you a little pail right here, just about your size—do you want to learn?" John didn't have to ask twice. Bill grabbed his little pail and was out the door and on the way to the barn. After an hour or so they came back to the house with their buckets full of milk.

Mary bent down and took Bill's bucket. "Well, now Bill, you are a big boy, milking and all. How did you like it?"

Bill looked her straight in the eye and said, "Well Mama, Dad showed me how to clean off their tails first cause if they have mud or poop on them and swing them around—they can get it on 'you' or in the milk, and that's not very good. If it's winter out and them tails get mud and stuff on them, it freezes like ice, then it can hurt you if you don't break the ice off before you start to milk. After that---we washed off the udders. Dad called them bags, but he told me that they are really called udders--you know, Mama, it's the bag that holds the milk inside." He was so matter-of a fact, that Mary had to hide a smile.

"Dad told me that especially in winter, it's important to take good care of the teats so they don't get sore and chapped from the cold." Bill's eyes got real big as he said, "Do you know what Dad did when he was milking? He squirted milk right here into my mouth!" Bill wiped his lips as if it had just happened. "I didn't like the warm milk too much Mama, but Jack and Rip liked it a whole bunch. Dad said that dogs and cats like milk any wheres they can get it!"

"When Dad squirted the milk into the pails it sounded real funny, like sss….ssss…..sssss as long streams of milk went into the pail. Dad can do that so fast----milk a cow. Boy, he's good!"

"Then Dad pitched some hay to the cows and I threw some in too. We had to check one of the cows hoofs—she was sort of limping. Dad said we had to check for a little rock, and you know what----he found one too! I think I like milking, Mama---it smells good in the barn. I thought it smelled like manure--but Dad said it smelled like money! The cows like to be milked cause it makes them feel better. I feel all 'growed' up when I walk to the house with pails of fresh milk!"

John patted Bill on the back, "That's right Mama, this Bill here is a right smart boy, I only have to show him once and he remembers how to do something."

Mary gave John one of her looks, then said, "It smells like money? You are incorrigible---you might have to look that word up in the dictionary!" She took the pails of milk and poured them into the hand-turned separator to separated the milk from the cream. The skim milk that came out was fed to the calves. Most of the cream went into special five-gallon cans that John took into town once a week to sell to grocery stores. Mary was sure to save enough whole milk and cream for the family's needs. In the summer, she saved a bit more cream to make ice cream which was always a big treat for the family.

~~~~~~~

After Mary put the children to bed, she and John sat next to the lantern---he read while she tended to her endless mending, trying to nudge just a little more life out of their clothing. "You know John, it's quite thoughtful that Jim takes to his room after supper to give us some time together. He's a good man. Are you going to send him or Herbie out with the sheep wagon tomorrow?"

John said, "Herbie is the herder for now. Jim is handling the farming operation, it's what he says he prefers."

Mary replied, "Where is Herbie going to take the sheep and how many dogs is he taking? I swear, we have so many sheepdogs around here that I am losing count---there is Rip, Teddy, Dusty, Joe, and---Checkers---right? They do keep the coyotes and the like away. I think Checkers tangled with a skunk the other night---he smelled really bad. He didn't even like himself, kept trying to rub the smell off in the grass. Mary paused and said, "You know, Bill and Ruth are still partial to the two dogs you gave them in Worland, Hank and Jack. They are very attentive dogs and I think they actually 'herd' the children, which is good—they are watching out for them when I'm not there."

John would nod his head once in a while like he was actually listening. Finally, he yawned and stood, "Are you ready to head upstairs, Mary? I've got a big day ahead of me tomorrow." John paused in thought. "I am going to buy a threshing machine of my own along with a steam tractor to run it, maybe after harvest this year, if we have a good one. It will pay for itself by me signing up other farmers to thresh their grain! I've got to study up on the way it's done before I go extending myself like that. Plan, think, then plan some more!"

Chapter Eight

THE GROWING YEARS

1905: *'There were several large sheep operations on the Bench including Morris Newcomer and John Wamhoff.'* (from **Wiley's Dream of Empire**)

Before John saddled his horse that morning, he took a curry comb and vigorously brushed the winter coat from the horse's back. The horse stood still as stone because it felt so good to have that toothed curry comb raked over his hide. John finished the task, saddled up, and climbed aboard. This was one of his favorite things---riding his horse, overlooking his farm, and seeing how each of his endeavors was running according to his plan. He reined the horse left at the road and headed out to the hills where his sheep were pastured. Before riding down into the camp, he pulled his horse to a stop and gazed at the pastoral scene of his sheep scattered over the hills, grazing. *This ---all this, is what my dreams were made of--- owning the land, the sheep, and orchestrating---overseeing it all. It's happening—it's all happening, right before my eyes. My head is filled with dreams and thoughts of what to do next. I'm now an officer in the church and the school district; people know to come to me to borrow money; I'm a mortician;—what can I do next to help Germaina grow? I think the threshing business could be very good.*

He rode up to the grazing herd and remained in his saddle, watching Herbie work the dogs to keep the sheep in the fold and away from any dangerous plants or drop-offs. He heard Herbie shout orders, "Gather, gather---back Rex. Fetch---drive--drive!"

When he was certain the sheep were settled, Herbie rode over to where John was sitting on his horse watching the operation. "Morning Boss---say, I've been thinking about building a few corrals and three-sided sheds out here to protect the sheep at night; also for protection when a storm comes up. We could use any old lumber—nothing fancy. I also noticed some Scab on a couple of the sheep. The wool isn't real thick yet—we might think about dipping this herd before it gets out of hand.

John said, "That's a good idea about the corrals. Jim is stacking hay right now; with a large crew. I might keep those boys on a few days more---have them ride out here and help you put up some decent corrals and sheds. It's all about protecting the herd. You take a look and see where you think might be the best spot and mark it off! I gotta be heading back now. About the dipping—I will leave that up to you and Jim. You'll have to bring them back to the home place where the tanks are, probably sooner than later. Thanks, Herbie—you are doing a right fine job. Remember to keep your eye out for any trouble with the cattlemen. That attack on the Gantz sheep camp, near Shell Creek last month by ten masked raiders was downright unthinkable. They dynamited and clubbed nearly 4,000 sheep to death, killed the herder, a team of horses worth $400, his sheepdogs, and then burned the sheep wagon--- that is just too darn close to home! Gantz claims that cost him near $40,000 and he's taking it to court! He claims he knows who did it." John pushed his hat back on his head and leaned over his horse, "My point is Herbie—you be damn careful and watch for trouble, don't take any chances, your life comes first, before the sheep."

Herbie said, "I sure will, don't you worry none. Say, before you head home, take a look at this wild paint horse I caught on the flats yesterday. He's a beaut! Only trouble is, he's not broke. I was going to give him a try out this morning, but I would appreciate having you here just in case I get throwed and he tries to stomp me!"

John rode over to the small fenced area where Herbie had the horse tied up. "Okay, I gotta watch you even get a saddle on him. He's doing the St. Vitas Dance with us just being close by! That is some good looking horse flesh."

Herbie said, "I'm going to take him bareback. I never told you before but I'm a half breed and I grew up amongst the Crow Indians. We know horses."

Herbie walked over to the horse, speaking some low Indian chant—as the horse just stood there waiting like he was mesmerized. Herbie managed to get a hackamore on him and swing upon his back. He clenched his thighs around the horse's middle and wrapped one hand in his mane. The paint's head went up and then he goose-stepped to the side before spinning to the left. All this time Herbie kept up the chant. The paint stopped, then crow-hopped four times before the back legs came up again and again. Then he reared so high that John thought he might fall backward onto Herbie.

Herbie stuck like glue to the paint's back. The horse bucked again then fishtailed across the small corral. He was breathing hard and the next time he paused, Herbie slid to the ground and whipped the reins around a post.

"Well, what do you think?"

John laughed and said, "I think I'd stick to herding sheep if I were you. That horse was born wild and it would take a lot of work to get it out of him. You were pretty impressive—knowing horses was born in you I expect. You decide what you want to do with him, just don't forget about your job---the one I'm paying you to do!"

John laughed and waved goodbye as he headed toward the home place. Herbie stood for a long time watching him. *He's right in that the horse is wild to the bone. What right do I have to take that from him just because I'd like to ride a beautiful horse like that? I gotta let him go, it's the right thing to do---I don't have the time to work with him like I should and that boy is going to take a lot of work to break. I'll do it tonight, by the light of the moon. I got to take the sheep out now.*

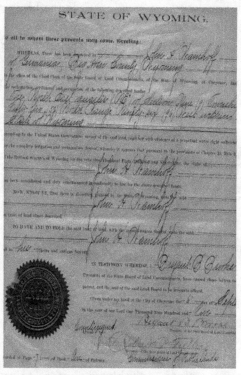

On the way back home, John thought about their new baby daughter born that March. *Mary wanted to name her Adella—it's a pretty name. She's birthed three girls in a row—we only have one boy and I have to say, I'm*

Courtesy:
Arnold Wamhoff

disappointed. I need sons to help around here. Well, maybe eventually we'll have us another son. I have to say those little girls are sweet things. Ruth is getting so tall, Esther is a little beauty, and now this new one. She is a good baby, I'll say that for her—got long legs already. Marie Grabbert has boarded with us all summer, helping Mary with the children.

John stopped off at Wegner's place and glanced through his mail until he spotted what he had been waiting for. He could hardly wait to get home. He galloped Trotter all the way, then jumped off and tied him to a post. John ran into the house waving the deed. "Mary, Mary---it's official---this place is ours!"

~~~~~~~~~

1906: As he did so many nights, John sat at the kitchen table going over the ledger accounts. He thought to himself— *we got nearly 45 bushels of oats to the acre off those two fields, and we did well to sell all them at $1.50 per hundred to the Wiley Project up by Cody, cash money! He scanned down to where it showed the names of those who had borrowed larger sums to help get their farms started. I charge them interest on the money they borrowed, but not as much as the bank ---some of these folks couldn't even get a loan at the bank. I like helping folks get started, it makes me feel good. Now, if they just get in the position to pay me back---that would help. Some are paying what they can, but times are hard.*

John recalled threshing with a horse-driven threshing machine where the horse would go round and round in a circle to get power to the threshing machine. It was hard work for

Threshing outfit owned by John Wamhoff. Courtesy: Robert Werbelow

everyone but easier than by hand as he well remembered. Now, he had a steam engine to run the huge threshing machine. There were three large threshing outfits in Germainia--- Cyrus Pearce, Beirman, and John Wamhoff.

Courtesy: Arnold Wamhoff

Farmers booked him up in the spring to thresh their grain crops in the fall, as he had a good reputation and they fought to get on his list. This was just another way he was making money, good money. John smiled as he thought of an old saying—*It takes money to make money! I am proof of that. That is what my plan was before we came here. I came to Germania with some money from the sale of my business in Germantown and I put that money to work, in the bank, and in the purchase of machinery and animals that would bring a good profit!* John smiled, *So far so good! I've been reading about cars and tractors of the future-who knows what will happen.*

~~~~~~~

In late spring when school was out, several settlers got together and set the little schoolhouse up on a large wooden sled. It took four teams of horses to drag the schoolhouse up the hill to the far northeast corner of the Wamhoff farm on Road Ten. John had gladly donated the little bit of land they would need for the schoolhouse. He thought *I am excited to learn that we now have two teachers because of the increase in the number of students. The school is still on a three-month term because most of the children are needed on the family farm in the spring and fall months. I am going to suggest to the board that we increase the length of school per term. Students aren't going to learn anything the way it is now, they must be in classes longer than three months. It won't be long and we'll need a bigger school, maybe two rooms. In time, in time........*

~~~~~~~~

On the way home, John rode past Grabberts place next to the quarter section that Reverand Wunderlich had sold to Bennetts. *That is a good piece of land and with a fine two-story white clapboard house already on it. I could make some additions to the house, build a large horse barn, chicken coops, pens for the hogs, cattle, and sheep---lots of sheep pens and sheds. Oh, and a fine large orchard out in the pasture right over in that marshy corner where Road Ten meets this east/west road. This would be an opportunity if it ever comes available.*

John was jolted out of his daydreaming by the sound of Mary's voice. "John, I think both Bill and Ruth are ready for more chores around the place. I know Bill helps you with the milking, but he could also carry slop to the chickens and pigs. Ruth is scared to death of the pigs ever since that big sow charged the fence when she was looking at the baby pigs. I told her to stay away from any animal when they have babies, especially hogs. But, she is a good little helper in the garden now and Bill is teaching her to gather the eggs. They trade off turning the crank on the milk separator too. Bill has been carrying the extra skim milk to the hogs now that they have all those babies—that calf in the barn likes it too. Bill knows better than to go inside their pens."

Mary paused in thought, "Say—John, I want you to look for an ice cream churn when you go to Garland or Basin City next time. We could make some ice cream—I'll use some of that ice we keep under the straw in the root cellar. Oh, mercy, that sounds so good my mouth is just watering!"

John replied, "That does sound good. I'll see if they have one, and if not I'll order one out of the mail-order catalog!" He leaned over and kissed her cheek and then paused in thought, "You know I get a downright wonderful feeling every time I look at that flock of sheep we've grown in a very short time."

Mary started laughing, "Speaking of sheep--I keep forgetting to tell you---remember at lambing time when you and the men were cutting off their tails, worming, and taking the testicles off the males that weren't going to be breeding, the 'wethers' sheep? Well now, Bill was on the fence watching it all and when Herbie took those testicles in his teeth and bit them off, that's all it took for Bill. He ran to the house and laid on his bed with his face in his hands."

Mary laughed, "Oh John, it was so funny. He, he was gagging and crying because —he thought he was going to throw up! He also vowed never to do that---so don't bother asking him!"

Courtesy: Arnold Wamhoff

John laughed and said, "Well, farm kids get a real education, first hand, don't they? He was a great help when we were shearing the sheep. Jim would open a gunny sack, throw a bit of wool in it, and put Bill inside the sack where he stomped down the wool so we could get more in. He lasted longer than I thought he would— he's a strong little guy! He kept asking me why we cut the lamb's tails off and so I told him right out. 'Bill', I said, "sheep have a problem lifting their tails high enough when they go poop. Pretty soon that thick wool back there gets full of urine and poop and then flies lay eggs on there and before you know it, the sheep has worms."

"Bill made the worst face you ever saw. Then he said, 'so that's why you just cut their tails off, huh? Is that why you cut the boy sheep's nuggets off too?'"

John said, "I laughed so hard when I tried to explain to him that we castrate all of the male animals that we don't want to use as breeders. That boy doesn't miss a thing! But frankly, I thought he learned enough for one day—no use going into all that business before he asks about it."

John gazed off at the corrals, "We got a real good crop of lambs, just have to get them up to around ninety to a hundred pounds and then off to market! I have to watch the market reports and see when the high point is predicted."

John cozied up and put his arm around Mary's shoulder, "Soooo, when are we going to try for another boy? I could use the help!"

Mary cocked her head and smiled coyly, "Oh, I 'spect about May we find out!"

~~~~~~~

Life on the Germania Bench was becoming more accessible---what with the mail and stagecoach line that ran from Garland across the hills to Germania and for a fare of only $2.50. However, they charged $3 to go to Burlington and a whopping $5 for a trip to Basin City!

~~~~~~~

May 1907: John sat reading the newspaper while drinking his second cup of coffee. "Mary, listen to this. It says here the average worker makes between $200 to $400 per year and the average wage is twenty-two cents per hour. Life expectancy is forty-seven years old and the leading causes of death are pneumonia/influenza, then tuberculosis, diarrhea, heart disease, and stroke."

John sipped his coffee, "I guess I better get busy---I don't have as long as I thought I did to get everything done I want to do!" He stood and kissed Mary on the cheek.

~~~~~~~

Marie Ida Wamhoff was born in the first week of May. Minnie Grabbert came over to help with the birth of Mary's sixth child and then left her daughter Marie to help with the children. Mary smiled up at Marie and taking her by the hand said, "I named the baby after you Marie. You have been such a good helper to me time and time again."

John couldn't help but show his disappointment. "You started pretty well birthing a boy, and since then it's been girl after girl---four girls now?" He leaned over to kiss Mary, "They are pretty little things, and I guess I'll just have to teach them how to farm and shear sheep!"

John walked out the front door just as one of his hefty Rambouliett rams came around the corner of the barn and charged Bill who was in the process of carrying water to the hogs. Bill lifted his head to see the big ram bearing down on him. He tossed the buckets of water into the air and ran for the nearest fence. Sitting safely on the fence, Bill began yelling at the annoying sheep at the top of his lungs. As soon as the sheep went back around the barn, Bill slid from the fence and headed for the barn where he picked up a shovel and just in time. When he came out of the barn, that ram was waiting for him. As the ram charged, Bill stepped aside and swung the shovel with all of his might, hitting the ram hard on the rump---which deterred the ram's further intentions, for the time being!

John went out to pat Bill on the back—"I was a watchin' you and that ram. You did good cause he was wantin' to give you a good butt with his head. Come on now, we need to load up manure from the corrals and go spread it out in the fields."

Sitting up on the seat beside his father, Bill said, "Manure spreading is one of my most favorite things. It's just funny to watch the manure flying out of the back of the spreader!" John thought to himself. *In a couple of years, Bill will be the one driving the horses—he is growing fast and he already has an understanding of machinery. He's a good hard worker too.*

~~~~~~~~~

One evening as Mary sat nursing the new baby, John said, "We all knew that Wiley was working on another project to the east of Cody. Now, word has it that he has moved his entire operation to what is now called---the town of 'Wiley'! That man must have an ego about the size of Wyoming! He's digging another 'ditch' up there, to bring water to that huge piece of flat land. He's been signing up people to buy the land and rights to the water just like he did here. Oh---and also, he and his entire family took one of those camping tours of Yellowstone country. They didn't take the coach with the common folks, but their 'own' automobile. When I have as much money as Wiley does, we'll have to do that too!"

Yellowstone Park,   Oct. 11, 1907

Out in the horse and buggy for a Sunday afternoon drive, John and Mary stopped by the spot where the new parsonage was going up on the land that Maylands donated. There were already plans to build the new church right across the road on land Grabberts donated. Herman Werbelow was in the process of laying out the grid for a large grove of cottonwood and alder trees to the west and north of the church. The decision to paint the church white had already been made. Fred Grabbert made it be known that he wanted to donate a large bell for the belfry. It was going to a fine church!

Mary looked off into the distance and thought, *it'll look just like the Lutheran Church in Germantown---a little bit more of my old home way out here in Wyoming.*

John laughed and said, "I've been thinking about putting that field to the south of the house in winter wheat. But, perhaps barley, because the horses are partial to it. Though, I hate threshing that stuff with all those stickery beards that make a man want to scratch all over! Gives me the heebie-jeebies just thinking about it."

Mary just looked up at him with an unsympathetic expression and said, "Well John, all these babies keep me up at night and make more work for me which I don't always love either. I know you have things to do which you don't especially love but don't we all? I hardly have a moment's peace what with all the cleaning, cooking, washing, gardening, canning, feeding the chickens and turkeys, tending the children—doctoring them and— you; helping neighbor women, church duties; I help in the fields if needed, and at harvest time I cook for days on end for the hungry threshing crews." Mary smiled sweetly, "It's the life we are blessed with, so we buckle down and we do what we have to do. Go plant your barley, I'll scratch your back for you after threshing!"

~~~~~~~~~~

The next morning Mary took Ruth and Esther out to help plant the huge garden. John had gone to Garland earlier in the week and brought back some nice pepper, tomato, and cabbage seedlings plus strawberry and raspberry bushes. First, the girls took the hoes and made long rows/ditches down the length of the garden. Then, Mary showed them how to dig a tiny ditch down the top of each row, sprinkle the seeds into the dirt then cover them up. It would take about two weeks before the garden would begin to sprout green with peas, beans, tomatoes, radishes, onions, lettuce, cabbage, potatoes, squash, and other seasonal vegetables.

Mary pushed herself to a standing position and stretched her back, "You girls finish up and don't forget to clean off the hoes. I have to go in and start supper." On the walk back to the house she thought, *We get the garden going, water it, hoe the weeds, then it's time to start picking and the canning begins. It never seems to end. In no time it'll be time to start filling those Mason canning jars, and it's not just the vegetables, it's fruit too: then we can the meat, like beef, pork, and making sausage. We just finished butchering a hog and the cellar is filled with smoked bacon and home-cured hams hanging from the ceiling. Mercy me, it never ends. But I thank God for the food, some good help, and a fine cellar to put it all in over the winter months. I must admit that the girls and I have some good talks and laughs when we are working together.*

~~~~~~~~~~

Bill and Ruth had been diligent in caring for the four dozen fuzzy baby chicks that came from the mail order catalog, about twelve weeks ago. Now, they were grown and ready to butcher. Early that next morning, John sharpened his ax while Mary built a fire under two huge cast iron pots outside. She sharpened her knives while Marie Grabbert laid out the big pans on the porch. John told Bill and Ruth to bring the fryers out of their brooder house. One by one he chopped off their heads and before you knew it, forty-eight chickens were hopping around the yard without heads. Bill laughed but Ruth had tears running down her face. "I loved those chickens. They were so soft. They would come running every time I fed them."

Bill said, "I didn't love em---they pooped all over everything and we had to clean out their coop all the time. I can't wait to eat them!" This didn't help the visual torment Ruth was experiencing but John explained, "When you live on the farm sweetheart, you can't get attached to the animals because they are food for us and we all have to pitch in and do what we have to do! We can't be friends with the animals we are going to eat."

Ruth looked up at her father and said, "Does that mean we are going to eat Jack and Hank too?"

John laughed and said, "We don't eat cats or dogs now do we? But---if we got hungry enough and we didn't have cows, sheep, pigs, or chickens, then I suppose we'd have to eat the cats and dogs!"

Ruth didn't think that was very funny. She made a face and ran off before anybody saw her tears.

~~~~~~~~~

1908: John sat at the kitchen table and with the light from the lantern went over his ledger; he kept meticulous business records, including a personal account of his business and spending. He thought to himself. *Every spring we run into this problem—the lack of forage for the sheep. Time to buy corn to feed them, which costs money, and now we have to borrow from the bank. Now, the other side of the coin is that $500 covers a month of corn for a bunch of sheep who have just given us $3,000 worth of lambs and maybe $6,000 in wool. It's good business to keep some [11]wethers around,* *just for their wool. So---bottom line—we have to maintain the sheep so they can give back to us!*

~~~~~~~~

John studied his plan for crop rotation the next year. He learned from his father-in-law the importance of crop-rotation so that one crop didn't suck all the nutrients out of the soil---there was a give and take with plants. He also studied irrigation and how you look at the lay of the land before you run your ditches. Water doesn't run uphill!

He looked up at his wife, "Oh Mary, some good news---I just learned that the U. S. Forest Service began zoning some grazing areas and is charging any wheres from five to eight cents per head of sheep—on federal forest land. It helps keep the undergrowth down and that helps with fires. That means the Bighorns! I am certainly going to look into that—we could take the entire flock up there all summer and let em get fat on that green grass for pennies on the dollar! I plan on talking to my herders, then heading down to Basin and get a permit."

~~~~~~~~

John thought about all the folks who had considered buying in with Solon Wiley and his new project. They had quickly become disillusioned and were now looking around in Germania for farmland. Just last week he had met John Davis, George Zorn, Frank Kellerman, the Watsons, Tranks, and W. B. Edwards. More folks were breaking ground and moving in, especially down on the east end. He and John Davis hit it off right away.

Courtesy: Robert Werbelow

That fall, Bill and Ruth went back to school—it wasn't a far walk for them because the schoolhouse was at the corner of their farm. Some kids rode horses or walked when the weather was good. There was a shed to shelter the horses, as well as an outhouse for the boys and one for the girls. Bill didn't often say much, but he hated it when it was cold and the teacher heated the cast-iron stove. Bill remarked, " If you sit near it, you cook, and if you sit far away from it---you get cold."

Ruth complained about the smelliness that filled the small room—which seemed to be the result of those unwashed children who sat close to the heat. Normally, most didn't take a bath but on Saturday night—if then. Ruth said, "I love recess, Mama. We have one in the middle of the morning, then at dinner time, we take our dinner pails outside--- if it's nice out, and then recess again in the middle of the afternoon. It smells so good outside, Mama. I can't wait—for recess every day."

That day after school Bill and Ruth saw Jim driving their father's dapple gray team of horses, pulling the hayrack filled with straw. Bill grabbed Ruth by the hand and pulled her along as fast as her little legs would go. All the way he was waving his hands and shouting at Jim. They wanted a ride on that big soft bed of straw! Jim pulled the team of horses to a stop, wound the reins around a post, and reach down to pull Bill and Ruth up beside him. Bill pleaded with Jim, "Please let me ride up on the top of the stack, pleeeease Jim! I promise I won't fall off."

Finally, Jim gave in to better judgment and let Bill scamper  back behind the seat to the center of the pile of straw. Bill stood up and raised his arms to the sky---"See how big I am—I can see clear to Burlington!" About that time, Jim flipped the reins and the horses moved forward with a jolt.

A moment later---there was no Bill! Jim panicked, pulled the horses to a stop, and wound the reins around the seat. "Ruth, you stay put, I've got to see what happened to your brother!" He jumped off the rack and ran around the side expecting to see Bill under a wheel or laying on the road. Jim almost wept with relief when he spotted twelve-year-old Bill hanging off the back rails of the rack, smiling like it was Christmas.

Jim squatted down in the road with relief, cursing up a storm-- in German. Then he grabbed Bill and pulled him off the back of the hayrack. "What in tarnation do you think you are doing? You scared ten years off me, boy! For that, you'll walk the rest of the way home. Yessiree—you just walk you smarty pants---no more rides with Jim!"

Ruth made sure to turn around and wave goodbye to Bill as they drove by!

~~~~~~~~~

In the winter when the temperature dropped enough to freeze the stock tank, it was Bill's job to get up with John at daybreak, light the kerosene lantern then go to the barn. Bill would check the animal's water and scoop out the manure troughs while John started milking before being joined by Jim and Chester, their new farmhand/herder. With Bill's help, Jim had put together a simple, cast-iron heater with a little firebox and chimney to help keep the stock tank from freezing completely. Meanwhile, inside the house, Mary stoked the stove downstairs and laid out the girl's clothes so they were nice and warm when they got up. She knew when they were awake because they squealed like baby piglets—as they scampered down the cold stair steps until they got to the warmth of the stove.

~~~~~~~~

After harvest that year, the hired help built a simple bunkhouse, just on the other side of the outhouse. Chester and Herbie took up residence right off. Later that fall, Jim decided to move out of the main house as John and Mary needed the extra room for their growing family. Jim moved into the bunkhouse and at first, he missed the constant commotion from the children, but then he got used to the peace and undisturbed quiet.

Bill liked to peek inside their bunkhouse when the men were gone—it was small and very messy. He thought. *Nobody makes them pick up their clothes and it smells different than our house and not in a good way, in fact, it downright stinks!*

~~~~~~~~

John spent many winter evenings looking at car magazines—his new fascination. Ford produced the kind of car most farmers wanted and could afford. It was a fifteen-horsepower Model N, introduced in 1906 for $600. In 1908, the famous Model T came out and sold for a whopping $850. The 'Tin Lizzie' as it became known, came in any color you wanted as long as it was black! It was a bare-bones, rugged, and reliable automobile. However, the Buick Motor Company was right up there with Ford, followed by Maxwell and Studebaker. Other cars were Cadillac,

Oldsmobile, and Rambler but Ford stayed in the number one spot until after 1913. At that time, the Model 10 Buick was the most popular model—as it was equipped with acetylene headlights, taillights, and a bulb horn! The newest thing was 'color'---the Buick was available in an off-white shade called 'Buick Gray'. Then, the competition started offering a full array of cars in color.

~~~~~~~~

That next afternoon when John rode into the yard on Trotter, Bill and Ruth ran out of the house, all excited. "Dad---Dad---one of the old mama pigs died. The other pigs are really mad too. We tried to go see it, but they squeal at us. Come see, come see!"

John put Trotter out to pasture and then went to see about the old sow. The boar and other pigs didn't like him either, so John diverted them into another pen by tempting them with food. He walked up to the dead pig while Bill and Ruth were hanging on the fence watching him. John bent down, and just by looking, could tell the sow had been dead for longer than possible to use it for food. He said, "Well, looks to me like she mighta been sick or died of old age. Anyways, she's been dead too long and we can't butcher her out--- I'll have to tie a rope to her legs and drag her out to the dump past the cemetery there!"

Bill and Ruth jumped up and down on the fence. "Can we come with you Dad, huh?" John turned to them, "Don't you two have school tomorrow?"

Bill pleaded, " But Dad, we want to throw rocks at the other dead and bloated cows and stuff! Sometimes we find good stuff that people throwed away!"

~~~~~~~~

That morning, John got up at the crack of dawn and said to Mary, "I am going to take that Percheron stud down to the Davis place. John Davis said his mare is in heat and he'd like a colt out of our stud. I think one of our mares already got together with that big boy—she is acting like it. I'll tell you that big fella must do a good job because everyone around wants to borrow him. The few dollars they pay for his service is good as well."

John thought for a few moments then added, "I also sold another draft horse to the fellas who are working on building the roads around here. They need lots of those horses---they are so strong and can work all day. I wish I had ten more to sell to them!"

Before he left, John said to thirteen-year-old Bill, "Go harness up the workhorses like I showed you and hook them to the harrow. I want you to harrow that field to the south of us. You can do that can't you? Climb up on the fence like I showed you to put the halter over their heads."

Bill had been out in the field for over five hours, driving the huge team of Percherons up and down the field, pulling the harrow. As he was making the turn on the far end, one of the harrow teeth got hooked up in old sage roots and the whole thing flipped over. Bill had all he could do to handle the spooked team of enormous horses, so they didn't run the field. The boy climbed down, tied the horses to a fence post, and started walking home.

When John returned from his trip down to the Davis farm, he saw Bill walking across the harrowed field toward the house and he rode out to meet him. John was furious when he found out about the overturned harrow. He had never laid a hand on Bill, but that day he did and it was a spanking to remember!

That night as John was sitting in his chair, Bill approached his father. "Dad, I want to tell you that I'm sorry the harrow got hooked up in that sage root, but I didn't see it and didn't know that could happen. I did the best I could to control the horses. That's all I have to say. Goodnight."

Bill started to climb the stairs to his bedroom. John said, "Bill, you did the right thing. I am the one who did wrong. That was no reason to whip you and I am sorry too. I love you son."

Bill went into his bedroom and laid face down. *Dad had no reason to whip me like that and I won't forget it, ever.*

~~~~~~~~

After supper that next evening, John looked over the rim of his eyeglasses and said, "Yesterday when I took the stud down to the Davis place it was smooth riding---looked like Charlie Myer just graded that road."

John sat up in his chair, "Say, Mary, Mrs. Davis was telling me that there is a new doctor in Greybull. Mrs. Davis said he makes house calls, even clear out here to Germania."

Mary smiled sweetly and said, "That's good news in case something serious happens but at this stage John, I think I do just fine with a mid-wife. I have already talked to Mrs. Grabbert---she helped to birth Marie and we worked together very well. There's just no sense in paying a doctor that kind of money to drive clear out here and help with something I've had a bit of experience with!"

John put his arms around his wife and said, "Mary, it's completely up to you. When the time comes, you can decide if you want the doctor from Greybull and if you do---I'll go to Wegner's store and call him!"

John went back to his newspaper, then smiling he said, "You'll never guess what Mrs. Davis said to me today. She asked why neither of us has a German accent like the others up here. She said, "Why, one could never tell that you are German.""

John said, "I told her that neither of us spoke the language very well, and we practiced speaking good English, like her!"

~~~~~~~~~

More and more people were moving into the available land on the east end of the Germania Bench. The folks down there finally built their own school in 1908 because it was six-eight miles to the Wamhoff Schoolhouse in West Germania and that was too far for their children to walk or even ride. The new school in East Germania became a part of School District #33, of which---John Wamhoff was president.

Chapter Nine

A NEW DAWN

1908-1917-- was the period of the 'country-living movement'. The State of Wyoming was granted statehood on August 10, 1890, and was coming into its own.

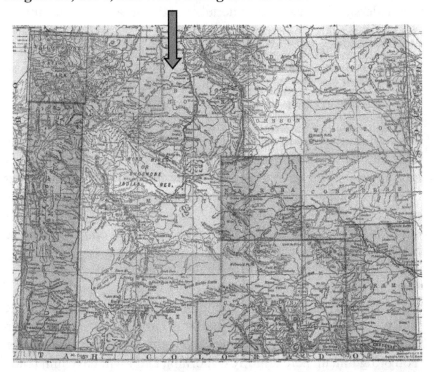

1909: John sat at the kitchen table, studying the recent map of Wyoming which indicated how the various counties were divided up. He was proud to see the name of Germania on the map.

On January 1, 1909, there was an article in the Greybull Standard which read---*A debating society has been organized at Germania where they expect to meet once each week and debate subjects that are chosen from time to time. Mr. Wamhoff was elected president and with this splendid man at the head, we expect a progressive organization, furnishing a great deal of enjoyment for all.*

~~~~~~~~

Wearing his worn bib overalls, John was on his way to the barn to milk the cows when he noticed two men riding into the yard. John set the milk buckets down on the ground and tipped his old straw hat in greeting, "You boys are up early, what can I do for you?"

"We just moved in on the east end of the Bench, Mr. Wamhoff--- and one of our hired hands done up and died last night. We understand you are an undertaker and can take care of him for us. We don't have much money and we'll be glad to dig the grave where you tell us to. We don't need nothing fancy like---a pine box would serve right fine. He wasn't a religious man that I know of, so we don't need no words said over him either. We can put the box in the grave and cover it up. So what would it cost for your services today."

John said, "I'm sorry to hear of your loss and of course I can take care of it all for you. Can you bring him up here tomorrow morning? Do you have a set of clothes for him? Or, on the other hand, just what he was wearing would be fine I expect. I'm in charge of the cemetery as well and I can show you where to dig a grave— that would cost two dollars. Since he isn't Lutheran, he will be buried on the far east side of the cemetery."

John put his head down, calculating what it would cost to prepare the body. "I tell you what---since you are going to do all of the work except for my preparation of the body, I will only charge you two dollars. I'd do it for nothing but I have to use certain chemicals as directed by the state of Wyoming and their guidelines. You bring him up here tomorrow morning and I will have him ready by noon for you to take to his grave."

The two men shook John's hand, "We do appreciate it Mr. Wamhoff and we will have the four dollars tomorrow. Thank you and good day!"

John wasn't called on very often to use his knowledge with the deceased, but every bit of money helped and he found worthiness in being called upon to help folks during times such as those. That afternoon, as he was going over year-end numbers, John thought-- *The pastor asked me to be Secretary-Treasurer for the church. Of course, I accepted---it was an honor, but I also know I'm taking on more responsibility, what with being president of the School District 33 board of directors too.* John smiled—*well, I guess that was a natural thing to do since everyone calls it the Wamhoff School! I just can't seem to say no when folks ask for my help.*

John's finger moved down the page to where he kept figures on his sheep. *I am quite pleased with the condition our sheep business is in. We got good money for the wool last spring. We've been diligent in dipping for Scab and other parasites, and all in all--they look to be healthy. Every ewe is pregnant and we should have a good lambing season in March-April. I've got to hire on another herder—even after we sell off sheep in the spring, Herbie, Chester, and Frankie have too many sheep to handle by themselves. With such large herds, we have to take better watch over our sheep or we are going to lose more of them to predators. Even with the loss of twenty sheep from eating that poison weed out in the hills last summer, the sheep are doing better than what I'd hoped for— making a nice profit and assuring me of a year-around cash crop, combined with the row crop sales and all. I figure I'll make a nice profit on hay this year—my profits are up ten percent from last year and rising. Last I heard it was selling at seventeen dollars a ton. Yes, sir, we're doing all right, if I do say so myself!.*

John looked out the window of the adobe house and thought about another recent brutal raid on a five-man sheep camp just south of Ten Sleep. *Raiders killed three men. Two were roasted in their burning sheep wagon, one shot, and two others were kidnapped. The raiders killed all of the sheepdogs along with a couple of dozen sheep. They burned the sheep sheds and corrals---and left a trail of* destruction. *I don't dare tell Mary about the raids, she'd just worry herself.*

John stood up, pushing the wooden chair back as he moved from the table. He reached in the drawer and pulled out the old box of cigars—*I could use a smoke about now. They say there are six million sheep in this state and we are still plagued with murderous raids like this. I shudder with fear every time my herders take the flock out to the hills. I pray the newly formed Wyoming Wool Growers Association can put a stop to this sort of thing. The law has six of those murders who did this last killing, in the Basin City jail. Now, to prosecute them to the fullest! This is the chance to teach them and anyone like them, a lesson. I heard that the association has hired two top prosecuting attorneys—Will Metz of Sheridan and Billy Simpson of Cody.*

NOTE: *The jury convicted one man of first-degree murder and sentenced him to hang. Five others were sentenced to serve lengthy prison terms in the Laramie prison.*

~~~~~~~~~

Mary sorted through the eggs that Bill and Ruth had gathered over the past week. She sat the cream cans, with the extra cream and milk--along with the eggs, on the back porch where John could see them. Since it was favorable weather and the roads were frozen solid, John harnessed up the team to his heavy farm wagon and stowed the produce tightly in the back so it wouldn't tip over or fall out. This was a weekly task which he thoroughly enjoyed; any excuse to get dressed up and go to Greybull, Basin, or Garland, was a treat for John because he got to catch up on what was happening around the Bighorn Basin and visit with people. That morning, John eagerly put on a store-bought, detachable starched collar over his white shirt. He opened a drawer and pulled out his striped garters to hold his socks up. He pulled on a pair of gray trousers, and finally, his polished high-topped, button boots.

John closed the door of the armoire and looked at his image in the mirror. A smile crossed his face, *I've got to look like a successful gentleman when I go to town to do business—what would they think if I walked in with them bib overalls on?* He smiled to himself and reached up in the closet for his best hat. As a finishing touch, he splashed a bit of aftershave on. Now, he looked and smelled, every bit the gentleman farmer.

On his way out the back door, John stopped in the kitchen to say goodbye to his wife. Mary stood at the sink, with suds and dishwater up to her elbows as he reached around her and kissed her soft, fragrant neck. "Don't hold supper for me—I never know how long these trips into Greybull will take. I want to stop on the way and see how our new Pastor Germeroth, his wife, and eight children are getting along. I am looking forward to the new leadership in our church."

John's mind was on the day that lay ahead. He thought, *When I'm in Greybull, I hope to see the new steam engine--- if it's in town.* As John neared the corner of Road Ten and the highway, he noticed unusual activity over on the farm which the Bennetts purchased from Reverand Wunderlich—the farmland which he had his eye on from day one. On a whim, John drove over to the farm and pulled the horses to a stop in the yard where Bennett was loading a wagon with furniture. John said, "Well now, good morning to you Mr. Bennett. Are you moving in or out?"

Bennett turned to look at his neighbor, "Good morning John, we've had some bad news from back east and we have to sell out and go back."

John straightened up in the seat of the buckboard---"You are---selling out? Who are you selling to?"

Bennett cocked his head and replied, "Are you interested in this farm? I need around $6,000 for it."

John wound the reins around the brake and jumped from the buckboard. "Would you take $5,800?"

Bennett shook his head, "No, I need to make $6,000 to cover all of the costs—well, you know. I don't need it all at once; and I would be willing to work with you, say—payments over three years. However, I'd like a down payment of say, $1,500."

John scratched his head, "Does that include the house and outbuildings---what about machinery?"

Bennett said, "Everything on the place including that cow and my team of horses. We have to ship the wife's furniture by train. I've got to get this handled quickly---we have to get back to Iowa as soon as possible."

John said, "You know I've been thinking about this 160 acres for a while—so of course, I am interested. Consider it sold! I am on my way to Basin City to take the cream and eggs in. I'll stop at the bank and see what I can work out with my banker, starting with the down payment and then paying you in full over the next few years."

John shook hands with Bennett and was surprised to feel his own hands shaking as he climbed back onto the buckboard. He said, "I'll see you in the morning, with the bank check for the downpayment!" John turned the team and headed back to the main road. He took the shortcut over Table Mountain, but the twenty-six mile trip into Basin City seemed to take forever. The stop at the bank didn't take as long as he had expected because of his excellent credit. His banker agreed that John needed more land for his sheep and growing industry and that this was a fine opportunity. It was done!

On his way home, John took the road through Greybull—*I want to see that big steam engine that is in town. When they finally get the passage cut through WindRiver Canyon, then we can ship our sheep*  *east from here and save a lot of money. This town is surely going to grow now. Looks to me like they've built two more buildings since I was here last. It isn't that Greybull is a thriving metropolis, but it's coming right along. It has a hotel, saloon; some small churches to try their luck at civilizing the population; a general store, post office, and rough board sidewalks to get folks out of the mud and horse manure in the streets. I did hear there was a brothel in the*

back of the hotel, for shame! But, I guess one could say that is a sign of progress! The streets are wide enough for a wagon to turn around in—they planned that right; and I like where they built the town-

-- right on the banks of the Bighorn River. From Main Street, John could see the two-span [12]Howe Truss Bridge that the railroad had abandoned and now it had been converted to a bridge for wagons and such. He thought, *that sure makes it easier to cross that river when one wants to go to Shell Creek and the mountains. We can also drive our sheep across rather than pay a ferry to take that flock across—that would've cost too much money.*

As John's rig climbed the hill out of the river valley and he turned west across the flats toward Germania, he thought about Greybull and its future. It was certainly closer as a place to shop than Basin City, and with the railroad and a bridge over the Bighorn River, it might be a pretty nice town someday. *I learned that they are building telephone lines from our area down into Basin where the main switchboard is located. If Otto and Burlington are getting phone lines, then I'll bet the farm that Germania is as well. Won't that be the day!* He snapped the reins across the horses as it was getting late and he couldn't wait to get home!

~~~~~~~~~

Just as the sun was setting to the west, John burst through the front door of the adobe house. "Mary, Mary---where are you--- MARY!" He ran from one room to the other and was about to go out to the garden when she walked through the back porch door. "Mary—Oh Mary!" John grabbed her around the waist and swung her around. "It's OURS---it's finally ours----all 160 acres AND the house too!!"

Mary said, "John---first, put me down, and secondly—what in the world are you talking about? Have you completely lost your senses?"

"The Bennett place---it's all ours, Mary---all 160 acres and the buildings too! They have to sell out and move back east. I learned of it first hand and talked to the bank in Basin today. I signed a note to pay it off in three years and then it's ours, free and clear! Bennett has agreed to it all."

Mary sank into the nearest chair, her eyes wide as she stammered, "And---and the white frame house too, John? The two-story frame house too?"

John was so giddy he could have turned somersaults! He knelt at her feet and taking her hands in his said, " Everything, Mary—the house, buildings, a team of horses—when do you want to move?"

Mary smiled as tears ran over her weathered cheeks, "Oh my John, that's a lot to think about. When are the Bennetts going to be out of the house?"

John looked out the window, recalling the conversation he had with Mr. Bennett. He turned and said, "They are taking a load of furniture and the rest of their things to the train depot today to store it. They have to wait for a train car so they can ship the rest of their things back to Iowa—so, they should be out by the end of the week! I have to go back to the bank tomorrow, to get the papers and a check for the down payment. then, we can move in, any time you are ready!"

Mary laid her finger along her chin in thought, "Winter is not the best time to move, but if the weather holds---as soon as possible; anyways before I get too big."

John whirled around, his eyes wide. "Wha---What do you mean—get too big?"

Mary smiled sweetly, "Another baby—in July!"

John pulled her to him and wrapping his arms around her, he said, "You got your house sooner than expected. Now we can put down some roots and fix that house up properly. "Oh Mary, Mary—

what a year this is going to be---a new house, a new baby---maybe, a boy this time? I'll talk to Jim and Herbie. We need to sit down and decide if Jim will need another farm worker or two. We are going to own two sections my dear—320 acres! I think we have enough herders for now."

John began to pace, his mind going a hundred miles a minute, "As soon as possible we will go over and look at the house. Maybe have a few things done to it before we move in, so it's all ready for us and our family. I want to see about building a horse barn to the east of the house as well. It already has a cow barn and some corrals, but we will have to build more sheep pens and a granary. We have these pens here—" John whirled around, "We could let Jim and the herders' bunk in this house and watch the sheep pens here while we build more at the new place. I was thinking of building more pens out here, but NOW---now we have the new place. We also will have more land to plant fodder crops, so the sheep will have plenty of food during the winter."

Mary touched John's sleeve to get his attention, "And John, what about a big outhouse. With all of these children in the house, we need something much larger than what we have now." Before John could reply, she added, "And John, perhaps one smaller hole, on a lower bench for the little ones. Now, when they have to go, they have a difficult time getting up without a stool; and they are terrified that they're going to fall down the big hole."

John laughed then took her hands in his, "Yes—a new and improved outhouse we shall have. See, our dream of building a fine new life here is coming true—it's all coming true my love!"

~~~~~~~~~

John's head was swimming with ideas to modernize the 10-year old white frame farmhouse. 'Opportunity' was his alcohol—he thrived on it, he craved it. First of all, he was going to tear down the adobe that stood to the west of the house. He planned on building an entire white clapboard addition to the two-story main house on the south side (on the opposite side of where the folks are standing in this photo). John envisioned a large gathering/dining room, with a grand leaded bay window, on the south side for Mary's plants. On the east side of the house would be Mary's kitchen with a window

Courtesy: Arnold Wamhoff

and view of the Bighorn Mountains. It would have a spacious back porch area to house the icebox, milk separator, and a place to wash up.

John began pacing the floor, we *will need a detached summer kitchen for canning, along with a root cellar. I think I will dig another well out near the spot where the large horse barn will be built and put a windmill close by to generate electricity for the barns and house. THAT is going to be a surprise for Mary--- electricity in the house. There is a cement cistern by the house, a good-sized one about ten feet wide by eight feet deep that catches groundwater and rainwater. It's got a good heavy wooden cover on it and a hand pump beside it for household usage. Mary can use that for washing clothes. There is already a well close to the house for drinking and cooking. However, I can rig up a hand pump in the house by the sink. She will love that!*

Mary walked a ways from the house, looking for just the right spot for her massive garden next year. *I need a certain number of rows for perennial plants like rhubarb, strawberries, raspberries, and asparagus. Then the main part will be plotted out for seasonal crops like peas, beans, tomatoes, cabbage, onions, radishes, potatoes, squash, and perhaps watermelon.* Mary thought, *I love my herbs, to use for cooking so I think I will plant a flower and herb plot nearer the house too.*

~~~~~~~~

The next day, John took his field crew over to the new place and they mapped out where to dig the livestock well, so there would be no more time wasted in hauling water up from Dry Creek. Jim, Herbie, and Frankie dug the well by hand, in less than a day. Two of them were down in the hole digging and shoring up the sides, as they dug, while the third was up on top. They fixed a bucket and pulley system where they could fill the bucket with dirt and send it up to the top where another would empty the bucket and send the empty one back down. The water well measured four feet by eight feet; and as they dug, they shored up the sides with two-inch-thick planks so it wouldn't cave in on them. When they got down about six feet the water started seeping up from the bottom. Jim grabbed a steel bar and rammed it hard into the hole and UP came the water. "Let's get out of here. We got us a well. Now, to get the wood cover built and we'll call it a day! Tomorrow we can attach the pump and we are in business. I'd say we have us a darn fine well!"

~~~~~~~~

Later that week, John sat down and drew up the rough plans for the horse barn. Jim walked in about that time and John said, "Look here at this horse barn with eight stanchions—two horses to a stanchion. That will accommodate our twelve Percheron horses plus room for the team horses, and my two riding horses, Buck and Trotter; as well as your horse, Rider. It will have a massive hayloft with an opening on the east end. John stopped and looked up at Jim, "What do you think about putting two holes in the floor to drop hay and grain down to feed the animals?" Jim said, "Sounds right convenient to me. That is going to be a fine barn, John. I might move in there myself!"

John replied, "I am fashioning it after the grand horse barn my father-in-law had on his place back in Germantown. I also drew plans for a six-stall cow barn to the south of the horse barn, and they'll have separate corrals. I want it to have a room where we can store bags of oats, two calf pens, and a large enclosure in which they can take shelter in the winter."

"We will build two chicken houses---one is a brooder house for baby chickens and fryers, and the other is a large chicken coop for the laying hens!"John spent the entire afternoon at the new Wamhoff farm, walking the grounds. He walked out in the marshy six acres that laid between the main road and Road Ten. *Now, I can plant my cottonwoods---from the highway, down road ten, and then on both sides of the lane to the house. They will suck the water out of this boggy plot. We should plant several around the house as well as the machine shed for shade. This spot will make a perfect orchard, the ground is too wet for row crops and the fruit trees will love it. I want to plant apple trees— like MacIntosh, Wealthy, and Crab Apple. Mary likes to bake sour cherry pies, so there have to be several cherry trees and she is partial to pears too. We'd have room for some plums, raspberries, and chokecherries out here instead of in her garden. I think along that fence that goes up the lane---that's where I'll plant my hops. Got to have a patch of hops for my beer---you betcha!* John smiled at the thought of an orchard and his hops.

The next thing I've got to do is get ahold of Herman Tyler. He just finished with the construction of the Zion Lutheran Church; and now, I've got another job for him---fix up this house for us!

John was nearly beside himself thinking about the new Lutheran Church, which was dedicated only a month ago, and

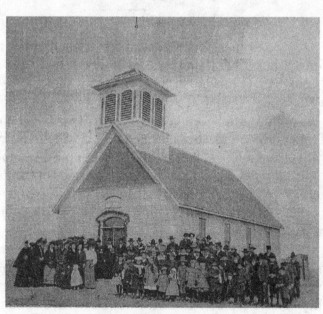

Zion Lutheran Church – Germania, WY

now, they had the farm they had always dreamed of.

~~~~~~~~

June 1909: John opened the door to the back porch of their newly remodeled frame house on what was now known as--the Wamhoff farm. Herman Tyler had finished work on the additions to the home three weeks ago and they had moved in immediately. Mary was in the eighth month of her seventh pregnancy and not able to do any lifting. Beaming with happiness, she waddled from one room to another, "Oh John, the house is quite grand. So much room—and, and the windows are so big, so much light compared to the adobe. Bill has his very own room upstairs and the girls are in the other. They are such nice, large rooms—big enough for two beds in each one. Now for us, I especially like having our bedroom on the lower floor in that northeast corner. The small room next to it will be perfect for a bathtub and washbasin. Someday, we might even have a bathroom right there. And, and John, the parlor is lovely, with carved oak double doors leading into it and all! We could use some new furniture in there---maybe the next time you go to Billings? Oh, John—perhaps, if you see a lovely red and blue Asian carpet to cover the floor in the parlor? Oh, and John, I love the hand pump over the sink in the kitchen and how you fixed it to drain outside. That is the most wonderful modern thing. It will save me so much time lugging water from the outside to the inside. It's all just more than I can wrap my head around."

Mary threw her arms around John's neck, at least as close as she could get---being so far along with her pregnancy. "I have to admit, I never dreamed of anything this wonderful. I must write to Mama and tell her all about it." Mary's eyes misted over with thoughts of her father. "Oh John, I so wish Pap were here to see this. He would be so proud of you!"

John nodded his head, "I wish he was here to see this too. We are living our dream Mary—living our dream and he was our inspiration! There is one more thing I am going to get you and that is a better wringer washing machine. I was figuring on digging a drainage ditch, just a small one running alongside the summer kitchen where you wash clothes, out into the pasture. That way you won't be carrying any buckets of water, and the wastewater won't be running in the yard and getting it all muddy. We'll pull it all away from the house. I want to get that done before our baby arrives."

Mary clapped her hands together in pure joy at the sound of the new set up to wash clothes. It seemed that every day there was something new and wonderful happening to them, making their life easier.

John took her by the hands and said, "Say now, the community is having a picnic down by Dry Creek next Sunday afternoon if the weather holds. Would you like to go to the picnic, Mary? I can take the children if you don't feel up to it."

Mary laughed gaily, and said, "Oh John, I am fine. The baby hasn't even dropped into the birthing position yet. I would love a picnic under the shade of the trees! Just to sit and chat with the neighbor women would be so nice and watch the children having fun. We must ask Jim to join us too, John. He has done so much for us and hardly ever asks for anything, he's like part of our family."

On the morning of the picnic, John took Mary by the elbow and gently helped her up into the front seat of the buggy as the children piled into the back seat. John climbed up, took the reins and they were off to the picnic! Jim insisted on riding his horse. "That way I can leave when I need to. I have a few things to do at the adobe to get it ready for the rest of us men to move into. I appreciate the invitation!"

The adults found themselves a shady spot and spread out a quilt to sit on. Jim offered Mary his hand when she lowered herself to the blanket. Mary directed Ruth and Bill to take the food over to the table where the other women were setting things up. Mrs. Jensen came over to where Mary sat. "How are you feeling Mary? Looks like you are about ready. Don't you concern yourself with helping---we have more help than we know what to do with. You relax, you need to do that!"

The children took off, chasing each other in all directions through the milling throng of people, in a game of tag.

They all had a grand time. The adults relaxed under the shade and caught up on the latest gossip, farm information, and local chitchat while their children played games like hopscotch, hide and seek, jump rope, wooden hoops, tag tug of war, and before the afternoon was over, there was a game of baseball—and some even splashed in the shallow part of Dry Creek---where there was no chance of quicksand.

The men enjoyed a few cups of beer---compliments of John Wamhoff who had made it in the barn with the hops that grew on his old farm. The tables were sagging with numerous covered dishes of sausages, sauerkraut, sliced tomatoes; and cucumbers swimming in sour cream, crispy scalloped potatoes, golden fried potatoes, fried chicken---you name it—it was there! Then, there were the desserts---pies of every flavor and cake of every type. German women are known to prepare enough food to feed an army for any gathering or occasion.

Sweating from the heat, John flopped down on the blanket beside Mary under the shade of the trees. "I brought you a cup of cold beer—thought that might just hit the spot on this hot day. Don't worry, some of those 'ladies' will think it's lemonade." John laughed and stretched his arms. "It's so good to see everyone out and having a good time. We have a wonderful community Mary, just like I'd envisioned it as we rolled across the barren prairie when we came here nine years ago. This Bench has evolved from a 'barren prairie' to a haven of prosperity and growing families. God is Good, Mary---he's been so good to us!"

Jim walked over to where the Wamhoff's sat, after making the rounds visiting the other farmers. With a mug of beer in his hand, he eased down on the blanket and stretched out his long legs. "What a day! This is so nice that everyone can get together and have some fun. Most of the time it seems like we just work. I remember when we rode up here about eight-nine years ago---was nothing but sagebrush, hope, and ambition!"

John said, "Jim, I want you to make a list of what you and the others need in the adobe, to make it real nice like---beds and such. When our crops come in this fall or we sell the wool first---whichever, you are going to get a nice check. I know you always said you don't need much, so put it in the bank or whatever. I owe you so much. We wouldn't be where we are if it wasn't for you."

Flushed, Jim stood and thanked John. "I better be getting back---I'll milk the cows tonight so you don't have to hurry none. And, thank you, John, I appreciate it!" He bent and kissed Mary's hand, then turned and mounted his horse.

Mary watched Jim ride toward the home place. "That was good of you, John, and I know it means a lot to Jim. You are so right; we wouldn't be here if it weren't for him and his help!"

~~~~~~~~~

July 26ᵗʰ, 1909: Helen Amelia Wamhoff made her presentation on the hottest day in July. Once again, Minnie Grabbert acted as midwife and Mary gave birth without any problems. Propped up in bed, she sat holding her beautiful, healthy baby girl in her arms. Now, that the coast was clear, John walked into their bedroom, "Oh my, oh my—look there. She is perfect, Mary, just perfect. She certainly has a set of lungs on her---we can hear her clear out in the living room. Her sisters and big brother can't wait to see her. Can I let them in?"

Mary had plenty of help with the new baby, with Ruth (nine) and Esther (seven)—they even learned how to change the baby's cloth nappies. Four-year-old Adella and two-year-old Marie weren't much help—so Marie Grabbert came over again to supervise the cooking and washing for the large family, over the next two months until Mary had fully recovered. One day, while she was nursing the baby, Mary thought to herself. *John has paid little attention to the new baby. He hasn't even mentioned he is disappointed she wasn't a boy. I know he wants a boy, but I can't wave a magic wand and make that happen! I know I must keep trying---for his sake—to give him another son.*

~~~~~~~~~

November 1909: John burst through the back door, "The east end of the Bench is digging their own canal system---and—and Mary---there are plans to form a drainage district to drain the boggy areas on the entire Bench! Hallelujah! It may all take a while, but it will happen in the next few years, so they say!"

Mary touched John's arm and said, "Let's go out to the backyard, I want you to hear something. The late evening breeze stirred the wisps of hair on Mary's neck as she pointed eastward to where their new church stood. Across the harvested fields, they stood silent in the coolness of the autumn evening and listened to the sexton toll their new bell "Isn't it a perfect way to end the day?"

John wrapped her in his arms as they stood together listening to the toll of the church bell. John said, "Look at this Mary—it's ours, all ours. There are times when you have to grab hold of what you want and never let go."

Mary replied, "Well John Wamhoff if you are known for anything, it's that. I'm getting chilled and supper is getting cold, let's go in before the children help themselves!"

They hurried into the cozy kitchen. There was no central heat but the kitchen and front room were always comfortable with the help of the coal stove and the cookstove. In the winter months, they all got used to warming their own bricks in old socks on top of the toasty coal stove. They would each carry their heated sock to bed and stick it down under the sheets. In the morning, either John or Mary—whoever was up first, would get the stove and kitchen oven cranked up to warm up the house.

Before Christmas, John had a meeting with his herders along with Jim who ran the farming operation. John said, "I want to first thank you all for your hard work—it's not gone unnoticed! Jim, come spring, I think it's time you hired another full-time man to help with the farming. In your next paychecks, there will be a bonus for Christmas and for doing a good job all year. "

The next morning as they were having breakfast in the adobe, Frankie, Chester, and Herbie discussed John's plan to take the sheep up, on the Bighorns for the summer. Herbie said, "I am thinking that after shearing, lambing, and selling off most of the old ewes and yearling lambs in the spring, we ought to be down to around 2,500 head, that's two and a half bands and we are allowed, three bands. John is writing to the government to apply for some of that land they have for grazing; I think with a flock this big that we qualify for use of that range. It would be a month or two after lambing that we start the drive up the mountain. If we get a week's head start and don't push them new lambs, we should be fine. I know for a fact that there are sheep ranchers up in Shell Creek that herd their flocks up on the mountain in the late spring, and it works for them."

A wide grin spread over Frankie's weathered face, "I sure would like spending my summers in the mountains, that would be right fine with me!"

~~~~~~

The seed catalogs came in the next day's mail and Mary couldn't wait to get her hands on them. She picked out seeds for the vegetable garden AND then---the flowers---like, columbine, bluebells, sunflowers, bouncing Betts, and even a lilac and spirea bush. She found herself daydreaming of what her flower bed would look like on the northwest corner of the house come next spring. Many of her neighbors had given her plants or shoots of lilacs and lilies to plant in her new yard, but there were a few favorites she would order. *I wonder if John might consider planting some grass out here---we could get the sheep to mow it? It would make such a nice yard for the girls to play in.*

Mary waited for the right time then said, "Now then John, when you plant your beloved beer hops, I was thinking, that it would be nice to plant a small yard of grass for the children to play on. Bill already volunteered to build me a nice picket fence to go around it."

John looked up at her. If he wanted his hops along the lane, he knew better than to say a word to the contrary; and so he planted a patch of grass to the east side of the house. The hops were planted beside the wire fence that lined the cottonwood lane from the road to the house and around the patch of grass. *Now that should give me plenty of hops for my beer. John Davis said his boy asked him why I would want a vine that was so scratchy? Well, it's not to look at, I'll tell you that---and if I ever catch the kids pulling off those hops and throwing them at each other, there will be hell to pay for sure! Wamhoff beer is the best in the county---that's what I'm told and I would have to agree!!*

~~~~~~

As he was carrying the two full buckets of fresh milk to the house, John saw Mary already out on the back porch. This was her domain---where she kept her pantry, her butter churn, cream separator, icebox, the washtubs, and a 'catchall' for various other household tasks. John set the full milk buckets on the back porch by the separators, "If you don't mind, Mary, I think I'd like a few scrambled eggs and toast before I head out to the fields to check on the men. The milk can wait."

Mary went to the stove and scrambled the eggs for John as he sat drinking a cup of coffee. "Mary, do you think you can get ahold of the 'stage', the mail carrier, and see if he will take the extra eggs and cream to town tomorrow? I have to ride out in the hills and see how the herders are doing."

Mary brushed a damp wisp of hair from her cheek and said, "Yes John, I'll get word to the mail carrier somehow." She dropped into a kitchen chair. "I swear, there are not enough hours in the day to get all my chores done. Ruth and Esther have learned how to hang the wet clothes on the line, they take Adella and Marie with them to hand them the clothes. They don't like doing it when it's so cold out---the clothes are frozen stiff when they bring them in. They help chase Adella and Marie around too---those two little imps get into more mischief than you can believe. The older girls are taking more and more of the chores. I've started propping Helen up in a chair to watch the older girls. She is such a good baby---I feel so blessed."

<p style="text-align:center">~~~~~~~~~</p>

That evening they sat close to the stove in the large parlor. John smoking his cigar while Mary was busy letting the hem out of a little dress. John was deep in thought. Mary looked up at him and said, "A penny for your thoughts, John."

John took another pull on his cigar, then said, "You've been looking at seed catalogs and I've just been daydreaming about automobiles---that Ford Model T. They want around $825 for one of them things. I think I'll wait for another kind of car. I read that there are several companies in a competition now, working on some other models. That would be a right handy way to travel to town and all, but right now, they are more trouble than they are worth. They scare the heck out of the horses when they backfire and the roads are less than dependable. I think for the present, I'll stick to my team of horses and the buggy—thank you very much! I want to see them perfect the automobile before I invest any money in one."

During the night John and Mary woke to find Bill standing beside their bed. He was in a bad way---tears rolling over his cheeks, holding his hand against his cheek, "Mother, oh Mother, my tooth hurts something awful!"

Mary wiped the sleep from her eyes and throwing on her bathrobe, took Bill into the chilly kitchen, turned on the electric light bulb hanging from the ceiling, and sat her fourteen-year-old son on the chair. "Open your mouth and let me take a took now."

She poked around in his mouth until she found the culprit—a molar. "Okay Bill, I think we can make the pain stop for now, but in the next day or so we will have to take you to town, to the doctor to have that tooth pulled. I'm going to put some clove oil in the hole in the tooth and that should fix it for tonight. Don't touch your tongue on that clove oil—it will sting plenty. Now---remember, if you forget and mention the tooth to your Dad, he'll get the pliers and pull it."

They all went back to bed. Mary was grateful her mother had taught her about the old home remedies for sickness and things like toothaches. But, it was all for naught as Bill forgot and mentioned the bad tooth to John while they were out in the barn.

Mary looked up from her task of bread making to see Bill standing in her kitchen with a smug look on his face and something in his hand. "What do you have there?"

Bill held out his hand, "It ain't nothin' Mother, just my tooth that Dad pulled with the pliers. It didn't even hurt! It is bleeding a bit. Do you have a rag I can bite on?"

Mary prepared a cold rag for Bill to bite on then ruffed his hair and kidded him, "See, I told you not to tell him about the tooth. You are such a big boy---bet you didn't even cry."

~~~~~~~

The next week after a trip over the hills to Garland and back, John sat down at the kitchen table as Mary prepared supper. "Boy, I tell you---that road across the hills was worse than terrible today. There was just enough thaw that the wheels went down in the mud and snow up to the hubs. I don't know what is in some patches of that dirt out there, but when it gets wet it gets slicker than snot!"

Mary huffed at him, "John Wamhoff---such language! Mercy me!"

John laughed and said, "When I was over in Garland today, I heard that the Shoshone Dam (later called the Buffalo Bill Dam) is expected to be finished around early spring. That dam will hold enough water to irrigate 90,000 acres of the Shoshone Project." John sipped his homemade beer while puffing on his ever-present cigar. "Guess what else I heard? They are about halfway finished with the road and railroad tracks through the Wind River Canyon. Maybe in another five years, we'll have us a way out of the Bighorn Basin on the south end. I don't know how they are getting through that solid rock, and with the river right there---madness. Why they didn't go up over the stage road where we went is beyond my thinking."

Mary stopped peeling potatoes. "Mrs. Davis has invited me and several of the other west end ladies to a meeting. We want to organize a Germania Women's Club or group to keep abreast of the latest trends in homemaking and simply to get to know our neighbors. I am most eager to go to the meeting, John, I think it is a wonderful idea---spending time with other women up here on the Bench. I told her she could count on me!"

John smiled and commented, "That sounds like a good idea for you ladies to get together once in a while---just so I don't have to sit and listen to all that hen chatter!" He pinched Mary's cheek and he started to go outside. John turned and said, "Ohhhh----you'll never guess who they hired to grade the roads between Germania and Greybull----[13]BLACK FRITZ!!! Now he has an excuse to wander all over the bench, even at midnight!"

Chapter Ten

THE YEARS OF PLENTY

1910: *The years 1910 – 1914 were referred to as the heart of the Golden Age of Agriculture.* **Farm prices were relatively high compared to other prices farmers faced. Many farmers joined their city cousins in enjoying some of the finer things life had to offer.**

John finished his breakfast, shoved back his chair, and said, "Mary, I am going to take a few days and ride up in the Bighorns to check on the herders and the sheep. I want to see for myself where they are and how they are doing up there. If you need anything, Jim and that new man he hired---Obie, will be around. I'm going to leave at first light tomorrow morning."

John pushed his horse until he got to the base of the Bighorn Mountains in mid-afternoon. He had enjoyed the ride up through the beautiful Shell Valley where cattle and sheep ranches sprawled over the fertile land. He began the climb on a narrow mountain road and was relieved to find Herbie and his sheep exactly where they were supposed to be. It was late afternoon when John slid off his horse and, rubbing his behind, walked bow-legged to the sheep wagon where Frankie was cooking up some grub. "Well boss, me and Herbie didn't expect to see you up here. I almost drew my shotgun on you! I've had a little trouble with bears, coyotes, and whatever else will spook sheep, lately. Those dogs are worth their weight in gold, keeping the sheep where they are supposed to be. Look out there, see how they've got those sheep spread out in good fashion right under that rock and timber ledge and away from deep timber or where a critter might be waiting."

"There's some good grazing up here on the mountain. I can't complain about that, not for a minute. We keep a keen eye out for bear scat, and paw prints---think there might be some cougars up here too. We killed a deer last week and enjoyed that venison; that's what I've got in the frypan for tonight. We have had a minor run-in with the Indians who want their share of mutton. We give them a couple of the old ones that will probably die anyway. Then they go away and leave us in peace. It shore is beau-ti-full up here, the air is so clean and fresh. I don't like them lightning and thunderstorms too much tho. They spook the sheep and us!"

John said, "Well, I just wanted to see how you boys are getting along and if you need anything from town? Looks like you have everything under control. I'll just spend the night; I brought a sleeping bag and I'll sleep by the fire under the sheep wagon tonight. Think I might enjoy it!"

Early the next morning after breakfast, John saddled up and headed back down the mountain, satisfied his herders had everything in control. "I don't think there is anything that you two can't handle! You boys let me know if you need Chester. He'd probably like to be relieved of cleaning sheep sheds and helping with the fieldwork."

~~~~~~~~~

Bill and Ruth dashed out the back porch kitchen door, followed closely by Esther and Adella. Ruth punched Bill in the arm and said, "Come on---I'll race you to the ditch—we can go wading and cool off." Before Bill whirled around to run, Ruth was halfway there! She had long legs and was thinner—Bill was having trouble getting used to his big feet. Ruth laughed and poked fun at her brother, "Come on slowpoke—get those big clodhoppers a-going!"

Finally arriving at the bridge that crossed their irrigation ditch at the entrance to their farm, Bill frowned and grumbled, "Dad-gummit Sister Ruth, do you always have to show me up?" Hearing an odd but familiar clanging noise, they looked down the road and saw a horse-pulled wagon all decked out with pans and household goods. They both turned and raced back to the house. Inside the backdoor, Ruth hollered at the top of her lungs, "Mama----Mama---he's coming. The Watkins Man is turning down our lane. Oh hurry Mama, maybe he will have a sucker or a piece of taffy for us this time!"

Mary was always happy to see the Watkins or Rawleigh Man pay a visit. They both had the most interesting wagons that looked like a stagecoach and smelled like a cook's kitchen. The Watkins Man pulled his one-horse wagon to a stop and climbed down from the padded seat. "Good morning Mrs. Wamhoff, I missed you last time around---'spect you might have a list ready for me?" With a showman's flair, he pulled open the side doors to display the interior of the mystifying coach. The air was instantly filled with the most wonderful aromas one could imagine. The interior of the wagon was filled to the brim with all sorts of exotic spices, ointments, oils, salves, and linaments. Of course, they were known to be a 'sure fix' for anything that ailed man or beast. Mary pulled the list she had made out of her apron pocket and scanned the row of penciled items.

Ruth wiggled her way to the front of the 'crowd' and said, "Oh my word, just smell all of those wonderful smells. I think my favorite is the cinnamon, but I do so love lavender too!" Esther pushed past her sister and stuck her face in front to get a better look. "Do you have lollipops today?"

Mary smiled at the Watkins Man and said, "Now then, I do have a few things on my list here." She ran her finger down the list---"Oh yes, some of that carbolic salve for the cow's bags. Then there are the usual things—salt, pepper, herbs, vanilla, nutmeg, and of course some of your cinnamon." Mary looked her list over and added, "Oh Mercy, I almost forgot some of that good linament you carry, for John's back!"

Mary felt Esther pull at her dress and she added, "Oh yes, and some lavender for Esther! She likes to put it in her bed—it makes things smell so fresh!"

At the end of the visit, the Watkins Man prepared to 'wow' the crowd of wide-eyed Wamhoff children as he reached slowly, very slowly--- into his candy bag. His eyes twinkled with merriment as he purposely tempted the upturned faces of the eager children, taking his time pulling out one piece of candy at a time. Today, it was the coveted salt-water taffy wrapped in paper, one for each child. Esther eagerly reached for her taffy and said, "Thank you ever so much. I am just going to lick it a little bit, every so often, so it will last for days and days!"

Adella said, "I'm not licking mine—I chew it up and it sticks in my teeth and then I can taste it all day long!"

The Watkins man closed up his wagon doors and climbed back up on the seat. He tipped his hat to Mary and waved goodbye to the children. "I'll be seein' you, folks, in a couple of weeks if the weather holds and all. Thank you for your business!---Oh my word, I almost forgot—the 'Limerick'—and I have a special one just for the Wamhoff children!" He smiled coyly, then leaned closer to tempt the children's great anticipation, as he began, "*There once were two cats from Kilkenny. Each thought that was one cat too many. So, they started to fight—and to scratch and to bite. Now—instead of two cats, there—aren't any!*" The children could hear him laughing until he got to the end of their tree-lined lane, where he turned south at the road and went on his way to the next farm.

~~~~~~~~

One could always tell it was spring on the farm when the smell of manure was in the air! Spreading it was the easy part, the fun part---filling the spreader with shovels of manure was the 'work part'. John and his hired men had to wait until the spring thaw set in to get at the deep manure. They were now wintering over two thousand sheep in the corrals; so between their droppings, the straw, and hay all mixed up, the depth was usually around 2-2 ½ feet deep. In the spring, it might be thawed on the top but was froze solid below, so they had to be patient and wait until it thawed all the way through to get it all. They also had to muck out the cattle and horse barns and corrals. There was never a lack of manure to cover the fields—John called it 'money'.

~~~~~~~~

Jim and John spent the morning out behind the granary working on the threshing machines. John handed Jim a wrench as he declared, "It's going to be time to start threshing before we know it. I took a look at our field of wheat yesterday and it's starting to ripen. Another week or two and we'll have to cut, it then bunch it into shocks so it can 'cure' before we get the threshing machine in the fields."

Jim kept working as he replied, "How many threshing jobs do you have lined up this year?"

John's eyes lit up at the thought of the extra work. "As of today, there are twelve farms that want us to thresh their grain and it's mostly oats, not that much barley, thank heaven. There is a real high market for oats and hay. I've marked them down according to how far away they live, so we can move easily from one to another and save time! I've got around twenty men lined up for the crew. I figure we'll need about six hayracks and drivers, plus, around twelve teams of horses to pull everything. We've got five '[14]pitchers' lined up to load the hayracks and I've hired a good man to act as the oiler. We have to make sure that those threshing machines are kept in top working order---I've used Jack before on threshing jobs, very reliable."

Jim added, "The thing is that some of the farmers supply their own hayracks and pitchers, so each job differs in what we are expected to do or not! It's up to the farmers to tell us if they want us to pitch their straw into stacks in their fields or if they want it taken by wagon to their farms. There are a lot of things that change, from one job to the other! What they want changes the final price we charge, so we have to stay right on top of it all."

Fifteen-year-old Bill stood off to the side taking it all in. He loved machines and was itching to get his hands on them, but John wasn't about to let the kid touch the expensive threshing machines—just yet. He knew his son was good with machines, he was amazing in fact, but he was still pretty young.

Bill said, "Dad, can I shock the grain this year? I know I can do the work, Dad—I'm a lot bigger this year."

John looked down at his son, "Sure Bill, we'll give you a try. It's hot, itchy work, but you are darn near big as any man now and I know you're a good worker!"

A grin spread over Bill's face, ear to ear as he stood silently, taking mental notes, and watching everything Jim and his father were doing to prepare the threshing machine for harvest. All the while Bill was thinking about the other one---the Minneapolis threshing machine ---the one they hadn't worked on yet. *I just want to take a look at it—that's all.*

~~~~~~~~~

Later that week, Bill was up in the loft of the workshop above where Jim and his father were working, when he heard Jim say, "Say, John, did you work on that other threshing machine, the Minneapolis machine?"

John raised his head and said, "No, I thought you did. I know when I checked it, it looked all ready to go to me."

Jim raised his eyebrows and replied, "Well it looks ready to go to me as well. If that isn't the darndest thing!"

It was all Bill could do to not laugh out loud. *I know, I did a good job on it—I saw them work on the first threshing machine, it was easy, I knew exactly what to do!*

~~~~~~~~~

Late August: At the crack of dawn more than one household was awakened by the steady clip-clop of horse hooves and the steady rattle of numerous empty hayracks and grain wagons. It was threshing time, and to make sure everyone within hearing distance knew it was threshing time, they would also pull the steam whistle--several times, for good measure!

The grain wagons measured 12 feet long by 4 feet wide by 3 feet deep. It was a thrill to watch the entire procession on its way along the dirt roads to thresh the ripe grain fields. The threshing crews were followed by the telltale column of black smoke as it rose from the brand new Rumley tractor which John had purchased in Billings. Its job was to pull the mammoth six-foot-wide Minneapolis-Fomain threshing machine.

Courtesy: Robert Werbelow

John headed up the entire operation, riding his favorite horse Trotter ahead of the tractor. *I'm excited to see how this Rumley tractor handles the separator. By golly, it's the first big tractor on the Bench! It's a huge, open-geared gas tractor--- a two-cylinder all steel machine. The power to run the threshing machines comes from a pulley on the threshing machine connected by a crossed belt to another pulley on the tractor. The kids get a kick out of that tractor and the sound it makes—pumpt-pumpt-pumpt! I've got one operator who watches the tractor and another man to keep his eye on the separator, watching the grain as it spills out and checking its cleanliness. We eliminated the need for a water wagon when we got rid of the steam engine! This machine should pay for itself in no time.*

Bill had proven his worth in his father's fields by stacking the bundles of grain together to make shocks. John ran the binder while Bill shocked the grain. John thought *we make a good team. That boy is going to be a big one, tall like the Westerhoffs. He doesn't know that I know he tinkered with the other thresher. He did a good job, he's got a head for machines that's for sure.*

~~~~~~~~~~

It was no small deed, getting a threshing crew together—a good one that would work and stay together throughout the duration. It was like a well-oiled machine if worked together well. The size of the crew depended on the size of the field and/or how many jobs were back to back. The largest crews consisted of 19-20 men. On top of that, there were 8–10 balers and 10-12 silo fillers (men that pitched the grain into the silos); and the shredders who numbered around seventeen. Each job took a different crew, depending on what the farmer wanted and all. John had each job outlined down to the most minute detail! They worked hard, in the hot sun, in storms, from sunup to sundown; and when it was time to come in to eat, they were thirsty and they were hungry!

The first day out during harvest was always a test. Timing and working with or around the weather was crucial. Grain could be cut before it was ripe as it continued to ripen after it was cut but the heads had to be off the ground—thus the shocking. This season, John didn't start with his field but started north of his place because their grain was ready first. They had approximately ten to twelve teams of horses working the field in some manner or another.

Throughout the day, John rode into the field with bags of freshwater slung over the backend of his horse. On this particular day, he was almost to where the threshing machine was set up when all hell broke loose. A new team of horses was pulling a hayrack, loaded with fresh straw. There was a wagon parked near the threshing machine's spout where the grain came out. The tractor backfired as it started up---that did it. The team pulling the hayrack bolted, dumping the straw everywhere, barely missing two pitchers on the seed wagon, as the driver finally got control of the team just as they got to the edge of the field.

John watched as the driver jumped from the hayrack and proceeded to whip the horses. John wheeled his horse, galloping hell-bent for leather across the field of cut grain. "Hey, hey there, what the hell do you think you are doing to those horses? Stop it—cut that out right now!"

John was off his horse before it came to a stop as he ran at the driver who was whipping his horses. The man took one swing at John before John caught him in the jaw with a left hook.

Both men were sweating and panting----John managed to say, "I don't know who you are, or who hired the likes of you to work with my crew. You are done. I don't hire and I don't work with horse beaters. Come by the house tomorrow and Jim will give you pay for a half day's work. Leave those horses here. Now get the hell out of my sight!"

The man pushed himself to his feet, 'Well, that's a fine thing. I was trying to teach those horses a lesson and I get fired."

John climbed back onto his horse and said, "And I am trying to teach you a lesson---never beat a horse for running away. It was your job to know how they would react around a threshing machine and tractors."

~~~~~~~~

It was the responsibility of each farmer's wife to provide the food for the threshers while they were working on their particular farm. For threshing day on the Wamhoff farm, Mary and her two oldest daughters along with Marie Grabbert started cooking and preparing for the threshing crew weeks ahead. It meant long days with grueling hours in the main kitchen and they even used the summer kitchen to bake the cakes and pies. As soon as the sun rose over the Bighorn Mountains, breakfast had to be served, only to the separator man and engineer as they prepared the machinery for the day ahead. When it was time to set up the long tables of food, Mary always included a tub of hot water, with some clean rags, for the men to clean up before eating. She thought to herself, *I'm so glad that John only has two fields of grain this year. It's heaven when he and the crew move on to another farm and they have to do the cooking, not us.*

After breakfast, the men expected a mid-morning lunch of some sort of sandwich, fruit, a cookie or two, and lemonade or tea, served in the field. When they were threshing on the Wamhoff farm, around 10 a.m. Mary sent Adella and Marie out into the nearby field with their light mid-morning lunch. At 12:30 thereabouts, the crews came to the house for the noon meal or dinner which was more extensive than the mid-morning lunch. Since the average crew was around twenty men, that meant setting up the long, board table outside under the trees at noontime. Once the crew was seated at the table, Ruth and Esther helped Marie Grabbert carry out bowl after bowl heaping with fresh vegetables, sliced tomatoes and cucumbers swimming in sour cream, cabbage with bacon, mashed potatoes, gravy, and some sort of meat—mutton, beef, chicken or pork. Desserts went over big—cookies, pies, cakes, pudding---whatever there was. This was all served up with lemonade, ice tea, or a cold mug of beer. It was thirsty work especially if it was a hot day! The men were usually in good spirits during mealtime, and the young girls heard all about the inevitable tricks and teasing which had gone on that morning. More than likely they heard a few things they shouldn't have, too. Sometimes, there was a hidden pinch or two involved!

Around 3:30 p.m., the crews expected another lunch similar to the mid-morning one. When it was 5 p.m., they called it a day and most went home to do chores and eat again before going to bed. The next morning they got up and repeated the action of the day before. Threshing was a busy time as well as a tense time because it was crucial to get the wheat/grain threshed while the weather held.

John watched the parade of food coming from Mary's kitchen. *I don't know how she does it on the stove she has. I think I owe it to her to get a stove that will serve her better. I've got an idea of what to do after harvest this fall!*

~~~~~~

In mid-afternoon, Mary let Ruth and Esther ride the old workhorse out to the field nearest the house and take more beer, lemonade, and cake to the workers. It was Bill's job to escort his sisters through the moving minefield of horses, wagons, hayracks, and tired men. The pretty little girls received a few whistles from the men, which Bill didn't appreciate. "Hey you, don't you be whistling at my little sisters or I'll have to box your ears!" It didn't bother the girls that much, as Ruth just ignored them and Esther stuck her tongue out at them.

The grown men meant no harm and were amused by this boy who was going to protect his sisters, but that didn't stop them from giving him a bad time either. "You are, are you? You and who else? Your sisters?"

At the end of the day's work, John noticed the storm clouds building to the north. The tops were billowy and the closer they got to earth, the darker they became. John sniffed the air and smelled the telltale pungent odor of sagebrush after a good rain. He thought to himself—*if the rain stays in the hills I don't have a problem with it; I just don't want it to rain while we are trying to thresh.* He looked at the heavens and said, "Lord, I guess you will do what you will do, but I would sure like that storm to pass us over this time!"

The storm clouds drifted towards the Bighorn Mountains, missing the 'bench' altogether which was exactly what John had prayed for!

~~~~~~

That night as they were getting ready for bed, John said, "Say, I got to thinking on the way home today. I'll talk to some of the other farmers and see if they want to have a harvest party or dance when we are finished with all of the fields on the Bench. We've got a few fellas around who can play the accordion, a fiddle, maybe a harmonica. It would be fun to let loose for once. What do you think?"

Mary looked up as she climbed into bed and said, "I'm sure there are folks who would think highly of the idea, John. It just depends if the weather holds and all."

Mary released a long sigh and said, "I'm glad we finished with our fields first because I have a garden that is groaning with ripe vegetables and fruit. The girls and I are going to get up at the crack of dawn when it's halfway cool to pick. Then we can sit in the shade to snap beans and shell peas. Mercy, it seems that everything comes due or is ready to be harvested at once, doesn't it?"

True to her words, Mary and her daughters rose just as the sun was cresting the Bighorn Mountains. They put on their long sleeve shirts, long skirts, straw hats, and gloves. Some of the girls broke all protocol and wore trousers which were easier to work in! Each grabbed a couple of buckets and headed for the garden. They devised a system where they would start at each end and meet in the middle, stripping the row of its ripe vegetables. They worked quickly and efficiently because the longer they took, the hotter it got.

By ten in the morning, they were all red in the face, sweating and complaining that they had enough work to keep them busy for the rest of the day. Mary said, "Okay then, let's head for the shade of the porch or under the cottonwoods. It's going to top ninety degrees today if I'm not mistaken. I'll go in and get the large tubs and pans and we'll work where it's cooler. When she came back out she also had large jars of iced lemonade and some butter cookies.

Marie sighed as she said, "Ahhhh Mother, you know how to keep us working, don't you. This is wonderful!" The girls kept themselves entertained when they worked by talking about boys, dress styles, and any juicy gossip that was circulating! Mary heard a few things that she wished she hadn't! By the end of the day, their fingers ached from snapping all of those beans and shelling peas.

They kept the snapped beans and shelled peas in the cooler overnight and the next day they canned all day long in the summer kitchen. By the end of the day, they had forty Mason jars of green beans, forty-five jars of tomatoes, and around thirty-five jars of peas. Mary gave a huge sigh as they all sat around the kitchen table, sipping cold tea. "In five days we'll repeat this all over as the second round of vegetables ripen. Then we have to wait for the root crops – the beets, potatoes, and carrots. Most of them we'll bury in the sand in the cellar, but I do want to can some of the beets and pumpkin. We'll have a few bushels of apples to can and make into jam as well. We will be eating good this winter, that's for sure!"

~~~~~~~~~

1911: That spring, Marjorie Trumbell Penn took a special photo of the children who were attending the Westend Germania School. (*Bill Wamhoff is in the back row in a dark suit, standing to his left, with the tie, is Bill Werbelow who would marry Ruth Wamhoff in a few years. Ruth is standing just to the right of the teacher, in a light-colored dress, and sister Esther is in the front row, hands clasped—dark dress with a white blouse.*)

Mary studied the photograph and smiling, said, "I am so proud of all of you. My sweet girls---you both take such a nice photo. My goodness Bill, you are the tallest lad in the photograph."

Bill replied without hesitation, "That's because I'm one of the oldest ones in school and I think it's time I quit and do what I like---farm and take care of the machinery. I'll be sixteen this year!" He thought for a moment then added, "Also Mother, the Germania ball team asked me if I want to play with them. I'd sure like to, but I don't know if I have time what with all the work I'm doing on this farm." A smile spread across Bill's face as he remarked, "Say Mother—did you hear about their game over in Otto last week? It was so funny when their only ball went down a prairie dog hole and they had to stop playing!"

Mary tilted her head and looked to the floor, then she raised her gaze to meet her son's. "Bill, you have a good point regarding school. I will speak to your father and see what we can do."

Ruth piped up, "Well and good, but did you see who pushed in beside me in the photo? Herman ----ugh! After the picture, I gave him a good kick in the shins."

Mary couldn't help but smile. "Now Ruth, you must conduct yourself like a lady and not deny someone to stand near you. He may have a crush on you," Mary teased.

Ruth threw up her hands. "I hate boys---except for brother Bill! Both Herman and that Menzel boy----they-they follow me around like puppies."

Mary patted Ruth on the cheek. "There will come a day, Miss Ruth, when you will meet a boy that YOU like, and then we shall talk about that! Until that time, please try and be pleasant. You have been taught good manners and to be kind and Ruth, that is exactly what and how I expect you to behave. Don't you forget that! You are a Wamhoff and we don't act that way!"

Mary wrapped her arms around her oldest daughter and kissed her soundly then turned to Esther, who, wanting attention as well, had climbed up onto her mother's lap. "So my little one, what did you think of the photograph?"

Esther turned her dark eyes up to gaze at her mother, "Well, it was exciting but what I want to know is--when I am going to grow? I am nine now, the same age as Illa and she is much bigger than I am." She put her little face into her hands as Mary stroked her daughter's dark curls. Mary heard a tiny voice say, "The other kids, they tease me—they call me a squirt!"

Mary hugged the dear child to her bosom. "Well now, some of us are just short and some are tall. I think you take after me and my sister Emma—we were always a little shorter than most others. It's not such a bad thing as you surely make up for it with your spunk---that you do! In the fall, Adella is going to start school, that will be fun won't it?"

Ruth said, "I don't know how I am going to like school in the fall. Fourth grade is hard now, especially in the spring when I can smell the new grass and Dad burning the ditches. I just want to be outside and not in some school room!"

Mary tried to change the subject, "Say, I think we need to plan what to take to the school picnic on the last day of school. What would you girls like to bring?"

Ruth and Esther thought for a moment then said, "I think fried chicken, of course, then some potato salad, red jello with bananas and some---lemonade. Yes, that would be a good picnic!"

Mary said, "Well let's get started on that potato salad and the jello ahead of time. I can fry the chicken tomorrow morning before the picnic. You'll have to help me pack up everything, including your three little sisters. Your father can't come, as he has to ride out to check on the sheep that day.

July 1911: Mary spent most of the morning over the hot stove, preparing food for another big picnic-- the Fourth of July picnic and community gathering. She thought about last year when John got up and gave a speech about everyone doing their part for the good of the community. *I was so proud of him. That man is a born leader—he just blossoms with the responsibility and duty of it all. I wonder who will give a speech this year? I can think of a few who I hope don't feel the calling! Oh, mercy me. then there are the races, like the one-legged sack race and other games for the children. And, the food—land sakes---so much food. I think we may all try and outdo each other. Cooking is so much easier this year what with that beautiful new stove John*

bought me! It is amazing and is such a wonderful combination of cooktop plus multiple ovens and even a warming oven. It just makes cooking for a big family and the threshing crews so much easier.

Sudden nausea flooded over Mary as she put her head over the dry sink. Nothing came of it and she recovered in no time. *It's just the heat and I didn't sleep very well last night.*

When nausea came back to greet her the next morning, Mary didn't need a doctor to tell her what was the cause. *It's not like I haven't been down this road before. Please, dear Lord, let this child be a boy—for John.*

The next morning John hitched the team to the wagon tongue and they all piled in the large wagon. Bill pitched in to help carry all of the baskets of food for the Fourth of July Picnic. After a huge dinner under the shade of a grove of trees, Mary sat on a blanket, holding Helen. John flopped down beside her with a jar of his beer and a fat cigar. He laid on his side and smoked and talked about the picnic.

Mary felt nausea rise with the smell of the cigar smoke. "Oh goodness me, John—please put that cigar out—have pity, I feel like I am going to be sick!"

John pushed himself up and cocked his head, "Since when don't you like cigar smoke?"

Suddenly he had a flash and he took Mary by the shoulders, "Now Mary, what's with this sudden nausea from cigar smoke?"

Mary lilted her head slightly to the left as was her habit. "I'm not positive yet, but all the signs are there. I am counting on around

Courtesy: Robert Werbelow

the first of February. And John, I am trying for a son this time but regardless, we shall be blessed by a healthy child!"

John pulled Mary to her feet, "Come along, they have a photographer over here to take a photo of the adults. Mary stood with the women, dressed in white, with her head tilted to the side. John stood to the far right with the men, wearing a new fedora.

~~~~~~~~~~

The next night, during supper, out of the blue, Bill asked, "I was wondering if it was alright if I went with a few of the other guys to the roadhouse tomorrow night? Bill Weberlow and some of the local fellas in their band are going to play for a dance upstairs there."

Ruth piped up, "Since when do you know how to dance?"

Bill shot back, "I don't know how to dance today, but that doesn't mean I can't learn tomorrow! I'd probably learn faster if I had me a nice sister who would teach me!"

Courtesy: Robert Werbelow

John tipped back in his kitchen chair and winked at his oldest son, "That's fine Bill. I guess you are old enough to be out having a bit of fun. But, fair warning, don't ever let your fun at night interfere with your work the next day, understood?"

~~~~~~~~~~

They had a good harvest that fall, the weather held and they were able to bring in all the crops without fail. Mary was relieved that harvesting and especially the canning season was almost over. *"Mercy me, that garden we planted last spring covered two acres at least. We had row upon row of potatoes, corn, tomatoes, carrots, turnips, onions, green beans, peas, lettuce, and peppers. Most of the root crops are buried in the sand in the root cellar, so I don't have to can them. Thankfully everything doesn't ripen at the same time so the canning is staggered throughout the summer and fall months. But then, there is the canning of the meat—I don't mind any of it except when we butcher the hogs. That summer kitchen becomes such a mess with all that fat and lard---I almost have to wear skates to get around in it. But it sure is good eatin' when it's put up in jars. I'm a lucky woman---most women around here don't have all the nice things that make my work easier. John might buy a lot of horses, machinery, land, and now cars, but he makes sure I have a few special things too---when we can afford them. He's not anything like my Pap was; John is more of a gentleman farmer—he likes to give the orders and set things up rather than get in his bib overalls and get dirty. He's very good at organizing and getting crews together.*

~~~~~~~~

November 1911: Winter came on early with a foot of fresh snow. John and his crew had their work cut out for them clearing it from the sheep pens. "Frankie, go ahead and take them out into the field to the east and see if they can get through to some of the fodder out there. If they can't we are going to have to feed them hay and corn-- and that costs money!"

The sheep were quite apt in finding areas where the snow wasn't as deep and then pawing through to the ground. They managed to find a bit of food, but not enough to sustain them for long periods That night Herbie and the sheepherders pitched hay to them and filled the feeders in their pens with corn. John said, "This is when these wooly critters cost us money---over the winter months. We don't dare take them too far out in the hills to forage, because of snow squalls. We've already put them out in the fields to eat what was left from the row crops. I've got to figure out what to plant that will leave more fodder for the sheep."

John knew this was a costly problem and he studied the most productive ways to manage it all. He looked up from the magazine he had been reading and stated, "I think that next spring I am going to try sugar beets. We'll leave the leaves and 'tare' in the fields; that way, the sheep might have a little more to eat over the winter. I think I'll give it a try and see how it works."

~~~~~~~

With Christmas music blaring from the radio, Mary and her children sat at the kitchen table, pasting, cutting, and knitting paper chains, stars, and circles; covering tin lids with shiny paper, while Bill whittled small wooden ornaments which the older girls painted with food coloring and red beet juice. After the dinner dishes were washed, Mary and the girls made Christmas cookies. Mary lost count of the number of knitted scarves, hats, and gloves she had made and hid away for presents; as well as two new gowns for the baby. They were all excited about Christmas, especially because John and Bill were going to go to the mountains and cut a real tree.

Mary was in her eighth month of pregnancy. *I'm always reassured when I feel my child move inside of me. This baby is strong for its age, and I swear, constantly on the move. I can't even let myself hope that it's a boy for John's sake. I just pray for a healthy child.*

~~~~~~~

John burst through the back door, shook off the snow, and then came into the room where Mary and the children were gathered around the stove. "Well, it's going to happen. We are going to have electric lights in the church! At the meeting of the church board, I proposed a gasoline-powered electric generator like the one we have. They are putting it in the adobe building next to the parsonage and it will take care of both buildings."

Mary's face lit up, "Oh John, that will be so nice when we have evening services, like on Christmas Eve and all. We won't have to worry so about the tree catching on fire from those candles. But it's only a matter of time until the Rural Electric Association makes its way out here to rural Wyoming and then we won't need generators!" She paused and gazed out the window, "I heard the other day that the telephone company is starting to run telephone lines out to Otto and Burlington, then on to Germania. We'll have several lines with several people per line, but it's better than having

nothing!" Mary added, "Will you see about getting a telephone for
our house John? It would be so useful and handy to be able to call
someone when we need something. I saw a picture of the phones, it
certainly is an odd-looking thing. Most are hung on the wall and
made from oak. It has this part that hangs down, the speaker---which
you talk into, then a receiver on a cord that you hold to your ear, a
ring crank, and a bell. If you want to make a call, you turn the crank
the number of rings you need for the number you are calling, then
speak into the cone affixed to the frame. You pick up the receiver
and hold it to your ear. Several houses are put on one line and have
various numbers or rings, like two 'shorts' and one 'long' ring
which you perform from your phone. Now, if you need to call
someone on another line, you must call 'central' and the
switchboard operator puts the call through to the other line." Mary
continued, "I also heard that only unmarried women are hired as
telephone operators and are forced to quit if they marry. I wonder
why that is?"

John smiled wickedly and said, "Because women are
supposed to be in the home fixing dinner for their man!" His head
barely missed the pillow thrown at him!

Chapter Ten

A FULL HOUSE

1912: When the sun pushed its way through the bank of low-lying snow clouds on February 10th, Mary had been up for hours, walking the cold floors with her shawl around her shoulders. She finally gave in and turned the heat on, so the oil stove might warm the room a bit. The children's school clothes were already laid out beside the stove in preparation for their school day. Mary had packed their dinner pails an hour ago.

In the back bedroom, John reached over in bed to find a cold empty spot. He jumped out of bed and throwing on his robe, he padded barefoot into the living room where he found Mary next to the stove. "Mary, what in the world, couldn't you sleep?" As soon as the words left his mouth, he realized WHY she was up, walking around the room. John crossed the cold floor quickly to where she stood with her hands cradling her extended stomach. "The baby? Are you in labor? Do you want me to call Mrs. Grabbert?"

Mary nodded her head, "Yes John, I think by the time she gets here, the children will be off to school and they won't be here to see or hear anything. I have started their breakfast. Ahhhhhh, ----" Mary doubled over as another contraction hit her. She reached for the nearest chair. Just about that time, Bill, Ruth, Esther, and Adella came running down the stairs, squealing as their feet hit the cold floors; they instantly surrounded the warm stove and hurriedly began dressing in their warm clothes.

Mary pushed herself up and out of the chair then walked slowly to where the children were dressing by the stove. "Ruth and Bill, I want you to get breakfast on the table. The mush and hotcakes are already made. You help the little ones. Get them bundled up in their coats and mufflers before you go to school. Dad will take you in the wagon this morning. It's my time and you will need to take charge of things for a few days. Hopefully, when you get home you will have a new sister or brother."

Bill put his hand on his mother's shoulder, "Is there anything else I can do for you Ma?

Bill put his arm around his mother's shoulders and said, "Since I'm not going to school now, I can watch Marie and Helen if that would help."

Mary smiled and said, "Yes Bill, that would be a big help. Mrs. Grabbert is coming over to help me and we'll be plenty busy."

Six-year-old Adella ran over to her mother, "Why Mama, what are you and Mrs. Grabbert going to do today?"

Ruth grabbed her little sister by the arm. "Now, never you mind, Miss Nosey! Here, let's get your muffler and mittens on. We need to get to school."

Mary went to the telephone and had the operator connect her on the switchboard with Minnie Grabbert. "Good morning, I hope I didn't wake you. If you can arrange it, John is on his way over to your house—it's my time and I would appreciate you being here with me again!"

~~~~~~~~~

John dropped the children off at school and then drove the wagon over to the Grabbert ranch where Minnie was ready with her black bag. On the way to the house, Minnie said, "This will make seven children for you and Mary. That is a fine house full of children. Mary is a remarkable woman to birth that many babies!"

John flicked the reins over the back of the horses, and replied, "Her mother was the same way, built for having babies. I am just glad I am not a woman."

Mrs. Grabbert looked straight ahead and quipped, "I'll just bet you are. If men had to have the babies, there would only be one per family!"

John didn't comment, he was smart enough to get her message.

Mary was squatting over the chamber pot when Minnie Grabbert walked into the bedroom. She reached down and hooked her arm in Mary's and helped pull her to her feet. With trembling legs, Mary staggered to the comfort of their featherbed. Mrs. Grabbert took her by the arm and holding her back, said, "Let me prepare the bed for the birth, Mary, you wouldn't want to soil those nice feather comforters." It took her only minutes to strip the bed and put down a tarp and old blankets for the birth. She put water on to boil and assembled her birthing aids on the bureau next to the bed. John headed for the barn---any place outside of the house. He couldn't stand to hear the noises Mary made when she was in labor—it tore him apart and flooded him with guilt.

Bill turned the radio up so his little sisters wouldn't hear their mother in the bedroom, having a baby. He tried to keep them at the far end of the house, in the kitchen, playing 'house' under the kitchen table. *I wish she would stop having babies. I'm worried about her. I know sometimes women die having babies.*

~~~~~~~~

Mrs. Grabbert put some midwife herbs and potions into the tea to ease Mary's discomfort. She had laudanum in her bag if necessary, but Mary Wamhoff usually birthed her babies quickly and without supreme effort. Mrs. Grabbert looked at Mary, laying in bed, with her eyes closed, breathing with the pains, not fighting what her body was doing on its own. *This is one strong woman who knows what she has to do and how to do it. She has such a steady faith, I admire her greatly.*

Mary motioned to Minnie that she needed to get up and use the chamber pot again. "Let me look first Mary, to see if the baby is coming before you get to your feet."

She looked under the cover to check on the progress of the birth. There was no head presenting so she helped Mary to her feet. The moment Mary stood up, a gush of liquid ran down her legs to the floor, followed by a hard pain. Mary's eyes opened wide. "I—I think I need to push, Minnie----I NEED to—it's coming."

Minnie took another look and said, "Right you are, that baby is on its way out and is coming, now! Lay back down and let's get this baby out here."

There was one more long contraction and push, as a wrinkled, red, squalling baby emerged from Mary's body. Exhausted, Mary laid back on the pillow, eyes closed—waiting to hear what the baby was—boy or girl. At first, she didn't believe her ears, then she said, "Wha—what did you say it is?" Minnie laughed with tears rolling down her cheeks, "You have a robust son and the first thing he did was to pee on me."

Mary pushed herself up on one elbow to have a look. "A boy—are you quite sure? For certain, we have another son? Oh glory to God, a son!"

At that moment John came into the room as Minnie laid the baby in Mary's arms. Mary's face was glowing with happiness--- "John, oh John—we have another son!"

John hurried to the bed and kissed Mary's forehead, then picked up the tiny bundle and kissed his son. "Thank you, Mary thank you for going through this pain again."

"What do you want to name him?"

Mary gazed out the window of their bedroom. "I have always been partial to Theodore---Theodore Adam Wamhoff. Do you like the name?"

John looked down at his new son, beaming with admiration. "Yes, yes I do---it fits him—a fine name for a fine, strong son!"

~~~~~~~~

1912 Spring: John walked into the kitchen for the dinner meal. "Well, it's official, they are pouring the concrete foundation for the new school over on the corner right across from where it is now. The order has gone in for several tons of white gypsum block. It is going to be a grand country school with two large rooms—one for the lower four grades and the other for the upper grades. The façade will face the rising sun to the east and have double doors, balanced by two sets of paned windows. Inside will be a double cloakroom with hooks for the children's coats and a shelf for their lunch pails. To the far north of the grounds will be the boy's outhouse, and to the south behind the school will be a larger building for the girl's needs. We have asked Herman Werbelow to plant five rows of Eastern cottonwoods and a Russian Olive hedge next to the fence on the north side of the school, as a windbreak. It will have a large playing field, and on the south side there will be room for playground equipment eventually." John leaned back in his chair and added, "It is going to be a fine school, it will last for generations."

After his meal, John stood and walked into the living room, sank into his easy chair where he continued talking to Mary as she nursed her son, "We figure the school will cost around $22,000."

John added, "I am proud to say that we will also teach the first year of high school in the upper-grade room. We already have fifty-one students enrolled for school in the fall. It's a tall order, but I think they may have it completed by September. We've hired two teachers—Miss Dickman for the lower grades and the widow, Mrs. Conger for the upper room. We are still teaching for only six months out of the year—someday soon, I hope to have a full nine-month yearly session. We don't have the funds for a teacherage yet---but that will come in the next decade or so."

Ruth spoke up, "Dad, I have decided this is my last year of schooling. Mama needs me to help more around the house. I've already completed the first year of high school, so with your permission, I am finished."

John smiled as he caressed Ruth's soft cheek, "Ruth, I agree that you are finished with the school. You have done well and are old enough to make your own decisions."

~~~~~~~~~

John saddled up and rode out early. *I want to see with my own eyes just what those men are doing out there with the drainage ditches. Also, I want to see that monster--the* [15]*Bay City Dredge at work.* It only took Trotter and John about a half hour to reach the western end of the Bench, where the men were working to drain the boggy land. John reined Trotter in, dismounted, and stood watching the machine open the boggy prairie ground.

Having seen what he came for, John put his foot up into the stirrup and swung his leg up and over Trotter's back. Easing down onto the saddle, John reined the horse toward home and urged Trotter into an easy gallop.

Drain ditching machine.
W.B. Edwards Collection

On his way home he rode past his fields of grain. *They look fine---I think we are going to have good crops all around this year! With a little water and hopefully no hail, we should have a fine yield.*

It was interesting in talking to those fellas—all of the drain ditches belong to the Bench Canal, except those that are going to be dug along the main east-west road---those ditches belong to the Wyoming Highway Department. I guess that makes sense since the ditch is probably on the highway department right-of-way.

~~~~~~~~~

John decided to try raising Great Northern beans that year. There had been several other farmers on the Bench plant beans with fair success. *I have the water and I believe in rotating crops—beans would do well in that field next to the house. The leftover plants will make good fodder for the sheep. Those girls can get out in that field*

and pull weeds from the beans. I'll pay them to do it, that'll get them out there!

The farmers on the Bench had a good summer, plenty of

Courtesy: Arnold Wamhoff

water when they needed it, no hail, and now a good threshing season. Jim cut the beans and they were ready to be raked into rows to finish ripening. John thought *I figure they will be ready to thresh in two weeks if we don't get any rain or wind.* For the Wamhoffs, there weren't any mishaps that fall and John made several healthy deposits into his bank account and paid off his bills. He had been reading about automobiles and liked the looks of the 1911 Chevrolet four-door. He thought, *next time I go up north to Billings, I am tempted to see about driving one of them.*

The next two years were good years for farmers, with good weather and good prices for their crops.

1914: John sat in his easy chair, reading the newspaper he had picked up in Greybull. He read aloud to Mary as she set the table for the dinner meal, "President Woodrow Wilson has pledged neutrality regarding the Germans and for the time being, that is keeping us out of the war over there. I'll have to keep my eye on this situation. If there is war, that will mean an increased need for agricultural products and that could be a good thing for us.

~~~~~~~~

Mary took to her bed on the first of January. John was worried about her and called Marie Grabbert to come over and help with the household. "Mary, what seems to be the problem, do you want me to call the doctor out from Greybull?"

"No, no John. There isn't anything much that he can do for me. I need to rest, stay off my feet and all."

John sat beside her bed. "Do you think it's the flu? What are your symptoms? You are so pale and seem without strength. You are not eating—you don't seem to be able to keep anything down."

Mary looked up at her husband of twenty years with tears running down her cheeks, "John, for heaven's sake, I am going to have another baby, and that's not all. I found four more gray hairs this morning. It looks like I am taking after my father and turning gray early. For pity's sake, I am only thirty-eight and look at me, I look like an old gray gunny sack!"

"Oh, Mary, no---it's soo soon after Teddy's birth—only two years. You haven't regained your strength as quickly as you usually do."

Mary looked up at her husband, "I know it's too soon and I don't know if I can carry this baby, John. I have been spotting, and I feel poorly."

John said, "I am calling the doctor. Perhaps he can give you some potions to help. We have to do something." He knelt beside the bed taking her work-worn hand in his, "Oh Mary, I am sorry to put you through this again. I love you so much! This will be our last baby if you can carry it to term. You can count on me to do my part, I can't bear the thought of losing you."

~~~~~~~~~~

That next week, the doctor from Greybull paid a special visit to the Wamhoff house. He took Mary's blood pressure, and other vitals, then he said, "I hear you believe to be pregnant with your ninth child, is that correct?" Mary looked up at the doctor and said, "After eight babies, I think I know when I am going to have another. I don't recall having felt this sickly with the others. I have the other children, the house, garden, and chickens to take care of; I don't have time to be sick."

On doctor's orders, Mary stayed in bed that day, but the next day, she was out, and the next—back in bed. That's the way it would be for the next seven months. Around the first part of April, John was approached by Jim Wegner who operated the general store, telephone, and post office. "John, I have a proposition for you. I am looking to you first—I have decided to stop running the telephone switchboard. I'm looking for somebody to take it over. Your home is centrally

A Rural Switchboard - Early 1900's

located and I was wondering if you might be interested in the purchase of it? Everybody knows and respects you and your wife. I think you would be a good choice." John's eyes lit up. "For certain? Well, let me speak to my wife first. She has been feeling poorly and I don't know if this is the right time? But I am very interested in it." John waited for the best moment to present this prospect. It was after supper that night when he decided to approach Mary with the new opportunity.

"Mary, Jim Wegner is giving up the switchboard and asked if we might be interested in taking on the telephone business and running it from our home? It would mean that someone would have to be here at the house day and night to put through the phone calls. Do you think this is something you might like to do? We can keep Marie Grabbert on full time to run the house and help with the smaller children. Ruth is fourteen; Esther and Adella are good reliable help in the house and garden, and I was thinking they could help run the switchboard at times too. Marie and Helen are in school all day—that would leave Teddy and the new baby to care for. I know he's a handful, but the girls can chase after him. It's up to you Mary—this is something you will be in charge of. We can find extra household help if you need it. What do you say?"

John continued, "Jim Wegner explained that on occasion, you might get a call that someone has a fire and there is a need to form a bucket brigade---again, you notify the community with the line ring. You should catch on in no time flat and if you need to, you can always call him for advice. He left this list of everyone's phone numbers. The first column is the line they are on

Telephone cal by numbers on all lines.			
Bell J. W.	3	1	1
Berry C. B.	1	2	0
Edwards W.B.	5	2	0
Gerber Paul W.	5	3	0
Hodson Wm.	3	2	1
Jensen Carsten	5	3	1
Jones Ralph R.	3	3	1
Kellersman Frank	4	0	2
Lipsey C. R.	4	3	1
Marcus Jacob	4	0	3
Meier Heinrich	5	1	3
Moeller Freh H.	4	2	2
Moeller Dick	5	4	0
Moeller William	5	4	1
Moeller Fritz	5	1	1
Neff J. O.	3	3	0
Olson C. S.	4	1	2
Pearce C. A.	3	2	2
Pegg M. N.	4	2	0
Peper William	5	2	1
Preis J. Adam	5	0	2
Penn S. G.	5	3	2
Redmon D. A.	3	2	0
Rehwaldt William	5	5	0
Shoemaker S. H.	3	1	2
Teyler H. C.	4	4	0
Walton Fred E.	7	2	0
Wamhoff J. H.	5 2 2		
Wegner Henry	3	4	0
Werbelow Herman	5	1	2
Werbelow Emil	5	0	3
Wilson W. W.	4	1	1
Woolsey J. RL	4	3	0
Zorn Geo. W.	4	2	1

and the second is the number of short rings---the third column is the number of long rings."

Mary didn't hesitate, "John, I think this is a wonderful opportunity to serve our community and earn some extra money. It IS something I can do from home, and I get to sit down while I do it which is a plus in my condition. They say it pays $75.00 a month and I could sure use that to pay for a few extra things our bevy of young ladies are convinced they need. As you said, Bill, Ruth, Esther, Marie, and even Adella are old enough to help when I can't get to it." She paused and looked down at her pregnant body. "I guess, John, that I will say it is something I want to do, but it might not be in my power right now. I'm not supposed to be on my feet as it is, so I could sit, just sit and answer the phone---put calls through for folks. I think I can manage that, if I get the help you mentioned!"

Mary learned quickly how to run the switchboard and to alert the entire community to any problem utilizing a 'line ring', which rang on every phone on one line, at the same time, and then the operator gave the message to everyone. There were close to eighteen phones assigned to the five-party lines.

John added onto the west side of their house, putting two small rooms where the large front porch had been—it turned out to be an ideal telephone room, right off the living room. They hung their oak wall phone beside the front door where it was handy.

Mary said, "This phone business is interesting, to say the least. With having several phones connected to one line, everyone complains that when they make a call, they can hear several folks pick up their phones to listen in." She laughed, "I won't name names, but there is this one woman over on the south line who has a loud ticking clock near her phone; everyone knows when she picks up to listen in because they can hear that clock!"

~~~~~~~~~

That spring, Mary was in no condition to be gardening or on her feet. She was carrying the baby low and her back ached like it never had her other pregnancies. She decided it was high time the girls took charge of planting the garden on the other side of the Russian Olive hedge. Mary thought. *It will be handy to care for, without walking out to the field where the old garden had been. We'll try it for one summer and see how it works out.*

~~~~~~~~~

After a long day in the saddle, overseeing his farm, John sat smoking his cigar and reading the newspaper when suddenly he began to laugh, "I'll be doggone. Montana just gave women the right to vote? "They are trying to keep up with Wyoming—Wyoming gave women the right to vote clear back in 1869!"

Courtesy: Arnold Wamhoff

Mary said, "Well, I say good for the women of Montana—you know, John, you men aren't the only ones with brains and a mind—think on that! Times are changing and women are bent on getting their fair share of things and that includes voting and jobs in the cities. We are good for other things than keeping house and bearing children!"

~~~~~~~~~

It wasn't two weeks later after supper that John announced, "Mary, I am going to do it, I am buying a car. I ordered a Chevrolet sedan from Billings and it will be delivered on the train next week. Now, you can ride in style and

Courtesy: Arnold Wamhoff

comfort, but they only come in black, so I suppose if you don't care for that color, we are out of luck".

Mary replied, "Well since you are ordering a car, I think perhaps I should order those black calf, sixteen-button, high-cut shoes out of the 'Monkey Ward' catalog. They are only $2.39---and I think I should order that hobble skirt to go with them—it's only another $3.99. That way I will be quite stylish riding in the new car!"

~~~~~~~~

Everybody loved the new car, Bill wanted to take it apart and see what made it work, however, John put the kibosh on that idea. Every time somebody on the Bench bought a new car it was big news, and as the telephone operator, Mary heard all the news first hand! Some people even paid extra for a windshield, speedometer, an electric starter, or anti-skid tires on their new car.

That evening the two of them sat at the kitchen table reading and mending by the light of the kerosene lantern. John said, "I read where over in Park County there are eighty-eight cars registered. I registered ours down in Basin and had to pay a $4 fee that goes to fixing the roads up. These cars go faster and faster. Why I had our Chevy up to forty-eight miles an hour the other day. That will surely cool you off on a hot day!" John laughed just thinking of the exhilaration of the speed of that car. "But I tell you this, in town you'd better reduce your speed to twelve miles an hour or the cops will tell you about it!"

Bill laughed, "Do you know that for a fact Dad? Did they catch you speeding in Greybull?"

John said laughing, "No sirree---they tried to, but they couldn't catch me!"

~~~~~~~~

In 1914, what was referred to as the 'stage' (the mail carrier from Greybull /Germania) changed from a horse-drawn wagon to an automobile. Various residents hired on over the years to drive 'the stage', carrying the Germania mail into the Greybull Post Office in the morning and coming back with incoming mail and packages to mailboxes and the post office in the afternoon. Folks who didn't have another way into town would often pay a few cents to hitch a ride with the 'stage'.

~~~~~~~~

Mary quipped, "In case you haven't noticed, this is going to be a big baby; it's so active, that I find it hard to sleep at night. I suppose I should call Mrs. Grabbert and let her know that I think my time is getting near." She looked out the window and John couldn't help but notice the fatigue and worry that lined her eyes and face. It was obvious this pregnancy was taking all Mary had to give.

He took her in his arms and said, "Mary, you are a strong woman. I can't believe this is your ninth pregnancy. Even though you are 38 years old, you are quite fit and I know you will birth this baby too—our last baby. I love you my sweet, sweet woman, mother of our seven wonderful children, and soon eight!"

~~~~~~~~

July 14, 1914: Mary tossed and turned in their bed, the weight of this baby was almost too much to bear. *I can't sleep on my back because it presses down on my innards and when I try to turn to my side I have to support my belly and hold it as I turn over.*

Oh dear Lord Jesus, please let this be over soon. This pregnancy is wearing on me. Please be with me when my time comes.

It was around two in the morning when Mary felt a sudden urge to use the toilet. She swung her feet over the bed and pushed herself to her feet—at that moment her water broke and the first pain began to squeeze the child from her womb. "John, John---come here---WAKE UP John!"

John had been sleeping in the other room because Mary was so uncomfortable and now when she needed him-------. Mary tried to walk toward the door to their bedroom, "JOHN, JOHN—I need you!"

Groggy from sleep, John came stumbling from the other room. The situation dawned on him like a bucket of cold water. "Mary---what—is it time? Should I call Mrs. Grabbert?"

Before she could reply another contraction hit her and her face went white as she gritted her teeth and a low moan came from her lips. "Ahhhhh John, yes, please go call Minnie now. I think this baby is going to come fast and hard—go now!"

It wasn't but two minutes and John was back in the bedroom, doing what he could for Mary. "She said she will be right here, she'll have her husband drive her over. She told me to stay with you and for you to hang on, she'll be right here!"

John tried to adjust the pulling ropes for Mary, so she could reach them as she pulled with each contraction. He watched as her body tense with each labor pain.

"Oh John, get the tarp and old towels—throw them on the bed and get some buckets, arrrghgh----Oh JOHN!" Mary started to breathe fast little puffs of air—panting like a puppy. When the pain subsided, she slumped back onto the pillow as John dabbed her forehead with a cloth. He went to the back window and looked out into the dark farmyard. "She's here Mary, I'll go unlock the door. Just hold on, hold on!"

Minnie Grabbert hurried into the bedroom with her bag in tow. "Well, now Miss Mary, it sounds like this baby is in a hurry. Have you counted how far apart the pains are?"

Mary's body went rigid as another contraction mounded her large belly until it was solid as a rock—pushing, pushing the baby down to freedom.

Minnie said, "Let's take a look and see what is going on."

After a quick examination, Mary had another contraction. Each one getting worse than the last. She flopped back onto the pillow, her face relaxing. "Is the baby coming, what do you see?"

Minnie Grabbert said, "You are ready and things are beginning to happen fast. I applied the oil and positioned the birthing pads under you. We don't have to concern ourselves with the water breaking because it already broke; which is why this birth is progressing so quickly." Mrs. Grabbert walked around to the head of the bed and used a cool cloth to bathe Mary's face. She reached for her wrist to check her pulse. But she didn't tell Mary that she was bleeding just a bit which wasn't normal at this stage and was cause for concern.

Minnie said, "I want you to take this Landanum for the pain. You are doing fine, just fine. Remember to breathe and pant through the pain and let it do the work, don't fight it." This went on for about another hour. John had gone to the kitchen and made some coffee for himself and Mrs. Grabbert. He knocked quietly on the bedroom door. "I made some coffee and thought you might like some."

She took the cup in her hands, cradling the warmth. "Ahhh yes, thank you, John. It shouldn't be too long now, but Mary is weaker than I have ever seen her. This has to be the last baby or you won't have a wife or a mother to your children!"

From the bed came a sound---a pure guttural cry, as another contraction squeezed the baby down the birth canal. Mary's mouth opened again but no sound came. Minnie looked underneath the sheets again, "I better a get a move on, this baby is coming. Breathe, Mary, calm---calm, drink just a little sip more of the Laudanum-- it will help. "

Mary managed to take a couple of swallows of the pain medicine before her body began to twist with the force of the contraction. She gasped, "Oh Minnie, I can't—I can't. Make the baby come—I can't!"

Minnie put her arm behind Mary's back. "I want you to sit up straighter, keep your knees bent and apart—that will help push the baby out. It's almost here now Mary, just a few more pains---- ohhhhhh---now, Mary, PUSH! PUSH---okay breathe, nice deep breaths, and relax." Minnie said, "We are so close now Mary, I see the head---so close. Hang on, work with me!"

Mary said, "Fe-el, like I—am, go—ing to faint---all closing in!"

Minnie grabbed a cool cloth and wiped Mary's face, trying to revive her. "Okay little mother, here comes another contraction—PUSHHHH!"

A howling sound came from deep down as Mary's face grew red. She gave the push everything she had left. Suddenly—Mary felt the pressure stop as her child slipped from her body. Exhausted, she fell back onto the pillow as Minnie worked with the baby, cleaning the mucus from his mouth and wiping his skin vigorously so that he cried and took precious air into his lungs. All the while Minnie was smiling and watching Mary out of the corner of her eye, as Mary's head fell to the side.

Minnie laid the baby down and rushed to the bedside. She took the cold cloth and vigorously wiped Mary's face, patting her cheeks as she felt for a pulse.

Mary's eyes fluttered open as she looked around the room like she didn't know what had happened. Then it came to her. Mary pushed herself up on one elbow, "Minnie—the baby---girl or boy?"

Minnie brought the tiny bundle wrapped in a soft blanket and laid it in Mary's arms. "He is exactly, what you prayed for---a strong, lusty, baby boy!

Mary began to weep as she pulled back the blanket to look at her new son. "Oh, oh—call John. Tell John to come in, but don't tell him what we have!" With that, she collapsed back onto the pillow.

With a stern face, Minnie Grabbert met John Wamhoff outside of the bedroom. "I must tell you, John, that if Mary would have had to do what she did for another fifteen minutes, we would have lost her. She is going to need rest—lots of rest and I'm quite sure you realize, this must be her last child. I think you are smart enough to know what I mean by that!"

John Wamhoff strode into their bedroom where Mary laid, holding the baby. She had her eyes closed and was deathly pale. Minnie Grabbert said, "She had a rough time of it John. I packed her insides and gave her some herbs that should stop the bleeding, but I want her to lie quietly for several hours, to give her insides time to relax and repair themselves. She should be quite fine, this is something that happens now and then, especially with later babies.

She couldn't carry another baby if her life depended on it. You might want to call the doctor out to take a look at her yet today."

John walked toward the bed and laid his hand along Mary's ashen face. "Mary, Mary, can you hear me? It's John—our baby is here, but I don't know if we have another daughter or a son. All I know is it's awfuly red and loud with a head full of dark hair."

Mary opened her eyes and faintly smiled. "Well, we have a son, John—we have another son! Our last son!"

John laughed as tears welled up in his blue eyes. "Another son. That's just fine, mighty fine and he is a good size boy. He looks so bright and ready to get on with life. Oh Mary, Mary---thank you. Rest now, the children want to come in to see you. Should they wait a bit?"

Mary managed another smile as she nodded her head, "It's okay. Let them come in and meet their new brother. I want to name him Arnold Johann Wamhoff. Arnold means strong as an eagle and the—the Johann is after you!"

John leaned down and kissed her again. "I like the name, it fits him!"

He walked Minnie Grabbert to the door, paid her, and thanked her for being such vital help to Mary. Minnie smiled and replied, "It's what I do for my fellow women and mothers. We all need somebody when the time comes. I am partial to Mary, there is no finer woman than your wife, Mary Wamhoff. Best you remember that!"

Mary reached for her son and held him to her breast. She gazed down at his tiny face and caressed his head of dark hair with her hand. "You are a fine big boy, that you are, and very handsome too." Mary traced her fingers over his tiny nose, ears, and soft cheeks; as she murmured, "Thank you, God, for delivering him and me."

Chapter Eleven

THE GENTLEMAN FARMER

1915: In an interview before he passed away, Arnold Wamhoff had this to say about his father:

"Dad was a very progressive man. He liked to have the 'first' of anything new on the Bench. He bought the first tractor up here, it was called a Rumley. Dad liked to go into town on Saturdays. He'd get all dressed up. I remember he'd put on a bow tie, a starched white shirt with a starched fake collar, spats, and his dress hat—he looked more like a businessman than a farmer. He was a good businessman but he wasn't crazy about going out into the field so he hired out most of the fieldwork. He was an excellent manager and he knew finances. Dad always had a couple of saddle horses because he liked to ride, he didn't want to walk. The sheep were my Dad's biggest moneymaker. In the summer they would take them up on the Bighorn Mountains to graze. He also liked helping folks out with loans, with harvesting their grain—most of them never paid him back—big names, here on the Bench—people he had known since the beginning. When he died we tried to collect from them and they refused-- said that they never signed a note. I've never forgotten who those people are. They go to church with me, shake my hand—they don't know that I know who they are and what they did to my father.

~~~~~~~~~~

February 1915: "Germany announces the unrestricted warfare against all ships, neutral or otherwise, which enter the war zone around Britain."

It was only a month later when John read in his newspaper that Germany sunk the William P. Frye. The German government apologized and called the attack an unfortunate mistake. President Woodrow Wilson feigned outrage but still did nothing. John slammed the paper down, "President Wilson knows about this contemptible act and he sits on his hands and pretends anger. What is it going to take for him to declare war against Germany?"

Mary sat back in the easy chair as she nursed Arnold. "You know John, being of German ancestry, and seeing how ruthless they are, makes me almost ashamed to be German American. We have to concentrate on the fact that now, we are American. I know our president is trying to keep us out of a war, but Germany continues to defy us. I agree, but have to wonder as well, what it will take to make him declare war."

John looked over the top of the paper as he replied, "I don't know, probably more American deaths. He is slow to move, we've all seen that and we've seen how aggressive the Germans are when they want something and they want more land for expansion in Europe." John sat for a moment watching his wife nurse his newborn son. 'Mary, you make a beautiful picture—you caring for our son. He seems to have a healthy appetite doesn't he?"

Mary smiled down at her dark-haired baby, "Yes, yes he does and I am glad for it. He weighs around fifteen pounds already and he is only six months old. That reminds me I need to write Mama a letter."

That evening by the light of a single electric bulb lamp, Mary wrote to her widowed mother whom she hadn't seen in the fourteen years since she and John left Nebraska.

Dear Mama,

I am slowly regaining my strength and vigor. Baby Arnold is growing like a weed and is already very spoiled by his sisters. Little Ted is now three and a half and he doesn't quite know what to think of this intruder on his spot at being the baby in the family. He stands and watches everything the baby does. He did bend over and kiss Arnold on the cheek the other day. They will grow up being the best of friends, I am most assured.

John's sheep band seems to be growing by leaps and bounds. The band averages about 1,800-2,000 sheep—when they have their lambs next month, that number will almost double. It is a very busy time as they must shear the sheep before lambing, then tend to the lambs after that. John sells off the wool and also the yearling lambs. I'll say this for him, he is a fast learner and he studies up on everything he does. He's hired good herders to care for them and two additional hired men to farm. He has his hands full just making sure everything and everyone is doing their job.

Last spring and summer when I was carrying Arnold, the girls planted the garden, harvested the vegetables, and did all of the canning. The only thing I had to do was answer their questions. They have volunteered to do it again this year, as I am slow to recover from Arnold's birth so I imagine I will take them up on their offer.

I am enclosing a photo which we had taken of our family at Christmas time. Since you aren't familiar with the children, I will tell you who is who: In the front row is Marie, Adella, I am holding

Arnold, Teddy, and Helen. Back row: Bill standing tall above everybody, Esther, John, and Ruth.

Oh, Mama, I hope you are ready for a visit from me and my two youngest sons. John is buying us tickets to come by train to Seward on March 15th. I am so very eager to see you again. It has been such a long time since we've seen each other. John and the older children can handle the farm and the house. I need a vacation. I need to see you and my sisters.

We are doing well running the telephone switchboard from our home. I am usually the one to tend it, and I don't mind because it gives me pause to sit down. Bill, Ruth, Esther, and Adella also know how to work it. It is one way to make a few dollars and keep up with everything that is happening in Germania.

I hope you are doing well Mama. I am comforted that Robert lives with you on the farm to help out with it and to keep you company. I have such wonderful memories of growing up there. I close my eyes and it seems like yesterday.

I think of you often with much love, Mary

~~~~~~~~

Mary spent the evening looking through the seed catalog. *Mercy me, spring is just around the corner and I haven't ordered my seeds yet.* "Ruth, Esther, Adella, Marie---you girls are going to plant the garden again this year. You did such an outstanding job of it last year that I have decided you are elected to the task!"

Ruth said, "When do you want us to start planting? Do you want it in the same place again this year? And Momma, do you think you can keep Teddy and Helen occupied with something else—they are such a nuisance—walking over our rows and all."

Mary looked up from her seed catalog, "When I go to Seward, you all are going to have to be in charge of the house and garden while I am gone and that includes Helen. You girls will have to figure it out. Perhaps Helen can walk along the rows and hand you the seed packets, which may keep her happy for a while. Dad bought tickets for Ted, Arnold, and me to go to Seward to visit my mother. Lizzie and Emma are going to be there too. Mercy me, it has been so long since I laid eyes on my family in Nebraska."

Ruth and Esther agreed that their mother needed some new clothes to go to Nebraska. "Mama, you never get out, and so we ordered you two lovely dresses from the Sears and

Roebuck catalog as well as a stylish hat. That should make you feel up to date."

John said, "I am going to go to Billings at the end of the week and I'll buy you that coat with the fur collar I told you about. Women all over are wearing those stylish coats. I saw a camel colored one with a dark fur collar in the window of a department store. Would you like that Mary?"

Mary replied, "I don't know if that's the real me. I'm not a fancy society woman. I'm just a plain country bumpkin!"

John lit up one of his cigars, "Well, I think you can pull it off and look very elegant in a coat like that. You will be as lovely as ever! When I am up there, I might even take a look at International Harvester's stand-alone threshing machines and they say they are also making a horse-pulled combine. I don't know if that's a good idea or not, but I'm going to take a look. We are between the age of the horse and the engine!"

~~~~~~~~

March 15, 1915: Mary kissed her six children goodbye, They were staying behind, as she prepared to leave for a visit to Nebraska with her mother. Teddy was all dressed up in a new suit and was very proud of himself; Mary had thought to pack a special bag for baby Arnold and one for Teddy with things they liked to play with. "I expect each of you older children to do your chores and to help your father when he needs it. I've taught you well, so you know what to do. Bill and Ruth, you are the oldest and are in charge, keep an eye on Helen, she gets into more mischief. I

**Courtesy:
Arnold Wamhoff**

wish you could all come with me, but perhaps next time."

John helped Mary into the car. She held eight-month-old Arnold as Teddy climbed in the back seat for the short drive to the Greybull train station. "Mary, are you sure you are up to the long train ride and handling two squirming little boys? By the way, you look lovely in your new coat and hat. I hope you have a wonderful visit."

Teddy piped up, "Don't worry, Dad, I'll take care of Mother! I'm a big boy now! We are going on this train, all the way to Nebraska to visit my grandmother."

John replied, "And you behave yourself, young man, do you hear me?"

John took Mary in his arms and kissed her soundly. "That will have to keep you until you return in three weeks. That seems like a long time, but it has been fourteen years since you have seen your family back in Nebraska. You deserve this trip—it's about time. Don't forget that I love you."

John disembarked from the train and walked towards his car. Mary looked out the train window holding her palm against the glass to wave goodbye, but he never turned around. The train began to pull away from the station as John backed his car out and headed west, out of Greybull. *I have to check on where those sheep are and also if Jim got the water set on that field of grain.*

~~~~~~~

With both children asleep, Mary laid her head back against the seat and gazed out the grimy window of the train. She thought about the last time she traveled anywhere. *I was down in this part of Wyoming fourteen years ago when we came over those mountains in a covered wagon. So much has happened in those years, six new children, a new life, and watching John run our farm---constantly improving it and himself. He has changed—he has changed so much that some days I hardly recognize him. I guess I have changed too— grown older, plumb wore out. I noticed my hair is almost all white like my Pap. We have a good life; it's a hard life, but we've accomplished so very much and I thank God for the blessings.*

Mary looked down at her sleeping sons. *Teddy has grown so big, has a soft heart, and such a happy spirit. And this little one—*

Arnold—strong as an eagle. With seven older brothers and sisters, he is going to have to be strong. I hope he and Ted will be close, be good companions. She thought about the six children she left at home.

Bill is so tall and quite smart----he can take anything apart and put it back together. John would be lost without him. He isn't interested in the girls so much, kinda shy and reserved, but he's a good man, a very good man.

Ruth is a lovely young woman, so slim and tall—so sweet. I have heard that Bill Werbelow is sweet on her, but she won't give him the time of day or she pretends not to. We shall see what happens there, sometimes the heart doesn't listen. Don't I know that!

Esther has dark hair like her father but she is smaller like me. She's complicated, very popular with everyone and she likes to care for people. She is too pretty for her own good---boys are attracted to her like bees to a flower.

Adella is going to be tall like Ruth. She is very shy and doesn't say much but she's such a good worker and student in school. Then there is Marie—she is built like her father, stocky and shorter. She loves to get out in the field or garden and work hard like a man, mercy me. She has such a good heart. And—Helen, is only five years old but already she is a hand full. She is very pretty but hard-headed and wants her own way—which she usually gets.

Mary stretched out her legs, I am feeling a bit drowsy with the constant hum of the train wheels and there is nothing to look at since we left the Wind River canyon. Mary gazed out through the dingy train window at the landscape that unfolded for miles and miles. *Mercy, I remember coming across here all those years ago—it is a God-forsaken part of the country.* Her head rested against the window as sleep came.

~~~~~~~~

A week later: Before John left for Billings, he told Bill, "You take that scythe and start cutting the weeds along the fence line in the field to the south of the house. I showed you the other day how to get a good rhythm going; otherwise, it will wear you out. I expect to see that done when I come home!"

John made sure everyone was managing their chores and duties before he left for Billings. He'd been thinking about the Gray Dort automobiles since he first laid eyes on them. Now, he was going to have another look. He gassed up the Chevrolet and told the children that he was going to Billings on business and he'd be back the next day. He had received a letter from Mary telling him that they arrived in Germantown in fine shape and were having the time of their lives---and that her mother was well and thriving.

During the two hour trip to Billings, John and his alter ego had quite a conversation about whether or not to purchase a Dort automobile. He had talked to the dealership the last time he was in Billings. John had a plan in which he intended on becoming a car dealer in Germania, and now was the time to delve further into that possibility.

John Wamhoff walked into the Dort dealership in Billings and went straight to the manager's office. "Good afternoon, Mr. Walker. Here is what I would like to do-- become a Dort automobile dealer in Germania, Wyoming. I propose to purchase two closed sedans with the [16]Lycoming engine listed at $1,065, but with my dealership, I figure they will cost me half that, and I will trade in my Chevrolet as well."

The Dort manager thought for a moment then said, "As a dealer, the two Dort sedans will cost you $862. I will take off $300 for the Chevrolet. How does that sound?"

John scratched his head and lit a cigar, "What if, I take the two Dort sedans for $862 and keep my Chevrolet. I am sure I can sell it for more in Germania."

The manager replied, "That, Mr. Wamhoff, is entirely up to you. I can have them shipped down on the next freight train---which will cost you an additional $50. So do we have a deal? I can get your dealership papers drawn up today."

John got out his checkbook and wrote a check! He walked down the street to his favorite movie theatre. This was his major weakness---he was mesmerized by the moving picture shows and went every chance he got, sometimes they even had double features. As John neared the theatre, he noticed on the marque that **Birth of a Nation** with Lillian Gish was showing. *Oh boy, I have been waiting for this movie, I've heard it is well done and I must say*

Lillian Gish is a great actress. The last time I was in Billings, I saw **Double Trouble** *with Douglas Fairbanks—superb!*

~~~~~~

After the movie, he went back to his hotel to freshen up, then decided to have dinner in the dining room, He was shown to a nice table by the window where he sat down and began to look at the menu. "I think your beef steak with mashed potatoes and red cabbage sounds pretty good," then quickly added, "Oh, and waiter, I would also like a stein of your best beer, to start."

John reached inside of his coat and took out the silver cigar case which Mary had given him for Christmas. Waiting for his beer, he put a light to his favorite Cuban cigar, then waited for his dinner to arrive. Out of nowhere, a scantily clad woman with dyed hair and

 too much makeup approached his table. John didn't need any explanation as to what this woman's profession was.

"Good evening sir, I see you are having dinner by yourself and wondered if you would enjoy my company?"

Never taking his eyes off of the woman, John took a long draw on his cigar and blew it out into the room. "Well now, I 'might' enjoy your company, but it seems I am happily married with eight children and my wife is the jealous type. She is also an excellent shot! So, I expect you might be wise to skedaddle."

~~~~~~

Before he headed back to Germania, John drove over to the general appliance store which he favored in Billings. He browsed through aisle after aisle looking at this and that. Finally, a clerk approached him, "Can I help you find something, sir?"

John said, "If you want to make a sale you can! I'm a regular customer from Wyoming and there are a couple of things I have been thinking about. I would like to purchase an extra-large copper soaking tub and a dry sink along with an attractive commode with a false door, hiding the chamber pot--all matching."

1915 Wringer Washing Machine

After choosing the tub, sink, and commode, the clerk said, "We just got three of these new wringer washing machines in too; they are the newest thing around. The ladies really rave about how much easier it makes their wash day. Are you interested?"

John said, "Yes, as a matter of fact, I think I would be."

John wrote another check that day and had the items shipped to Greybull.

~~~~~~~~~

On the long drive back to Germania, John thought about how much Mary was going to like the wringer washing machine and especially the soaking tub, that is if she could get her daughters out of it long enough for her to have a soak. *Those two items will look so well in that room, it's perfect as a 'bathroom'. Someday when those new porcelain tubs become affordable, I am going to buy one of those with a toilet and sink to match. We'll have to have plumbing installed to handle it all and hot water with a septic tank. Only the very rich can afford them now, but someday—we will have them as well!*

    John turned down the lane of cottonwood trees to where their home stood. Pride swelled inside of him as he looked at the sprawling white clapboard house and all of the barns, granaries, and chicken coops; as well as the vast number of machinery parked in the back.

    Bill and the girls were waiting for him as he turned the car off and climbed out. "What did you bring us, Dad---show us!"

    John doled out the candy and silk headscarves for the older girls. "I also bought a new copper soaking bathtub and dry sink for the bathroom. You still have to carry hot water to it, but it's a dandy

Exceptional high quality of coach-work—graceful lines—distinctive appearance—with unbeaten economy and real comfort—mechanically right

GRAY SED.
$895

and I know there will be fights over who gets to use it. He took Bill off to the side and handed him a box, "I thought you were old enough to have a couple of nice neckties of your own. Say, you will never guess what we are going to do next! WE—you and I are going into the car business---we are going to sell Dort automobiles and maybe even Chevrolet. I bought two Dorts in Billings, one for us and one to sell. I am also going to sell this Chevrolet or give it to you until somebody wants to buy it. How do you like that?"

    Bill's eyes opened wide and his mouth as well. "Say, Dad, that's a great idea—I could get jazzed about something like that--- and if the folks we sell the cars to need help with the motors, I can do that too!"

    John smiled and replied, "When the cars come in on the freight train, we'll go down and drive them home. In the meantime, I'm going to start telling people they can buy their cars through us instead of going clear to Billings. The Dort has a fine reputation and that was part of the reason I chose it. We'll sell this Gray Sedan for $895, their big sedan for $1,065, a convertible sedan is around $815, their five-place open tourer is $695, and the Fleur-de-Lys roadster costs $695---that's the one you'd like! As dealers, we get them for half price, but we have to pay freight on them from Michigan. I don't think we can let folks make payments on them. We need our money upfront, at least at first."

"We will have to compete with the Ford Model T's that are selling for $440, but they are massed produced and don't have the latest details or features that the Dort has. Folks are used to only black cars because that color cures faster and the factories only have to stock one color. Nowadays, folks want to have some real color in their cars and Dort offers that as well."

Bill was grinning ear to ear, "I can hardly wait, thanks, Dad! I think this is going to be good for us! I like that new Chevrolet Series D sedan. They have a D V8 internal combustion engine that is liquid-cooled—a brand new idea. It has an impressive profile and chassis which we could do well with."

John said, "You know Bill, I've been thinking of trying a battery-powered radio for the house. What do you think of them? We still have to use that windmill and a battery system for electricity in the house. Some day the Rural Electric Association will get around to putting up lines for us farmers, way out here. That will be the day, that and plumbing in the house!"

~~~~~~~~~~

Ruth said, "Dad we had a letter from Mama and she said she and the little boys are taking the train out of Seward tomorrow and expect to be in Greybull in two days. She enclosed a photo that Grandma Westerhoff took of Arnold in front of her leaded window. Here it is, isn't he just the cutest little thing? He's walking all over the place and I guess she wants to keep him----he really took to her too is what Mother said. Grandma bought him the little suit that he has on, and he looks to me like he is going to be tall like Mother's

**Arnold 'Jimmy' Wamhoff:
Toddler**

brothers." Ruth paused and added, "You might check with the depot to see what time they get in. I miss Mother so much— it's not easy running this house and making sure everyone does their chores! I'll be so glad when she is back home!"

~~~~~~~~~

John picked Mary and the boys up at the train station after her trip back from Nebraska. He held her for a long time. "I've missed you so very much; and, I ahhh--- when I was in Billings last week, I bought a few things I think you might like."

Mary sat up straight, "What in the world did you buy now? Another tractor or machinery of some sort? There are so many things we all could use."

~~~~~~~~~

Once they arrived on their farm, John parked the car and opened the door for Teddy and Mary, who was carrying little Arnold. John picked up her suitcases and led them into the cool interior of the house. John said, "I am sure you need to unpack and perhaps freshen up after the long trip. I'll wait out here for you."

Mary made her way to the back bedroom, but she had to pass the bathroom on the way. John heard her let out a small scream, "OH JOHN, what have you done?"

John was grinning ear to ear as he walked back to the new bathroom. "Well, I see you have spotted your new soaking tub and commode. I couldn't resist buying the dry sink as well. There is also a new wringer washer out on the porch. Bill rigged it all up so it drains out to the back lawn. The girls sewed a nice cover for it. Just a few things to make your life more comfortable my dear! The new icebox is also coming on the train from Billings. I bought the biggest one I could find. I'd say it is about nine feet tall by ten wide and three feet deep. It comes with several compartments where we store the ice to make it cold. It is going to be worth its weight in gold and it'll keep my beer nice and cold too!"

Mary laughed and said, "That is the real reason you bought it--- admit it. But I do feel the need for a larger icebox---this family could certainly use one. Thank you, John." She paused a moment then added, "Now, what's this I hear about you and Bill going into the 'car' business? Like you don't have your fingers in enough pots already? As you explained it, I suppose it is a good venture, however, what worries me is that you will think you have to be driving the latest automobile, to advertise!"

~~~~~~~~~

That fall, it took the herders, Frankie, Herbie, and Chester just over two weeks to bring 1,800 sheep off the Bighorn Mountain grazing land. The sheep looked good--- fat, and healthy. Frankie pulled John aside, "I hate to tell you, but we lost one of our dogs up on the mountain. There was this rattlesnake; and well, Chester took a shovel and chopped the head off, and left it there. Rex, one of our best dogs decided to pick up the snakehead and play with it. Well now, the head still had the fangs and venom in it---like it weren't dead! Somehow it bit down on Rex's paw. There weren't nothing we could do for the dog. I never seen anything like that in my life---was a queer thing."

John patted Chester on the back and said, "I'm sorry to hear that. Rex was a great dog, but accidents happen and we have to pick up and go on. You look around and get us a couple more dogs if need be."

That afternoon Frankie and John sat down to go over the sheep count and the figures on the herd. Frankie said, "Well now, as usual, we gave five sheep to the Indians. Other than that, I figure we lost about four to coyotes and mountain lions. The dogs do a darn good job keeping those critters away most of the time, but them are cunning wild animals."

Before John could get a word in edgewise, Frankie scooted to the edge of his chair, "Boss, we saw the darndest thing on top of the mountain this trip. Way over on to the north there, above that Kane/Dayton road there, we came to a fine mountain top meadow to graze the sheep in. There was a large, treeless hill rising out of the meadow. Herbie and Chester walked up on top of to it to have a look at where the next grazing spot might be and what do you think they found? The top is all smoothed out and there's this huge round wheel-like thing made with rocks, all laid just so. It's like a giant wheel--there's a center then the spokes go out, radiating from the center to a circle of stones. To tell you the truth, I got the heebie-jeebies just being there. It's some sort of Indian shrine. We didn't stay too long, you can bet on that!"

"When we was all walking down that hill, I swear we could hear chanting. I'm steering clear of that place. It's damn spooky—the Indians told us it has big medicine and is a holy place to them! But I tell you, we could see all over the whole basin from way up there and it was a beautiful sight, it shor was!"

Frankie said, "Say, boss, did you know about those wild horses on the Pryor Mountain? Those Crow Indians told us there must be around fifty head of wild mustangs up there; the ones that originally ended up here from some exploring Spaniards or something like that!?

Chapter Twelve

THE COMING STORM

May 7, 1916: John threw the newspaper down and swore at the top of his voice. "Damn stupid Germans, now they've done it, sank the Lusitania with 2,000 people on board---including 128 Americans."

The next day, John listened to the President speak on the radio. "The United States is quite distraught over the sinking of the Lusitania by the Germans, but we are at this time too proud to enter a European fight! Army reserves have been increased as well as exports to Britain and France."

John stomped out of the house muttering to himself. "I don't know what it is going to take to get Wilson off his fat butt—too proud indeed! But eventually, we will get in the war---already wages are on the increase and the prices we get for our crops have gone up substantially! Europe needs grain and hay for their war efforts, and many farmers over there can't farm, so they need our food products too. The price I can get for my Perchons has skyrocketed, as the French are using them to pull their war wagons and guns."

"World news is anything but good, it's becoming obvious that Germany is provoking a fight, pushing for expansion." The next edition of the local newspaper reported ---*without warning, the Germans torpedoed the British-owned Lusitania ocean liner off the coast of Ireland. Over 1300 people were killed, including 128 Americans.*

John growled, "The newspaper states Germany claims the ocean liner was carrying munitions, which it was NOT. Before this event, President Woodrow Wilson always forgave or made excuses, waffling to stay out of the fight. However, this time he is demanding an end to German attacks on unarmed passenger and merchant ships." John looked up at Mary, "He's merely giving them another chance which is lunacy! I am telling you now, the Germans are not going to stop and we will end up going to war with them! Wilson claims he is maintaining a policy of non-intervention, avoiding our participation in the conflict, and trying to evoke peace. I'd say that initially we Americans wanted neutrality, but as time passes and the Germans continue with more brazen and heinous acts, that mood is changing. Folks like it that he is keeping our economy at normal levels, but he is also ignoring our military preparedness. Mark my words, this pot is coming to a boil!"

Mary looked up from her crocheting, "Oh John, I hope not. Knowing our oldest son Bill, he would want to sign up to fight."

The year, 1915, continued as before---day in and day out of struggle, work, and more work. The possibility of world war loomed overhead, it seemed imminent.

1916: *"Get the farmers out of the mud!"* Headlines in the local paper said it all. Both city and farm dwellers had put pressure on the federal government to do something about the abominable condition of rural roads. The Federal Aid Road Act of 1916 created the Federal-Aid-Highway program and now, funds were available on a continuous basis to state highway agencies, to get busy with rural road improvements. Gasoline was inexpensive and automobile makers were targeting the farmers as well; good roads would help their cause.

John put the newspaper down on the polished side table. "I'll believe it when I see it. They always find one excuse or another to delay fixing the roads out here. This time it will probably be the war we are about to get ourselves into!" He walked to the back door and watched as the older children saddled their horses and headed to the hills for their Sunday afternoon ride—to Coon Creek where they would have lunch under the trees, then head back. They rode all over those hills to the north and west, it was an inexpensive and popular source of entertainment and exploration. Mary tried her best to console Helen and Teddy who were left behind, explaining they weren't big enough to go riding that far yet.

Before they left for mountain top summer grazing, John gathered his herders, including the hired men, "I've applied for and been granted a special brand which we are going to brand our sheep with before you leave for the Bighorns. That way we can prove

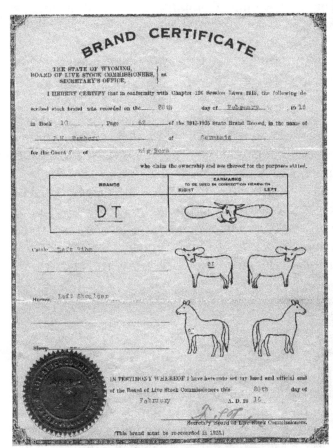

Courtesy: Arnold Wamhoff

which sheep are ours or not. It's going to take a week or more to brand all of these sheep, but it's something we have to do."

Old Jim asked, "We got to get some sort of assembly line going, once they are sheared; maybe herd them through the chutes, trap one, brand it, and send it on. What do you think?"

John said, "That is exactly what I was thinking. I'm not partial to putting a hot branding iron on the sheep so I am leaving that up to you men. The certificate doesn't signify exactly where sheep should have the brand---it's up to us."

Old Jim said, "That would be the easiest spot to make a fast brand. I see where on cattle it's the left rib and horses on the left shoulder. Maybe since those are all on the left, we should put our brand on the left hip?"

John replied, "Good point Jim. After you brand the sheep, they will probably give you the 'stink eye' for a few days until they calm down. You boys get started on that as soon as you can. Also, we can hope they finish up on that new bridge over Dry Creek on the road to Greybull. The County Commissioners are furnishing the material and as we speak, and some of the local farmers are building it"

The Wamhoff farm had a good crop of lambs and the wool yield was better than last year. As soon as the lambs were able and branding was completed, the herders started pushing them towards the Bighorn Mountains and their summer grazing land. John sold 1000 yearling lambs and 50 old ewes before they started the long monotonous journey through Germania, across the Bighorn River bridge, and up through Shell.

John sat on his horse out in the field as the sheep headed up the road toward the Bighorns. *I am glad to see those bleating creatures heading for the mountains for the summer. They have been good to me—the wool and lamb predictions were outstanding, but that branding about did me in. Now, Jim and I can concentrate on the crops.*

~~~~~~~~

At supper that night, John said to Bill, "We've sold a few of our Dorts---one to Martin Oleson and the other to Charley Oleson. They like them fine. Martin said to me the other day, "We hit a flat section of road out there on that Greybull Bench and I opened her up. Son of a gun, before we knew it we were going forty miles an hour. Now, that was pure fun. That is one fine automobile!"

John sorted through his papers and pulled one out. "This here is an order for a new Oakland car for Dr. Gorder in Greybull. The garage in Billings just got it in and I'm driving up tomorrow to pick it up and deliver it to Dr. Gorder. Say, Bill, come with me and follow me to Greybull in our car, so I can deliver the new car!

~~~~~~~~

July 4, 1916: Bill said, "Some of us are going to take a picnic down to the ballpark on Sunday after church and watch Burlington play our Germania baseball team in their new fire engine red uniforms. I've heard they look mighty fine. I'd play, but my feet are too big and get in the way of my running. Maybe I just need to hit it over the fence every time, then I could trot around the bases and wave at the girls. I'm just not a runner---maybe they should suit Ruth up. That girl can run like the wind!"

Marie piped up, "That's just what you need to do Bill, I'd even pay to see you do that! Ahhh---say, would you mind if Adella and I tagged along with you on Sunday afternoon, it sounds like fun. After all, it is the 4th of July Picnic!"

Bill didn't hesitate. "NO Can Do! See if you can hitch a ride with Dad and Mother."

Marie complained, "Why is it that we only celebrate three holidays a year-- Christmas, Thanksgiving, and the Fourth of July; and our brother can't be bothered to give us a ride to have some fun too?"

Arnold Wamhoff – Age 2

Bill gave her the evil eye and said, "I don't want no little giggling girls following me around like a couple of puppy dogs. Go find yourselves another ride! Anyhow, you don't even watch the game, you just sit and make google eyes at the boys."

~~~~~~~~

Mary said, "Will you check on Arnold and his bunnies. He is out there in the yard. He could sit there for hours petting them and letting them crawl all over him."

Marie opened the screen door and looked out, "He's right where you left him, Mother. You should take a photo of him, he's so cute!"

Mary picked up the Brownie camera and snapped a picture of her youngest son and his cherished bunnies. She sent a copy to her mother and the family back in Nebraska.

~~~~~~~~~

After John returned home from supervising the fieldwork, he checked in with the family. The girls were busy making supper and Bill was out in the machine shop, working on the harrow. John walked to the horse barn, straight to Trotter's stall. He put the bridle and saddle on his favorite horse and swung up into the saddle. John reined the horse out of the barn and urged him into a fast trot--up the lane to the main road.

Courtesy of W. B. Edwards

He headed southwest to where the Bench's main canal was located. *I need a good ride today and I've heard rumors that some folks are worried there isn't going to be enough water for all of the benchland. I want to see for myself.* John took the road to the south as far as he could go, then turned to the west. After riding several miles, John rode Trotter up over a hill and there it was---the Bench Canal in all its majesty running about as full as it could. John pulled Trotter to a stop and got off to stand and watch the freshwater rolling down through the canal—destination—Germania! *It looks to me like we have more than enough water. I am glad they built that new concrete diversion dam and headgate. It will pay for itself and hold up for many years unlike the previous dam, that's for sure. There is also talk about building another holding reservoir up in the mountains at Sunshine where our present reservoir is. It's good to plan for the future.*

I just sold another Dort to Price Johnson this week. That was a good move on my part to create a dealership here in Germania. It's convenient for the customers and is proving to be quite profitable for me.

~~~~~~~~~~

Fall 1916: John sat at the kitchen table far into the night going over and over his ledgers and talking aloud. "Because of the war in Europe, grain prices are up by fifty percent! Wages have risen substantially, as well, because of the shortage in the workforce. Even though we aren't at war with Germany, there are a number of Americans who have already signed up to fight with the Brits and the French. I am quite certain we will be in the war come 1917. I've decided to open a bank account for Jim, regardless of what he wants or not, next time I'm in town. I can't just listen to what he said about not paying him for all of his work. That's not right—he's an important part of this operation. I know he wouldn't take a cent if I didn't insist. "

He stood up and shouted into the telephone room, "Mary, I'm going down to the barn to check on that new calf. Call me when supper is ready."

Mary laid out the mail and local newspaper beside John's easy chair for him to read that evening, as he relaxed after a day in the fields. It wasn't long before John opened the back door, washed up at the sink on the back porch, then strolled into the kitchen where Mary was cooking supper. "What's to eat tonight?" Mary pushed back the stray wisps of hair off her face and said, "One of your favorites. John, fresh liver and onions." John's face lit up as he walked over and kissed the back of Mary's neck. "I think I'll have me a beer before supper and read the mail."

Mary said, "Pour one for me as well. I've had one of those days—you know like the old woman who lived in a shoe, had so many children she didn't know what to do---days!"

Mary was about to put supper on the table as the girls were pouring the milk and getting the bread and butter on the table when John let out a roar! "What in blazes are they trying to do to this country? A lot of farmers are struggling as it is and the dad-blamed government is talking about passing prohibition laws that take away our barley money that we get from the breweries? This is gonna hurt a lot of farmers, might even break some who haven't diversified their crops and income." John slammed the paper down on the table.

"Well, I'll tell you one thing, I'm gonna make my beer in the barn until hell freezes over. I say to hell with them bigwigs in Washington---and what's this going to do to the saloons and places that count on the sale of liquor? This country is going to hell in a handbasket! Somebody is always trying to change things and I'm sick to death of it all!"

~~~~~~~

Actual Letter: Dear Lena and all, I got your letter some time ago. John thinks we are going to get in the war so he is beginning to make preparations here on the farm. Our Bill is considering he might join up if it comes to that.

Ted is starting first grade this year and Arnold is going to miss him so much. You know Jim, the man we've had since we moved here? Well, Arnold has taken a particular liking to him and follows him everywhere he goes so that folks now call him Little Jimmy. Of course, Old Jim thinks that is just fine as he thinks highly of our youngest son. John brought home a little white fuzzy puppy for Jimmy to play with. He decided to name it 'Snowy', and he does love that puppy. They chase each other all over the yard.

Germania had a big celebration on July 4th and most everything was donated—it all went to the Red Cross. There were 250 people there. Has Germantown changed its name yet? I think we are changing Germania to something else like 'America' or 'Emblem'. They have even considered stopping our German-speaking church or school---everything will be spoken in English. It suits us just fine. I hope this letter finds you all well.

Tell Ma hello for me, Love to all, Mary

~~~~~~~~

The United States was beginning to tighten its belt. There were more and more shortages, with sugar the first one to go. As if folks were afraid they might not have another opportunity, they bought new cars like there was a 'fire' sale on them. John sold several cars and made a welcome profit. There was the threat of a steel shortage with the anticipated war, thus, the production of passenger vehicles reached an all-time high of 1.75 million cars--darn near double of what it had been the previous year.

John just shook his head in disbelief when he read where women were entering the workforce in place of their men who had signed up to fight. They complained because they didn't receive as high a wage. John said, "It's because they don't do the job as well as the men, plain and simple!"

The look which Mary and his daughters gave him did not go unnoticed!

~~~~~~~~

Bill took the back steps two at a time and burst into the kitchen where his parents sat at the kitchen table. "I just came from the store and they said that the United States just broke all diplomatic relations with Germany. As I was about to leave there was a message that the Germans sank the American liner Housatonic." Bill paused to catch his breath. "I'll bet you anything we are going to get ourselves in that war. Germany is just baiting us, daring us to get in it—sinking our ships like that!"

February 22, 1917: *Congress passed a $250 million arms appropriations bill intended to prepare the United States for an inevitable entry into the World War. At the end of March, Germany sunk four more American merchant ships and the writing was on the wall!*

John met his oldest son, Bill on his way out to the south field. "Mornin'n Dad, I rode out here to check the ground and have decided to wait a day to two to give it time to thaw a little more before I start plowing that sheep manure into the ground. As soon as I get it plowed, I'll go over it with a disc to break it up, then harrow it in real good. By then the manure in the corrals will be thawed and we can spread that manure before we plant. That is if the weather holds and all. There are three fields I plan to get to--- Old Jim said he would work the upper place."

John said, "Well I guess I wasted a trip out here to see how you were getting along. Sounds like you know just what to do. I'll see you back at the house!"

Bill spoke up, "Say, Dad, I've been thinking about this war that we are probably going to get ourselves into. I'm pretty serious about signing up—you know, it might be an opportunity to see the world. Besides, it would be one less belly for you to feed. I know times are tough and probably going to get tougher. I'm going to sleep on it and I'll let you and Mother know for sure."

John sat at the kitchen table, deep in thought as he went over his ledgers again, trying to decide which crops would be the best bet against the continuing drought and what markets might be highest with the war demands. *Crops are producing just half of what they previously had, and the government is paying almost twice what they had been for grain and food products because of the war. We need to have some rain and some good harvests to take advantage of this opportunity.*

I guess we will have to tighten our belts and not be buying any more cars or machinery. I'll probably have to borrow some money from the bank to get the sheep through the winter months. Dad-blame it! If it isn't one thing it's another.

April 2, 1917: President Wilson called for a declaration of war against Germany. In four days, he had his answer from congress----WAR! It's not as if it wasn't expected. Now, it was official and men were leaving their jobs in droves to sign up to serve.

"Mary, the next time I go to Billings I am buying one of those good tabletop radios. We need to keep up with what is going on in the world faster than relying on the newspapers which is usually old news. We can run it off the electricity from the generator by the windmill."

Mary lifted her attention to her husband, "That sounds like a good idea, John. I know the girls have been wanting one, to listen to their music. They've also been asking for a Victrola and some of those Shellac paper records. You probably know more about that business than I do. They mentioned Al Jolson, and the broadway star Nora Bayes who sang *Has Anybody Here Seen Kelly*. Esther and Adella especially love songs like '*By the Light of the Silv'ry Moon*' and '*Alexander's Ragtime Band*.'"

John perked up, as there wasn't anything he liked to do better than to go shopping for his girls. Money was tight, but he had ways of finding some when he needed it. When he came back from Billings the next week, he had a beautiful Victrola along with twelve records for the girls. Esther squealed with delight, "Oh look it's a Victrola XI! I read where this is the largest selling victrola of the day. I love the beautiful mahogany finish. Thank you, Dad, we love it so much. Come on, let's put a Rudy Vallee record on the Victrola." The girls played the records over and over again until Mary wanted to scream! At times, Mary thought the upstairs floor was going to fall in as the girls jumped and hopped with great vigor, practicing the latest dances.

Finally driven to her wit's end, she shouted up the stairs. "You girls turn that thing off, get down here and get your chores done or I'm going to have Dad put it all in the granary!"

That evening after supper, Mary said to John, "I know the girls especially love that Victrola, but it is about to drive me crazy. Have you seen the dances they are doing? Some of them are not fit for proper young ladies, showing their legs and jiggling their bosoms as they do, to some dance called the *Shimmy*. It's positively disgraceful."

John looked over the rim of his eyeglasses, "Now Mother, let them have a little fun. Just be grateful we live clear out here in the country and not in a big city. Then you would have something to be worried about. I have seen some of the popular dance halls in Billings and I suppose you might say I was shocked. But our girls are growing up and these are concerning times with young men going off to war and all. I suppose they have to have some fun. Don't worry, it will pass."

John stood, stretched, and walked to the table where the new Philco radio sat. He turned the dial to 'on'. It made the most ungodly sounds as it warmed up, screeching and growling—until finally it zeroed in on the station and began speaking. All everybody could talk about was that WAR had been declared on Friday, April 6, 1917, and everyone wondered what would happen next. John said, "President Wilson announced, "Those whose jobs are essential to the war effort will not have to serve."

John turned to Mary and said, "That means us--our sons— farmers and ranchers. I guess I won't have to go down and sign up, but I hear talk that our Bill is seriously thinking about signing up!"

Mary gave him one of her 'looks' and said, "Yes, I'm quite sure that Bill and a few more of our Germania boys will be signing up to go, even though they don't have to."

John put his head near the radio to listen to what the President had to say. President Woodrow Wilson announced, *"On June 26, the first U.S. infantry troops will land in France to begin training for combat with the French forces. These 14,000 Americans will be a most welcome addition to the French and British troops which have endured four years of a bloody stalemate in the trenches along the Western Front. The morale of the British and French*

soldiers are indeed lifted with the addition of our well-supplied forces. It is hoped that our troops may help turn the tide of [17]World War I into an Allied Victory. The United States intends to send another 20,000 men in two months and more after that until we help to end this terrible world conflict. We ask your support with Victory Gardens and the moral support of our soldiers during this time."

~~~~~~~~

The wind shifted and was blowing hard, directly from the north. John looked at the horizon and saw gray, low-riding billowy snow clouds gathering somewhere over the Montana-Wyoming state line. *Those look like snow clouds if I ever saw any.*

After supper, John and Mary were sitting in the parlor as usual, when Ruth appeared in the doorway with Bill Werbelow, a local young man her younger brothers constantly teased her about. Bill stood ramrod straight and after clearing his throat, he approached John. "Uhh---Mr. Wamhoff, uhhh, I would---I would like to ask permission, to marry your daughter, Ruth. I will be a good husband to her, I have the means to support her and give her a good life. I own 160 acres of fine farmland over there on the south line. It has a modern house and all. We would like to be married as soon as possible because your Bill and I have signed up for the army."

John looked over at Mary who had scooted to the edge of her chair. Mary smiled and nodded her approval as John stood up and shaking Bill's hand said, "Yes, of course, you have our permission. You are a fine young man and I have to say, you made a good choice for a wife. We hope you and Ruth will be very happy. I assume you will be getting married in the church here in Germania.

Mr. & Mrs. William & Ruth Werbelow

Courtesy: Robert Werbelow

Let us know what we can do to help out in any way. Congratulations!"

Bill picked Ruth up and swung her around and kissed her soundly to seal the deal! Ruth recovered and said, "Thank you Dad and Mother—I was thinking perhaps the 20th of July at the church here in Germania. I've already found a wedding dress in the Sears Roebuck catalog that I like very much. We know it seems a bit sudden, but we have been dating for a while now and it just seems like we don't want to be apart any longer. We want to be married before Bill and brother Bill leave for the service."

Mary was smiling ear to ear. "We are very fond of you Bill and we welcome you to our family. I will miss my Ruth around here, she is such a good cook, you will be pleased I'm quite sure. We wish you many happy years together."

~~~~~~

Bill Werbelow along with his new brother-in-law Bill Wamhoff were two of the 2.8 million American men who enlisted in the United States Armed Forces. After a short stint in boot camp, they prepared to ship out of New York for France. Ruth was beside herself, she cried for days, and Mary was worried about her. "Ruth,

I want you to move back home here while Bill is overseas---you being with child and all."

Ruth replied, "I will be fine Mama, besides I told Bill I would stay home to make sure his father had his meals on the table and his clothes washed. Mr. Werbelow is a fine man, he appreciates everything I do for him. He's been such good company for me, he's always fussing at me to take it easy—to get my rest."

Mary shook her head, "Well, you always did have a mind of your own. But when your time gets close, please move back here until after the baby comes."

Ruth said, "We'll see Mother. Now don't worry about me."

Private William

Courtesy: Robert Werbelow

Many Americans of European heritage felt the strong anti-sentiment since the United States went to war with Germany, especially those from Germany. They were harassed, spit at, and called names--it was not a comfortable situation. They tried to keep their heads down and declare their allegiance at every instance.

Mary received a phone call around noon from the Home Guard from Greybull. They wished to speak to a Mr. John Wamhoff---it was urgent.

Mary hurried out to the machine shed where John was working on a car. "John, come quick, there is a phone call for you from the Home Guard and they say it's urgent. The man on the other end of the line sounds very angry!"

Mary stood to the side and listened as John spoke to the voice on the other end of the line. "They did what? Oh my word, why in the world would those boys do something like that?' Yes, yes, of course, I will meet you at the parsonage in about half an hour! Now, we must remain calm and sort this thing out, no need to go to extremes now! We will certainly get to the bottom of this, I assure you."

Mary stood to the side as John, muttering to himself, headed to their bedroom to change his clothes. "John, what is the matter, why is the Home Guard calling you?"

John slipped on clean overalls and shirt then said, "It's Pastor Germeroth's boys. It seems someone hung the American flag from the cross on top of the church steeple. The Pastor's two teenage sons climbed up there, removed the flag, and nailed it to the outhouse!" John was fuming. "Of all the stupid things to do, they need a good thrashing. As a community of Germans, we are already in the Home Guard's bull's eye, and now this. They are ready to lynch the Pastor and those dumb kids. I'm serious, they mean business! I gotta go down to the church and try and talk some sense into them." Mary heard John's car roar up the lane toward the highway.

An hour or two later the screen door slapped as John stomped into the house. He slumped down into his easy chair. Mary poured him a cold mug of beer as he tried to relax a bit. "I think we just saved our Pastor from getting hung! Those Home Guard fellas were hot under the collar, for sure! They didn't take kindly to the fact that our American Flag was nailed to the outhouse by our German pastor's sons! They also demanded we stop speaking German in and out of the church."

John continued, "W. B. Edwards was really good. He got right in there and said, "I can tell you that only a particular group of older folks speak in their native German tongue when talking about personal matters. We all love this country and our community and we are loyal to the United States of America. The Guard was so worked up, they made threats about German books kept in the church and the fact that some of the Sunday sermons were given in

German. They were ready to gather up every German book and have a bonfire!"

"Those two boys of the Reverends are pretty cocky. When I started to reprimand them, the one sassed me and I told him, 'You sass me like that again and you'll be pulling grass outta your teeth. Maybe what you two need is a good swift kick in the pants! I'd be first in line for that!"

Sitting on the edge of her chair, Mary said, "I sure wouldn't want to be in the Reverand's position. It's pretty serious what those boys did and us being German and all!"

John muffled a chuckle then said, "It was getting pretty hot and out of hand when Edwards took out his gun and ordered the Home Guard to leave, telling them our community would take care of the matter. As an elder in the church, I suggested we make a change and hold most of the sermons in English—only an occasional one in German. And, we have to change the name of our community of Germania. After several suggestions, we all agreed on calling it 'Emblem'. As noted, several of us have purchased war bonds and have sons and husbands serving in the army. We might be of German blood, but we are Americans and most of us were born in this country!"

The next morning John received another phone call. After speaking for a short time, he hung up and walked into the kitchen where Mary was baking bread. "You will never guess what happened last night while we slept---Pastor Germeroth and his family have left Emblem! That's right, not even a simple goodbye, thank you, or final paycheck. They skipped town! Which on second thought might have been the best thing to do."

John couldn't help but chuckle as he walked out the back door. Mary could hear him talking to himself, "So, now we have to find us a new pastor--and, one that speaks English, and preferably, one doesn't have snotnose teenage sons!"

NOTE: *Because of the common sense intercession of W. B. Edwards, Adam Preis, and John Wamhoff, who were closely associated with the English-speaking business community, a peaceful transition was brought about. Sunday sermons were given in English and for those who spoke predominately German, another sermon was given during the afternoon; until 1943, when the new English speaking Pastor, Ralph Temme, arrived in Emblem.*

~~~~~~

It was reported that American military units weren't deployed onto European battlefields on a large scale at first. They required education in trench warfare! John and Mary received a postcard from their son, Bill.

Dear Mother and Dad. So far so good except for the haircut they gave all of us. I don't think the barbers had any education in barbering. We all looked like someone ran over our heads with a lawnmower. It was a comical sight for sure but we were all in the same boat. Speaking of boats, I didn't like the ride across the ocean on the ship that much. I did better than most who spent their time puking over the ship's rail. We should arrive in France in another few days and I will be glad of that. Brother-in-law Bill went on a different ship so I don't know if I'll see him over there or not. They don't tell us where we are going—to a camp or the battlefield. Keep me in your prayers. Love Bill

~~~~~~

John and Mary didn't receive many letters from their son. Both their son and son-in-law were not good letter writers and besides, they were rather busy fighting a war. However, Bill Wamhoff sent his four-year-old brother Jimmy a special postcard from Paris.

"My Dear Little Brother. Well, what are you doing now that Theodore is at school? I'll bet you do some playing when he is at home. When I get home again, Theodore and I are going to fix everything up and the cars too, and you can help too, and then we'll have a few rides. Well, I guess that is all for this time. I am well and hope that you are too, so long. From your brother, Private William Wamhoff COH,306INF American E. F. – France Vin New York.

NOTE: *Jimmy* kept this fancy decorated postcard from his older brother for the rest of his life--- he was very proud of it.

Actual Card

As predicted, the war in Europe created a sudden shortage of steel and a boom for agricultural products. Armies need many things, but foremost, the troops need to eat and they had thousands of horses that needed oats. John sat in his chair reading the newspaper, "Sure, the government will pay top dollar for what we grow, but the problem is we are in the second year of a bad drought and we aren't harvesting the crops that we did two years ago. Why that soil out in the field is like flour, it's so dry! Hopefully, we will have a wet winter and we'll have us some ditch water come spring to grow some decent crops." John slapped the newspaper down on the table. "These terrible dust storms that we hear about on the radio--- it's because those knuckle-headed homesteaders plowed up everything they could. Before they could plant something in it, the weather turned bad, now the topsoil is just blowing away in choking dust storms. All those years that dry-land farming was successful is gone—now it's a disaster! I remember how your father would leave the grain stubble in the fields over the winter to catch the snow. He planted hundreds of trees on his property to hold the snow. That man knew what he was doing!"

March 1918: John drove his Chevrolet Model D into Basin that Monday, to tend to some business. *This might be just the opportunity I've been waiting for--- to take a look at that plot of land I've been thinking about, located on what they called the Airport Bench. Mary has always said that someday she would like a section of land in her name, for retirement security. This land I have in mind on the airport bench has a great deal of potential and it's close to*

Greybull which will only increase its value someday. I'm going to see if I can homestead it before I talk to the banker.

That afternoon when John arrived home he found Mary, hanging clothes on the line, "Mary, well, they finally got it built—the courthouse in Basin. It is a fine looking building with four two-story columns out front. It's built of stone and has this fancy stonework on the corners. We should all be mighty proud of our Bighorn County courthouse. They claim it's fireproof and it has rooms for all of the officials. Everybody who's anybody has a room in that courthouse! And, it's not hard to find---biggest darn building in Basin!"

~~~~~~~

Europe had experienced a record-breaking winter. At the end of it, Americans began to swarm the battlefields in Europe and the tide quickly turned. War efforts on the home front were also intensified. By the beginning of fall, the war was winding down and things were looking good—folks had hope that their soldiers would be home soon. However, they were in for another, a bigger, and deadlier foe that was beginning to sweep the globe---The Spanish Flu.

~~~~~~~

John and Mary's youngest son, Jimmy was growing up and that boy didn't miss much—he paid close attention to everything that went on in the house. He *learned a lot of stuff that way, especially when he listened to his sister's talk and they didn't know he was hiding and listening to them.* The lad was five going on sixteen. A few days later, he was standing beside his father, holding his hand as John talked to the herders, Chester, Herbie, and Frankie. John said, "Are you taking the sheep down to graze on the range close to Burlington tomorrow?"

Frankie laughed and said, "Yeah, we thought we might check out those Mormon girls as long as we're down there when we have some free time of course."

Chester, "Well now, you know they wear that long underwear year-round."

They all laughed and went about their business---- nobody paid any attention to little Jimmy who was taking it all in; this conversation piqued his curiosity!

~~~~~~~~

Two weeks later John had to check out his crops up on the other place, across the road from the Preator farm. He said, "Say, Jimmy, would you like to come with me this morning? I'm going up to the other farm." Across the road lived a good family of Mormon folks with whom John had become friends as he and Mr. Preator had helped each other numerous times over the years. "Well, good morning Mr. Preator, how's the family doing?" Jimmy was standing close to his father, intently watching the Mormon neighbor and----THEN---he spotted the long underwear sticking out of the man's shirt sleeve. Curious as most five-year-olds, he edged closer. Still holding his father's hand, he got as close as possible so that he might get a better look at the underwear.

John said, "Well, I guess we better get over and take a look at that headgate, you have yourself a good day now!" He gave a tug on Jimmy's hand and began to walk back to his wagon when Jimmy pulled away and ran back to where Mr. Preator stood. He reached up and pulled on the end of Mr. Preator's s underwear. "Is that your long underwear sticking out there?"

Mr. Preator pushed his work hat back on his head and smiling, he pulled his sleeve up, showing more of his Mormon underwear. "That's what it is, right there!"

"Well, I have another question, what's under-----

John could see where this conversation was headed and it wasn't going to have a good ending. He grabbed his young son by the arm and hoisted him up on the wagon in the middle of the sentence. Waving goodbye to Mr. Preator he gave the horses their rein. Jimmy slumped down in the seat. He had a real bad feeling he had done something wrong, but he wasn't sure what it was. He noticed his Dad's face was beet red and he looked funny. About a half-mile down the road, John let go, and as Jimmy later recalled, *"I've never heard Dad laugh so hard or so long."* Finally, John turned to his young son and said, "Arnold, you'd better not be such a good listener or learn when and where not to say what's on your mind. Mr. Preator and other Mormon folks wear long underwear because of their religion. We don't believe the same way, but that doesn't mean he or they aren't good people, they are just different than we are. So, next time you have a question, you ask me first. Okay?."

Realizing he had done something wrong, Jimmy said, "I am sorry Dad, I didn't mean anything---- I just wanted to see what that underwear looked like. From what I could see, it wasn't any different than ours, except we only wear ours in the winter!"

~~~~~~~

Note: *Even though Lutherans and Mormons had distinctive religious differences, they worked and lived side by side in the community to make it a productive place to live. They both got a kick out of teasing each other once in a while, yet they got together for picnics and visiting over the years. They were neighbors and were there for each other.*

~~~~~~~

The family had not heard from their son, Bill, for months, and Mary couldn't help but be worried. Finally, in the middle of May, a letter came:

Warfare Trenches of World War I in France—Western

Dear Mother, Dad, and family, I am sorry that I have not been able to write to you for many months. I contacted the Spanish Flu and I was so sick with it the doctors thought I had died and sent my body to the morgue. I woke up with a sheet covering my face. I threw it off and swung my legs over the edge of the bed and to my horror, the room was filled with bodies, all with sheets covering them. That is when I realized where I was. You have to believe I headed for the door with haste and burst through it into the hallway. A watchman was sitting in a chair near the door and when I came bursting out, he was so startled and alarmed that he stood up and just stared at me—his eyes as big as saucers. Finally, he stuttered, "My - my God, man, we thought you were dead so we put you in the morgue! You nearly scared the life out of me!"

I am feeling fine now, still a bit weak, but much better. Thousands of servicemen have died from this flu, so I am most thankful to God that I am alive and he saved me. Now, it's back to the trenches for me, and believe me, I am sure to take the gas mask with me at all times. Continue to pray for me.

With my love, your son, Private William Wamhoff

~~~~~~~~~

NOTE: Bill was careful to avoid telling his parents, Anna, or anyone he wrote about how terrible the war experience really was. How horrible it was to see your buddy get ran over by a tank—then, digging through the mud to try to find his dog tags. Watching friends being sent home in body bags, or losing an arm, a leg, or both. And what he couldn't understand is why he was still unharmed? Oh sure, he had lice crawling up his back and doing the jitterbug in his groin. But just how it felt not to have a bath or even wash your teeth or hair for months. How sticky blood was and the smell, dear God---the endless smell of it all! That the seemingly continuous roar of the big guns, and explosions of bombs, one after the other, after the other, never left him! He was thankful that he never saw the faces of the men he killed. Bill knew the sounds, smells, and horror of it all would haunt him—until the day he died.

~~~~~~~~~~

Slowly and methodically, John pushed his way through his milling herd of over 1,800 sheep to get a good look at their overall condition. His herders were getting ready to take them up on the Bighorns for summer grazing. He thought to himself. *We're in one of the worst droughts I can remember down here in the Basin. If we weren't getting such good prices for our crops I might be forced to consider selling off half my herd. But farm prices have remained steady for the last year.*

John walked along the end of a grain field. *What I'm having a problem with is the lack of labor. First, a lot of the farmhands signed up to fight and now they are coming back and looking to do other things. I'm darn lucky my herders stayed; and of course Old Jim and his newly hired hand, John is a good guy—a hard worker. I got a bad feeling that farm prices are going to hit the bottom here pretty soon. What goes up so high eventually comes down with a crash!*

~~~~~~~~~~

Mary rose before dawn, pushed open the back screen door, and walked out to where her dry clothes hung on the clothesline. She paused and inhaled the sweet heady scent of the copper roses in bloom. As she reached for the first clothespin, she heard the sound she loved the most in the early morning, the turtle dove's *whoo-whoo-awwhoo. I think I like to hear their call almost better than the Meadowlark.*

She rushed through the task of removing the dry clothing, something she could do with her eyes closed. The girls could fold them later. Right now she had to get breakfast going and then later it would be a full day in the garden, kitchen, and canning.

Mary was in the middle of canning tomatoes and corn. She and the girls had been at it since daybreak, picking the vegetables fresh, then getting them into the Mason canning jars to preserve as quickly as possible. It was around three o'clock when the phone rang. Mary wiped her hands on her apron as she walked from the kitchen to the phone room. She reached for the receiver.

"Hello,--hello, I can hardly hear you, who is this? Can you speak louder?" The person on the other end of the line spoke louder and the blood left Mary's face. She slumped onto the nearest chair to the phone. "What did you say, Lizzie—did I understand you right—oh Lizzie—MA?—Oh no---not Ma. I didn't even know she had the Spanish Flu. When did she die?" Lizzie said something on the other end of the line, Mary replied, "So, it came on sudden like and you found her down by the pond, laying on the ground in the morning? Oh, Mercy me, that is terrible. When is the funeral, will I have time to come?"

Mary said, "I'll have to call the train station and see if I can get a train out tomorrow. We are right in the middle of canning, but the girls can handle it if I come.

"I'll let you know Lizzie if I can come. Thank you---thank you for calling me. I miss you and love you. It's so hard to think of both Pap and now Ma—gone. How is the rest of the family—no flu? We haven't had it and way out here in the country we don't see many folks. Okay, Lizzie, I will call if I can get a train in time. Thank you. I love you, sister! Goodbye."

~~~~~~~~~~

Mary sat on the chair, gathering her emotions and thoughts before going back to the kitchen. The girls turned when she walked into the room. "Mother, what on earth? Sit down, you're white as a sheet. Who was that on the phone, what's happened? It wasn't Bill, say it wasn't Brother Bill."

Mary shook her head, "No, it wasn't Bill, it's my mother. She got that flu and was gone in two days. I'm going to try and get a train to Seward, to see my sisters and brothers. Robert is still in the army hospital in California with the flu, he's getting better, but still, I have a powerful need to see my family."

John took over and got Mary a ticket on the next train to Nebraska. "You will have to change trains in Cheyenne, but you will make it in time for the funeral. Mary, I am sorry that I can't leave the farm right now, in the middle of threshing and harvesting. I am sure the girls can handle the meals and tend to the little ones. If we need to feed a crew for a couple of days, they've helped on it before. You have a good trip and tell your family, hello from the rest of us. I'm so sorry, Mary, your mother was a wonderful woman and she lived for eighteen years after your father passed. She didn't suffer for long. I'll be at the train station in Greybull to pick you up in a week. Be strong Mary, she had a good life and a wonderful family. I love you."

~~~~~~

Mary made the trip and was back home in less than a week. During the train trip back to Wyoming she had pause to think. *I have been back to Garland several times over the years, but John has never been back since we left there in 1901. I suppose he sees no reason to go back—mercy, such a shame it is.*

She didn't have time to grieve, she had a big family. It was harvest and canning season and the Spanish Flu threat was growing worse by the day. It was only a matter of time before it came knocking on their door.

~~~~~~

Fall: The cottonwood leaves were beginning to turn yellow and there was a crispness in the morning air. John said, "I'm going to run up to Wegner's store and collect our mail. Is there anything you need me to pick up for you?" Mary wiped her hands on her apron and said, "No, I can't think of anything unless you find a few women there who need some work. I could use some help with this canning." She laughed as she waved John on.

There was a sense of urgency in the air to stock up for the coming winter, get the crops in, and take care of any last-minute preparations. The nights were getting colder, but the days remained pleasant, for now at least. The cellar was filled to the brim with jars of meats, vegetables, and fruit. Mary could take a deep breath now that the canning season was coming to an end. The granary was full and Ted and Herbie had mucked out the barn and added fresh straw in preparation for winter when the animals would take shelter inside. Jimmy liked nothing better than to climb up and sit on the corral fence, watching them work and kid each other.

~~~~~~~~~

The kitchen was filled with the yeasty smell of baking bread. Mary looked up as John drove back into the farmyard, parked the car, and started up the sidewalk to the back door. She thought to herself. *He hasn't been gone that long, that's not like him, he usually spends time talking to whoever is at the store.* John walked into the kitchen and without saying a word, handed Mary a letter---a letter from Bill. Mary's hands were shaking when she opened the letter from her oldest son. She hadn't been able to put her finger on it, but she'd had a dark feeling about Bill's wellbeing for the past weeks:

Dear Mother and Dad, I am sorry that I have not written sooner. I have good and bad news---good news first, I am coming home. The bad news is, a couple of months ago, I was shot in the foot while fighting in the trenches in France. It's going to take some time to heal and so they are shipping me home.

I can't tell you how eager I am to set foot on Wyoming soil again and sleep through the night without bombs going off and the sound of rifle shots. So many of the fellas I have met, joined up because it meant a job with food to eat and a place to sleep. We all got more than we bargained for, I guarantee you that! War is simply put, horrible. There is a thin timeline between life and death and one can turn into the other in the flash of a bullet. The area they refer to here in France as 'No man's land'—is exactly that. It is a place where no man would or does ever wish to go. When you are walking through it, it is like the worst nightmare you ever had, ----

endless mud, dead animals and dead and dying men lying everywhere, rusted, twisted razor wire—leafless, dying, twisted remains of trees, nothing is moving, except the maggots and rats. I had no idea the extent of cruelty or insanity that men can go to in a war. It is the most horrible and disappointing example of mankind. I have seen things I never in my worst dreams or thoughts imagined possible.

I think probably the thing that tore my heart out the most was the way the horses were treated. They were harnessed day and night to the guns or wagons until they dropped dead of gunshot, explosion, starvation, hunger, or overwork, and then left to die beside the road. If they were wounded, they were unharnessed or left as was, to suffer and die. I was sick to my stomach more than once, I can tell you that. My heart goes out to the fellows who are shell-shocked. Some can't talk, walk, and they shake constantly as if they have palsy---they have this wild look in their eyes. I only got a few whiffs now and then of mustard gas and some of the chlorine gas. The mustard gas leaves nasty blisters and the victims often end up with internal bleeding as it attacks the bronchial tubes and all. It is a gruesome weapon. I thank God I am coming home. It's rumored that the war is about to end, but regardless, they are sending me home early. How is everything back in God's Country? I cannot wait to see the glory of the Bighorn Mountains again and taste Mother's cooking.

I ship out of Antwerp, Belgium around the first part of October. So after going through all the discharge rigamarole, I will hope to be home in time for Christmas! By the time you read this letter, I will be on my way home.

I miss and love you all so much. Your son, Bill

Mary's hand shook as she read the letter from Bill, "Oh, thank God, he is coming home to us! Our boy, our boy Bill!"

Bill Werbelow was still in the army in France. He had hoped he might make it home before his child was born. However, on October 20th, Ruth gave birth to their first son. "Oh Mother, I feel so bad that my Bill isn't here to see his first-born son. I hope it won't be much longer and my husband will come home to us as well!"

John and Mary were quite aware of the influenza epidemic which was now a worldwide catastrophe. It wasn't particular what age the person was—it hit every age, killing hundreds of thousands of people. There were cases where entire families died from the flu and it was deemed the worst epidemic the United States had ever known. The Wamhoff family would not go unscathed.

John sat in his easy chair, near the radio, reading the Greybull paper. "It says here, Mary, that the flu is spreading with astonishing rapidity in Greybull. They have over 500 cases so far—two of the town's doctors are sick with it including Dr. Gorder and Dr. Minnis, leaving only Dr. Hamilton to take care of the many cases. The hospital is full and they have turned to the Red Cross which has converted the Rinker Apartment house into a temporary hospital. The Burlington Railroad has even brought in a couple of doctors and nurses from Cheyenne and Denver. On October 4th there were a total of twenty-five deaths in Greybull. Emblem has been especially hard hit---five persons in one household on the lower end, have died from the flu."

John looked up from the paper and said, "It also says city authorities have closed all businesses and or places where people congregate---like churches, the theatre, pool halls, schools, dance halls, and saloons." John said, "I don't think we have any reason to go to Greybull right now---it's closed!"

Young Ted walked up to his mother, "Say, Mother, I heard a funny rhyme at school today, it went like---'I had a little bird named Enza but it flew away. I opened up the window and---IN FLEW, ENZA!" The little lad paused for a moment then said, "Mother, what is 'influenza'? Isn't that funny?"

Mary pulled little Ted onto her lap and said, "Influenza is a bad sickness like a very bad cold and we hope we don't get it. So, let's let Enza stay outside shall we?"

Ted jumped down and ran off to play not the wiser as to the seriousness of his little rhyme.

~~~~~~~~~

Mary always kept a good supply of home remedies which she stored in a tapestry carpetbag in the back closet. To get a fever down, she usually gave several drops of Laudanum, sponging the body often with tepid water. For diarrhea, she gave paregoric and tannin; or perhaps a dose of tannin with Laudanum repeated every three to four hours. Mary soon discovered that none of her home remedies had what it would take to go to battle with the Spanish Flu.

Nine people were living at the Wamhoff home, with all five girls sleeping in one bedroom upstairs and the two boys in the other. When the Spanish Flu hit the Wamhoffs, it hit them one after the other, like dominos falling over. At one point they were all in bed, each in a different stage of the flu. They were in a bad way when a knock came at the back door. With a blanket wrapped around his body, John managed to stumble to the door and opened it a crack, holding a towel over his nose and mouth. He said, "Mrs. Preis, we all have the flu, or I'd invite you in." She pushed her way into the house as she said, "THAT is why I am here---to take care of you folks. We already had it at our house and so I won't get sick. Now then, Mr. Wamhoff, you get yourself back to bed and I will make the rounds and see what is to be done first." John knew better than to argue with Johanna Preis.

Mrs. Preis stayed until everyone was on the mend and then she went back to her home. This is how Emblem folks watched out after each other---it's who they were. She even managed the telephone business as well as the post office during her week-long stay at the Wamhoff's!

The Spanish Flu: A tenth of the world's population of more than 500 million took ill with the flu, which killed more than 50 million people worldwide, more than the World war. In October 1918 alone—over 100,000 Americans died. It was known as the Great Influenza or the Spanish Flu although there was nothing Spanish or great about it. Death from the flu came with astonishing speed and death was horrifying agony—bodies turned blue from a lack of oxygen. The victims' lungs are filled with fluid. as if they had drowned. This flu began in the spring as perhaps any ordinary flu—sickening victims with fever and chills for an average of three days. In the fall it returned, with a new mutation and the power of a juggernaut! The second round is the one that caught the Wamhoff family, but blessedly went away from that house, empty-handed, as they all recovered! In the end, the Spanish Flu killed over 675,000.

November 11, 1918: World War I ended! Headlines in the Greybull newspaper read---"It's "All Over but the Shouting!"The war to end all wars was over, and the soldiers were coming home. Churches and businesses reopened and folks were relieved they had their lives back! John and Mary already knew their son, Bill, was coming home, and Ruth heard from her husband. Everyone in Emblem was making plans to have a big celebration when their soldiers were all finally home.

The Spanish Flu was in its prime and by the time it had run its course, it killed 548,000 Americans in the trenches and at home. An estimated 50 million died worldwide, as it infected a third of the world's population (632 million)----more than died in World War I.

~~~~~~

December 12, 1918: Mary was at the switchboard, it had been a busy morning. She had just taken a sip of hot coffee when the board buzzed—it was for the Wamhoff phone. Mary sat her cup of coffee down and answered the call, "Hello, Wamhoff's, this is Mary, what can I do for you?"

The voice on the other end said, "Well, just being home for Christmas with lots of presents, your home cooking, and hugs from my family would make me happy, but I will be happiest when I can wrap my arms around you again--- Mother of mine!"

Mary cried into the phone, "BILL---is that you? Are you okay? Where are you?"

Bill laughed on the other end, "Hello there Mother. I am in Cheyenne, getting ready to catch the next northwest train to Greybull. I expect to be rolling in around 10 tomorrow morning. Do you think somebody can pick me up?"

Mary cried into the phone, "OH Bill, Bill my boy. Yes, yes, of course, we will be there to meet the train---with bells on you can bet! Oh, son, I am so thankful that you are back home. How is your foot?"

Bill said, "It's good to be back Mother and my foot is coming along as well as can be expected. After I get settled in, I might take the car and go down to the baths at Thermopolis, which should make it feel better. I'll see you tomorrow! Bye for now." The line went dead and Mary just sat there, looking at the phone with tears running down her face as she said a silent prayer of thanks to the Lord for sparing her oldest son.

The next morning, John and Mary, their five daughters and two sons were all at the train station. It took three cars to get them all down there, but nobody was going to miss seeing Brother Bill get off that train! Through a cloud of steam and smoke, a huge gleaming black steam engine screeched to a halt in front of the station ---it was so loud that most folks covered their ears. It pulled a long line of passenger cars filled to the brim with soldiers on their way home. The Wamhoffs crowded onto the platform, trying to catch sight of Bill---and suddenly, there he was. Tall, thin, and with the biggest smile you ever did see. He wrapped his mother in his arms and lifted her off her feet. "OH Mother, I missed you so much, thank you for writing to me as often as you did---and Dad, oh Dad." None of them could hold back the tears of happiness as the Wamhoff family welcomed their soldier son and brother back from the theatre of death.

Bill felt something pull on his coat and looking down, he saw his little brother Jimmy. Bill reached down and grabbing Jimmy by the waist, threw him up in the air, and caught him. "Oh that was fun, do it again brother Bill! You sure are big! I got bigger too since you've been gone---that's what Dad says! I am four and a half years old now, bet you didn't know that!"

Back home on the farm, they turned on the Victrola and Mary brought out platter after platter of Bill's favorite foods. John supplied the beer as he was known to do! As soon as Bill could excuse himself from the festivities of his homecoming, he walked across the barnyard and escaped into the dark musty confines of the barn—a place where he always found peace. Bill closed and latched the door so he could address his emotions in private.

He sat on an old milking stool, head in his hands, as the tears came in a flood. *Will I ever be able to forget what I've seen and heard over there? Never in all my life did I imagine human beings could do such things to each other; and the horses, oh dear Lord— those poor poor horses with open wounds, broken limbs, left to die in the mud and barbed wire. I still hear the order screamed to don gas masks, the look of the mustard gas as it floated over the trenches like the plague. It was God's blessing that I got the flu, and then the German bullet in my left foot which was my ticket home.*

~~~~~~~~~

John had been out feeding the horses and when he walked in the kitchen, he found Mary sitting at the table, her face buried in her folded arms on the tabletop. John noticed the sharp rise and fall of her shoulders, her body convulsing with the sobs. Rushing to her side and fearing the worst, he took her by the shoulders and pulled her to her feet. "Mary, Mary, what in the world has happened?"

She stood, wrapped in John's arms, still sobbing as she laid her head on his shoulder, "Oh John, John---it's Minnie—Minnie Grabbert. She's died from the flu. She was there for me during my last five births and now there was not a thing I could do to help her. I feel so bad for the family, she was such a pillar of the community— always there to help in any way she could. This Spanish Flu has turned out to be much worse than most folks thought. It took my mother, Bill almost dies from it, and my brother Robert still isn't over it, and now Minnie!" She turned and sat down at the kitchen table, cradling her cup of coffee in her shaking hands. "We are so blessed, John, that we all recovered from that flu, it's a miracle."

John said, "Did you know that down in Greybull they are running out of places to put the dead and are using the Presbyterian Church as an emergency morgue. Mr. Cassel is the undertaker, and I hear he doesn't even have a hearse. They are having three to four funerals a day and the services are being held right at the gravesite because they are so backed up. The word is that the families don't hang around for long because people are scared to death of getting the flu." John shook his head, "I never heard of anything like this in all the years I was a mortician. I'd help if they needed me to, but I have to say, I'm plenty glad I'm not in that business anymore."

Mary said, "John, about Christmas—I simply don't feel in the mood to decorate a great deal like I usually love to do—Bill's first Christmas back home and all. I know Arnold and Ted will expect Santa Claus to come and all—I can order a couple of little things for them out of Sears & Roebuck. I can order the girls some hair combs and brushes---things like that from the catalog! I saw the cutest little wooden carved horse, hooked to a wagon so that when you push it, the horse's legs move as if it was galloping. The boys always like a little shovel and bucket. I will figure it out. I thought I'd just tuck colored cotton balls on a large tumbleweed for the Christmas tree. I know you said you'd go to the mountain and cut one down, but that is so far and you are still weak from the flu. We'll make do John. No worries!"

Spring, 1919: The HOMECOMING PARTY! Because the Spanish Flu was still around in January, folks waited until spring to have a homecoming party for the soldiers. Word got around fast and Mary sent out several line rings on the telephone to everyone in Emblem, Burlington, and Otto. There were posters at the post office and grocery stores that there would be a big celebration and carry-in dinner, that next Saturday afternoon, to 'Welcome Home' the men who had fought sp bravely. It would be held upstairs at the old Wiley roadhouse in Emblem, and dancing would follow the ceremony and meal!

It was a big deal---the Homecoming Party. Girls curled their hair, sought out their best dresses, and polished their shoes. Everybody dressed up for the occasion. Bill was now sharing the other bedroom upstairs with his two younger brothers, Ted who was almost seven, and little Jimmy was almost 5. They couldn't help but hear their sisters giggle and fussing from across the hall. Bill said to his brothers, "Do they act like this all the time?" Jimmy hastily replied, "Well, usually it's not this bad, it's just that they are excited about the party and seeing their boyfriends there I guess. Oh, and you gotta be careful and close your eyes when they run around in their underwear. Ted and I peek accidentally, sometimes"

Surprised, and trying his best to suppress his laughter, Bill said, "In their underwear? And, they have boyfriends? Does Dad know about this?"

Little Jim piped up, "Yes he does because I told him! I'm his 'little spy'!"

Bill and Ted burst out laughing and Bill said, "Well, remind me never to tell you about my girlfriends then!"

Jimmy's eyes grew large and he questioned, "You have more than one, girl?"

Bill exaggerated, "That's right, I have them all over the place! France, Nebraska, ---everywhere they see me walk into a room, especially when I was wearing my uniform!"

Bill ruffled his little brother's hair, "No Jimmy, I haven't found any special girl yet, but I am looking!"

~~~~~~~~

The hall above Wiley's abandoned roadhouse was all decorated in red, white, and blue with flags, candles, and colorful bunting. They had a special long table for the honored soldiers who were home from the war. It was covered in white paper and set with people's best dishes and pretty glasses. Everyone else sat at plain tables with no covering and they had to bring their tableware. The large table with the food was sagging, it was so heavy, with the steaming platters and bowls of the soldier's favorite dishes. All the women made plenty of their best dishes, and some of the farmers, including the Wamhoffs, and several others, butchered a cow, pig, or sheep---for the dinner.

There were people there that Bill had never seen before. It didn't take him long to spot a very pretty, brown-eyed girl. Not wasting any time, Bill walked up to her and said, "I don't think we have met, I'm Bill Wamhoff."

The girl opened her big brown eyes wide as she looked up at the 6'4" man who stood in front of her. "My, you are a tall 'drink of water', aren't you? No, we haven't met, I am visiting my cousins in Greybull. My name is Anna Sievers and I'm from York, Nebraska."

Bill slapped his knee, "Well I'll be darned. I know where that is. My folks came from Garland, above Seward----that's where I was born. Well, if that isn't the darndest thing. " Bill looked her straight in the eye, "Well, I have to go sit with the rest of the men now, but when they start the dance, save one or two for me, 'brown eyes', okay?"

Anna blushed and coyly replied, "Ok, I sure will!"

After dinner the local musicians broke into familiar songs, as the tables and chairs were pushed to the side of the room, clearing the floor for dancing. Most of the older folks took their little ones and the leftover food, and called it a night! Just in time, the band broke into 'I'm Forever Blowing Bubbles' followed by 'Red Wing'. The couples flooded the dance floor and began to mix it up!

Much to their annoyance, Marie, Helen, Ted, and Jimmy had to leave with their parents. On the ride home, Jimmy said, "I sure wish we coulda stayed a while and watched them dance. Say, I think Bill found a girlfriend. He was acting all mushy, he even told me to beat it!" John and Mary exchanged glances and amused smiles.

Seventeen-year-old Esther had a serious boyfriend, as she and Walt Blank had been seeing each other for a year or so. Walt Blank was a local man and they made a great looking couple. She didn't think her parents knew about him, but little Jimmy heard things and he didn't keep much to himself.

As usual, a local band played the music—with someone on the piano, a couple of guitars, drums, and a hot sax. Bill waited until the second song, then crossed the floor to where Anna stood with her friends. He tapped her on the shoulder and said, "Hello, brown eyes, may I have this dance?"

Bill had to stoop down to hold a conversation with her. "Say, how tall are you?"

She looked up at him and said, "Oh, I last time I checked I was around 5 foot 2, tall enough I guess!" Bill chuckled and replied, "Sure, I guess you are, uhhh, how old are you?"

She threw back her head and laughed, "You are something Bill Wamhoff—how long have I known you, and you ask me how old I am? Is there anything else you'd like to know about me?"

Bill leaned down and whispered in her ear, "Everything, there is to know, and I have all the time in the world!"

~~~~~~~

Weeks later: Supper was eaten, the dishes were washed and Mary and John sat reading and chatting in the parlor. Out of the blue, John announced, "The new Pastor, Walter Rehwaldt is coming in February, by himself. His wife Martha and their two sons will join him after school is out in Minnesota. It is going to be difficult for some of the older members to adjust to the new rules. It was discussed and we decided that the early sermon would be in German and the later one in English. As agreed with the Greybull Home Guard, there will be no German school and the Lutheran Catechism will be taught in English. I know there are a few of the old-timers who are going to kick and scream about this because they don't want it changed. But we need to prove we are loyal Americans and as always we'll persevere as times change!"

They were almost ready to call it a day when Bill walked in the parlor with a silly grin on his face. "Evening folks, I just had another swell date with that little brown-eyed gal from York, Nebraska. I think I'm kinda keen on her. She is something special, but she is going to be going back home pretty soon and I sure hate that! Uhhh-I've been thinking, I sure would like to have me a car and I was looking at that old Dort you have parked out back in the junkyard, Dad. I would like to take it apart, then bring it in here and work on the parts. I want to fix it up for my own. I'd also like to make my bedroom down here, where the parlor is. I'm too old to be sharing a room with those two little knuckleheads. It won't be forever; I can have the car done in a month!"

The next day Bill moved his bed downstairs into the parlor as well as the Dort car—part by part. Mary watched him walk back and forth, carrying the 'car' into what had been their parlor. Finally, she cornered him in what was now his bedroom and machine shop. "Bill, sit down, I want to talk to you. First of all, I hope this isn't going to take too long---you putting this car back together and all because I am rather partial to my parlor!" When there was no reply from Bill, she stood and walked to look out the window, then turned and asked, "Bill, what is wrong with you? I see it in your eyes, you look haunted, sad, not quite here, with us?"

Bill looked at his mother, then at the floor and swallowed twice, "In my eyes, huh? I suppose it's going to come out someplace even though I've tried to forget, tried to wipe it out of my mind. You see the war in my eyes, Mother—that's what you see. You see what I saw every day I was over there. The brutality, the inhumanity, the horror of it all. I haven't been able to forget or wipe it out of my mind. Little things, silly things like the gunny sacks of grain in the granary—remind me of the trenches lined with bags of sand like that, just like that. I see them and it flashes back in my mind, the sounds, the terrible smells of gunpowder, of unwashed bodies, of blood and death, of men, yelling, screaming for their mother. The mice in the granary turn into the millions of rats that lived in those trenches with us! I know, I know---in time I will forget about it, but

I've never talked to someone who has been in a war who has forgotten about how it was!"

Mary walked over to her oldest son and held him to her. "Bill, oh Bill. I remember my father saying some of the same things to my mother about the Civil War. I wish I could tell you that you would or will forget it, but I don't think that ever happens. It all will fade over time and perhaps once you find love and start a family— make a new life of your own to take its place, it will not haunt you so."

Bill said, "That's what I'm trying to do Mother. I thought maybe occupying my mind with rebuilding this car would help, and then I have met this Anna from Nebraska and, I don't know, something just clicked. Can you fall in love in two weeks?"

Mary smiled, "Anna, huh? Yes, Bill, you can fall in love in one night, after one kiss!"

~~~~~~~

At the end of almost every day, when their work was finished, the girls headed upstairs, where their prized Victrola sat at the top of the landing. Esther, Adella, Marie, and Helen cranked up the Victrola and played it as loud as possible, and danced to the music. When the lamps started shaking and dust fell from the ceiling, John had all he could stand. He walked over to the bottom of the stairs and yelled up, "You girls up there, turn that blasted thing down. I've told you before. We can't hear ourselves think down here and you are making the house shake! I can always take that thing out to the granary, you know!"

Esther was the only brave one--- well, she was brave because she knew she was the apple of her father's eye. She skipped down the steep stairway to where John stood. "Oh, Dad—we are so sorry. It's just that we lov-v-v-v-e that Victrola so much and we were practicing the new dances like the Charleston, Fox Trot, and the newest dance—the Shimmy!!! It's ever so fun. We'll try not to disturb you and Mother. That Helen, she might be the youngest, but that girl can dance. We showed her the steps and away she went. She does love to dance! You ought to see her do the Charleston!! When she is old enough, she is going to 'wow' them on the dance floor."

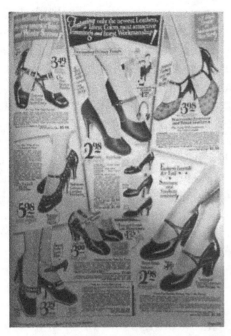

John said, "I am glad you girls are having such fun, but I don't think much of some of those dances. They are pretty indecent if you ask me---showing your legs and wearing such short skirts. I don't know what this world is coming to?"

Esther sat on the arm of his chair and putting her arm around his shoulder, said, "Ahhh, Dad---that reminds me, dearest Dad---- Adella, Marie, and I want a pair of the new dance shoes so badly. See, they have a whole page of them right here in the Sears and Roebuck catalog. We all bought new dress patterns and we are sewing our own dresses so you won't have to spend so much on us. The thing that we love is that wearing those horrible corsets is 'OUT'. It feels so free, and breathing is so much easier, especially when you are dancing all night."

John just shook his head in disbelief, "I can't understand what you girls see in those crazy dances. But I see them in the movies too and it's what they are all doing! You all act like you have a screw loose if you ask me!" John looked up at Esther and said, "Okay then, order one pair of those shoes and you all take turns wearing it!" He laughed so hard he almost choked.

Esther said, "Very funny father, we each need a pair, and you know it. Thank you very much!" She bent over and planted a kiss on his cheek.

~~~~~~~~~

In from the field, John slumped down on the step outside the back porch and pulled off his boots. Mary had been working in her flower bed and walked over to where he sat. "So, sitting down on the job now are you?"

John took off his hat and ran his fingers through his hair. "Oh Mary, we are in big trouble all over the Bighorn Basin and the country. Everything is so dry and there is NO water left in the reservoir. There was hardly any snowmelt up in those mountains this year and we are really in for it now. The herders tell me that the mountain is tinder dry. We get one good lightning storm up there and we'll have us a heck of a fire. The problem is when those goofy sheep get spooked, who knows where they are going to end up.

We are right in the middle of what they are calling a nation-wide drought. All I can hope for is that we have a good lamb and wool market. That is all we have going for us except those two fields we planted in winter wheat---they look like they might make it without irrigation. Plant the garden close to the well and cistern. We will have to pack water to it if we are going to have anything!"

Mary put her arm around his shoulder, "Ahh John, we will make it through this somehow. We've had bad times before. We just all came through the war, the flu, and rationing. We've had tough times, but we are tough people and we always find a way of making do! We are all in this together and it makes us appreciate the good times when they come to us! The thing about living on the farm is that we always have plenty to eat."

Suddenly they heard Jimmy scream! John and Mary ran to the screen door and there was Jimmy, down on his knees in the lane. His little white dog, Snowy, was lying in the road and she wasn't moving. Jimmy picked his little dog up and turned to walk to the house. John ran out to meet him. "What happened, is she hurt?"

Jimmy sobbed, "I don't know Dad. She was having fun, chasing a car and I think it ran over her." John said, "Here, let me have her and check to see how bad she's hurt?" John felt for a pulse, pulled open the dog's closed eyes, and----nothing!

The next day, Ted helped Jimmy make a crude little coffin out of a few boards they nailed together. They also nailed a cross together and Mary gave them some pretty flowers to put on the grave. Ted and Jimmy walked out to the edge of the pasture, under the cottonwood trees. Ted dug a small hole, and Jimmy laid Snowy in the grave. They pushed the dirt over the grave and put the cross at the head of it. Jimmy said, "Ted, do you know of a prayer we can say for Snowy? I think that's what they do when they bury someone." Ted looked perplexed for a moment and then said, "Well now, not really but we could say the prayer we say when we go to sleep, that's a real nice one!" The two brothers held hands and bowed their heads and said, *"Now I lay me down to sleep, I pray the Lord my soul to keep. If I should die before I wake, I pray the Lord my soul to take! Please Dear God take care of Snowy, she was a real good little dog."*

With tears in his eyes, Jimmy said to Ted, "Do you think dogs go to heaven with Jesus?" Ted put his arm around Jimmy's shoulders as they walked back to the house and said, "I don't know about that but I do know they go to Dog Heaven!"

~~~~~~~~

That afternoon when Ted and Jimmy gathered eggs, it didn't take them long to figure out the chickens had mites or lice. They hurried as fast as they could, screaming and scratching as they ran to the back porch, sat the baskets of eggs on the step, then commenced to hosing each other off. Jimmy said, "Yee gads, I hate the feeling of those creepy things crawling up my arms. Gives me the willies---all over! We need to tell Dad to spray the chicken house. It seems like they get them about this time every year!"

That evening at supper the two boys told their father about the lice. John had a good laugh, "Well now, I'll ask one of the hired men to get that chicken house sprayed tomorrow. In a couple of years, you two can tend to that chore as well." Jimmy looked at Ted and Ted looked at Jimmy---neither was eager to get to that age!

~~~~~~~~

Esther was moping around the kitchen while Mary was trying to get dinner on. "Esther, what is wrong with you, get busy and peel those potatoes and carrots. Ever since that dance we gave the soldiers, you act like you are in another world. What's gotten into you? "

Esther put her hands over her face and started bawling! Mary went over to her and took her hands away from her face. "Are you in trouble?" Well, that didn't help at all! Esther cried even harder. Mary said, 'Okay, tell me what it is and maybe we can figure something out!" Esther flopped down in the oak kitchen chair, 'Oh

Mother, I got it bad for Walt, I just have the blues today. I want him to ask me to marry him. Did you feel like this about Dad at one time when you were young?"

Mary threw her head back, laughing and remembering those days. "Oh, I guess I did. So you are telling me you are in love with this Walt Blank? Well, you could do worse. He comes from a good Lutheran family and he's a hard worker. But Esther, you are only seventeen."

Nevertheless, Esther and Walt Blank were married in the Lutheran church in early December. John had ordered a special new wedding suit which fit him to a "T". He looked quite handsome as he walked another daughter down the aisle. The reception

Courtesy: Arnold Wamhoff

was held at the Wamhoff house and as usual, it was quite the affair. The Wamhoff's held a huge dinner for the wedding guests. There was NO dancing, but guests played cards, visited, and the kids were outside having fun playing games! There wasn't supposed to be any liquor but John didn't consider his beer or cider to be inappropriate for this occasion, so he provided the beverages from his 'personal' supply. There was snow on the ground which they shoveled out of the way for the group picture.

That night several of the guests who had drunk a bit too much cider and beer, bedded down on the floor of the Wamhoff house. John Wamhoff was known for his potent apple cider—and several discovered this fact a bit too late in the day.

Several days after the wedding, they had a 'chivaree' for the newlyweds. They put Esther in a wheelbarrow, decorated with cowbells, and made Walt push her up the road to where the party was to be held. It was another carry-in dinner and dance where the men had to pay Walt, for them to dance with his bride. This was one of those times when the community came together to relax and let loose! After the wedding, Esther and Walt set up housekeeping on the farm in Emblem. In a year they had their first child, a girl—Betty June who was the apple of her grandfather's eye from the day she was born.

~~~~~~~~~

January 1920: Mary sat in her rocking chair, crocheting while John read the Billings newspaper. Suddenly he wadded it up and threw it across the room. "John, what in the world caused you to do that?"

John stood up, his face was red and he was mad as a hornet, to say the least. "Those dad-blamed idiots have no common sense to pass an Amendment like that. 'The 18th Amendment to the Constitution of the United States prohibits making or selling any alcoholic beverage.' How do you like those bananas? At least there is a clause that doesn't prohibit the consumption of it! Now, how the hell is that going to work?"

Mary's eyes opened wide, "So then John, does that mean you are breaking the law by brewing beer and cider in the barn for our personal use, but you can drink it?"

John said, "Well, no, that's not how it reads---"the act allows for 'personal production and consumption' of an alcoholic beverage—you just can't go into a store or a bar and order a drink. Those senators and such don't know what the hell they are doing. And I thought we lived in a free country. This law doesn't go into effect until 1920, so that gives us time to think up a plan! But, I'll tell you this, I AM growing my hops and my barley and my apples, and I AM going to continue to make beer and cider, for my personal use. I certainly won't sell it, but on second thought the money would come in pretty handy. I might put it in Mason jars and store it in amongst the jars of your tomatoes and such down in the cellar, but I guess I can still make it and drink it, I just can't sell it! I'll be damned if I am going to stop having a beer and my apple cider just because a bunch of old biddies say it's wrong! I can't even imagine how many establishments this is going to force out of business or they are going to have to get extra creative! All together, it makes no damn sense!"

John walked over to where Mary sat and tweaked her cheek, "Oh now, you'd have mercy on me—your husband and bail me out if the cops throw me in the hoosegow? Wouldn't you?"

Mary continued to crochet and cocking her head to the left, she softly said, "Well now, I might give it a couple of days, you know, let you cool your heels. But, eventually, I would scrape up the bail money for my beer-drinking husband!" She smiled sweetly up at John, whose eyes were wide with disbelief.

"A couple of days? Are you serious? You'd leave me in there for a couple of days? Well then, I'm going to have to be more creative if I want to go into town and have me a drink or two!" They both had a good laugh over it, but John was considering putting his 'now, semi-illegal brewing system' out of plain sight.

Chapter Thirteen

THE ROARING TWENTIES

The "Roaring Twenties"--- the decade which followed World War I was a time of excess and wealth for many. Post-war optimism enticed rural Americans into the cities in vast numbers. They all had dreams of finding a better life in the industrial sector. The cities prospered during the decade, while the overproduction of agricultural goods created widespread financial problems and anguish among American farmers. In March of 1929, a small crash occurred ---investors began to sell stocks at a rapid rate---then the economic 'crash' began to pick up speed!

April 19, 1920: It was official, Henry Wegner was moving on---closing the Wegner store and post office and was looking for someone who wanted to take on the post office. Henry spotted John Wamhoff out in the field and stopped to speak to him. "Good Morning John, I have a proposition for you! I am closing the store and I need to find someone to take the post office. Well, the first name that comes to mind is you and Mary since you already have the telephone-- it just makes sense you might consider taking it. You'll be making about $100 a month or so, depending on what the government thinks it's worth." He started to walk to his car, then turned. "Say, John, I was wondering how you like that new Prohibition Bill the government passed? Guess you will be tearing out all those hops now?"

John's eyes narrowed, "Well, I tell you, Jim, I don't think too much of that Prohibition business, just a bunch of old battleaxes trying to keep their husbands home! And, I will not be tearing out my hops---not on your life! They like it fine, just where they are! I'll talk to Mary about the post office offer and let you know."

When John returned home that day he and Mary discussed Wegner's offer. Mary said, "Let me think on it just a bit and I'll talk to you later."

After supper, they were sitting next to the radio as usual and Mary said, "John, I have been thinking about the post office opportunity. We've already closed in that front porch to house the switchboard and folks could just walk in the door to mail a letter or collect a package, we might put a bell above the door to let us know when someone comes through the door for their mail. We have to be on-premises all the time as it is—so why not add the post office too? I do have experience with the post office back in Germantown."

John said, "Okay Mary—you are the boss where those two businesses are concerned and that money is yours too. The bell is a good idea—that way if you are in the kitchen or we are sitting in the parlor, you can tell when someone comes in. I'll pick one up in town. We also need a good lock on that door in case Black Fritz wants to check his mail at midnight! Another thing I thought of is to post your open/closed hours on the door so folks realize we're not open 24 hours a day."

NOTE: *The Wamhoffs accepted the task of running both the post office and the telephone switchboard. The two enterprises remained on the Wamhoff farm for the next thirteen years. Folks often remarked about how lovely Mary Wamhoff's voice was over the switchboard; and no matter the time of day, she was usually there, ready and willing to help.*

~~~~~~~~~

Mid Summer: Mary and John remained at the kitchen table, taking their time with the second cup of coffee while everyone else was off to take care of their chores. Mary said "I see we have new neighbors, the Blank family; they have a boy about Arnold's age. I'll have to take Arnold over and introduce him to Albert, who's our son-in-law, Walt's youngest brother. One thing for sure, I always know where to find that boy of ours, he follows Old Jim around like a puppy. I asked Jim if it bothered him and he said he liked having the little fellow around!"

John said, "I have to run into town today. Going to take the eggs and cream in, and I need to check in with the elevator and see what prices look like for grain this fall. I should be back in time for supper!"

~~~~~~~~~

It was an unusually hot day, Mary wiped her hands on her apron as she finished up with the dinner dishes. She looked out the kitchen window and noticed Jim working in the field to the south of the house. *It's too hot for him to be out there on that tractor at his age. I think I'll put some ice tea in a Mason jar and take it out to him---maybe a little of that banana cake too. I know he likes that.*

Mary put her straw hat on and headed for the end of the field, waiting for Jim to make his turn and head back towards her. Jim shifted gears and slowed the tractor when he spotted Mary walking at the end of the row. He cut the engine and looked down at her, "What in the world are you doing out in this heat, woman? Is something wrong up at the house?"

Mary smiled and said, "No, no—everything is fine. I just noticed you out here and it's so ungodly hot today that I thought you might like to take a break, sit in the shade of the tractor and have some ice tea and a slice of cake."

Jim slid down off the tractor and winced when he put his weight on his bad hip. "Mary, Mary—you are a godsend! This heat is about to get me down, I'm getting too old to be doing this. Must be the hottest day of the month. I am most grateful you brought this ice tea out to me. Here, sit under the tractor with me in the shade for a spell---I'll share the cake!"

They both laughed as Mary scooted under the shade of the tractor and sat next to Jim. She noticed something about him seemed different today, he had a pained expression on his face as he ate the cake and drank the tea.

"Jim, is something wrong? You seem a little down today, are you feeling okay?"

Jim laid the cake down and hung his head. When he looked up there were tears in his eyes.

Mary put her hand on his shoulder, "Jim—why, Jim, what on earth is the matter? Are you not feeling well? I've seen you favor that hip of yours---or is it something else? Jim, I have to be honest, I have had a feeling for a long time that there is something in your past that you don't share, that you are trying to forget? I have no right to ask Jim, but is there something you've been keeping to yourself, all these years? Sometimes it helps to let others who care about you, share in the hurt."

Jim shook his head and wiped more tears away. "Well, now, I suppose you might say there are things that happen in a man's life that even time won't change."

Mary took hold of Jim's hand, "Jim, how long have we known you—that you've been a part of our family? Will you please share what it is that troubles you so—it might help some. It will stay just between the two of us, I promise."

Jim looked down at the soil and ran his fingers through it, then lifted his head. "It's that --- it's so hard to talk about, to think about. It's something one never gets over---losing one's family, all in one day, without getting to say goodbye! It was on this day, so many years ago and it brings it all back when this date rolls around."

Mary's hand flew to her mouth. "Oh mercy me, dear Lord, Jim---you lost your family? You had a family and now you don't? Jim---what, when, did this happen? How long?"

Jim lifted his head to look at the clear blue sky and took a deep breath. "It was in Kansas—around 1890—we had us a nice little farm, a good life. It was a clear day when my Sally and our three little ones—Mandy, Robert, and James—when I seen them that morning before I took the wagon into town for supplies. I noticed the clouds building as I drove the team, but then, that was Kansas. I went on into town, not thinking anything about it. The storm came out of nowhere—folks that lived through it said they never saw such a huge funnel and without warning, it seemed to drop out of the seething black clouds directly onto our place. It was a monster!"

Jim rubbed his hands over his face and back through his hair. "Mary, when I got home—it was, as if—there weren't ever a house there. They didn't even have time to get to the storm cellar. There was no sign of the house, outbuildings, or any of my family, just Mandy's doll laying on the bare ground. I don't remember much of the next few days. Neighbors took me in until I could talk about it. I never knew it possible to hurt that bad, Mary---or that it would never leave me be. At first, I had such bad dreams, I tried everything, the Bible, whiskey, and then I decided to leave, I ran from it. The memories of my family were everywheres and I was going out of my mind. Then I met you and John in Cheyenne---I do believe that God sent you to me because without you and your family, I think I would have ended my life, what there was of it. You and John gave me a family, a home, a life---I owe you so much. And that little one of yours, Jimmy—that folks started calling him, Jimmy after me, because he follows me everywheres. Oh, Mary---you will never know what you all mean to me!"

Mary wiped the tears from her face and put her arms around Jim. "Oh dear Jim, I knew---I knew you held some terrible secret deep inside you, something that haunted you. I could see it in your eyes when you weren't on guard. You,---your little girl's name was Mandy? Our first baby was a girl,—Amanda—she died right after she was born. We have a connection Jim—we both had our little Amandas'!"

Mary stood and said, "Jim, I'm sorry if I bullied you—but maybe it'll be easier now that I know. I won't tell John if you don't want me to. It can be between us. I don't want to cause you any more hurt, I am here for you and I also understand losing someone you love. Life can be so very hard—we all have disappointments, hurts, things that stay deep inside of us."

Mary picked up the Mason jar and tucked it under her arm. "Jim, are you alright now? Are you sorry you told me?"

Jim stood and wrapped his arms around Mary and held her to him, "No, no—I'm glad you know, I'm glad to know you understand. There's no need to speak of it again. Thanks for the ice tea and cake, Mary. John doesn't know how lucky he is to have you and those children. I know I shouldn't, but I envy him."

She stood there at the end of the field and watched as Jim started the tractor up and turned it to go back down the field. She waved, then turned to walk back to the house. Her heart was heavy with Jim's secret but now she knew for certain there was something terrible which he was hurting from. *I hope sharing it with me will ease his mind somehow. He's such a good man and to have something so terrible happen is beyond my understanding.*

~~~~~~~~~

The next morning Mary was up early, ready for a full day's work. "John, I think tomorrow I want to butcher those 40 fryers that I've been raising in the brooder house. I'll get the girls to help me pluck feathers, gut them, and cut them up if you will take care of chopping off their heads. I'll get the scalding pots set up if you can have their heads off, say—by nine, later this morning?"

John grinned, "Your wish is my command. There is nothing funnier than seeing all those chickens jumping around the yard without heads!"

Mary said, "Well, you'd better let Ted and Arnold help you, they get such a kick out of that; but after that, you can take them with you for the day, if you would. I don't want them around those huge pots of scalding water."

"I'll get the Mason jars out tonight and get them all washed and ready to can the chicken tomorrow. That will be good eating come this winter."

The next morning, John crawled out of bed while it was still darker than a stack of black cats. He dressed and headed for the shed where he sharpened his ax. When Mary said she was ready to commence the chicken killing, John grabbed his 'chicken catcher', a metal rod with a hooked end that fit over the chicken's leg. He'd snag a fryer, chop its head off and go after the next one. Ted and Jimmy stood to the side for a bit, taking it all in, then Ted said, "Dad, would you let us try to snag a chicken? We've been watchin' you."

John handed Ted the 'chicken catcher' and the boy proved he was a natural. The boy caught the chicken and John chopped its head off. Then it was six-year-old Jimmy's turn---the three of them got an assembly line going and soon there were no live fryers anywhere on the farm. When they were finished, John patted his youngest sons on the head, "You did real well, boys. Now you can come with me, out in the hills to check on the sheep herd."

Jimmy's face got all screwed up and tears came to his eyes, "Ahhh, Dad—I wanted to help pluck chicken feathers off and watch them gut the chickens!"

John slapped his thigh, "Well, maybe next year. Today we have to get our horses saddled and check on the sheep!"

~~~~~~~~

August 18, 1920: John held up the Greybull Standard to show Mary an article. "Well now, did you know you have the right to vote? It's right here in the paper. The Nineteenth Amendment to the U.S. Constitution was ratified ---giving women the right to vote.

So Mrs. Wamhoff, who are you going to vote for in the next election?"

Mary bristled, just a bit, and then replied. "Well now, I think that women have had the right to vote in Wyoming since 1869—right? I will have to study the reports won't I, so I make an educated decision. I will tell you that I am quite impressed with William Harding, but I may change my mind. That's what we women do, change our minds on a whim, or at least that's what you tell me! You are a pretty smart man John, but you still have some learning to do when it comes to women!"

Mary went to the backyard to take the clothes off the clothesline. *I smell the rain and it looks dark across the hills there. I'd better hurry or I'm gonna get wet too.* Just as she put the last clothespin in the bag, the wind picked up and she felt a cold drop of rain on her neck. Lightning tore through the gathering clouds as a volley of thunder rumbled across the farmland. Mary just made it through the back door with the basket of dry clothes when the first hailstone bounced in the yard.

"John, John---it's fixin' to hail. John ran to the back door, I'd better run for the barn and get the milk cows and those two horses inside. He put a bucket over his head and watching the ground, ran for the barn but not before several hailstones stung his back and the backs of his legs. The hail drummed on the bucket until John could hardly hear. After getting the animals under shelter, he decided to wait it out in the barn.

Lightning flashed across the sky as Jimmy sat on the porch and counted slowly, "one and a bucket,—two and a bucket, —three and a bucket,"—and then they heard the low rumble of thunder as it echoed across the bench. "The lightning struck about three miles away. Jim taught me how to count how far the lightning strike is by counting real slow like. Try it Ted—that works swell!"

Another explosion of thunder rattled the doors and windows. Mary stood at the back door and watched as the hail bounced in the yard like hundreds of small white balls of popcorn. Mary listened to the little balls of ice slam against the windows and almost as soon as it started, it was over and the sun peeked through the clouds. Mary opened the windows to let the fresh air into the house. She stood at the screen door and breathed deeply of the clean fresh rain-washed air. She recalled storms like this in Nebraska when they would head for the storm cellar. Then she thought of Jim and his secret—*what storms must do to him, the poor poor man.*

When John decided it looked like it was over, he opened the barn door to let the cows and horses back out. He turned and started back toward the house. The small hail crunched beneath his feet. *I'll be gol-damned---I hope it didn't hurt that field of wheat. I think it's still pretty green. That's the thing with farming---every day is a gamble if you are going to make it past what mother nature has in store. A farmer works all spring and summer to raise a crop and in five minutes it can all be gone. This hail storm didn't amount to that much though, thank God!*

~~~~~~~~~

September: The threshing crews were all set and John had contracted with Grabberts to thresh their grain for them on this day. Now, Brother Bill didn't drink, but he did get a kick out of watching other people and how they acted when they drank. So, he took some of John's good cider out for a few of the men---to get them ready for the day of hard work. He said to them, "Come on boys, take a break and wet your whistle with a little Wamhoff cider to start the day!"

The Trumbull boys were running the hay racks that day. They along with a few others were partial to John Wamhoffs cider so of course, they couldn't resist. After a half-hour, they all started dancing and whooping on the empty wagon bed. Well, in turn, that scared the horses and off they went. Everybody, who was sober, was afraid the hayrake wouldn't make the turn at the lane, but it and the dancing men made it, in tack. Minus a couple of men, most of the workers were still dancing on the hayrack as it pulled into Grabberts farmyard.

Mary answered the phone at the switchboard. "Well hello Mr. Grabbert, and how are you doing today. I guess you have a big threshing crew all ready to harvest your fields." Mary listened to what Mr. Grabbert was saying on the other end of the line then said, "I'm so---I'm so—so, uh, sorry about that, I will speak to John immediately. Thank you for calling!"

Mary went to the door and called, "Jo-hn, Jo-hn. I need to talk to you, NOW."

John came to the back door and said, "What now, I have a big day of threshing ahead of me, I don't have time to stand and jabber. We got to get the threshing machine over to Grabberts, we've already lost half the day."

With a devious smile, Mary said, "Well now, I don't think that is going to happen. It seems somebody got into your cider and passed it around to the threshing crew. Mr. Grabbert just called to say that some of the crew were over there, and they didn't know where they were or what day it was!"

John saddled his horse and said, "I don't know when you can expect me, I've got some behinds to kick!"

~~~~~~~~~~

John looked at his six-year-old son, Jimmy as he sat on the floor playing with the toy soldiers Bill had brought back for him after the war. John put his paper down and said, "Arnold, come here!"

The boy stood and walked over to where his father sat. "If I'm not mistaken you will start school in the fall. I think it's time to cut off those long baby curls. You don't want the other kids to make fun of you, do you?"

Big tears ran over Jimmy's cheeks. "Mama likes my curls and my sisters comb them all the time. I don't want to get them cut off---I don't!"

John could feel Mary's eyes bore into him. This was her baby and she spent hours, winding the curls up and fixing his hair.

John said to Mary, "Tomorrow, you take this big boy down to our son-in-law, Walt Blank. He's a barber and he will do a good job---and I don't want to hear another word about it!"

The next morning Mary put Arnold in the car and Bill drove them down the road to where Esther and Walt lived. Walt said, "Now Jimmy, you are a big boy and going to first grade. If you keep these long curls, the other boys will tease you and pull them and put them in the ink wells. You decide, do you want to be a girl or a boy? Sit up here right now,—they are coming off!"

Jimmy sat real still when his brother-in-law was using that scissors. He felt the long curls fall to the floor, one by one until---- he looked in the mirror. Everyone was holding their breaths. Jimmy said, "Is that really me? I like the way I look now, I look like Ted. Thanks, Walt"

On the first day of school, Mary laid out a new pair of knickers and a white shirt. Jimmy fussed, "Why can't I have bib overalls like the other big boys?" Mary replied, "Because, you aren't that big yet—soon you will be. Remember when it's time for lunch, you run home with Ted, Helen, and Adella. I'll have it all ready for you!" Mary paused and smiling said, "Now Arnold, remember that if you have to go to the bathroom and you can't hold it until recess, you hold up your arm and when the teacher looks at you, hold up one finger if you have to make a quick trip to the outhouse and hold TWO fingers if you think it will take longer."

~~~~~~~~~

First Day of School: Jimmy held sister Helen's hand as they walked a quarter of a mile to the schoolhouse. It had two rooms—the lower room was for grades one through four and the upper room for grades five through eight. All the way there, Jimmy thought about the stories he'd heard from his brothers and sisters about how strict and mean some of the teachers were, and that they would spank you with a paddle if you were naughty. He was a bit scared, but that didn't last longer than the first day.

Arnold Wamhoff and Albert Blank shared a locker where there was a place to hang their coats and a small cubby overhead. There were four rows of desks, one for each class ---1st through 4th. Arnold was assigned a desk in the first row, and Albert sat right behind him, near the teacher's desk which sat in the corner. In the front of the room was a large blackboard with the ABC's bordering the top. A black iron potbelly stove sat over in the far corner of the room, near the door to the cloakroom. To the left of the blackboard was a floor to ceiling bookcase. School supplies were paid for by the parents—like books, tablets, pencils, etc.

At recess, Albert asked Jimmy, "I wonder why the girls get a bigger outhouse than the boys? We have a two-seater and they have at least a six-seater and it's closer to the schoolhouse. "Say, Jimmy, I'll bet you are too chicken to peak through the cracks in the girl's outhouse!"

Jimmy looked at Albert, "You do it first, that sounds like your kind of trouble to me! If I want to see a naked girl all I have to do is look through the keyhole at my house---I have five sisters you know!"

Now, Albert was a bit of a mischief-maker. During the second day of school recess, Albert and Jimmy were sitting on the ground playing a game of Tic Tac Toe when Jimmy spotted Albert cheating. Jimmy said, "Hey now Albert, you can't do that—that's cheating!" Albert stood up and kicked dirt at Jimmy, "Well, now if you don't like that I'll just slap you around the belly, you baby you!"

The teacher, Mrs. Shoemaker heard this and said, "You two will stay after school and wash the blackboard. We will have none of that kind of talk here at school!" After that there wasn't any more talk like that, at least the teacher didn't hear it! And the oddest thing, after school that day when Albert put his foot into the stirrup to get on his horse, the saddle came down on top of him. Somehow, that cinch belt pulled loose all on its own!!

~~~~~~~~

It was mid-morning, near the end of October. Mary had just finished hanging the laundry on the backyard clothesline when she spotted Arnold, running down the lane and into the house without stopping. She dropped the wet shirt back into the basket and hurried into the house. There stood Arnold with the telltale stain running down his front pant leg. The minute he saw his mother, he burst into tears!

Mary said, "Oh dear, you had an accident. Why didn't you raise your hand with one finger as I told you to do?"

Arnold said, "Well, there was others before me and I just couldn't wait to go. I am never going back to that school again. All the kids laughed at me!"

Well, word spread through the Wamhoff house, and that day at supper time, Bill came in from working in the field with a stain down the front of his pants. Mary said, "What in the world happened to you, did you go in your pants?"

Bill put his head down in a sheepish motion, grinned, winked, and said, "Yeah Mother, I didn't want to have to stop the tractor to go and when I couldn't hold it any longer, I stopped but I couldn't hold it."

Jimmy laughed and laughed, "You are just like me brother Bill. That same thing happened to me in school. I guess it just happens sometimes, huh?"

~~~~~~

1920 - Fall: For the first time, the school in West Emblem had a school bus/wagon, well that's what they called it. Otto Blank built the truck bed with seats along the outside edges and offered to drive around and pick  children up who didn't want to ride their horse to school. Unfortunately, it only had a canvas cover, so the children were still cold and out in the elements. It wouldn't be until 1933 that the school district established three bus routes for the Emblem Grade School, but Jimmy and the rest of the Wamhoff children didn't get to ride the bus because they lived so close to the school.

~~~~~~

1921: John sat his coffee cup on the breakfast table and said, "Mary, I don't know about you, but I am starting to regret we gave Bill permission to use the parlor in which to work on his Dort." Every time Mary peeked in the door all she could see was a mountain of clutches, joints, spark plugs, gaskets, heaters, piston rings, door bumpers, and other things that belonged to the car.

The second week in February, Bill sat down at the kitchen table for his breakfast and announced. "Well, I think it's time to move the clean and assembled parts of my Dort outside to the machine shed or else we'll have to take a wall down to get it out.

And Mother, since you've been so good to let me use your parlor, I'll move back upstairs and bunk with my little brothers. At least they don't snore and who knows, maybe one of them will get married soon".

Mary chuckled to herself and thought, a*t seven and nine, marriage wasn't in the cards just yet for Ted and Jimmy!!* Carrying his first load of car parts, Mary could hear Bill laughing on his way out to the machine shed!

As tears filled her eyes, Mary thought about what their oldest son had been through in the war and the terrible memories it left him with. She thought of the day he left for war, how enthusiastic and proud he'd been, and now he seemed haunted and even sad. *Time will help, but he has seen and gone through so much that even we can't imagine or help him forget. I am sure working on those cars occupies his mind for now. I know soldiers see so much death and cruelty, I remember little things Pap would tell us about the Civil War.*

A couple of weeks later, Mary was out in the back yard hanging up freshly washed clothes in the brisk March wind. John walked up behind her and took Mary by the shoulders, turned her around, and said, "Mary, I've been thinking about it since the last harvest and I am going to do it. I know we are a little tight in the budget, but I

Courtesy: Arnold Wamhoff

think I can swing it. Today is the day. I'm driving to Billings to buy one of those Minneapolis Moline tractors. I know it will pay off in time. It's a beast and it will come in right handy during threshing time and in the spring when the ground is rough and we need a lot of horsepower to break it up. That behemoth weighs 22,500 pounds and is seventeen feet long! I need something with that much power to pull the new threshing machines now too. That Rumley tractor is about tuckered out!"

Mary said, "Well John Wamhoff, that is no surprise to me. You have been talking about those tractors for a couple of years now. If I know anything, I know you and when you set your mind to something---you are like a river. Once it gets to flowing in a direction, it won't change for nothing!"

About that time, Bill walked up. "What's going on?"

John answered, "Bill, I am going up to Billings and buy one of those Minneapolis Moline tractors, you know the one I've been looking at. You said it was their best design—how they enclosed the gears to keep the chaff and dust out of the engine. I can afford it, even with the bad crops, those sheep are the thing that's keeping us afloat! I can't afford NOT to buy that tractor because it will make us more money, faster!" He turned to walk to his car then stopped, "It will take several months to fill the order. When it comes in on the freight train, We'll drive into Greybull to the train station and you can drive that beast home. Would you like that? In fact, why don't you come with me today, up to Billings? There isn't much for you to do around here this time of the year. You can help me look the thing over!"

Bill slapped his cap on the leg of his pants, "By George, that would be just dandy. Let me change my clothes and I'll be more than ready!"

Mary smiled and waved goodby to John and their oldest son. They didn't have many opportunities to have time like this together. It would be good for both of them, as it seemed they didn't have much in common except farming. Both men walked a different path. John was impulsive, a risk-taker, explosive, a leader---while Bill was like a calm river, deep and moving. He kept things inside and was slow to anger and he certainly wasn't a risk-taker.

~~~~~~~~

Around the end of April, John's new tractor arrived in Greybull on a flatbed railroad car. It was the impressive beast he had predicted and more. When they unloaded it from the flat car, Bill twisted the hand-crank, the engine gave a thunderous roar and windows rattled for a block away. Everybody in town came running to see what was making all that noise. With a big grin on his face, Bill climbed onto the seat, waved his hat, then taking the dirt back roads through Greybull, he headed for the road to Emblem. He had to drive next to the road in most spots because the iron teeth on the tractor wheels carved up the graded road and highway. It was slow going and it took most of the day to go the eighteen miles on and off-road, back to the farm.

Around supper time, Mary heard the tractor coming down their graded dirt road. Mary and the children stood behind the fenced-in-yard and watched as Bill proudly drove the mammoth machine into their farmyard. Nobody was quite sure everything this tractor was capable of doing! But, it certainly was BIG and it was LOUD!

That tractor arrived just in time for the fall harvest which was going to be short because of the [18]drought, but the tractor would have an opportunity to show what it could do. Every time John started that tractor up—it made the ground shake as it belched smoke and roared to life like some prehistoric beast.

That next Saturday, John made one excuse after the other to take the horses and wagon into Greybull instead of the car, saying he wanted to see the new bank building on the corner of Main Street. He also needed to deliver all the eggs and cream in town and had too many to take in the car. Bill said, "Now then Dad, you are making a lot of excuses not to take the car, what do you have up your sleeve?"

Courtesy: Greybull Standard

John winked at Bill and said, "Now, just you mind your business, I got a surprise for your mother, something really special I have to pick up in Greybull. I think you better get yourself out to the field and see how the men are coming along plowing that wheat field. Check and see how that Moline tractor is working out, I don't trust them bozos to drive that beast."

After he finished his chores in town, John decided to take a few minutes and headed to the 'Smokehouse Saloon'. He bellied up to the bar and ordered a chilled mug of beer. John turned and looked around the pool hall. With his back to the bar and one heel resting on the foot rail, he watched as several fellows had a card game going while others shot pool. John walked over to the card table where some men he knew were playing Pitch.

One of the men said, "Say there Wamhoff, how about a game or two of cards?"

John smiled and slapped the fellow on the back, "Naw, I gotta get on home. I just stopped in for a cool beer before heading out. Maybe some other time. Have a good day gentlemen!"

It was half-past four when Jimmy heard the rumble of the big freight wagon and the team of horses, "Mother, Dad is coming down the lane!"

When John saw his youngest son run up the lane towards him, he pulled on the reins, "Whoa there." He reached down to give Jimmy a hand up. "Well now, I guess you can ride the rest of the way with me."

Jimmy climbed up and squeezed in beside his father. He turned around and saw something big under a tarp in the back. "Dad, what is under that tarp back there?"

John pinched Jimmy's little cheek and said in a low voice, "It's a big surprise for your Mother, something she deserves."

John pulled the horses to a stop in the yard, close to the back porch. Bill was walking in from the barn. John called to him, "Say, Bill, come on over here and help me with this surprise for your Mother."

Suddenly the wagon and the 'surprise' was surrounded by all the children and a couple of hired men. John said, "Where is your mother?" Jimmy said, "Why she's at the switchboard where she has to be."

Adella said, "Tell me what's under the tarp and I'll go take her place." John whispered what the surprise was. Adella ran inside the house and yelled, "Mother, Mother come quick, Dad is back from town and has something for you!"

Mary tucked some stray gray hairs back into her bun and adjusted her apron as she pushed open the screen door. Everyone was gathered around the wagon where the most beautiful cookstove sat under the tarp, waiting for approval.

John did a grand swoop of his hand toward the stove. "A surprise for the lady of the house and the best cook in the Bighorn Basin and all of Wyoming, if I say so myself!"

Mary's eyes opened wide and her hands covered her open mouth, "Oh John, John---oh my, it's grand. Look at this, there is even a place to warm the hot irons when we are ironing and to heat water for a bath or washing dishes. Oh, hurry and put the old one in the summer kitchen and sit this beauty in my kitchen. I can hardly wait to start cooking on it." Bill and the hired men removed the old cookstove and put it in the summer kitchen where Mary would now have two old stoves to do her canning on. With a grand gesture, they

moved the spanking new cookstove into the kitchen and hooked it up to the chimney.

Mary ran her hands over every part of that stove. "Oh John, it's a beauty—so modern and so big. Mercy me, I don't know what to say except, thank you with all my heart!" John hugged her tightly. "When we get electricity out here, I'll get you the first electric cookstove on the Bench!" Mary laughed, "That big oven door will be just right to keep the bum lambs and sickly calves warm when we have to."

~~~~~~~~~

January 1921: John had been gone for nearly two hours, attending a meeting of the church board and Pastor Rehwaldt. Mary spent the time sorting through the day's mail. *Oh, such a mess. I don't know who it was that dumped the mail sack out in the middle of the floor. THAT is not how I attend to the mail, not at all! I take this job seriously; after all, I have sold $100 to $200 worth of goods almost every week, from stamps to boxes, to wrapping paper and such. I am also keeping the books for the post office and the telephone. It sure does help with the household costs—that extra money every month and John doesn't need to know about my little stash. I hid it where he would never look, not in a month of Sundays! It's growing fast and I just like to know I have an emergency fund if needed.*

Mary kept a plate of food warm for John. It was well after supper when she saw the lights of their car come down the lane;

minutes later, John walked into the house. "Well now, that was a very interesting and fruitful meeting if I do say so. Pastor Rehwaldt called a special meeting of Walter Jensen, F H. Moeller, and myself to tell us that we are to be assigned the task of translating the constitution of the congregation from German into English, so those persons not familiar with German could read it! I'm glad to do it, not that I have anything else to do!"

Mary's smile went ear to ear as she said proudly, "Well, now, wasn't that just the best vote of confidence you could get. I am very proud of you dear!"

John sank into his easy chair and said, "That's not all. The Reverand has asked for a release from his call so that he can accept one from Casper. We decided to grant the release and also to call a student pastor from the seminary to serve the remaining ten months of this year, giving us time to find a suitable replacement. Well, I guess that is all for the day, did you save me any supper, I am famished!"

~~~~~~~~

Spring 1921: John pushed open the white-picket gate and walked up the board path leading to the back porch. Mary stood

Courtesy: Arnold Wamhoff

outside watching Jimmy and the girls trying to catch some of Jimmy's bunnies that had escaped their pen. She lifted her head as

John walked up. "Well, so there you are. I didn't know where you went, I noticed you took the car. What's going on?"

John took his hat off and washed his hands at the dry sink. "I guess you might say it's not the best of days. I just got word that Mr. Grabbert passed away last night. He was only seventy-four. I admired that man. He was a good neighbor and he was very successful—he made something of that place over there. Now, it's up to Fred and Smokey to take the reins. I guess they've already been to the bank and talked to them about the family debts. The bank has consented to transfer it all over to the boys and his children all signed."

~~~~~~~~~

It wasn't three days later that John stomped into the house at dinner time. "You know I told you that the bank consented to let the Grabbert family assume the debt. Well, just today they foreclosed on them. You can't trust them bankers is all I can say. So anyway, Mrs. Jim Yorgason from Burlington heard about it and she loaned Fred and Smokey the money to pay the damn bank off and save the ranch. Then, Mr. Newcomer was wanting to retire and get rid of his sheep and he sold them to the Grabbert boys. He said they could pay as they went."

John sat down at the table, "There are good and bad folks in the world; it's when the chips are down--- that's when you see their true colors! Those Grabbert boys will do just fine, they have gumption—got it from both their parents!"

~~~~~~~~~

That next evening they were sitting in the parlor when John remembered seeing the new theatre in Greybull that morning. "I tell you I can hardly wait to attend the Grand Theatre; they built it next to the Pavilion dance hall. Why they say it has the only pipe organ in all of Northern Wyoming! It's a fine-looking building with a ticket booth and everything. That will be right handy to take the grandchildren to and then take them home to their parents afterward!"

~~~~~~~~

~~~~~~~~

Spring: John told the girls that they would be going into the bean field to pull the weeds before the rows closed. Mary volunteered to go with them, just to get some time with her girls. They walked up and down the rows of Great Northern Beans, bending and pulling out weeds like Horseweed, Ragweed, and Russian thistle. "Dad said, "Pull anything that isn't a bean plant."

Courtesy: Arnold Wamhoff

Working hard, they also enjoyed sharing the local juicy news and updates on boys! Mary hung in there with her daughters for half of the day, then retreated to her kitchen.

~~~~~~~~~

October 1921: Bill was out in the big field next to the house, driving the Minneapolis Moline tractor, pulling the iron-toothed harrow over the rough ground. Seven-year-old Jimmy was on his way home from school when he spotted Bill out in the field. That was about the same time he noticed a ragged-looking man with long hair walking down the road towards him. Of course, images of the Boogie Man exploded in his head, and in his panic, he ran straight toward where brother Bill was, out in the field. He stumbled and fell once but picked himself up, running as fast as his little legs would carry him---he knew that Boogie Man was behind him.

He tried to yell to Bill, but the tractor made too much noise and Bill didn't hear him. Running alongside the big tractor, Jimmy reached up in desperation and grabbed onto the canvas water bag that hung behind the tractor seat. He felt the pull of massive tractor wheels grinding through the soil in front of him and the sharp spikes of the harrow behind, nipping at this pant legs as he clung to the bag for dear life.

Bill felt his canvas bag move and turned to see what was the cause. He was horrified to see his little brother hanging on for dear life. Bill stomped on the tractor's brake with both feet, reaching for his brother at the same time. Jimmy heard the tractor's roar come to a stop only to be replaced by his brother's roar. "What in the holy hell do you think you are doing, Jimmy? You could have been ground to a pulp by that harrow, not to mention the wheels of Big Bess here!"

Young Jimmy had been scared to death, he was shaking and fighting the tears which threatened to explode from his eyes. "I—I uhhh- buttt, I saw the Boogie Man coming down the lane, honest I did! All I could think of was that you could save me."

Bill looked in the direction of the house and to his amusement saw the familiar figure of the old peddler who occasionally walked house to house selling his wares and fixing broken pots! Bill couldn't help but laugh as he said, "Ahhh Jimmy, that's only Ole Homer the peddler---he won't hurt you none and he sure ain't the Boogie Man, but if there was such a thing, he does look like one! I got me a feelin' that Ted has been filling your head with Boogie Man stories again. You have to remember to be more careful around machinery like this. My God, I can't even think about what might have happened if I hadn't felt the pull on my water bag!"

Well, that cured Jimmy from running behind a big iron tooth tractor but he still kept one eye peeled for that Boogie Man!

~~~~~~~

July 14, 1924: Since neither of them had any chores to do and it was a nice summer day---and Jimmy's birthday, Jimmy and Albert agreed to saddle up their horses and take a ride out in the hills to see if there were any antelope to chase. Jimmy said, "I heard Brother Bill tell Ted that there's never been a horse born that can outrun a pronghorn antelope. Them suckers can run circles around a horse and turn on a dime. Even if you had a fast horse, you'd not stand a chance because those pronghorns never run in a straight line either. They remind me of those barn swallows—dodgin', dartin', jumpin' all over the place until you are plumb dizzy. Why he said even a flash of lightning can't hit a pronghorn antelope!"

Albert punched Jimmy in the arm and laughed, "Now you are pulling my leg—you can't fool me like you think you can---I know you. But, I 'speck we might as well ride out and see if we can spot any antelope this side of Coon Creek."

Albert said, "Say, Jimmy, did your mother bake you a birthday cake since today is your 10th birthday? Are you going to have a party?"

Jimmy puffed out his chest, "You bet she did—one of her special chocolate cakes with sour cream frosting and ice cream too. We are going to wait until Brother Bill and Dad are in from the fields—going to have a big family party tonight! You can come over if you want, Albert, since you're my best-est friend and all."

Albert said, "Do I have to bring you a present if I come?"

Jimmy said, "Well now if I was coming to your birthday party would you like it if I brought you a present?"

Albert blushed and replied, "Well now, I guess I would. I'll look through my sock drawer and see if I can find a decent pair—one that hasn't been darned!"

Jimmy said, "I suppose you can just come on over without a present. Knowing you, you'd wrap up a rock for a present!" Ahhhhaahaaa

Albert said, "Real funny Jimmy. I wouldn't bother with a whole rock, just a bunch of gravel for you!"

~~~~~~~~

After a full day of riding the hills between Garland and Emblem, Albert and Jimmy started for home. Albert said, "By gosh Jimmy, you weren't foolin' me this time. Those dad-blame antelope we seen ran like the devil was after em'; I never knew that about those animals. How do hunters get a shot in and kill 'em? It looks to me like they could outrun a bullet. That's probably why there are so many of them!"

The two friends had a good laugh and kicked their horses into a trot as the afternoon was getting late. As they neared their homes, they pulled up their horses beside a ditch, so they could have a drink. Jimmy said, "Say, Albert, we will have to take a ride up to my Dad's other farm and look at his corn. He says it's as high as his biggest draft horse. We could play hide and seek in it all morning!"

Albert said, "I'll have to see if my folks have any chores for me to do. Dad gets plenty mad if I play around too much and don't tend to my chores. I don't get to lay around and just ride horses most of the time like you do. I'm not the baby in the family---I don't get spoiled like you!"

Jimmy's eyes opened wide, then narrowed as he felt himself getting mad. "Baby, huh? Well, I don't know why I'd want to spend my 'baby' birthday with some old slobberguts like you!"

Albert's face got red as he rebutted, "Well you, you slimy booger eater----"

Jimmy shot back as he mounted his horse, "Stinky pus gut"!

Then Albert came back with---"Turd Bird!"

Jimmy reined his horse toward home, kicked it, then shouted the ultimate retort--- "TURKEY DINK!"

Jimmy ducked his head just as Albert's dirt clod whizzed past his head.

The next day they were buddies again! And, Albert didn't have to worry about a birthday gift.

~~~~~~~~~

1925: Every single day in the '20s was a struggle on the farm, but the Wamhoffs were holding their own. They had a little water for the crops but were still in what was considered a drought. Most farmers planted crops that would grow with a minimum of water, like winter wheat and other grains. John said, "It's those sheep that are keepin' us afloat--- best decision I ever made—to make sheep a big part of our operation. Folks are doing their darndest to dig themselves out of debt. However, even the prices I get for yearlings and the wool has dropped. It's just that during the war, we couldn't produce enough grain, meat, and wool and got top

dollar; now, the market is saturated and we get bottom dollar."

"And Mary, I must say, I am certainly glad that you don't wear your skirts as short as our daughters and as some of the younger women do. It borders on indecent if you ask me, annnnnnd those hats---I guess you all wore big hats when you were young too, but some of these look like they took a bucket and put it on their head!"

Mary laughed and said, "You should just hear the girls when they are looking through the Sears and Roebuck catalogs. *Oh, Marie, look at this—isn't that just the Bee's Knees!*

"Helen is all upset because as she says, she doesn't have any 'bubs' yet and wants to know 'when' they will grow?" Mary threw her hands in the air.

John just shook his head and muttered, "Those girls are your territory, I'm going to the barn for safety! I liked them better when they were little. What gets me is that out here on the farm, we are working our can's off and in the cities, they are doing the Jitterbug, Charleston, Fox Trot—and don't get home until the sun comes up. We get up when the sun comes up and work like the devil all day long. They play all night and sleep all day. We work all day and sleep at night! There's something wrong with that business!"

~~~~~~~~~

Two weeks later: John held up a picture of a car for Mary to take a look at. "I just ordered one of these Chevrolets, it's a dandy—will make a nice car to drive to Yellowstone Park when we go next summer, wouldn't you say?"

It's a beauty and I get them for half price because I'm a dealer. That's the other venture I've made that has sure paid off. As much as we like cars and all, especially Bill---and how he can work on them just amazes me. Anyway, I know we have talked about taking a trip to Yellowstone Park for a long time and I think now that Ted and Arnold are old enough, and out of their nappies, that they'll enjoy the scenic drive and adventure of staying in the park for a few days too."

Mary clapped her hands, "Oh John, that is so exciting, but I thought we had to watch our spending; and here you are buying a car and planning a vacation? I don't understand, but I'll leave all that up to you. I have wanted to take that trip for so long and the boys will be 'to the moon'." John said, "I think we should just take Ted and Arnold, Bill needs to stay here and run the operation. By the way, Mary, have you talked to Old Jim? I know he hasn't been feeling that well lately and refuses to go in to see the doctor."

Mary said, "First of all, I'll call Marie and see if she can come out and stay at the house for a few days and handle the switchboard and post office. Ruth said she would come over if they needed her, but she has her hands full with her own house and those babies. Bill needs someone to cook for him too. I have to admit I miss Adella since she married Richard Smith and moved to Pratt, Kansas. She was such a hard worker; I'm afraid I have lost my household help as they all went off and got married. But I'll figure a way to get it all done---it also means less washing, cooking, and cleaning! I might even find some time to enjoy myself a little bit!---Oh, and no, I haven't talked to Jim, but I've noticed the way he moves—like he's hurting real bad."

~~~~~~~~

They loaded up the new Chevrolet and headed for Yellowstone Park. John pulled out onto the highway and turned the car to the west. About twenty miles out of Emblem, they noticed a dust cloud rising above the prairie, not far from the road. When they got close enough, they were thrilled to see it was the Macalla Peaks band of wild horses, and they were right near the road.

Jimmy and Ted yelled, "Dad, slow down, slower so we can see them. Look at that black one and the paint. They look good for wild horses don't they, Dad? How do you suppose they got out here?"

John said, "Well now, there are several opinions as to just how they did get out here, all wild now. Some say they are leftover Indian horses and others say they are from hundreds of years ago—Spanish conquerors or something and another. I can't say for sure where they did come from, but that is a handsome bunch of horse flesh if you ask me. Some of them look to have a little Arabian blood in them."

John said wistfully, "There is just something about horses that tends to get under your skin. You never forget how they smell and how it feels to climb on their backs and let them run. How it feels when they are running hard---the way their muscles push and pull—their strength. They are all pretty darn special if you ask me."

They drove west for fifty miles where they stopped and had lunch in a Cody restaurant which was a treat in itself for Mary and the boys. After lunch, they followed the one-way road up the canyon, where hundreds of men had built the Buffalo Bill Dam by blasting, digging, and cutting through the stone canyon to the most narrow spot, where they poured the cement dam. There was a man in a 'lead' car that took five cars through the narrow one-lane, one-

way dirt road up the canyon. On the other end, he would turn around and lead those waiting cars back the other way.

Courtesy: Arnold Wamhoff

Mary said, "Well now, I could have done without this narrow road. I can see why it took them so long to build that dam—they had to build a road to it first!" While they waited their turn in line, Ted and Jimmy entertained themselves by throwing rocks over the edge down into the Shoshone River below.

The boys loved going through the narrow tunnels. Once through the worst part, John pulled over and they all got out to see the vastness of the concrete dam and how it was built to hold the water back. The mountains rose majestically out of the beautiful grassy valley to the west, where the snowmelt and rainwater from the mountains were channeled down into the reservoir. Every so often, John stopped to let the car cool down. Mary took the opportunity to walk along the road and pick wildflowers. "Oh John, just smell the air up here. It reminds me of when we came over the Bighorns all those years ago, and how wonderful the air smelled then and how cool it was—remember that?"

John said, "I could kick myself for not thinking to bring a fishing pole. Maybe we can buy one where we are staying tonight at Fishing Bridge Cabins."

It took them another hour to reach where they would spend the night. There was a long bridge that crossed the meandering Yellowstone River below---Fishing Bridge! There were some ideal ponds and spots where the fish lingered, and all along the bridge, people stood patiently fishing. Jimmy laughed and said, "Gee, I guess that is why they call this place Fishing Bridge. Are you going to buy some fishing poles here Dad, so we can fish too?"

John said, "Right after we register for our cabin, we'll check in the store for fishing poles. Now, boys, I don't want you to be

Courtesy: Arnold Wamhoff

scared, because these 'cabins' which we are going to be sleeping in, are large tents with wooden walls built around the sides so the bears can't join us in bed!"

John warned, "Remember, the bears are wild and if you see one, don't try and pet it. It would just as soon take a chunk out of your arm as hunt for food; especially don't go out at night alone. They have outhouses for people in the daytime, but they also have chamber pots in each of the cabins!" Just as they were driving through the rows of tent/cabins, they spotted a bear searching through the garbage cans for a snack. Jimmy squealed, "Oh my gosh, look, look over there, it's a real live bear!"

~~~~~~~~~

John was successful in buying a couple of fishing poles for the boys and they spent an hour fishing from the bridge while Mary took a nap before dinner. They both caught two fish, which the cook at the lodge was kind enough to fry for their dinner.

Mary folded her hands in her lap as she watched her sons gobble down the trout. "Maybe you should have caught a few more, those were sure tasty. I am sure we will get another chance to fish up here in the mountains. I so enjoy having somebody else fix supper, this is such a treat!" Mary paused and said, "You know John, I don't think I have tasted fresh trout since we came over the Bighorns back in 1901. Oh, land sakes, that was a spell ago, wasn't it?"

John reached over and squeezed her hand. "I am sorry Mary, that we haven't been able to travel around the country more. At first, we didn't have the means or the money, then the babies kept coming and I had more land and more work just to put bread on the table. Perhaps these next years will slow down a bit for us. With all of our daughters except Helen, married now, that leaves only the boys at home. I've been thinking, since you have to spend so much time at that telephone switchboard, perhaps we need to hire a girl to help with the house and garden. I know you aren't canning as much as you used to, but there is still too much work for you to do alone."

Mary put her head back, closed her eyes, and sighed, "Oh my goodness, you have that right. I don't have so many to cook for anymore, but there is still a lot of work to do and I am not getting any younger. I am lucky that Marie can come out from Greybull whenever I need her. That telephone and post office keeps me tied down."

They drove all through the next day. Mary said, "I had no idea Yellowstone Park was this big, it is so beautiful, I can see why they made it a National park. It is a special place. We've seen hot water come out of the ground at Thermopolis, but never so many geysers and mud pots as what's up here. But to think, that we are probably driving and walking right on top of what might be a vast lake of boiling water and mud is frightening in a way." They drove all day over graded dirt roads to their destination, the Old Faithful Inn. Mary stood in the lobby of the immense log building, turning around and around, looking up at the incredible hotel roofline. Jimmy said, "I sure do like those stuffed heads of bears, elk, moose, buffalo, and all the Indian things they have here. I never knew they could stuff a dead animal like that."

John said, "They built this structure in 1904 for $140,000. This lobby is seventy-six feet high and the style is called 'Parkitecture'! I read that this is the largest log structure in the world and is on the National Historic Landmark register. It sure is something isn't it?"

Mary replied, "It's amazing and so beautiful. How lucky we are to be standing here and we get to spend the night in it!"

After breakfast, the following morning, John, Mary, and the boys strolled around the boardwalk laid over the unstable crusty ground where mud spurted and hot water bubbled up in colorful pools. Everybody hurried to get a spot when the Old Faithful geyser began to sputter and burp--then it shot three stories up into the cool mountain air. They all clapped and their eyes were wide with wonder. Ted said, "WOW! It's hard to imagine the water goes back underneath us and we are walking on top of it. I wonder how deep it goes under the ground." John said, "Yes, it's like when one of your mother's pots begins to boil---when it gets to a certain temperature it blows—like her tea kettle"—he winked, "and her temper!" For that remark, he got a good solid sock on the arm!

They spent another week driving around the Park, seeing deer, elk, moose, eagles, and more bears; eventually making it to Jackson Hole. Mary took one look at the majestic Teton Mountains and commented, "I am most grateful we don't have to go over those mountains. My word, I never---have never seen anything like that! The next morning they piled in the car and headed for home. John said, "I hope you boys enjoyed yourselves and learned a lot about the park."

Jimmy said, "It was a swell trip, Dad, thanks for taking Ted and me along with you and Mother. We've never seen anything like this before in our lives! I wonder how many bears we will see along the road on the way home? We saw forty coming up."

Several days later they arrived back at the farm. It had been an amazing trip, but they were all glad to be home. Bill had done a good job, keeping the farm running smoothly and he welcomed them back with open arms. "It's swell to have you all back home, just in time for harvest. Jimmy, you have school starting in a couple of weeks—sixth grade! Boy—where does the time go. And Ted, your first year of high school. You two are going to miss out on all the harvest work, lucky ducks!"

~~~~~~~~~

That fall was a good one and the harvest season went smoothly; except for Old Jim, who was having a hard time with his back and didn't do any of the heavy lifting. John kept an eye on him and thought it was probably hurting him a lot more than he let on. "Say, Jim, when we are done with harvest, maybe you should make an appointment with the doctor in Greybull and get checked out—see if there is something they can do for you."

Jim shook his head, "Don't worry yourself none on this, John, and I mean it! I have already been to the doctors and there is nothing they can do for me except give me some pills to keep the pain at bay. I'll let you know when I've had enough! I just appreciate you letting me stay on here even when I'm not worth much."

John put his arm around the older man's shoulders, "Jim, this is your home, and don't forget it. I couldn't have done any of this without you, my right-hand man! You have been a blessing to us all and you never wanted much or asked for anything. I bought you that car ten years ago and I doubt if you have driven it fifty miles."

Jim grimaced as he tried to stand up, "You and Mary have been the blessing in my life---you gave me a reason to live. The opportunity to build this farm with you, John. It made all the difference to me. And, and John---the way you and Mary always include me in your family. Why you will never know what that means to me!"

~~~~~~~~~

The holiday season came and went with lots of cooking, laughing, and memorable family times around the table heaped high with good farm cooking! As soon as the natural springs in the hills froze over, all the kids who lived on the Bench were quick to grab their home-made wooden ice skates and head for the hills. Jimmy told his mother that night, "It was sure a swell night, we built a big bonfire and it wasn't cold at all. That natural spring sure is running a lot of water over the ground this winter—that ice skating pond was big!"

That winter was a good one too, with lots of snow in the mountains---which meant water in the ditches come next spring. Ted wasn't that fond of high school and he begged John and Mary to let him quit and work on the farm. "It's what I am going to be, a farmer—it's what I want to be anyway, so why do I have to waste time with more school?"

John said, "You finish out this year and we'll see. I think you have confirmation coming up in May, isn't that right? Have you been learning the Lutheran catechism at Saturday School?"

Ted sat up straight, 'Yes Dad, the pastor has been grilling us every Saturday when we gather to study it. I'll be glad when that's over too."

Mary said, "Well, we will have a big family dinner for you on your confirmation day---everybody will be here who lives close by." Ted added, "Do I get a new suit like Bill did—and maybe shoes too? I've growed out of the ones I have now, my toes are about to poke through the ends any day!"

Mary laughed and said, "Yes, of course, you get a new suit of clothes---you are growing so fast, Ted, I can hardly keep you in shoes. I think you are going to be as big as your brother Bill."

Ted laughed and said, "I hope I grow bigger than him, then I can whoop on him once in a while and win!"

~~~~~~~~

April 1926: First thing that spring, on a whim, John bought a white Aryshire bull with brown patches. Mary took one look at the bull and said, "John, what in the world did you buy that bull for?"

John scratched his head and looked at the ground, "Well now, I don't rightly know except they are a good dairy breed and I figured I want to see what kind of a calf we'll get when he breeds our Jersey cows. I guess you might say, it's an experimental purchase!"

Mary said, "Well, he isn't much to look at, and that sound he makes when he is bellowing at the cows is enough to peel the paint off the barn. It sends chills down my back it's so high pitched and all! It looks to me like he is plenty onery as well---see how he butts the other cows. I don't think he's a very good buy but we will see what kind of calves he produces!"

~~~~~~~~

True to her word, John and Mary gave a big family dinner for Ted when he was confirmed into the Lutheran church that spring. Later that month, Mary wrote her sister Emma a letter and sent a picture of Ted and Jimmy on Ted's confirmation day.

Dear Emma,

Well now, our Theadore has been confirmed and that leaves one to go. Ted is getting so tall, he's like watching corn grow. He and Bill have the Westerhoff height, just like our brothers do. Arnold hasn't started to grow yet, but he has that long lean Westerhoff body. I 'spect that he will shoot up here any time now. He's plenty worried that he isn't going to grow tall.

We enjoyed that trip to Yellowstone Park last summer. Traveling on dirt roads all the way wasn't the best, but I'm not complaining.

Courtesy: Arnold Wamhoff

I am going to try and find time to make another trip to Nebraska to see Charlie and Lena and their new baby. Maybe you can come over from Mitchell for a few days and we can catch up. Ruth and Bill have three little boys now, Esther has a boy and a girl and we love having them live close. Betty June is always over here tagging along with Jimmy and Ted or going to town with John who takes her to the movies. John loves his grandchildren and always has a 'big nickel' in his pocket for them! Adella is going to have a baby soon. Our Bill has a girlfriend—she lives in York, Nebraska. He met Anna at a dance here in Emblem. He fell hard for this girl.

She is a very sweet girl and I hope they will get married someday. Bill wants to have enough money to buy them a house right away.

John and I are doing fine. My arthritis has been acting up—mostly in my knees. I guess that's life. My hair has gone to white, just like Paps. It makes me feel old, but I like it quite a lot when the girls fix it up for me. I will let you know when I will be in Garland next.

With Love Mary

May 1926: Mary said, "I'm cutting down on the size of my garden since it's just the boys at home now. I also decided to keep around 200 laying chickens—but we'll eat the rest of those fryers. That egg money comes in handy!"

John said, "I am going into town today, so I'll take the eggs and cream in if you want me to."

Courtesy: Greybull Standard

Mary replied, "That would certainly help. Any reason why you are going in today? Perhaps a movie or two? What's playing." John hugged her and said, "The Flying Ace" if you must know!"

Spring 1926: Jimmy and Ted inhaled their breakfast, but before they could make their get-away out the back door, John said, "Now, just hold it you two! Before you go riding out in those hills again, you need to check with me to make sure you have all of your jobs done. Ted, did you muck out those stalls in the cow barn like I told you to do?"

Ted looked down at his feet and shuffled them a bit. "Well, no, I was waiting until tomorrow morning, after milking. There's no harm in waiting another day—just more manure!" He laughed at his joke. But his father wasn't laughing.

John stood, pushed back his chair from the table, and grabbed Ted by the arm. "When I tell you to do something, you get it done and you don't wait another day, or until after you take another ride out in the hills." John grabbed his razor strap off the wall and swung it across Ted's behind, then he kicked him in the pants. "Now get out there and clean out those stalls, and when you are done, I'll have a look at them to see if they are done right. NOW!" John gave Ted a shove out the door and turned to find Mary and Jimmy staring at him. Jimmy quickly wiped the tears from his cheeks. "I'll go help Ted, is that okay Dad?"

John just grumbled something and went back to the kitchen table.

Mary said, "Now John, was it necessary to use the strap on him for that?"

John whirled and shouted, "Don't you ever criticize the way I discipline my sons. They need to learn to get their chores done before they take the day off!"

Mary stood her ground and looked him straight in the eyes, and declared, "Now, John, I don't ever say too much to you at all about disciplining our children, but using that razor strap has gotten to be a habit with you and I don't like it one bit. There is no reason to use that thing on those boys for forgetting a chore!"

John's eyes blazed as he shot back, "I would advise you to mind your own business. Those boys have to learn to get their chores done when they are told to do them and that's the end of it!"

Mary stood nose to nose with him as she drew herself up straight and got right in John's face. "Don't you ever, tell me, to mind my business, when my sons are my business, as much as they are yours. You don't tell me what to say or what to do. I've been married to you for a long time, John Wamhoff, and always went along with what you decided on, but today you drew the line and I won't have it. I won't stand by while you whip our son like one of your animals, not in a month of Sundays, I won't!"

John had enough sense to see that he wasn't going to win this argument. He turned his back on her and stomped out of the house, making sure to slam the door harder than usual.

On his way to the barn, John met up with Ted who said, "Dad, come and take a look at the job Jimmy and I did in mucking out the stalls. If it's good enough, can we go riding now?"

John stuck his head inside the barn door and back out in a minute. "That will do. You boys go on now."

John stalked off toward the field. Jimmy looked at Ted and said, "Boy, something got under his saddle. I think him and Mother had a fight—I heard them yelling at each other!"

Ted said, "Well, that explains it—he musta lost!" They both giggled as they saddled their horses.

Jimmy ran up to the back door to let their mother know they were leaving. He bumped into her just as she was coming out with a basket of wet clothes. He kissed his mother on the cheek. "Ted and I finished with our chores and are going to take that ride to the hills now. I'm glad I have such a good brother, we always have fun together. We'll be back in time for supper, Mother, bye now!"

Mary watched as her two youngest sons galloped up the lane between the large cottonwood trees John had planted fifteen years ago. The boys whooped and hollered until they were out of earshot.

"Ted and I had lots of fun together—he was two years older than me and used to tease me a lot too. We'd be over across the road there at Albert Blank's house and on the way home, Ted would say, "I think I saw something under that bridge, it was all hairy and had big shiny teeth". Then he'd take off running, he was bigger than me and knew I couldn't catch up with him. All that time I was looking back over my shoulder to see if anything was chasing me!

I remember Ted warning me about the threshers. "They will give you some chewing tobacco and tell you that you have to chew it to work with them. When you have it good and chewed, they will try and give you water to drink. IF you drink that water, you'll swallow the chew juice, and man, that will make you barf plus probably give you the' two-day' trots!" **Arnold Wamhoff on his brother Ted. 2003**

July 1926: Albert helped Ted, and Jimmy finished their chores early. Albert said, "Say, my sisters and some of their friends from over on the south line are in the back bedroom, looking at catalogs and talking about boys. I say we sneak over there and hide in the closet and listen to them. I snatched one of them catalogs my sisters look at too and it's full of women in panties and bras---it's really something, just wait until I show it to you!"

One look at the three of them and even a dummy would know by the silly grins on their faces, those boys were 'cookin' up a bunch of trouble. Ted was older but he liked hanging around Albert and Jimmy, and they knew the girls gossiped about juicy things when they got together and sat on the bed. The boys figured that a little excitement wouldn't hurt, it was a boring day anyway. So, off they ran, up the lane and across the road. They crawled under the barbwire fence and crept up to the backside of Blank's house. Albert opened the back screen door real careful like and they tiptoed inside. Sure enough, the girls were right there, sitting cross-legged on the bed just like Albert said they were. They had their backs toward the door. The three boys hit the floor and crawled until they reached the safety of the dark closet. They crammed themselves inside and waited---waited for the 'good' talk to start.

Alberts's sister was holding a catalog, "Oh my golly, I can just see myself in this dress. It shows a little cleavage but not too much of the bubs. You wanna give them a peek but not the whole show if you know what I mean." They all giggled.

Albert's sister said, "I wanna find something that will pop boy's peepers when I walk in the room. I don't want to look like some moll or nothing, but I wanna turn heads—you know—a sweet patootie!"

Albert and Jimmy had to put their hands over their mouths as they started to get the giggles. Ted gave them both the elbow and ran his finger across his lips to 'zip it'!

The girls started talking about which boys they would like to go out with. One girl, Ruby Mae said, "I can't wait to go to high school, there are so many cute boys. I wish Bill Wamhoff was going to high school. He's so tall and manly."

Then this girl named Betsy propped herself up on her elbow and said, "Have you seen those Lovell guys—well there is this one Korell fella, he has the prettiest blue eyes, and when he smiles they like crinkle up in the corners. He makes my knees go weak,--he's got it!"

The other girls covered their mouths and giggled, "You got that right!"

Well, Albert, Ted, and Jimmy couldn't keep quiet with that one as they exploded with laugher. The closet door flew open and the three eavesdroppers made a beeline for the door, all the while squealing with laughter and mocking---- "Ohhhheeeee, I really like those Lovell boys---ohhhh, me too!"

The girls stood up and looked at each other as the three boys ran from the dark safety of their closet and out the back door. "Ohhhh I hate those little devils! Little snipes---wait until I catch that Albert---I'll give him what for!"

On their walk back to the safety of the Wamhoff farm, Albert said, "What do you wanna do now? I got some Sears catalogs. We could look at the underwear pages---they got some really good ones in the new catalog!"

Ted said, "Naw, we gotta get home and get those eggs gathered or Dad will take the strap to us. He says if the skunks get the eggs because we didn't get to them in time, he'll swat us one time for each egg the skunks ate!"

Jimmy said, "Yeah, and I don't like going down to the chicken coop in the dark because Ted always runs away from me and yells that the Boogie Man is coming!"

Albert said, "Yeah Ted---you are the one the Boogie Man is going to get first because he's waiting at the corner of the granary for the first one by!"

They all laughed like it was some big joke, but truth be had---they all believed in the Boogie Man and avoided going out on moonless nights ---just in case that Boogie Man was hangin' around!

Albert said, "Well, now, I've been saving the ends of my dad's cigars. Have you ever smoked a cigar, Jimmy? Well, you come on over tomorrow!"

Jimmy's eyes got real big. "No Albert, I can't say that if have, but I've watched my Dad plenty!" He sat up real straight and using his two middle fingers, imitated smoking a cigar.

The next morning Jimmy didn't waste any time after chores to run across the road to where Albert lived. The boys crept out behind the barn where Albert had hidden the cigar ends. He pulled the gunny sacks off the can and proudly withdrew several 'two-inch long smoked cigars butts' along with a book of matches. The boys were real careful with the matches—they knew they would get the tar whipped out of them if they started a fire. Jimmy said, "You go first Albert, since, ahh, they're your cigars and all!"

Albert took a cigar butt and put the match to his, then to Jimmy's. Albert threw the match in the dirt and ground it out with his foot.

Both boys puffed out their chests and sat real straight like— like dignified men! At first, they both sucked in on the cigar, let the smoke roll around in their mouths, and then blew it out. After several puffs, Jimmy said, "I think my Dad breathes it in deep, then—blows it out, real far like!" Next round, they both inhaled, pulling the cigar smoke into their lungs and before they could exhibit their ability to blow it out into the air like their fathers, they began choking and coughing! After catching his breath, Albert tapped the ash off the end of his cigar and announced, "I would say, Jimmy, that we've got the hang of it, no problem!" They sat behind the barn for about another ten minutes, until the novelty of cigar smoking wore off and the butt-filled can was empty.

Albert propped himself up on one elbow and said, "Now this is livin'---we look like a couple of 'swells' I do believe we do. We look like we've been doin' this forever!" About that time' Albert turned a peculiar shade of green and said, "Awwww, I feel sorta dizzy and not so good!" Jimmy went to stand up and swayed a bit, "I don't feel too good either, I feel like I might barf!"

Jimmy said, "Let's go to my house and have some cold lemonade." They managed to make it back to the house where Mary intercepted them in the kitchen. "What have you two been up to?"

Jimmy said, "We don't feel too good Mother, I think we drank too much pop!"

Mary said, "Is that a fact? Let me smell your breath." She backed up with a sly grin on her face."That's not pop, that's cigars that got you sick. You two just go outside and suffer it out!"

After an hour or two of not knowing if they were going to live through the experience, the two boys decided to call it a day, but planned to go riding horses the next morning---Albert said, "Say about ten o'clock? Why don't you ride that big black one, Rex? He's a beauty and I'll bet he can run pretty fast."

Jimmy made a face and said, "Nah! Rex might be a good-looking horse but he has one thing on his mind and that is to find a lady horse. He doesn't want to work in the fields, pull a wagon, or go riding. He's too busy looking for a mare! I think Ted might like to come along with us---I'll ask him."

The next day was a Saturday, so the three of them decided to ride up and see the 160 acre-farm John had recently bought. It was about a mile west and then a mile south. Brother Bill was up there irrigating the bean and beet fields. It was a hot day and getting hotter as the boys trotted along the main road, then turned at the section road to the south. Ted said, "Let's race, last one to those trees, bites sheep nuts!"

Albert and Jimmy kicked their horses and leaning forward in the saddle, rode like the wind, hooping and hollering as they tore down the road. Albert and Ted were head to head as they thundered across the old board bridge that covered the canal. Jimmy was right on their tail riding old Bess-----and, then he wasn't. When Albert glanced back, there was no Jimmy---and he could see old Bess was lying on her side on the bridge!

Albert screamed at Ted while pointing behind them, "Something happened to Jimmy---I don't see him and there is his horse. Come on—we gotta see if he's hurt or playing a joke on us---maybe the Boogie Man got him!"

All joking stopped when they saw Jimmy's crumpled body lying on the other side of the drainage ditch. Old Bess was on her side with one foot down in a hole in the bridge. She was in bad shape, flopping all around.

Ted jumped from his horse and screamed at Albert, "Go, get Bill, tell him Jimmy is hurt. Oh, Albert---he's not moving—I think he's hurt bad, real bad. I'm going to jump the ditch and get to him. Ride! Find Brother Bill, he's over in that next field!"

Ted jumped the ditch and in seconds was beside his younger brother. Jimmy wasn't moving. He was unconscious. Ted held his finger under his brother's nose and saw that he was breathing. He patted Jimmy's cheek, gently, as tears rolled from his eyes over his ruddy cheeks. "Ahhhh Jimmy, brother---wake up, please wake up. Please don't be dead!"

Ted knew better than to move him—he knew he had to wait for Brother Bill who was strong enough to pick Jimmy up. Ted slid down to the ditch and threw his shirt into the ditch water, wrung it out, and scrambled back up the ditch to where his brother lay, not moving. Ted wiped Jimmy's face and laid the wet shirt across his forehead. Then, he prayed. "Oh Dear Jesus, please, please let my brother be alive, don't let him die. Please, dear Lord!"

The next thing Ted knew, Bill was kneeling on the ground beside Jimmy. After only a minute or two, he turned to Ted and Albert. "Jimmy's hurt real bad, it's his leg. I can't tell if it's broken or what, but it doesn't look right and I think he got knocked out. He's starting to moan so I think he's coming around."

Jimmy drew a long ragged breath as he clawed his way out of the darkness. He tried to move and felt a pain rip through his hip and leg. A red world of pain broke over him and he felt everything start to spin again as he cried out.

Bill stood up, a tower of a man, "Now look, you two ride like hell is chasing you and for hell's sake be careful. Get Dad and a wagon. Tell Mother to call the doctor from town. We got to get Jimmy across that ditch, but I don't want to move him till he comes around, he's in a world of trouble. I can carry him, that ain't the problem. Go NOW, RIDE!"

Chapter Fourteen

PRAYING FOR MIRACLES

1926: Mary stood at the kitchen sink preparing a fresh garden salad for supper when she saw Ted and Albert gallop full speed into the farmyard. *Oh, those boys, probably racing again or Ted told Jimmy a Boogie Man was coming! I guess boys will be boys—I certainly remember my brothers and the tricks they played on each other.*

Mary watched out the kitchen window as Ted leaped from his horse and ran for the house while Albert rode around the yard in circles, seemingly looking for John or somebody. Suddenly alarmed, Mary wiped her hands on her dishtowel and met Ted at the back door. "For heavens' sake Ted, you act like the devil was after you." She teased, "Was that Boogie Man chasing you, boys?" Mary took a look at Ted's face and knew in an instant, this was no joke or boy's game. "What is the matter, you are white as a sheet? Did something happen? Where is your brother?"

Ted grabbed Mary and propelled her through the dining room toward the switchboard. "Mother, it's J-Jimmy. His horse stepped in a hole in the bridge when we were racing and threw Jimmy over the drainage ditch, he's laying on the bank. Brother Bill is with him now, and he being in the army and all said we shouldn't move Jimmy until he comes to—he's knocked out. Bill said for you to call for the doctor from Greybull and for Dad to bring the wagon or car to get Jimmy home--- and-- and for him to come fast as he can."

Ted burst into tears---relieved that his message had been delivered—now all the emotions came bursting out as he sniffed his nose. "Mother, he said for you to get a bed ready for Jimmy. I'm gonna see if Albert found Dad."

Mary said, "I'm sure he did, I saw him head to the barn and that is where your father is pitching hay to the cows. Just go now, quickly--- and take your Dad to where Jimmy is." She threw her arms around Ted and said, "Don't worry son, you and Albert did what you could. These things just happen, I'm sure he will be just fine, don't worry yourself. You go now and I'll call the doctor! Say some prayers on the way!"

~~~~~~~~

Albert found John Wamhoff and between gasps of breath, filled him in. John Wamhoff decided at the last minute to take his Chevrolet, it was faster and gave a softer ride than the rumbling old wagon. Albert was told to go on home, or he could wait at the house with Mrs. Wamhoff as Ted jumped in the front seat with his father. "John said, "What the hell were you boys doing—racing again?"

Ted looked down at the floorboard and said, "Yes Dad, yes, we were, but it wasn't anybody's fault. That old Bess just happened to step in a hole in the bridge, and she's in a bad way too, Dad. I'm scared Dad, real scared. Jimmy was so white and laying there all crumpled. Bill said he knew what to do, learned it in the Army and, and---."

John slapped Ted alongside the head and said, "I told you, boys, not to race like that—somebody was going to get hurt, now didn't I—DIDN'T I? You never listen, and now your brother is hurt and it sounds bad."

Ted sobbed, "But Dad it wasn't my fault, it was an accident, we weren't doing anything we haven't done a hundred times. It wasn't my fault Dad, it wasn't!"

John pulled up to where he saw Bill squatting on the other side of the ditch. He braked hard on the Chevy and it skidded to a stop as a cloud of dust rolled on down the road. John and Ted opened the car doors and ran to the edge of the road. John said to Ted, "You go see if Bess is dead or not."

John slid down the steep bank and jumped the small drain creek then clawed his way up the other side as Bill stood. "Dad, thanks for coming so fast. Jimmy was knocked unconscious, but he has come to now. I remembered what the orderlies did in the war and I asked him what hurt and if he could move---all that stuff. He says his right leg, his hip hurt. I think he musta landed on that side. His arms and other leg are fine, he can move them all, but I think he hurt that leg pretty bad, he mighta broke it. Is Mother calling the doctor?"

John bent over his youngest son, "Yes, Bill, the doctor should be on his way out from Greybull." John put his hand under Jimmys' head then looked at his eyes and face. "Well then Jimmy, sounds to me like you tried to fly today and landed a bit hard. Don't worry, we'll get you fixed up in no time. You're a tough fella and you gotta be brave cause Brother Bill is going to pick you up, Jimmy; and it may hurt a bit, but we gotta get you across the ditch. I brought the car and we'll get you home in a jiffy where Mother is fixing a bed and the doctor from Greybull is coming out to check you over."

Bill kneeled on the dirt bank. He put one hand under Jimmy's head and slid his other hand slowly along under Jimmy's back. As soon as he reached the hip/left leg area, Jimmy cried out in pain. "Dad, I need a board to put under Jimmy's backside. We have to keep that hip immobile as I carry him. John grabbed an irrigating backflow board that was lying close by. Bill said, "That should do the trick. When I lift him, slide it under his hips."

Bill took off his shirt and wrapped Jimmy's lower body to the board so he was immobile. With one fluid movement, Bill stood put one arm under Jimmy's head, the other under the board, and lifted his brother in his arms. Jimmy let out a groan as Bill bent his knees to slide down the steep bank; wade across the stream, and carefully climb up the other side—all the while holding Jimmy as steady as he could. "Now then, Jimmy, I'm not going to lay you in the car, I'm going to sit in the back seat and hold you just like this— so we don't move you any more than we have to."

John opened the back door for Bill as he put one foot inside the car and fluidly moved his body, with Jimmy's broken one, into the backseat. Even with all that, Jimmy still felt it and let out a howl. John said, "Just a minute, Bill, I gotta check on Bess. Ted, you go on and get in the car."

Ted got into the car and watched to see what his father was going to do. "OH Bill, oh my gosh----he's gonna shoot Bess!" Ted put his face into his hands---"ohhh Bill." They both jumped at the sound of the pistol's report. John walked slowly back to the car. "Her leg was broke—she was in a bad way. There's nothing to be done for a broken leg in a horse. I couldn't let her suffer any longer. I saw the hole her leg went into, it wasn't a big one, just the right size to snap it. Ted come with me, let's see if we can pull her off the road just a little bit. I'll have Jim and Herbie come out with the wagon and take her out to the cemetery hill dump. Now, to get this boy home. How are you doing there, Jimmy?"

Jimmy managed a weak reply, "Okay, Dad---it hurts something awful. I wanna go home—to Mother!" Tears started again, making trails down his dust splattered face. Bill patted his brother's shoulder and said, "Now don't you move, the ride will be short and we'll be home. Be brave my little buckaroo!"

~~~~~~~~

Dr. Gorder arrived at the house about ten minutes after John and Bill eased Jimmy onto the bed Mary had made up for him in the parlor. She was pale, worry etched her face and her eyes were wide with fear.

Mary smoothed her hand gently over Jimmy's dark hair. Slowly and with purpose, she ran her hands down his leg—on the side he said hurt. When she got to where the femur goes into the hip socket, he let out a cry. "Oh Mother, no—that sure hurts there. What is the doctor going to do to me?"

John moved beside the bed and took Jimmy's hand, "Now son, I don't want you to worry. Your Mother and I are going to do everything we can for you. We want Dr. Gorder to check you out first---I'll drive you to Billings if I have to. We'll get you fixed up in no time."

John met the doctor at the back door. Explaining what had happened, he led the doctor into the bedroom where Jimmy lay on the bed. John and Mary stood near the bed while Bill and Ted waited over by the door. Bill put his arm around Ted's shoulder---"Ted, I know you are feeling bad about this but it was an accident, nothing more or less. It sure wasn't your fault. You did good, to get me over there right away."

Ted wiped the tears from his cheeks, then sniffed his nose and said, "Gosh almighty Bill, we was just having a race like we always do. Albert and I went over that bridge and our horses missed the hole---but Jimmy's horse hit it. I'll just never understand that. It makes me sick to my stomach that Dad had to shoot Bess too—she was a good horse."

~~~~~~~~~

Dr. Gorder pulled up a chair at the kitchen table and Mary poured him a cup of coffee and laid out the spice cake. John and Mary sat across from him. Dr. Gorder said, "Well now, I suspect he's cracked or broken something in the hip area—it's very tender and he can't put any weight on that leg. We have no way of seeing inside and telling what it is exactly. I would recommend keeping him off that leg as much as possible, use cold compresses and I'll leave a medicated rubbing ointment for it. I also gave him some laudanum to keep him calm and help him sleep. Give that to him to keep him quiet for a couple of days to give the leg a chance to heal. It could also just be a very bad bruise. I'll be out to check on him on Friday and we'll see how he is doing. Call me if he gets worse." After the doctor rose from the chair, he paused and said, "Whose idea was that to secure the boy to that board?"

John said, "It was our oldest son Bill—he served in WWI and saw a lot of injuries and what the medics did. It was his idea."

Dr. Gorder said, "He might have saved that boy from becoming a cripple by doing that when he did!"

John started to pay the doctor and he said, "Not now John, let's see how this goes. I can always send you a bill. No worries, you always pay your bills."

John and Mary walked the doctor to the door and thanked him for coming out so quickly. Mary walked slowly to the kitchen sink and looked out the window, her hands gripping the edge of the sink. John waved goodbye to the doctor, turned, and walked back into the kitchen where Mary stood shaking. John went to her and turning her around, he wrapped his arms around her. She laid her head on his shoulder and sobbed. "Ohhhh, John, I got me this feeling that he's hurt worse than we think or know. He doesn't remember things or recognize some things. "

John patted her back and wiped the tears from her cheeks, "Mary, now don't go getting yourself all in a state. We have to give it a couple of days and see."

Ted walked into the kitchen, "Dad, Mother—I want to ask if you will let me sleep on the floor next to Jimmy's bed tonight. I can get you if he has to get up or something. Please let me do that—he's my little brother and I feel like I'm responsible for him getting throwed and all!"

Mary said, "That's very sweet of you Ted—I think that might work out just fine. I'll show you how to use the urinal for him when he has to go to the bathroom or needs some water." She turned to go check on her youngest son, "And Ted, I do not ever want you to blame yourself. I know you do, but you weren't doing nothing you didn't do before---you boys were just having fun and it was an accident!"

Ted wrapped his arms around his mother as she comforted him. "None of us meant for that to happen, for Bess to step in that hole. Why didn't my horse or Albert' step in the hole? Only Jimmy's horse!"

~~~~~~~

Ted spent the night on a pallet on the floor next to his brother's bed. He helped Jimmy when he needed to pee and wanted water. Day after day, Ted never left Jimmy's side---he tried to entertain him and get him to remember things. "Hey Jimmy, remember when we was little and we'd pull up those big horse weeds, take the leaves off, leave the roots, and then pretend they were our horses? We called them our pretty dappled gray horses and even gave them names. We'd have races with them and just trot them up and down the lane."

Jimmy looked at Ted blankly replied, "No, I don't remember that, are you kidding me?"

Ted looked up at his mother with a worried face. Mary said, "Don't worry yourself none, Ted, that he doesn't remember. He took quite a bump on the head and sometimes it takes a spell before folks regain their memory."

A smile spread across Jimmy's face as he saw Old Jim standing in the doorway. "Is it okay if I pay the patient a short visit?"

Mary smiled and said, "Oh Jim, of course, come on in. He is about the same, not much change. We are trying to get him to remember things—he had a pretty good knock on the head too, but he remembers you, so that's a good sign."

Jim reached down and ruffled Jimmy's hair. "So you tried to fly over the drain ditch I hear? I know it hurts pretty bad right now

Jimmy, but you just gotta do what your folks and the doctor tell you to do. Say your prayers and you'll be up riding those horses before you know it. Promise me you'll take it easy now!"

Jim said, "I'll check in on you every day, but I gotta get to work or your Dad might fire me." Jim bent over and kissed Jimmy's forehead. "Be tough, mind your Mother!"

After Jim left, John went over to the bed and said to Jimmy, "Do you want to get out of bed, son, and see if you can walk on that leg?"

Jimmy's face went pale and he said weakly, "I guess Dad, but it hurts just laying in bed. I don't think I can stand on it."

Mary put her hand on John's arm. "John don't, it's too soon to try and get him to do more. Please don't!".

John pulled the covers back and started to help his youngest son out of bed and even before the boy was on his feet he was in greater pain and crying, "Dad, I can't, I can't stand---please Dad, don't make me!"

Mary intervened and said, "John, this isn't helping. It's too soon. I have been thinking since Dr. Gorder doesn't know what is wrong, we should take him to Billings, to that new Billings Clinic up there where they have better doctors and machines to check Jimmy out. We need to know what is wrong with his leg and back."

John slid his hand under Jimmy's neck and said, "Son, remember how you liked to hunt for bird's nests out in the orchard. Where is that Meadow Lark's nest, the one that was hard to see— can you remember that? Think hard now."

Jimmy closed his eyes and then he smiled and said, "Yes, I remember, it was up there by that alfalfa bush!"

John laughed and said, "THAT'S right! You can remember, yes you can! Your head is getting better, now we got to do something about that leg. Son, your mother and I want to take you to Billings to the clinic up there where they have doctors who know about accidents like this and trauma problems. How does that sound?"

Jimmy looked up at him with tears in his eyes, "Fine, Dad, fine; if they can help me to walk again."

~~~~~~~~~

Mary called the Billings Clinic and made an appointment with Dr. Arthur J. Movius, the head of the clinic. Two weeks later they sat in his office. After examining Jimmy he said, "The trouble is with the boy's hip—it's possible it was traumatized and cracked in the fall; the accident also may have injured his spine. We want to use this new machine on Jimmy to see inside, it's called an X-ray machine." They laid Jimmy on a table and pushed him under this big machine that could take pictures of his bones. When it was over they

Dr. Arthur J. Movius

waited for an hour or more and Dr. Movius came back into the room.

"Mr. and Mrs. Wamhoff, the X-ray shows that your son's hip socket is badly cracked and when he tries to stand on it, the big leg bone, the femur, pushes up into that hip cup. That socket or cup is packed with nerves, that is why when he puts pressure on it, he experiences great pain. He also has a slight curvature of his spine. He is at a crucial age in his skeleton development when his bones and tendons are growing the most. I suggest putting him in a body cast that will stabilize that leg and hip so they grow correctly.

John looked at Mary and before she could respond, he said, "Absolutely not. We do not want our son put in a cast because then he WILL be crippled for life!"

Dr. Movius shook his head and said, "I strongly disagree, but he is your son. The second-best thing I have to suggest is that you take him home and keep him in bed—off that leg for the next year."

~~~~~~~~

For the next nine months, twelve-year-old Jimmy laid in bed, in the small room next to his parent's bedroom---(the room that later became the family bathroom).

NOTE—from Jimmy's 2003 interview: '*I laid in bed in that tiny room for so long—that was a terrible thing for a young kid to go through, but I did it'*.

It was about two in the morning when Mary woke from a sound sleep to hear Jimmy sobbing in the next room. She climbed from their bed, threw her chenille robe on, and walked barefoot into the small bedroom where her youngest son lay on his narrow bed. She knelt beside him. "Arnold, son---what is the matter? Are you having trouble sleeping, are you in pain?"

Jimmy pushed himself up on one elbow, tears running down his thin adolescent face. "Oh Mother, why did God let this happen to me? Why did he let me be crippled like this? Why doesn't he fix me? I believe in him and he lets me suffer, lets me lay here and I hurt all over Mother. There isn't one place down there that doesn't hurt. I don't understand why he would do this to me?"

Mary took his tender young face in her hands and stroked his cheeks. "Oh Arnold, it wasn't God that let this accident happen—it was God that let you live."

Jimmy looked up at her and said, "I wish he hadn't Mother. I wish this had never happened to me. It's too hard, I don't have any hope of ever getting to do the things kids my age do or even to grow up like Bill and Ted. I am useless, Mother, do you understand? Why me, Mother, why did this happen to me?"

Mary stood and looked down at him. "Arnold, it was something that just happened—God didn't make it happen. Sometimes in this life, bad things happen to us and we try to blame him. I never told you this, but the first baby I had was a beautiful little girl. She didn't live. She died right after she was born---there was a problem with her that we couldn't fix. God didn't make that happen and later he gave us eight other children. I want you to understand that this too shall pass. You have to believe and will yourself to walk again; you will have a life. You only have to have faith that God will lead us to the healer. God is near, he is going to help you recover, he sees you, he hears you and he will answer our prayers in his time."

"Did you ever think that perhaps you were meant to die that day and God stopped that---he let you live? You have a purpose on this earth, Arnold, and you have to find it deep inside you to gather the strength to rise and overcome this. Pray on it, son, pray very hard as your father and I do every night."

The next morning, Old Jim walked into the house and made his way back to where Jimmy lay on his bed. Jimmy perked up when he saw his favorite fellow. Old Jim kelt beside the bed and ruffled Jimmy's hair. "So, how's my best boy doing today? I hear you are in a lot of pain---I wish there was something I could do to make it go away!

Jim pushed himself to his feet and said, "I know this has been the hardest thing you have ever been through. I know a few things about making yourself go on even though you don't think you can. I have lots of faith in you boy, that you will try your best to get that hip back to working real good again. I just wanted to tell you that I'll be praying for you Jimmy, every night I do! You are a strong young man and I know you will get the job done! I wait for the day that you are up following me all over this farm again."

Jim bent over Jimmy's bed and ---he hugged the boy, the boy that had taken a likin' to him ever since he could walk. Jim walked out of the room with tears in his eyes and a prayer in his heart. *Please, Dear Lord, heal our Jimmy, give him his life back. Don't let him suffer anymore. We both know what a lifetime of suffering does to a man. Amen.*

~~~~~~~~~

A few days later, John walked into Jimmy's bedroom and said, "I've been talking to Mr. Grabbert and they all think the mineral baths in Thermopolis might help you. I know lots of people who go down there often; so your mother and I are going to drive you down there to see if that might give you some comfort and help you walk."

John and Mary discussed what an extended stay in Thermopolis might mean. Mary said, "John, I've arranged for Ruth, Esther, Marie, and Helen to each take a day working the switchboard and taking care of the post office. Even Old Jim said he could handle that job, as he wasn't much good for anything else anymore. I know you could find others who would be willing to come in and help out."

Mary said, " I realize we are not in the best of financial situations either, times are so hard right now. Can we afford this? I don't know how long we will have to be down there. We'll have to rent a room and there's food and all."

John clenched his jaw and said, "I don't care if it takes two years—three years, we'll get along here on the farm. I know it will be hard on you Mary as well, to stay down there with him, but I also know you wouldn't be anyplace else. He is our son, our last son, and we are going to see him get better. End of story!"

Two days later they made Jimmy comfortable in the back seat of the car and headed for Thermopolis. John's hands gripped the steering wheel until his knuckles were white. "It's worth anything to get our boy well and back on his feet. Mary, don't you worry about the farm, telephone, post office, or garden--we will handle it all from there. What's important is that you are there with Jimmy. We have to hope and to pray that this is what God has in store for our son!"

~~~~~~~~~

Thermopolis 1927: Jimmy sat in the hot sulfur water baths for several hours each day for several weeks and then a masseuse worked on his muscles and ligaments. It helped some, but he still had trouble and pain when he stood and his walk was not fluid. The masseuse took Mary aside and told her that he didn't think the boy would live to be seventeen, but Mary wouldn't have it.

"We are going to find a way to help him live a normal life. I'll take him to the end of the earth to find somebody, something that will help him!"

The next day Jimmy was playing cribbage—a new game he'd learned between treatments. He got up from the table and walk unsteadily across the room to speak to his Mother. A new doctor who was staying there was watching him. Dr. Arnoldus walked over to Jimmy and said, "I'm an osteopathic doctor and I think I know what is wrong with you. You and your mother come up to my room in an hour."

In an hour, Mary walked with her youngest son up to the new doctor's rooms where he put Jimmy on a long skinny table. He moved his hands over Jimmy's legs and hips. He smiled and nodded his head---he knew what he had to do. Then, he began to massage and adjust Jimmy's bones. "This is called Chiropractic medicine and it is the medical movement or adjustment of bones, muscles, and ligaments—coaxing them back to where they belong. With my hands, I can feel that you have a bunch of things we have to put back in their place, then you will feel better and walk better. I want you to come back tomorrow to see me and I will give you another treatment. I want you to sit in the hot springs an hour before I work on you and an hour afterward. We'll see how you feel in the morning and if I am right, you will already feel better by then."

Dr. Arnoldus put the boy on an all-milk diet—"He needs calcium and lots of it. This accident couldn't have happened at a worse time in his life—these next few years are his main growth period---adolescence. His bones need a great amount of calcium, especially because he is going to be tall. We will begin with one quart of whole milk a day." By the end of that year, Jimmy was drinking eleven quarts of milk a day—every day. (*He didn't have a cavity in any of his teeth until he was 65 years old*).

The next morning Mary awoke to the sound of Jimmy's voice, "Mother, Mother, come here. Oh, Mother, that is the first time I have slept through the night in as long as I can remember, without pain. Ohhhh, Mother, I'm getting better, I am, I am!"

Dr. Arnoldus and Jimmy

Mary hugged her son and sat with him for a while and then excused herself to the bathroom. She leaned against the wall and let the emotion come out in choking sobs of gratitude and relief. 'Oh dear Lord Jesus, thank you for bringing us down here and for this doctor. Our son, our Jimmy, is going to be okay. Thank you!" Mary slumped to her knees and continued to cry until there were no more tears.

She tried to fix her face as well as she could when she heard a knock on the door.

"Hey Mother, I have to get to my doctor's appointment."

Mary rented a room for more than a year at the hotel in Thermopolis and stayed there with her son while he had daily treatments from Dr. Arnoldus. John came down when he could get away, and one day they even had a photo taken—the three of them.

Every day, the doctor would adjust the young boy--- morning, noon, and night to keep his growing bones straight and strong, and most important of all, he said, "We can make these corrections and try to

Courtesy: Arnold Wamhoff

teach the bones and ligaments to function as they should. He is growing so fast at this time of his life, that this is most important we stay on top of these adjustments and guide his bones so he will walk straight. I am afraid he might have one leg shorter than the other because of the trama and lying in bed for so long. However, by putting a small lift in his one shoe, he will walk straight like any other young man, maybe a slight limp. He will most likely have periodic pain for the rest of his life, but the lift will also help make up for the difference in the length of his legs, so his back doesn't take the brunt of it."

Arnold Wamhoff: *"I stayed out of school one year, during the sixth grade. Mother stayed with me down at Thermopolis. She got school books and lesson books from the teachers for me and also* *she helped me study the Lutheran Catechism, so I could be confirmed when we went home again. We were quite poor and the chiropractic treatments were $1.25 each, so that added up to $3.75 a day. That was a lot of money back then. Dr. Arnoldus wasn't concerned with payment, he said we could pay it off over the next years. I grew about six inches during the time we were down there. My legs grew long and strong. We had to eat and stay there at the mineral springs hotel---that added up to a lot of money. When I got better and came home, I went to high school. I remember one time Dad asked me to run up a hill. I couldn't do it! Dad didn't want me to be a farmer. He said I was good with numbers and I should be an accountant or a banker. He believed farming would be too hard for me. But I loved the farm and that is what I chose!*

~~~~~~~~

Mary and Jimmy had been gone from the farm for over a year. Over that time, John developed some new ideas about the small bedroom where Jimmy had slept for those months after his accident. He converted that bedroom into their modern bathroom. He had it and the kitchen plumbed, a septic tank put in, and ran more lines with power to the house---which came from the huge windmill driven generator.

~~~~~~~~

1927: Dr. Arnoldus decided Jimmy was ready to take on the world. He gave him two pages of exercises and suggested he take a hot bath every night. "I think you and your Mother can pack your bags and plan to go back home by the end of the month. You have done well Arnold, and I think you should have a good life. You will have some pain and I would suggest you work at something other than being a farmer—that will be hard on you. I would like to see you every two weeks for a few months, then once a month, just to keep you adjusted while you are growing so fast. I would also suggest that you see a good chiropractic doctor throughout your life to keep your body in line and adjusted!"

Jimmy shook Dr. Arnoldus's hand and said, "Thank you, Doctor, you have made me feel so much better---almost like my old self. I can't wait to get home and see my old pals and my horse Buck."

Dr. Arnoldus said, "I don't want you to trot on that horse, nothing must jar your back right now. You can ride your horse, but only at a walk. You will have plenty of time to ride your horse later on--just like old times, but later."

Summer: John packed up the car with all of the belongings which Jimmy and Mary had accumulated over the past year. He made sure Jimmy was comfortable in the backseat, then he opened the front passenger door for Mary. "I almost forgot to tell you that your cherry trees are in full bloom. The onions, lettuce, and radishes are up and the potatoes are about two inches high. The girls did a right fine job of planting that garden for you. Okay now, we are all ready to make the drive to Emblem. I have waited for this day for oh---so long. It just didn't seem like home with you both gone."

John could hardly wait to get Mary and Jimmy home---he had a big surprise for them and he kept giving out little hints until Mary was about to clobber him.

"John Wamhoff, what have you gone and done now? You didn't paint the house red or something did you?"

John reached over and kissed her cheek, "No Mary, but you are going to love this--- it's actually a gift for the whole family and especially our young man here!"

Finally, they drove down the shaded lane, between the huge cottonwood trees to the white farmhouse. John pulled the car to a stop. "Well, here we are—home! Are you ready to see the rest of the family AND the surprise?"

John carried the suitcases into the house where Bill, Ted, Helen, Marie, Ruth, and her family were waiting. After the ceremonious hugs and kisses, Jimmy said, "Okay Dad, where is the surprise?"

John winked and said, "Your first clue is--- it's inside the house. You find it!"

Mary went to the kitchen first---nothing new. Then to the back porch and summer kitchen—nothing new. She hurried back inside the house and into the dining and living room---nothing new. Mary walked toward their bedroom and on the way, THERE it was! The new modern bathroom with candy pink fixtures!

Mary held her hand over her mouth and Jimmy pushed everyone aside as he walked into the small room where he had spent a year of his life. They were speechless. John was grinning ear to ear as he said, "I---I bought you a bathtub, not just any white bathtub—this one is a candy pink with claw feet—the latest thing out—colored tubs sinks, and stools---the whole shebang!"

Mary's eyes grew large and a bit moist as she replied, "Oh John—really you bought us a matching bathtub, sink, and toilet? But Candy 'pink'? Honestly, John—we are going to have neighbors come over just to use the toilet!"

John stood her up and wrapped his arms around her. "I had them put in all the plumbing, including a better hand pump, which you missed, in the kitchen sink. The water comes from the well, and when you flush the toilet it goes into a septic system and tank. Can't you see yourself just soaking in that tub with steaming water and bubbles up to your neck? It's made by Crane—top of the line!"

Mary smiled as she shook her head, "THAT, was the last thing I imagined you buying. I can't wait—it will be wonderful, and especially for Jimmy---now he can have a hot bath every night as Dr. Arnoldus suggested. " She paused in thought then said, "But really, John, what will the neighbors think about the extravagance of a bathtub not to mention a pink one?" John replied, "Well now, we won't care what they think when we are soaking in that tub!"

Bill said, "I don't think I will use those pink things---that outhouse is still just fine by me as long as I've got the Sears catalog to wipe with. 'PINK' is too girly for me? That big bathtub might not be too bad if I keep my eyes closed!"

Helen piped up, "I think it's gloriously exotic, and Bill you can continue using the outhouse---fine with me! And also, now we don't have to go outside to the outhouse in all sorts of nasty weather!"

~~~~~~~~~

When Mary found a spare moment, she wrote to her favorite sister Emma in Mitchel, Nebraska.

Dear Emma, Jimmy and I are back home now after spending a year in Thermopolis where he was attended to by an Osteopathic doctor and took the mineral hot bathes. I am so grateful to say, that he is so much better. He will never be the same, but he can lead a normal life and do everything—almost—that other kids do. John surprised us with a new bathroom and a hand pump at the kitchen sink. I am almost embarrassed to tell you that the tub, stool, and sink are pink. YES, pink---such luxury!

I am sending a photo of our Arnold standing straight and tall between Adella and Helen; see how tall he is for thirteen. He grew about five inches during the past year, thanks to that doctor. He is quite thin and I am concentrating on putting some meat on him again. Oh, Emma, it was such a frightening experience. We thought we might lose our dear youngest son. God indeed heard our prayers and delivered Jimmy. We are so thankful. I hope this letter finds you all well.

Love, Mary

Courtesy: Arnold Wamhoff

Mary got right back into the swing of farm life. By mid-June, the cherries and strawberries were ripening. After everyone ate their fill, Mary began canning them. When the raspberries started producing in July, Mary canned the cherries with equal parts of raspberries—her favorite recipe which she used to make pies with. It was the girl's job to pick the berries and Mary canned them –three to four quarts every other day for several weeks. Ted and Jimmy were kept busy hoeing and cultivating the sweet corn until it got to be a certain height. Jimmy couldn't keep up with Ted yet, but he worked as long as he could.

Jimmy walked into his mother's kitchen holding a squirming fat worm by the tail. "Guess what Mother---I found this big worm on your cabbages and he wasn't alone!" Mary reached up into the cupboard and brought down a carton of cornmeal. "You take this out to the garden and carefully sprinkle a little over each head of cabbage---that should stop those cabbage worms!"

The Wamhoff kitchen and summer kitchen was in full canning mode. John brought a bushel of peaches from Greybull where they were selling them off a truck. Mary got twenty quarts of peaches from that bushel. She canned another twenty-two quarts of tomatoes and about ten quarts of pickled beets. There was quart after quart of beans and peas, squash, pumpkin, and around fifty pints of jam. She did the majority of it out in the summer kitchen where she could make a mess and it didn't affect the family meals. When she was canning, Mary left the daily cooking to the girls or the hired girl.

After the first frost, Mary sent Jimmy and Ted out into the garden to pick the green tomatoes. A family favorite was Mary's fried green tomatoes. The rest she made into relish and chutney. Nothing went to waste!

~~~~~~~~~

In the fall, Jimmy went back to the small grade school in Emblem. Because he had been studying on his own during the past year, the teachers gave him a test to see if he was at the same level to enter the eighth grade, which Jimmy passed with flying colors. "Does that mean that I will graduate next year and get to go to high school the year after that?"

His teachers and the County Superintendent of Schools gave the thumbs up and he couldn't have been happier. "Thank you so much, that is the 'bee's knees', I get to be with my friends in high school!"

Courtesy: Arnold Wamhoff

Standing at the kitchen sink where she loved to look out the east-facing window and gaze at the broad expanse of their fields and the Bighorn Mountains, Mary about dropped the dish she was washing when she saw Jimmy sitting on a Percheron horse in the yard, proud as punch. She practically ran to the back door, wiping her hands on her apron as she went.

Flinging open the back door, she said, "Arnold John Wamhoff, what--in the world do you think you are doing? You shouldn't be on that horse!"

Jimmy had the biggest grin on his face. "Ah Mother, come on. I have been dreaming of sitting on Buck's back for so long and here I am. It feels swell! It doesn't hurt none and don't you worry, I won't race him---me and Albert are just going for a ride, no trotting like the doctor said—just walking the horses, Mother. I don't want to hurt my back, not now, not ever again!"

Mary waved at him, "Okay then, you go ahead and take it easy. Please. Have fun son---have fun!" Mary watched him ride around the yard as tears of joy and thanksgiving rolled down her face. "Oh my boy, you are growing so tall and you have such an amazing spirit and strength. You are going to be just fine!"

Mary turned and walked back into the house as she heard the switchboard buzz. *I love being back in my life---even with all of the work. It gives me a purpose!*

Halloween: Mary noticed Abert and Jimmy whispering and laughing over in the corner, but she didn't put much stock in it. Those two were always cooking up something. After a bit, Jimmy peeked around the corner and said, "Albert and I are going to take a short ride, we won't be gone long."

Mary winked and said, "I know it's Halloween and I expect you two to stay out of trouble, understand me?"

The two boys climbed up on their horses and rode up the lane. A half-hour later they were both back at their respective homes, sooner than expected! Jimmy took the saddle off his horse and after taking his sweet time currying her, he put her out to pasture.

Mary was at the switchboard when Jimmy peeked around the corner and said, "I'm going to go to bed now, Mother, see you in the morning."

Mary said, "JUST a minute, young man. You come here, I want to talk to you."

Jimmy walked slowly into the room, eyes to the floor.

"You and Albert—you know the teacher, Miss Edgar? Well it seems, she was IN her outhouse when somebody tipped it over early this evening."

Jimmy just couldn't help himself, as images danced in his head of the outhouse going over with the teacher inside, screaming her fool head off. He burst out laughing.

Mary cocked her head and tried in vain to subdue a smile that crept from the corner of her mouth. "Arnold John Wamhoff---- was that you and Albert who tipped her over?"

Jimmy said as meekly as he possibly could fake, "Yes Mother, it didn't hurt her none. It is Halloween and we were just having a bit of fun now!"

Mary shook her head and said, "I guess nobody was hurt and boys will be boys. I wouldn't tell anybody you did the deed---you could get in trouble with the school board and you KNOW who is on the school board---your father! This entire shenanigan would not sit well with him! I think I'd go to bed before he gets home if I were you."

~~~~~~~~~

1928: They had good snow that winter, the first time in a long time and the reservoir was full which assured Emblem of having enough water for their crops. That spring, John planted mostly grain, but also a couple of fields of Great Northern beans and sugar beets. John continued to rotate and diversify crops—not planting the same thing in the same field year after year, as that sucked the natural nutrients from the soil. He and Bill decided to 'fallow' two fields (plow them under for the summer) and to 'strip farm' to reduce damage to topsoil and keep it from blowing away. Bill said, "Dad, with gasoline-powered tractors we can cultivate larger fields at a lower cost per acre."

Mary knew it was springtime when Jimmy walked out along the ditch banks searching for asparagus and wild spinach or lambs quarter. Proudly, he carried his large basket brimming with the fresh spring greens."Land sakes, look at this mess of greens and asparagus too. We are going to have us a nice supper. Whatever made you do something like that?" Mary asked.

Jimmy said, "Ahhh, I was just walking along the ditches before I set fire to them, to burn the weeds like Dad told me to do; and I saw all that asparagus and the wild spinach and it made my mouth water---I got to thinking how you would cook that up and all!" Jimmy left his batch of greens and went back to his work along the ditches. *Dad said he likes his ditches clean of weeds, that way the water flows faster and the weeds don't slow it down. To me, it's the mark of spring, the smell of burning leaves, and clean ditch banks. I just have to be careful not to let the fire get away from me.*

By mid-summer, John and his crew knew they were going to have a bumper crop of grain---something they hadn't had in previous years of drought. The grain, beans, and beets all looked good. John said, "Come on Mary, Jimmy, Helen, and Old Jim---let's go out in the field and get a picture of just how high that grain is. It's the best we've ever had."

Old Jim didn't show up for breakfast the next morning, so John drove over to the old place where Jim was living with the other hired men. John knocked on the door and there was no answer. He pushed it open

Courtesy: Arnold Wamhoff

and went into the adobe house. It was cool but had an odd odor. John walked to the back bedroom and noticed Jim was still in bed---the room smelled terrible.

"Jim, are you alright? Are you having a bad day, it's okay if you take some time off if you need to."

Jim opened his eyes and for a moment he didn't recognize John, then he said, "Ahhh it's you, John. I feel like hell today---worse, worse than--- than it's ever been. I couldn't get out of bed by myself now. Do you think you can help me to the outhouse?"

John said, "Have you been eating?"

Jim said, "Not much, can't seem to keep anything down and I got a bad case of the shits to boot!"

John said, "I'm calling Dr. Gorder to come out and take a look at you. This has gone on too long. I know you don't take to doctors, but he might be able to help you—give you some medicine."

Jim looked up at John and weakly said, "Don't waste your money, John. I told you that I saw a doctor a while back. I got cancer and it won't be long now. I want to thank you for taking me on when you did. You've treated me right fair and gave me a place to live and a purpose---you always made me feel like I belonged. I never told you this before, but I was at loose ends when we happened to meet up in Cheyenne. I'd considered taking my life a few times.

You offered me a new life, something to live for, and included me in your family. I could never try to repay you for what you have given me. We made a good team, we carved this beautiful farm out of the prairie and got that huge herd of sheep going. Now, I'm afraid it's time for me to bow out. I ain't gonna make it through this— cancer is all through me. If you are gonna call someone, call the undertaker! Oh, I----" Jim had a spasm of coughing and he laughed, "I guess you are the undertaker!"

John's face paled as he moved a chair near the bed. "Are you in pain Jim?"

Jim replied, "No, John, the doc gave me some stuff called morphine and it helps some. I might go into the hospital now, they could keep me drugged up better. The doctor up in Cody said I'd know when it was time to come to the hospital."

John said, "Let's go now---I'll drive you up to Cody. You don't have to get dressed, I'll just throw a blanket around you and get you out of the car when we get there."

Jim said, "Let me stop at the outhouse first, don't wanna mess your car up! Then, we can go!" When he was upright, he paused to look around the room. "I remember when we built this two-story adobe, best on the Bench!"

John didn't have time to call Mary or let anybody know where he had gone—he just went. *I owe so much to this man. I don't think I could have taken on the sheep and all when I did if it weren't for Jim. I owe it to him to get him some medical care now. I wish to hell he had told me sooner, there might have been better doctors in Billings.*

Jim made it crystal clear he didn't feel like talking, so John left him be as they drove the 35 miles to the Cody hospital. John pulled up to the emergency room. Jim reached over, barely able to speak, "One more---one more thing John—you should know---I loved her too—I loved that sweet Mary—a damn fine woman!"

John waved to an orderly to come out to the car. They loaded Jim in the wheelchair, but he died before they even got him inside the hospital. As a licensed mortician, John made arrangements to pick the body up the next day.

Stunned, John pulled his car into a parking spot and laid his head against the steering wheel, as his emotions overwhelmed him.

~~~~~~~~

It was a long drive back to Emblem. John pulled the Chevrolet into the farmyard and parked it. He sat in the car for a bit, gathering himself before he went into the house. Walking into the back porch, he stopped to wash up. Mary came from the kitchen where she was washing the supper dishes. "John, for pity's sake. Nobody knew where you were and so we went ahead and ate supper. Where were you? You are peaked as a ghost, what's going on?"

John took Mary by the hand and pulled her outside to walk in the yard. Mary knew enough to let him find the words, whatever it was. Finally, he said, "I've been with Jim. I stopped over this morning and he was feeling poorly, so I drove him to Cody to the hospital. He died before they even got him inside the emergency room!" John walked a bit and then said, "Mary, did you know he loved you? Did he ever tell you?"

Mary stopped short and a bewildered look filled her face. Her eyes filled with tears as she looked up at John, "He didn't have to, I knew. He was an honorable man and he never acted on his feelings, but I knew. I think, our family took the place of the one he lost all those years ago and I am grateful for that."

Mary stopped walking and turned to John. His ruddy cheeks were wet with tears. John put his arms around her, "You and I've been with that man for most of the last 25 years. He was like a brother to me, I couldn't have done what I did----none of this, without him. He had cancer, Mary, and he's known it for a while, he just didn't want to burden us with it."

Mary squeezed John's hand, "I just don't know what to say, I had no idea he was so sick. He was special to me too. He was family and I was very fond of him. I will tell you this now-- before he met us, he lost his entire family, wife three children, in a Kansas tornado. He was at loose ends and he said we gave him a reason to live. Do you know if he wanted a church burial?"

John said, "No, no he didn't, but I want to bury him in the cemetery up the road. I am going to lay him out, I still have my instruments. I just feel it's the least I can do for him. Just a month ago, we designated an area where non-Lutherans could be buried at our cemetery. I also want you to get ahold of Adella, see if she can come. I'd like all the family to be present and maybe we can have a family picture taken at that time. He was with us for six of the eight children's births. I know Jimmy is going to take this hard. I'll talk to Reverand Leasch and see if he would say a few words at the grave, if not, then to hell with it--- I will. Let's set his burial for two weeks from today."

~~~~~~~~~

Most Emblem Bench people turned out for the graveside burial ceremony for Jim. Reverand Leasch agreed to say a few words and John finished the service with a tribute to Jim. Later, after a short reception at the house, the Wamhoff's went into the parlor for a long overdue family photo. The five daughters stood in the back row: Helen Prugh, Adella Smith, Ruth Werbelow, Marie Yates, and Esther Blank. John sat in the front row, next to Bill, Arnold, and Ted. Mary sat on the far side with her hands folded demurely in her lap.

Weeks later when John saw the photograph, he sat for a long time, looking at it. "Mary, we produced a fine, fine family. I realize it's been hard on you, having this many children and all. But for what it's worth, I appreciate what you gave up, the pain you endured to birth our nine, and bearing the loss of our tiny Amanda. We've made us a good life---I'm so thankful for you Mary. I remember the first time I saw you—I knew, you were the woman for me, and I hope you feel the same. I think this life has been harder on you than on me but we've both done our best. I know Jimmy's accident and all that time you had to spend in Thermopolis with him aged you--- the daily worry and stress were hard on you. Just know this, I love you and I always will!"

Mary looked into John's eyes. "Yes John, I look at this picture and I feel so much. I look at each of our children's faces and remember their births, taking care of them, fighting so hard for Jimmy to get well---our Bill coming back to us after the war and the Spanish Flu. I know you have done what you could, to make this house and all easier for me to take care of and I appreciate it. We have built something good here, together for our children and our grandchildren. Just like all those years when you tried to convince me that we could do it---build a beautiful new life out on the prairie. Oh, Mercy, it was so ugly when we first moved here, sooo ugly."

Mary studied the photo a while longer and said, "I've gone gray early like my Mother—it makes me look so old. I might look better if I used that 'shoe polish' on my hair like you do." She laughed and pointed at her husband, "And John, don't you deny it, I've seen you put that on your hair for the past four years. Yes, you look younger, but you cheat!"

John said, "Okay, you've got me, I do put color on my hair, so shoot me!"

That Friday, John was gone all day. Mary wasn't sure where he had gone, just that he and John Davis had some business to take care of. That evening, after supper, John reached into the inner pocket of his suit coat and pulled out a document. He handed it to Mary, his grin reached ear to ear.

Mary looked at the document, then at John. "What is this? What have you gone and done now, John Wamhoff?"

John beamed as he said, "Well, Mrs. Wamhoff, this document says that you are the proud owner of two sections of land on the Airport Bench. I know we have talked about this—you owning some land of your own—like your mother did back in

Nebraska. John Davis and I both filed on some several hundred acres down there—it was a homestead situation like we had here. All we have to do is continue to make improvements on it and in five years it's yours. There will be property taxes and things like that, but someday that land is going to be worth a lot of money. John Davis and I are talking to J. T. Doty about digging a canal with his dragline for our 'first' improvement. It might take a few years to improve the land, but it's good soil and it's close to Greybull. We both believe it is worth the effort and now-- it's all yours!"

Mary said, "John, I don't know what to say. I know we spoke of it, but with everything else---all this land we have here in Emblem and what it takes to run this farm—now, more land?"

John said, "As I said, we won't try and farm it for a few years—just make a few improvements, but you know that it is your land when the time comes."

Mary threw her arms around John's neck. "Oh John, thank you. It's sort of a way to make me feel like I have something I can call my own, and security---my very own land. I am so grateful, thank you for thinking of that!"

~~~~~~~~

Like all the other farmers on the Bench, the Wamhoffs had a special spot not too far from the house where they had a charred steel barrel in which they burned their trash. It was usually Jimmy's job to take the paper trash out and set it on fire. Ted took the slop bucket and threw it to the chickens. Everybody had a job. One day, Mary said, "Go through the house and empty the trash cans and then burn the trash. After that I want you to hoe the potatoes—mound the dirt up around the little plants and take care you don't hoe any plants off. Singing as he went about his chores, Jimmy accomplished it in record time, his mind was on the song he was singing and not on what he was doing. He dumped the garbage and set it on fire, then headed to hoe the garden.

As he was hoeing and singing, he thought he smelled smoke. Ahhh, it's just the garbage I set fire to a few minutes ago. The breeze felt good on him as he began to sweat in the morning sun. Then the smoke smell became stronger—to his horror, he looked up and saw that the outhouse was on fire and it was spreading through the dry grass toward the field of grain.

Jimmy dropped his hoe and ran for the house. "Mother, Mother---FIRE!!! Call the fire truck, I'm going to get the hose---it's the outhouse!!"

Everybody who was close by, came running with wet gunny sacks and the garden hose. Soon, he heard the clang clang of the small Emblem fire truck as it turned down the lane. By then the outhouse was a total blaze. In no time they had it out. Jimmy squatted on his haunches, head in his hands.

Ted came up and patted him on the back. "Hey brother, it's all okay now. That breeze just happened to pick up an ember out of the can and spread it to the dry weeds. We needed a new outhouse anyway!"

About that time John walked up. "Well now, I see we've had a bit of a mishap here. Who used that outhouse last?

Jimmy stepped in front of his Dad. "I set the garbage on fire and some flew out and started the outhouse on fire. I'm sorry Dad, it was one of those accidents, maybe we need a lid for the fire barrel?"

John scratched his head and said, "Well, well, an accident or not, I think you can start digging the hole for the new outhouse right about there, here's the shovel!"

Bill and Ted joined in because they all knew digging wouldn't be good for Jimmy's back.

After a few days of digging, they got the hole big enough and John came over to inspect. "Well now, all we need is to slide the new outhouse over the hole. I'll get a couple of the herders who are working on the corrals to give us some muscle power. We'll put it on board skids and just slide it over the hole. To do that, we'll wrap a cable around it and hook a chain up to a cross board and a couple of those Percheron horses. We'll layout poles so many feet along the ground to where we want to slide that outhouse. I get to use the new outhouse first since I'm the head of the family!"

By the end of the day, the new outhouse was in its final resting place---over its new hole. They all stood around as John Wamhoff marched up to the newly painted white outhouse and closed the door. Moments later they heard the expected roar!

"Who in Sam Hell put vaseline all over this hole? You better run for the hills when I get my behind wiped off!"

Mary dropped the jar of vaseline into her apron pocket and headed back into the house with her head down. She was laughing so hard she could barely catch her breath.

~~~~~~~~

That evening as they sat in the living room, listening to the radio, John put a light to one of his favorite Cuban cigars and said, "Say Mary—I just heard on the radio that a doctor by the name of Alexander Fleming has just discovered a new drug that will cure about any infection, it's called penicillin—or something like that! The announcers said it was going to change the world of modern medicine! Now, THAT is some great news amongst all the usual bad news!"

John took another pull on his cigar and blew the smoke out into the room. "After that outhouse trick, did the boys come back from the hills yet?" Both he and Mary laughed and Mary replied "Yes, they did and I hope you can show for once that you can take a joke, John. So, you are sure it was the boys? You also have daughters you know---maybe it was me? Anyway, they were just having a little fun!"

John said, "Actually, it made my behind real nice and soft, wanna feel?"

Mary slapped him with the newspaper, "Not especially but thank you for asking!"

John said, "Well okay, be like that. You know, Joe Taggert who moved in the Blank house across the road, he and J. T. Doty are doing a right fine job of digging that new drainage ditch. Did you know that they even work nights when the weather is decent? They trade off so one of them isn't up all night or every night. They are almost to the corner of our orchard, right across from the school now—you probably noticed them over there. They are digging more of those drainage ditches everywhere on the 'bench' where there is a sign of bog. This is going to be even better land when they finish their system of planned ditches." The Wamhoff's had a good harvest that fall. Raising sugar beets was a whole lot of hard work and John decided he would have to think long and hard about raising them

1920 Chevrolet truck
Courtesy: Arnold Wamhoff

again. The best thing about raising beets was that his sheep would have good winter forage since he left the beet leaves and waste beets in the field. John only hired field help from March through September and was paying sixty dollars a month plus room and board. Most of them were single, men just trying to get their bearings.

~~~~~~~~~

October 11, 1928: Noted the Greybull Standard: *Friday afternoon W. H. Wamhoff of Emblem and A. Gregg of Greybull had a mix-up of vehicles at the old C. L. Say corner, now occupied by Father Marley in which Mr. Wamhoff's large Graham truck, loaded with something like 8,000 pounds of beans turned over. Mr. Wamhoff sustained a cut about four inches long on his forehead. Mr. Gregg was not injured; one spoke was broken out of the rear wheel of his car.* **Courtesy: The Greybull Standard**

John received the phone call from his son Bill around 2 p.m. Mary took the call and listened in because she could tell Bill was upset.

"Dad, I'm afraid there has been an accident. The truck is on its side and the load of beans is lying in the street in Greybull." John started to rage at his son and Bill said, "Dad, save it for later—right now I need some help in getting the truck right side up, and those beans back in the bed so I can take them to the elevator before they close tonight."

John stomped his foot and his face was beet red as he shouted into the phone receiver. "If it wasn't for thousands of dollars of our beans laying in the street, I'd tell you to figure it out yourself. I'll grab a couple of the hands and another truck or two and we'll be down there shortly. After this is over, you and I will sit down and have a serious talk."

Bill said, "I appreciate the help, and oh----I only have a four-inch cut on my forehead, other than that I am fine, thanks for asking! You are right--- you and I need to talk, and I guarantee that it will be serious, Dad!"

Bill hung up the phone before John could say another word. Mary disconnected her line and sat back in her chair, looking out on the newly-grassed front yard. *Well, I knew sooner than later this confrontation was bound to happen. Ever since Bill got back from the war he's been different—he grew up over there and he's no longer a boy that John can boss around. He knows his mind and I know that he doesn't want to be on this farm. Once he and Anna are married, things will change—if not before!*

It took the two large farm trucks and the help of a few others in town to get the Graham/Dodge truck back on its four wheels. Then came the task of getting 8,000 pounds of loose beans back into the truck. The elevator operator heard about the accident and came to their aid with a front-end loader. The street dirt they scooped up would fall out later when the beans were bounced across the conveyor belt at the elevator. Bill thanked the operator, "That was a hell of a lot easier than us fellows having to scoop all those beans with scoop shovels. I'll buy you a beer the next time I see you in the Smoke House!"

John went on home with the other two Wamhoff trucks and the hired hands, while Bill drove the truck of beans to the elevator. Bill thought *That's a good thing---cause what I have to say to him is best put on the back burner for at least a day. But, trust me—it will be said—it's time it was said—and the sooner the better! I have had it with him treating me like I am twelve years old. I am his son. I am a man who has gone to war and seen things he hasn't dreamed of. I know what I want, and it is NOT his farm. I want to invent, I want to work in the city—word has gotten around of my talents and what he doesn't know is that I am going to interview with International Harvester in Minneapolis next month. I will decide what my future will hold---and that future will be with Anna and not on the farm!*

~~~~~~~

Early the next morning Bill rose and milked the cows. He walked toward the house with two heavy buckets of milk. As usual, he sat the buckets next to the separator on the back porch for his mother to separate the milk from the cream. Bill walked over to the sink and washed up. Now, he was ready for breakfast and perhaps the confrontation with his father.

Mary was standing at the stove. "How do you want your eggs this morning Bill?"

"Oh, I'll take four, sunny side up. Say, Mother, did you make any bacon or ham to go with them and maybe a few fried potatoes?"

Mary smiled as she set his coffee in front of him. "If you are wondering where your father is, he had to run into Greybull to settle up with the elevator on that load of beans you took in last evening. I'm sorry that happened, it must have been very frightening. What happened that you and that car collided?"

Bill put his head down and then poured a bit of cream into the coffee. "Well now Mother, first of all, thank you for being concerned. Yes, that old man turned the corner wide and I had to swerve to avoid hitting him broadside and perhaps killing him. Perhaps he didn't see me or wasn't thinking about what he was doing. I don't know for sure, it all happened so quickly."

"I got quite a cut on my forehead from the window glass breaking when the truck rolled but I put some iodine on it last night and I think it'll be fine. It was pretty late when I finally arrived at the bean elevator and we got the beans sorted from the street gravel. The fellas there were real nice---told me it wouldn't be a problem at all!"

Bill didn't even ask what time his father would be home. He figured he would see him sooner or later and then they would have their talk. After breakfast, he headed for the machine shed where he had some welding to finish on the plow. Bill worked for a couple of hours---he never heard his father approach, but saw the shadow on the floor of the shed. He turned off the welder and turned to confront his father. He smelled of sweat and his piercing blue eyes burned with intensity.

John loosened his necktie and unbuttoned his collar in the heat. He started to speak and Bill held up his hand. "I am fine Dad, thanks for asking, and as you know, the beans were delivered and weighed as usual. I looked the truck over this morning and it is none the worse for wear. I know that you didn't ask, but I am telling you now Dad---that old boy turned right in front of me. If I had driven straight I would have hit that old man in the side of the door and probably killed him. I had a moment to decide and I decided to turn out of his way. That truck was top-heavy as it was and it didn't take much to roll it over. It was an accident pure and simple, but you look at it like you want, as I expect you will."

John cleared his throat and took another drag on his cigar. "Yes, well, the bean count was good and I put the money in the bank account this morning. We can be happy that it didn't turn out any worse."

Bill said, "I am going to cut to the bone Dad, and not waste any more of your time. It's like this---we don't work well together. You treat me like a hired hand and certainly not like your grown son, or like a man. I have gone to war, seen things you have no idea of, but that's not here nor there. Fact is, I don't want to farm—I am not cut out to farm. I have decided to go to Minneapolis to the International Harvester plant where they have offered me a job on the engineering line. The pay is good and Anna will join me there in a short time after we are married next fall."

Bill looked off in the distance and said, "This situation is not good for either of us Dad. We don't think the same, the writing is on the wall and it will be for the best. I won't leave you in the lurch right in the middle of harvest. If you need me, I'll stay around until I interview with International Harvester, which may not be until next summer. I want Anna to come with me to see how she likes the big city. After we are married, we'll live in Emblem for a while until we figure out where we are going to live, where I have a good job. I also have a letter from Boeing Aircraft in Seattle that looks promising. Either way, we have solid plans to move to the city."

John looked Bill dead in the eyes and said, "I am grateful you have a job or think you do before leaving this one. I wish you well. You are good with the machines—you can figure it all out and I will miss your expertise. We wish you good luck and you are welcome to stay on as long as you can, it's entirely up to you."

John turned his back and walked out of the machine shed as he called back, "I'll write you a check for your wages to date, tonight. If you do any other work for me in the meantime, I'll pay you for that as well."

~~~~~~~~~

Fall 1928: John shifted into low gear as the Ford truck loaded full of grain, groaned and grunted as it climbed out of the field onto the highway. He turned toward Greybull to take this last load of grain to the elevator in Basin. It was slow going with a truckload of grain and he prayed he didn't have a blowout. Finally, after a little over an hour, he turned in at the elevator, pulled the brake, and turned off the ignition. He adjusted his good straw hat and went into the office. "I am just checking in---John Wamhoff--I called the other day about bringing a load of wheat in today. Which ramp do you want me on?"

John jumped into the truck, backed out, then turned onto the plank ramp leading over the cavernous belly of the grain elevator. He shifted down into low as the truck complained loudly with the heavy load. The wheels rattled across the planks and iron grid to where the hoppers were positioned underneath. After the truck rolled into position, John pulled the emergency brake. Another man came alongside the truck and together, he and John released the chains holding the sidewall of the truck bed with a mountain of grain inside. The grain began slowly, to slide out into the hoppers, like bits of gold, into the holding tank beneath.

John listened to the sounds that rumbled up from the bowels of the elevator as the auger groaned and pulled the grain up into the storage towers. John sneezed as grain dust boiled up from below. He watched a disheveled man with sausage-like fingers set the counterbalances and weights. In no time it was done and he chained up the side of the truck, climbed inside, and drove down to the office to settle up.

The man in the office was working on other papers as John stood patiently at the counter. John said, "I saw in the paper that you were giving $1.25 a bushel up until this Thursday. Like I said I called three days ago and told you I was bringing in a load today."

The man turned to him and said, "Well now, things do change unexpectedly, don't they?"

John felt the heat growing at the base of his neck. "So, what is it today---this being only Tuesday?"

The man said, "We've had a run on that price and we're getting full. The best I can do is $.95!"

John slapped his fist on the counter, "Now listen, you sure as hell didn't tell me that on the phone or when I drove up now did you? You sit there and wait until I unload my grain and then tell me the price is less than advertised? You aren't dealing with some old clod hopper here. I know what is right and what was advertised. Don't think you are even going to try and short change me now! You better sit by that advertised price or there will be trouble and I'm not whistling 'Dixie'!"

The elevator man looked up at John, "Well, I suppose you do have a point there Mr. Wamhoff and because you are a good customer and all, I'll honor that price, but as soon as you walk out that door it drops. Agreed?"

John signed for the grain and the elevator man said he would send the check. John said, "Agreed—I appreciate that. Have a good day. I'd advise you to put a sign in the window relating to the price. Thanks." He turned, opened the weathered door, then loudly pulling it closed, and headed for his truck. Waiting until he got inside and started the engine, he hit the steering wheel with the palm of his hand and laughed.

~~~~~~~~~~

It was an unusually cold winter evening, Mary watched patiently, as John sat, grim-faced, reading the local newspaper, the Prairie Farmer, and Better Farming magazine. Finally, she broke the silence and said, "John, what does it say in the paper about how some banks are making it hard to get a loan and such? It is worrisome and I don't understand it."

John slowly and deliberately folded the paper and laid it on the table next to his chair. "In a nutshell, Mary, the financial sector of this country is blaming this whole mess on overproduction of agricultural produce--- which they say, has been causing financial troubles throughout the decade. If all else fails, blame the farmer! Gol damn idiots! Every spring we put seeds in the ground and gamble there will or won't be a market for our crops, gamble on the weather—good or bad, if and when we'll be able to harvest. Now, they lay all the blame on us because we had a few good years of abundance and their warehouses are full of our crops. We've got to hope and pray that these financial geniuses get it all worked out eventually! I guarantee you those bankers and traders are just as much to blame in all of this—all over the world. They've had economic warning sign after sign when the stocks were bouncing around like a ball. They tried their dirty tricks to manipulate the market and the people. What they were doing is playing 'Russian Roulette, with the gun pointed at us!"

"I did take most of our money out of the bank, but that doesn't help when I need to go in and take out an operating loan for the summer after shearing as I've always done. I don't know what I'm going to do. Guess I'll sit here and twiddle my thumbs---not much else I can do. The entire country is just hanging on, but I have me a feeling we haven't see anything yet---not anything! This is only the calm before the storm if you ask me!"

Chapter Fifteen

THE DEPRESSION YEARS

"---the only thing we have to fear is---fear itself."
Franklin Delano Roosevelt, 1929

1929: In Arnold Wamhoff's words: *Living through the depression was unbelievable – you just wouldn't believe what we learned to do without. We were so poor we had to put cardboard in our shoes, even though Dad had a lath, and one of those stands to put shoes on to fix them. He would repair our shoes the best he could. He even had this special sewing machine which he used to repair harnesses, shoes, anything that was leather. But, my gosh, if you would get a new pair of shoes, it was very unusual. We kids went barefoot all summer---the soles of our feet would get almost like leather!*

We always had plenty of good living and eating here on the farm. Mother would plant the garden and Dad made sure it had water and plowed it in the spring and fall. We lived off the garden all summer long and still had enough to preserve for the cold months. She did an awful lot of canning – her cellar was always full of canned goods. We had a potato bin in there that was eight feet wide and six feet long—it held a wagon load of potatoes. We kept turnips and carrots down there as well-- all buried in the dirt so they didn't freeze. Why they came out of that cellar tasting like fresh vegetables. The meat was kept out in a big cement building beside the windmill, and where we used to store water. They would smoke it and put salt on it to keep it from spoiling, it was so good.

We had lots of chickens and sold the eggs we didn't need— sometimes for 9 cents a dozen. During the Depression, we'd only get 3 cents or so a dozen, that's when Dad stood on the corner of Main Street and gave the eggs to the needy. When the chickens stopped laying or got too old, they ended up in the best pot of chicken and dumplings you ever tasted. Sweet cream was skimmed off the buckets of milk and was a cash crop. It too was taken into town and sold at the grocery store. Lard replaced butter for bread and cooking because we had plenty of that and we could sell the butter.

We didn't have good crops for ten years or more, but everybody pitched in and made do. The community got together for carry-in dinners and dances, playing cards, socializing. That's when kids like me started getting up little bands and having dances of our own, sometimes we'd charge five cents or so, and other times it was free. Everybody was in the same boat—the one with the hole in the bottom!

One of the things I remember is the Spiegel catalog. They came up with a program whereby you could order clothing or whatever from them and make small monthly payments. If somebody had a Spiegel catalog laying around, you knew they were making payments. We kept ours in the cabinet! Folks were proud and didn't like to be in such a situation where they had to ask for charity. Mother liked Montgomery Ward catalog sales---she could order a bundle of assorted pieces of fabric or remnants in all lengths and widths and colors, for two dollars. You just can't believe the things she could make from that $2 bundle of fabric.

I guess once you go through something like that, it changes you. Those of us who grew up that way—we never took anything for granted, always looking over our shoulders for signs that it was going to happen again. We saved everything, like in that junkyard we had behind the granary. We learned to make or repair things out of old parts, we were pretty good at that. We always had a hard time trusting banks after the Depression, especially when they started foreclosing on farms—folks you knew personally. Early on and for years, Dad had loaned Emblem folks money, a little here a little there and sometimes it was quite a lot. He liked to help people but he trusted that people would pay him back when they could. He never charged them but a penny on a dollar interest if that, but they turned their back on him when the chips were down.

~~~~~~~~~

During the time Mary and her youngest son spent in Thermopolis, she had been adamant with her intent to keep Jimmy up with his classmates in his school work as well as church confirmation. She remembered how she often pleaded with him----

"Come on now Jimmy, you need to study your Lutheran Catechism, you don't want to fall behind your friends. You read and memorize it and I will quiz you on it, just like Reverand would."

Jimmy was confirmed into the Lutheran church that spring,

Courtesy: Arnold Wamhoff

along with his friends of that age. Even though money was tight, they had a big dinner for him on that Sunday, to celebrate. Somewhere or another, they found the money to buy him a nice suit of clothes and new shoes, just as they had done for their other children.

Mary looked at Jimmy and thought about all the young man had been through. *He's so determined to be a farmer. It's got to be his decision! He's going to be quite tall like my side of the family, and he is very handsome with that dark hair. I don't think he'll be as broad and beefy as Bill and Ted, they get that from their father.*

Little did the Wamhoffs know that life was going to become a lot harder on the farm and everywhere else in the United States in the coming years. The Roaring Twenties were about to turn into the Dirty Thirties!

~~~~~~~~

It was the end of the month, Mary spent the morning going over her telephone books to make out the bills for folks who had made long-distance telephone calls during the month. *With the way everything is now, I don't know if folks are going to be able to pay their phone bills. What do I do then? I don't have the heart to cut them off.*

On her way to the kitchen to prepare supper, Mary happened to glance in the mirror. Her face was damp and flushed from the heat, deep wrinkles creased her eyes. Little tendrils from her bun laid curly and loose on her neck. She reached up and smoothed back her white hair and taking her apron, blotted the sweat from her face. Her finger traced under her eyes where there were bags and dark circles. Her hands were veined, dotted with age spots, chapped, and calloused. Mary put her face in her hands and for an instant let the tears come. Mercy me, *so many worries, will it ever end? It seems like we go from one crisis to another and I'm so very tired of it all.*

~~~~~~~~

John came home from the church meeting later than he usually did. Mary lifted her head from the fancy piece she was working on and said, "That took longer than it normally does, any problems?"

John ran his fingers through his hair, "Well, I'm not going to name names but it seems one of Emblem's divorced young men----from one of the first families, has been seeing the Reverand's wife on the sly. I'm sure you know who it is. He's got a reputation as a Casanova and he considers himself quite the ladies' man. He's been bragging to the wrong people about his most recent conquest. A lot of people know about him and what he's doing, but so far, nobody has had the nerve to go to the Reverand."

Everybody went to church that next Sunday and the young Reverand's wife sat in the front pew like she always did. Right in the middle of his sermon, the Reverand announced, "This will be my last Sunday!" He closed the 'good book', turned, and left the pulpit. The next day he and his wife were gone.

It wasn't but a week later when Mary pulled John aside and said, "You will never believe what I just heard over the phone. It seems that our 'Casanova' hasn't learned his lesson regarding his bad habit of 'smelling the wrong flower'. Now, he's set his cap for a neighbor's wife, but it seems 'the neighbor' got wind of it all and interrupted it with the muzzle of his shotgun, aimed at a very vulnerable portion of 'Casanova's' anatomy!" John doubled over with laughter, "What I would have given to see that!"

Mary said, "Well, he is mighty lucky that the neighbor didn't pull that trigger. I suspect he will be keeping his distance from here on." It was a few months later when 'Casanova' married and this seemed to curtail his extracurricular activities to some extent, but he still had a roving eye when it came to the ladies.

~~~~~~~~~

Mary was in the kitchen cooking flapjacks for breakfast. It was wash day so she already had a pan of Faultless starch simmering on the back burner of the cookstove. She looked out the window as a breeze caught the sheer curtains and ruffled them. She saw John drive up in his car, get out, and slam the door. Mary watched with concern, the way he walked up the dirt path to the house. *Something has gone wrong, he is mad as a hornet, I can tell just by the way his jaw is set and the way he walks.*

John opened the back screen door and let it slam shut. He stopped to wash up and then stomped into the kitchen. Mary continued cooking and casually asked, "Got some hornets under our bonnet this morning, do we?"

John poured himself a cup of coffee and sat at the kitchen table. "I fired that one old sheepherder we hired a few weeks ago and hired this new fellow ---Redondo something or another. He claimed to be 'one of the best herders to ever watch over sheep'. Well, come to find out, he was supposed to take a band of sheep out in the hills to the west. Long story short, he lost the sheep! We figure he got rip-roaring drunk and ---the sheep just took off. So, Frankie and another herder spent that day and part of the next rounding up what was left. They found about 1,000 head around dark and decided to corral them for the night. The next morning they went looking for the rest. They were scattered all along the divide, Frankie said it looked like coyotes got to them, and killed about 25. With the help of the dogs, they rounded up another 600 and got them back to the corral."

John poured himself another cup of coffee as Mary sat his breakfast in front of him. "What I want to know is, just how in the hell can a man conduct his ranching successfully with such worthless help? Now, I will say this, I've been lucky that this is an isolated situation for us, but it happens more often than you'd like to hear."

Mary turned from the sink where she was washing breakfast dishes and said, "John, something dreadful has happened over on the south line at Black Fritz's place. I took the call and switched it on to Greybull. They found Sophia at the bottom of the cistern. Folks think she fell in and drowned. Some say perhaps she had a heart attack or a stroke and fell in. Of course, others speculate that Black Fritz may have just happened to push her in. He has been acting extra queer for a while now, walking around the Bench at night, knocking on people's doors, peaking in their windows. To tell you the truth he gives me the willies! I don't think he is playing with a full deck!"

John said, "Well, this will really send him over the edge. Not that they got along that well, but he was proud when he went back to Germany and married a 'German woman'. I never could figure him out. As treasurer for the church, I can't tell you how many times he's given me a check, for an outrageous amount, and it was no good. I have to report those checks. I don't know whether to be sorry for him or what. Jimmy asked me once if Black Fritz was related to the 'boogie man'! I guess he could be, at that, the way he creeps around scaring folks!"

~~~~~~~~~

The Wamhoff family gathered around the dining table that evening for supper. John said grace, then they passed the food. Jimmy was intent on loading up on the fried chicken and mashed potatoes until he looked up and found his father staring at him. 'Now then, does anybody at this table know anything about a neighbor's watermelon patch getting raided the other night?" The two youngest boys began to squirm in their chairs. Ted managed a quick peek at his father and felt Jimmy kick him under the table. Jimmy dug into his food without acting like he heard a word of what was said.

John said, "I was thinking that a nice cool piece of watermelon with a sprinkle of salt would be just the thing after supper. I couldn't say where it came from, now could I? Who am I to say?"

Jimmy said, "It was Ted and Albert's idea—I didn't want to go, but they called me a sissy. Mrs. Rhoerkasse is a real nice lady and she sure has a big garden. I never seen so many watermelons in one patch, ever. We only took what we could carry, honest!"

John choked on his ice tea at that explanation. "Well, boys will be boys, but I don't expect that will happen again—BUT, that is stealing you know. I think it would be nice if you three volunteered to muck out Mr. Rhoerkasse's barn or hoe her garden ----in the next few days."

Ted and Jimmy put their heads down and tried to muffle their giggles.

John said, "Now, about those watermelons ---got any left?"

March 9, 1929: Mary met John at the back door as he walked up to the house after milking the cows. "John, I just heard over the switchboard that there's another ice jam, this time up by Sheep Canyon and it's backing the Greybull River up so fast that any town along its course will be flooded in a few hours. They said folks in Greybull are grabbing what they can and are gathering up there, on airport hill, watching it all. When that river flooded before, it usually hit the low spots first, like the north and south streets. But this time, the speed of this flood and rising current is forcing all of Greybull to head for higher ground. They are going to need some help."

Mary stood on the front porch and watched her husband drive down the dirt road to the highway and turn towards Greybull, to see what he could do for the people out of their homes. She paused for a moment and gazed up at the bare, crooked, and gnarly branches of the cottonwoods which seemed to claw at the sky in the soft morning light. *I don't know what it is about those trees, their branches have such an interesting shape, not straight and gentle as some trees, but twisted as if in pain. The bark of the cottonwood is identifiable as well---cracks thick and deep as an old woman's hands. Soon they will be leafing out and those leaves will soften their look--like fine green lace.*

The sun was setting to the west when John returned from Greybull and drove down the tree-lined lane to his home in Emblem.

He parked the car and hurried up to the back door. "Mary, Mary—where are you?" He found her in the telephone room.

She waved a 'hello' at him as she plugged another call in at the switchboard.

John took his suit coat off and hung it over an oak chair. "I'll tell you, Mary, that is the darndest thing I ever saw. I'd say three-quarters of Greybull folks are out of their homes, but most of them have a place to sleep tonight. The word I got is that Joe Carey called Cody Airport and they are sending down a two-seater Eaglerock by-plane. Get this---they are going to drop dynamite on the main jams. I heard them say that Floyd Buchanan is flying that plane with George Scott and they are dropping over 700 sticks of dynamite on the two jams, one below the gyp plant and the other just this side of the gyp plant. That dynamite is wrapped in bundles of 25 to 70 sticks---can you imagine that? Floyd is flying the plane and George is lighting and dropping the dynamite in specific places."

In the next issue of **the Greybull Standard**, it read: *"The first bomb, according to George Scott, missed the whole damn river and the second landed on the left wing of the two-seater Eaglerock by-plane and remained there for a few seconds, then dropped off when Buchanan 'fishtailed' the plane. The last shot was a bundle of 70 sticks and the effect of that explosion was felt plainly by the people here in town. Within an hour after this shot, water began to recede here in town and within two hours people were able to wade about the streets uptown.*

Buchanan flew at an elevation of about 500 feet and when Scott would light the fuse of the dynamite bomb in his lap, Buchanan would dive down to something like 30 feet above the ice, then Scott would drop the dynamite until twelve drops had been made. Out of twelve drops, ten were perfect hits!"

Buchanan later remarked, "That was the most dangerous and difficult job of flying I ever had to do!" The water had covered the town from a few inches to fifteen feet deep. Flood damage was widespread and the hardest hit was the downtown area. After the water level dropped, cakes of ice measuring 6 feet by 8 feet, and some up to 8 feet by 15 feet were left behind in people's yards and the streets. It would be weeks before the huge cakes of ice melted.

NOTE: It wasn't until 1956 that the town of Greybull reached an agreement with the federal government to have the Army Corps of Engineers build a 10-foot high, 12,300-foot long levee along the banks of the Bighorn River.

Courtesy: Greybull Standard

~~~~~~~~~~

WALL STREET CRASH: All hell broke loose beginning in September of 1929 and escalated in late October when the New York Stock Exchange collapsed.

Note: *Winter started six weeks earlier than the average, in October of 1929. Long, unusually cold months followed and ended in April with a snowstorm worse than the storm of March 1878. Over two-thirds of the livestock in the state didn't make it, which included 25% of Wamhoff's band of sheep. Then, wool fell from 80 to 25 cents a pound, followed by the sheep market from $18 a head down to $12, then to $3.*

Bill remained on the farm after the Minneapolis job fell through. The Boeing Plant in Seattle was still interested in him and that was the job he and Anna were counting on after they got married in the fall. In the meantime, he gave his father a wide berth and went about doing his work. These were tough years for the farmers in particular. John kept borrowing from 'Peter to pay Paul'—'one step ahead of the tax collector and the bankers' as he liked to say. Every spring he needed to borrow operating money to get the farm going during the summer when there were no crops to sell. They had the wool to sell, but John watched the market and tried to hold off selling until the price was highest. That didn't always pan out the way he intended and as each year of the Depression went by, he found himself a little deeper in debt. He had a particular philosophy of dealing with the bankers. He told his sons, "You go in to see them, show you have confidence. Let em' know right off that there are five other banks who have already agreed to take care of you until things work out."

Jimmy said, "Does it really work like that Dad, or are you messing with us again?"

John said, "Well now, I suppose you will have to find that out for yourself now, won't you!"

~~~~~~

Back in 1922, John had taken out a mortgage on the home farm, the section of land where they lived. He faithfully made the payments every year after harvest. It was tough times and everybody was feeling the pinch, not just the farmers. John was good with figures and kept impeccable ledgers on what he owed and his assets, as well as money, expected to come in at harvest, along with the price of wool and sheep. He carried several large outstanding debts from other farmers on the bench—farmers who had asked him to harvest their crops with the promise to pay later.

~~~~~~

1929: Bill and Anna had been writing letters back and forth since he met her at that dance after the war. It had been love at first sight for both of them. Bill was counting on Boeing Aircraft in Seattle to come through for them in the fall after they were married.

(Actual Letters) *Anna, I am saving every penny I make for our future together. We can live in a house here in Emblem until we decide if we want to take the job in Seattle. I'll guarantee you this, we will not make our permanent home here. We will have 'the great' adventure and strike out on our own in the city.*

If you can believe it, my little brother, Arnold, or as all the rest of the family call him---Jimmy, is going to high school. He is quite the scholar and I know he will make something of himself. I want you to choose a date in November when we can be married. I don't want a big church wedding, just something simple. How about you? It's going to be an awful rush when the harvest starts.

I want to tell you in this letter Dear, that you have been a big help to me in getting my work done with a happy thought on my mind that I am doing it for a person that means everything to me, Anna Dear, I can't put it in writing how much I love you, I just don't know, how. Will close, all my love is yours. Your William

~~~~~~~~~

(Actual Letter) *My Dear Anna---Last night I received the best and dearest letter in all of my life, it was from you, the one where you had the date of our wedding set for the 5th or 6th of November. We had a storm and it set us back some with threshing. I sure do hope that there will be enough time. We threshed only about 3,000 bushels of beans and will get to the rest of them this week. Beans are about $4 a bushel now. We started to harvest our beets last Wednesday they sure look good. The ladies in Emblem have had some nice 'bridal shower parties' for you. Mother is keeping the gifts in a room for us.*

October 30th: The big rush is all over this week. I am sending my wedding clothes to your address in Omaha. I will try to be there on November 3rd sometime. I am getting more anxious than ever to see you and them brown eyes of yours. My Sweetheart, I am going to close with lots and lots of love for you,
Your William

Bill and Anna- October 1929
Courtesy: Arnold Wamhoff

NOTE: Bill and Anna were married in Omaha Nebraska, on the 5th of November, 1929. They honey-mooned in Peoria, Illinois, and then returned to Emblem where they made their home for another year before moving to Seattle.

To celebrate their marriage, John and Mary invited all their friends in for a special evening of socializing which included plenty of John's apple cider and beer. People brought small gifts to help the young couple set up their first house. It was late when the last car drove out the lane and onto the highway.

John helped Mary clean up just a bit before they went to bed. It was a dark night, no moon,---around two in the morning, Mary heard something and sat up in bed. For a moment she was too terrified to scream, but finally, she DID. BLACK FRITZ MOELLER stood as still as a statue, at the end of their bed, not saying a word, just watching them.

John jumped from their bed like his pants were on fire. "WHAT? What the hell do you think you are doing, coming into our house in the middle of the night and standing in our bedroom? Are you completely mad? Get the hell out of my house, and don't EVER set foot on our farm again. Do you understand me? OUT!!!

Black Fritz didn't say a word as he turned and calmly walked out of the front door and up the lane of cottonwood trees, blending into the darkness. John stood at the door until he couldn't see him any longer. He wedged a chair under the doorknob and then managed to make his way back to bed. Mary was still shaken, to think the man came into their home and their bedroom in the dead of night was unnerving, to say the least!

The very next day, John drove into Greybull. He went to the hardware store and bought locks for every door in the house. That incident didn't happen again at the Wamhoff house, but everybody on the Bench had their stories of the bizarre behavior of the notorious, Black Fritz Moeller. You might say that he was Emblem's –Boogie Man. He lived in Emblem for a few more years and then disappeared. Some say they saw him in Cheyenne a few years later. To say the least, Mary and most of the other women on the Bench were relieved that he no longer roamed the community in the night, scaring the women and children, peeking in windows, and sending chills down the backs of many of the farmers. Now, Ted and Jimmy didn't mind going to the outhouse in the dark of night, when the inside bathroom was busy. Even gathering eggs after dark wasn't so scary, now that BLACK FRITZ was no longer around!

Fifteen-year-old Jimmy packed his suitcases and looked around the upstairs bedroom he had shared with his brothers for as long as he could remember. He was off to high school in Greybull, eighteen miles to the east. There had been times when he didn't believe he would ever walk again, much less be going to high school. Bill, Ruth, and Helen had all gone for a year, then dropped out. Jimmy planned on getting his diploma, the first Wamhoff to do so.

Jimmy thought about his mother, *I could never have done what I did if it wasn't for Mother. She was determined I would walk again and she left her home and every obligation, all for me---to take me to Thermopolis for those treatments and it was where I got better. All the while she kept me up on my school lessons, so I wouldn't fall too far behind. Everything I am is because of my Mother! She never gave up on me. Of course, Dad and the rest of my family held the fort down, here on the farm—everything—the treatments, staying at a hotel, meals--it was so expensive. We were getting by on a shoestring as it was, and they all gave up things for my treatments.* Jimmy was only a year behind his former classmates, thanks to his mother who tutored him and kept him up on his classes. He passed some tests and was able to skip one year he had missed.

~~~~~~~~~

John and Mary couldn't afford to drive Jimmy to and from school every day, so Mary decided to get an inexpensive one-room apartment over the creamery in Greybull. She stayed in town with Jimmy during the weekdays while he was going to high school. The only problem was, it was close to the grain elevator and the railroad tracks. Mary and Jimmy weren't used to the sound of the train or the horn, so it took a while to adapt. She watched every penny. Haircuts were 35 cents, milk was 10 cents a quart, and for herself---beauty parlors charged 50 cents for a shampoo and set, plus 50 cents for a finger wave.

Jimmy liked high school and he received very good marks. The only problem was he wanted to play sports, but he wasn't able to because of his hip. He made friends easily and spent hours sitting in the stands watching football practice. One day in October, Coach

Mortimore climbed up in the stands where Jimmy sat. "Say there, I see you out here at every practice. Do you want to play?"

Jimmy looked down for a moment, then said, "I sure would like to Coach, but I got thrown from a horse a couple of years ago and I can't run very fast---got a cracked hip and all. Thanks for asking though. I just like watching how you all set up the plays and how everyone does their part to get a touchdown."

Coach Mortimore said, "Well, I'll tell you what. We need us a good 'ballboy' and I think you'd fit the ticket. What do you say?"

Jimmy's face lit up like a Christmas tree, "Gee, that would sure be swell, but I need to ask my mother. See, we're from Emblem and my folks got an apartment here in town so I could go to high school—my mother stays the week with me, cooking and—well you know, things that mothers do. We go home on the weekends. I'll ask her tonight and talk to you tomorrow. Thanks, Coach!"

That evening, Jimmy sat at the kitchen table, doing his mathematics homework. He laid down his pencil and turned in his chair. "Uhhhh Mother, I have something to tell you. I joined the boy's glee club and I sure do like it. The other thing is, uhhh, the football coach asked me to be a ball boy for the team. He asked me if I wanted to play, but I told him I couldn't. If I am the ball boy, that means I have to be at practice every night after school and especially during the games on Friday nights. I know you like to get home right after school is out on Fridays. Therman Sherard said they have plenty of room at their house and I could stay there on Friday nights. I've gotten to be friends with those guys on the team; that LaRoy Coguill can sure play football, he's our star player.

Jimmy stood up and walked over to where his mother sat in the wooden rocking chair, mending his pants. "It makes me feel like part of the team, Mother. I can't play, but if I am a part of the team that way, it makes me feel good. Maybe we can talk it over with Dad when we go home this weekend?"

Mary looked at her son's face when he was talking about the team. She knew what it meant to him to feel included. "Of course, we can talk to Dad. We want you to enjoy high school and feel like part of the crowd---that's important. We'll talk it over and figure out a way, don't you worry."

~~~~~~~~~

It all worked out and Jimmy became the ball boy for the Greybull Buffalos football team, and when basketball came around he was back being a helper on that team too. He liked to get involved and be a part of everything. Girls were becoming visible to the 'looker' from Emblem. He said to Albert, 'Sure, I had sisters, and we looked at those catalogs until we were cross-eyed; now I am starting to check out the real thing and see who I might like to ask out on a date. Maybe we should double date sometime—that way we have each other's back!"

~~~~~~~~~

John sat in his easy chair, reading the Greybull paper, catching up on local news. "By George, they keep talking about closing the banks. One good thing for us, Mary, is that we don't keep that much money in the bank." He read another article and burst out laughing, " By golly, it says right here in the Greybull paper that J. C. Penny Co. is advertising they have 'Dainty Vests and Bloomers' of an improved rayon that looks like silk for 79 cents, AND, Bloomers, elastic OR yoke top, elastic knee for, 98 cents."

John shook his head, "Mighty fancy items to be hidden away! I read somewhere the other day that these short skirts the young women are wearing have boosted bloomer and fashion hose sales--$30,000 last year." John laid down the newspaper and said, "I'm in the wrong business, Mary. What say you, if we sold out and bought a lady's fashion store?"

Mary raised one eyebrow and remarked, "Well, I for one would like to see that; I don't think that's quite up your alley!"

~~~~~~~~~

December 1, 1930: John waited until the boys had gone up to bed then he pulled Mary aside. "I've been thinking about something for quite some time and finally got all of my ducks in a row to make it happen. "

Mary cocked her head to the side and questioned, "Okay John Wamhoff, now what have you been cooking up?"

John said, "I probably should have done it sooner, but I've arranged for us to have a hot water tank put out on the porch, on the other side of the bathroom, and close to the kitchen. We are going to be the first on the Bench to have running hot and cold running water in our home!"

Mary sat like a stone, too shocked to say anything for a moment, then----"Oh John, what a dream come true. I can't imagine not having to put those pots on the stove to heat bathwater and dishwater and a 1000 other things where I need hot water. When is it going to be put in?"

John said, "They think they can have it done by around the 18th of the month, in time for Christmas. That's my Christmas present to our family!"

Mary said, "Not to change the subject, but Christmas is coming and, John, everyone is having a hard time dealing with this Depression and I think it'd be nice to just invite our children and their families for a Christmas buffet. We can't get them all around a table, so something like an open house where they come over and I'll have a nice table set up where they can help themselves. What do you think about that idea? What we might do is everybody brings one gift or we draw for gifts."

They had a lovely Christmas day and the drawing for gifts was such fun, especially when Jimmy got a pair of bloomers; he turned every shade of red possible. After everyone had gone home, John went out to the barn to milk the cows. An hour later, Mary heard the back door open and close and she went to take care of the milk. She looked around the room and didn't see John, then the door opened again and he carried in a large box and set it down. Mary said, "What on earth is that?"

John hugged her and said, "It's for US."

John broke open the box and there was the most beautiful floor radio Mary had ever set eyes on. "When I went to Billings last month, they were having a sale on this Majestic Motorola Highboy radio. We've listened to the old tabletop radio for over ten years. We don't get many entertainment opportunities out here in the country and I know we love to listen to our favorite programs like Abbott and Costello, Jack Benny, Edgar Bergen, Burns and Allen, Fibber McGee and Molly, Jack Benny, and Kraft Music Hall. Now our boys, Ted and Jimmy tune in the sports stations---the baseball games, the Lone Ranger, and The Shadow".

1931 Majestic Model 62 Highboy

Mary threw her arms around his neck and kissed him soundly. "Oh, John, running water in the house and now a beautiful new radio---it's too much. But I love it all, thank you, sweetheart! Merry Christmas"

~~~~~~~~~~

That evening, John and Mary sat as they usually did, he reading and she mending or crocheting a fancy doily. Mary said, "John, what do you think of this Franklin Roosevelt? I hear he's running for president next fall. People are tired of President Hoover and the mess he made with prohibition and foreign policy and all."

John straightened up in his chair and puffed his cigar. "I like him, Mary. It sounds like he has a plan for this country, for getting us out of this damn depression and prohibition nonsense. He's nobody's political puppet, like Hoover. He's a good German—strong character, and he wants to help the farmers and the people who are having a hard time of it. He knows how to play with the politicians---he might be in a wheelchair, but he's nobody's fool!"

Everybody had worked hard, they had rain, and they had plenty of water---this year the farmers got a decent crop from the land in the fall. John thought about his crew this year. *They have learned to rely on each other strengths, that's why they work so well together. That is the secret of a team.*

The mechanical augers made it so much easier, not having to pitch the straw and the grain. John liked to stand and watch how it picked up the grain and with the spin of the center cylinder,

Courtesy: Robert Werbelow

brought it up to the top of the stack or the upper bin in the granary for storage. *I've got a good crew of hard workers.*

1931: The great brunt of the Great Depression came like a thief in the night to most people except the farmer. The farmers had already suffered through a decade of falling prices and privation. It hurt the farmer in small ways rather than crushing them as it did those living in the cities. On the farm, they had to put cardboard in their shoes like their city cousins; the difference was--they could grow their own food. Most folks had been living high during and after the war, but those wartime prices soon collapsed and they were back in the soup. Farmers were used to 'making do' with what they had and had been doing so for years.

~~~~~~~~~~

John pushed his reading glasses down on his nose and said to Mary, "Can you believe that over 1,345 banks have failed this year---people are drawing out their savings or trying to. Those banks that haven't gone down yet are calling loans and restricting lending. Do you know what that means for us? Come time to borrow stake money to take the sheep to the mountains, like we usually do, we may have to keep them down here this year and hope to hell they find something to eat out in the hills. I may even have to sell some of them off to pay the shearers, and who knows what wool prices will be this year. Who knows if the bank's doors will even be open?"

John stood and looked out the window at the cottonwoods he'd planted eighteen years ago. "They are predicting that by the end of 1932, twenty-five percent of the workforce is going to be out of work. Even if I were to sell some of our land to make the bank payments, the land isn't worth what it once was. We need another truck to keep on farming this much land but I don't see how that is going to happen."

~~~~~~~~~~

Spring 1931: It was time for the Sadie Hawkins Dance at Greybull High School. Jimmy said to Albert, "What does that Sadie Hawkins thing mean?" Albert said, "I heard some guys talking and they said it's when a girl asks a guy out instead of us asking them---and they pay for the date! That's a pretty keen idea if you ask me!"

As it turned out, Jimmy and Albert double-dated with their Sadie Hawkins dates. Somehow or another, Jimmy was allowed to take the family car into Greybull for the double date. John had warned, "I know you are a careful driver and if you aren't, you know what will happen. Understood?"

Jimmy grinned from ear to ear and said, "Thanks, Dad. This is a big night for Albert and me. We've talked about double dating but never got up the nerve until now. I'll be careful and be home before midnight."

¹⁹**1931 Chevrolet**
Courtesy: Arnold Wamhoff

The next night Jimmy picked Albert up in the Chevrolet, they were both dressed to the nines. They had slicked their hair back---and had not forgotten to slap on a little Old Spice to enhance the effect. They drove into Greybull to pick up their dates for the dance. Since the two girls were staying at the same house, Jimmy drove to the address and he and Albert walked up to the door and knocked. Alice and Virginia came to the door and were acting all giggly. Jimmy looked at Albert and rolled his eyes—Albert hid his face and stuck his finger down his throat in the act of gagging!

Albert said, "Well, we better get going, do you have coats?" The girls picked up their coats and the four of them walked out to the car. The girls started to climb in the back seat together. Cocking his head to the side, Albert stood outside the car and said, "I don't think this is how it works. Virginia, you get in the front with Jimmy and Alice—you're in the back with me."

The rest of the evening went smoothly as they danced the night away. Jimmy's hip hurt just a little, but he was having so much fun that he ignored it. After the dance, they drove around a little and Jimmy said, "Well, I guess it's time we take you home."

Virginia said, "Home? Already? I think you should drive up on the hill above the river so we can see the night lights. I've heard it's beautiful!"

Albert said, "That sounds like a great idea, let's go!"

Jimmy's hands got a little sweaty as he maneuvered the car out of town and up the secluded hill. He found a spot and parked where they had a good view of Greybull's night lights. He pulled the emergency brake on and then--acting like he was stretching his arms, dropped his right arm around the shoulders of Virginia. That's when she put both her arms around him and laid a big wet kiss right smack on his mouth. He thought, W*ell, that wasn't too bad---uhhh, here comes another one*. The second kiss lasted a little longer and it then became obvious Virginia had a bit more experience as she slid her tongue into Jimmy's mouth. It was all he could do, not to gag.

Jimmy straightened up in the seat and turned back to Albert. "Say, Albert, I heard that this is when we switch dates." The girls just looked at each other, like --- 'well, this might be fun' and being about as inexperienced as Jimmy----Albert was game. "Okay, on the count of two, Virginia you sit in the backseat, and Alice, you come on up here with me. One, Two---trade!"

Jimmy figured it only took about two minutes after that for Virginia to slide her tongue in Albert's mouth. There was the rustle of bodies, then Albert said, "Jimmy, you son-of-a-gun! Okay, it's time to trade back and I suppose we should take you girls home as we have to drive way out to Emblem."

On the way home, Albert said, "Jimmy, if you ever do that to me again I'll pop you one, even if you are my best friend! I darn near gagged!" Jimmy laughed so hard he could hardly catch his breath as he stammered, "Well, I -I-I was just trying to be a bbbb-uddy and share---I know you are more experienced than I am and I figured you would know what to do with that!" The two of them laughed and kidded all the way home.

~~~~~~~~

Sept. 24, 1931: John strode in the backdoor and threw his straw farm hat on the chair. He washed up for dinner and went into the kitchen. "What's for dinner today---same as yesterday?"

Mary said, "Nooo, this is your lucky day, it's leftovers from two days ago, dressed up a bit!" Mary put his plate on the table in front of him and sat down with a glass of lemonade to sip on.

John shoveled in a few spoonfuls and then said, "Got some news, seems like some fellow, a 'short of stature' gunman robbed the Burlington State Bank last night—got away with $1,800 in cash 'money'! They found the car he had been driving, parked alongside the Greybull River. Looked like he waded across and somebody was waiting for him on the other side. Made a clean getaway—no more clues, so they say!"

Mary said, "John, not to change the subject, but some of us ladies are gathering up any spare garden vegetables, maybe a chicken or two, and taking it down to the Reverand and his family.

The church picnic is next week and since it's a potluck supper, it would give us a chance to give them a few boxes of food and some clothes. We don't want to make a scene of it, that might embarrass them. These are hard times for all of us and we need to help each other out when we can. They have sons about Jimmy's age and I have a box of clothes he has outgrown. I 'spect they will be able to use them just fine."

John said, "That sounds fine. I met with the school board the other day and I think we might have to board our school teachers this year---we just don't have the money to pay them. We can spread them around so it's not a hardship on any, one family. That's about the best we can do for now!"

~~~~~~~~~

Since Jimmy's two sisters, Marie and Helen, were married and living in Greybull, Jimmy's parents decided he could stay with one of them while attending his sophomore year in high school. Marie married James Yates in 1930 and Helen had married the local music director and bandleader, Merle Prugh. There was a room for rent next to the apartment where Marie and James lived and that was perfect for Jimmy. He didn't mind being alone, *I feel like a grownup, having my own place and all. If I need somebody, Marie and James are right upstairs and she invites me up every other night for supper.*

Interview: In Jimmy's own words: *I remember one 'boy's night out' in particular when I was staying at the apartments down on the south end of Greybull. It was early fall and a Saturday night, so some of the boys and I decided to take in a movie and whatever other excitement we might come up with. Well, the name of the movie playing was "Dr. Jekyll and Mr. Hyde", with John Barrymore. We'd heard that it was real scary, but 'heck' we were in high school and we figured we were pretty tough!*

The three of us slicked back our hair and splashed a little 'Old Spice' on, just in case we'd get lucky, and headed down to the theatre. Back then it was down on Main Street between the Smokehouse Saloon and Brady's Drygoods Store. Well now, that movie was pretty scary. There was quite a bit of gripping of the chair arms and swallowing of screams, but the really scary part came on the walk back home.

We all lived in the south part of Greybull and since none of us had a car that night, we walked. Well, it wasn't too bad when we were all together---safety in numbers, you know. But before I knew it, we reached the other two guy's houses, and wouldn't you know it was me, that lived the furthest! We all said goodnight and I continued—rather quickly—on to my place. I had eight dark blocks to walk, alone, before I was home. There was a fretful breeze blowing through the bare-limbed trees and a full moon casting suspecting shadows along the darkened street. It wasn't too bad at first, but by the third block, memorable visions of the movie now accompanied by the shadowy night were starting to make the hair on the back of my neck stand up and shivers scamper down my back. By the fifth block, I broke into a slow trot – sometimes frontwards and sometimes backward, just in case somebody was tryn' to sneak up and 'get me from behind'. Well, by the seventh block I was in a full out panic! I shifted into overdrive and I ran as fast as I could on my bad leg. I was never so glad to reach a doorway—my doorway---and believe me, I didn't waste any time getting inside and locking the door!

~~~~~~~~~~

November 1932: John took his hat off and slapped his leg. "Now we got somebody in that White House who will make something of this country and who has the farmer's back. I liked Mr. Roosevelt from the first day I saw him. He's more of a businessman than he is a politician. I like what he has to say and I like what he's done as governor of New York state! I say we are in good hands. Just the other day he said, '*Men are not prisoners of fate, but only prisoners of their own minds!*' Let's hope he can do something about the price of wheat at 36 cents a bushel. Nowadays, a 340-pound pig brings $2 if you're lucky. Butter sells for 15 cents a pound and eggs have dropped down to 4 cents a dozen.

Now, listen to this—it sums it all up pretty well. 'A bushel of corn makes a gallon of whiskey which normally sells for $16.80. From that, the government gets $4.40; the manufacturer takes $4; the railroad takes $1; the drayman is paid 15 cents; the store owner got $7---the consumer got drunk, his wife went hungry, his children wore rags, and the farmer put 25 cents in his pocket!" That, pretty much nails it on the head, don't you think?"

John slapped the tabletop---"That's about damn right!"

Mary shook her head and gave him 'the look'. "Now John, don't be swearing, one of the boys might hear you."

"Mary, in case you haven't noticed, all of our children are grown up except for Jimmy and he's at high school. So, I can swear to my heart's content, if need be---and I FEEL the need-- BE!"

John added, "Just for your information, I happened to take a tour of 'the establishments' the other night—we have one if not two gin mills or speakeasies in the thriving metropolis of Greybull. There is this one small shop on the west side of town where the front is normal, but in the back, the road drops down to a hidden garage under the shop. With all the bushes and stacked boxes, you'd never know it was there."

John said, "Once they get the hooch in the garage, there are a series of tunnels leading from under there to the Alamo Hotel, then to the shop next to the Bank building where they stash the moonshine. I went down inside of a speakeasy under Joe Carey's hotel on the east side of the main street. You act like you are going to the men's room but then turn down this dimly lit hallway to a certain door. You open it to a stairway and go down the stairs. There was another door with this little sliding porthole so they can see who you are. Inside, is a raging speakeasy all set up with a bar and stools, tables, and the like. Sometimes they even have music—a piano, horn, you know. I asked what the bright yellow stripes on the floor were for, leading to what looked like a wall. They told me that if the cops raided it, and they turned out the lights, the yellow paint showed up in the dark and showed you the way out! Now, don't that just beat all!"

"So, I was standing at the bar talking to this fella, can't remember his name. Anyway, we were talking about what we'd do if the cops raided the place. He went off on this long explanation of just what he would do and then he said, 'how about you?"

"I just laughed and said, 'Well now, I'm the cut and shoot type." I straightened my tie and explained, 'When trouble starts, I cut through the alley and shoot for home! I don't stick around to see how it ends if you know what I mean!'

Mary laughed behind her hand, "Oh John---did he believe you?"

~~~~~~~~~

John said, "In his 'Fireside Chats', Roosevelt laid out some ideas he is willing to try to jump-start this country, like the new idea of a five-day workweek. I still don't understand why teachers can't be married---he says it's to allow only one person in a family a job. I guess he has to start someplace with eleven million Americans out of work. President Roosevelt started putting men to work in this WPA where they build government dams and national parks--- things like that. 'Smile- smile, smile----he says.' Well, it's darn hard to 'smile', when that's all you got to give!"

"His other idea is to get the banks back in business. They are going to begin to reopen and we as citizens are to do our part and make some deposits. He hopes our deposits exceed withdrawals and then we are back in business—the panic will be over, and hopefully this country can get back on its feet. He is pumping an unprecedented mass of legislation through Congress to prevent foreclosures, reform banking, and financial markets, provide emergency relief for folks, and other things to put people back to work. Hot digitty dog---it sounds good enough to succeed!"

~~~~~~~~~

John went to foreclosure after foreclosure sale of farms and businesses of people he had known for thirty years. It sickened him to hear the prices they were selling a man's livelihood for. He saw so many of the women, the wives, standing alongside their husbands, with a stricken look of disbelief, as strangers pawed through their belongings.

Albert and Jimmy rode out early and were gone all morning. Mary was out working in her garden when she saw them ride their horses down the lane. They had been out in the hills between Garland and Emblem. As they neared the Wamhoff house, Jimmy waved his arm in the air and called out, "Rabbits here—we got rabbits here!"

Mary walked over to the wire fence covered with John's hops. "What have you two been up to this morning?" She looked at the string of dead rabbits hanging from their saddle horns. "Well, mercy me, looks like the great hunters have been busy! I thought you two might have outgrown shooting rabbits. Bring them around to the kitchen. We are having fried rabbit tonight for supper."

~~~~~~~~

Two days later, Mary cooked up a fine supper of Hasenpfefferr (or pickled rabbit), mashed potatoes with sweet gravy, and pickled beets. Jimmy was home for the weekend from school and was shoveling the food in his face as fast as possible, when he got real serious and said, "Say Dad—did you hear about what happened the other day? This farmer was going into town and picked up a young hitchhiker along the way. Well, they say that the farmer had this jug of hooch under the seat and he invited the young fella to have a drink."

"The young man said, 'No thanks, I don't drink, I just want a ride to town.'" Well, the farmer insisted until he became frustrated with the youngster and pulled a gun on him. 'Now, I said--- take a drink or I'll blow the top of your head off!'

At that point, Mary held her hand over her mouth, "Mercy Sakes, then what?"

Jimmy said, "I heard that the kid decided to take that drink, then the farmer said, 'What do you think---real good ain't it?'"

"The kid was afraid to say no, so he stammered around and said, 'Yeah, it's, it's pretty good.'"

"About that time, the farmer handed him the gun and said, 'Okay, now YOU point it at me and make me drink some!'"

John looked at Mary, and Mary looked at John---they just shook their heads!

Chapter Sixteen

PROHIBITION REPEALED

February 2, 1933: The controversial 18th Amendment was repealed by President Franklin Roosevelt. John Wamhoff didn't waste any time pulling his beloved stills out in plain sight and began brewing his beer and popular apple cider again. *Boy, it certainly feels good to be able to brew my beer without hiding it. Finally, President Roosevelt got his point across to the political folks. That bill did nothing but create a vicious community of crooks and gangsters not to mention putting a lot of good folks out of business.*

~~~~~~~~

It was no secret that H. D. Fiene from Emblem was the staunchest of Democrats. Now that his party was represented in the White House, he exercised his political influence, and next thing folks knew, he appointed his son, Walter as the Postmaster in Emblem. When Mary Wamhoff was given the news, she smiled with relief as she gladly handed over the keys. "That job entailed a lot of work and overtime! Now, I will have a bit more time to do other things and won't be so tied down—I'll just have the telephone to tend to, of course, we will miss that extra income from having the post office, but we will get by."

~~~~~~~~

Spring 1933: The years in high school flew by and it seemed that before Jimmy realized it, graduation day was upon him. John took his youngest son aside and had a heart-to-heart talk with him. "Now Arnold, you have your education and you have done very well. We are proud of you, the first Wamhoff to graduate from Greybull High School. After graduation, what have you decided on doing? Have you given thought as to what business you would like to go into---maybe accounting, or into banking? I know a lot of folks and I am sure I can get you on with somebody to teach you the business. You have a good head on your shoulders and a high school diploma—you are set!"

Ted and Alleen Wamhoff, Nov. 1
Courtesy: Arnold Wamhoff

Jimmy said, "Dad I wouldn't disappoint you for the world, but I think you know I have always said that I want to farm. I love the land and planting and harvesting. It means something to me. I don't want to spend my life indoors sitting in a revolving chair, dealing with people's problems. Dad, the thing is---Ted and I want to farm this place together someday. Ted has love in his eyes and is asking my classmate, Alleen Hartman, to marry him this fall after we are finished with that harvest. Can you please understand this?"

John had hoped that with the high school education Jimmy would choose a profession that would be easier on his hip. He realized his son was still in a great deal of pain and would be for the rest of his life. Nevertheless, John and Mary gave a big party, celebrating their youngest son's graduation from Greybull High School in May. Jimmy was glad and sad, that his high school days were over, but it was time to

Courtesy: Arnold Wamhoff

be an adult and take on some responsibility on the farm.

~~~~~~~~

Fall 1933: John sat at the table with his accounts and debts spread out before him. *How am I supposed to make a living with these kinds of prices for our crops? I keep thinking President Roosevelt is going to raise the prices or some miracle from heaven will change all of this, but when? There just aren't good markets out there, not enough need. People need to eat, they are starving in the streets of the cities, but the government doesn't pay us anything to grow food and the people can't afford it.*

John called Jimmy and Ted over to the table, covered with bills, payments, etc. He threw his hands over the table. "This--- This is why I don't think you boys can make a go of this farm. Maybe, with the sheep—you have a chance to ride this out. I believe in the pendulum swing---so many years of good then it moves to bad, and eventually back to good. Think long and hard about wanting to take on this farm yourselves, after I'm gone!"

~~~~~~~~

1934: John wadded up the newspaper and threw it as hard as he could across the room. Mary walked into the living room just about the time to see him throw the paper. "John Wamhoff, what in the world is wrong with you?"

John stood up, his eyes bugged out of his head and his face was red as a beet. "Gol damn meddling government, now that they have us, sheep growers down, they are set to kick us to the curb. For some of us, having sheep or cattle is the only thing that has been keeping us afloat and they want to put shackles on us. This is a death sentence! Our wonderful, all-knowing government has seen it proper to put an end to the old free grass system that allowed us to send our sheep out into the hills and let them graze on whatever they find to eat; and this includes the national forest, for which we already pay a fee. The Taylor Grazing Act is imposing a system of land leases and per-head grazing fees on the unclaimed public land. Sheep growers like us now need to own at least a small piece of land where we are set to graze our flocks. That means I would have to buy some land up in the mountains, to graze my sheep up there. I'll bet you five dollars those panty-waist senators wouldn't know a sheep from a cow! Little do they understand or care about what it takes to run a sheep or cattle ranch! This all came from the money-grabbing political idiots. They claim that this Grazing Act will result in improving range management and provide for better animal husbandry practices, whatever the hell that means!"

John stood and paced the floor, "Of all the dad-blamed, one-sided gobbly gook, political mishmash ideas! Animal husbandry??"

He strode angrily over to the window to look out at their farm. "I guess I'll have to do what President Roosevelt said on one of his 'fireside chats' the other night---' *When you get to the end of your rope, tie a knot and hang on!'* Anybody here, have a rope?"

Jimmy said, "Dad, we'll work through this, we'll find a way to make money; and even if I did have a rope, I wouldn't give it to you right now, not the mood you are in!"

~~~~~~

Summer 1935: Jimmy could hear his sisters, Esther, Ruth, and Marie downstairs, laughing and talking to his mother. He was getting ready to play at a dance that night and he wanted to look especially good. He pulled out a freshly ironed white shirt, white twill trousers, a black belt, and his favorite red stripe suspenders. Jimmy slicked back his dark hair and splashed some Old Spice on his neck—just in case. He turned and went down the narrow stairway and into the living room where his sisters and mother sat talking.

Esther took one look at him and

Courtesy: Arnold Wamhoff

said, "Va-va-voom! Got a big date tonight, big boy? Who is the lucky girl?"

Jimmy blushed, as he countered, "None of your beeswax!"

Jimmy continued, "No, no, I just have a dance to play for. Say, we are making some decent money and it sure is fun. I get to meet some swell girls and, it seems, they like guys who play in a band!"

~~~~~~~~~~

August 14, 1935: John sat listening to a message from President Roosevelt over the radio. "Well, finally, they are doing something for the elderly folks in this country—they passed what they are calling the Social Security Act which is going to give folks past the age of 65 a monthly check to help with living expenses. Now, that makes good sense to me. We have a moral obligation to take care of the older folks who have paid taxes and worked their entire lives. I like that, I like that a lot!"

John took a deep pull from his cigar and added, "The sad thing is what our teachers get paid---a high school teacher gets $125 a month while a grade school teacher only gets $100. They are expected to put in long hours and live on those wages? But I guess we are all in the same boat, getting less money for wages and everything costs more. Something is bound to happen to bust this injustice, mark my words!"

About that time Jimmy came in from milking the cows. "Say, Dad, I have been thinking of going into the chicken business. I've been reading all the magazines and articles I can get my hands on. There is a good market out there for chickens and eggs. I want to convert that big horse barn into the main chicken house and then I will build a smaller brooder house for newborn chicks. I'm ready to go. I've saved most of my money from the band and I will be able to pay cash. I've settled on Leghorns for the laying hens and White Rocks for fryers. I'll wait until they get to be about four pounds and then the fryers will be ready to sell. I'm going to work in four different cycles of growth—so they all don't mature at the same time and I spread my income out that way. I've contacted some grocery stores and restaurants and have signed them up."

From Personal Interview with Arnold Wamhoff: "*When I got the operation up and going, I had over 1,500 chickens. It went* *well and I bought so many Purina products that I won a trip back to St. Louis to tour their plant and all. That was my first time in a big city and I got kind of lonesome because almost everybody else was married. When it came time to go out on the town, I remember kinda standing aside and this one fellow came up to me and asked if I was going out with the bunch and I told him I was single. He said, "Heck, I'm single. My wife doesn't know it, but I am single tonight and I'll go with you. So we went out nightclubbing.*

It was my first time in the clubs, and being from Wyoming I was a friendly person, so I walked up to the bar there and started talking to some fella, another gent turned to the bartender and said, "Who is this guy here, by gosh he sure is friendly and knows how to get to know people!"

I stayed in the chicken business for about three years, made some decent money, and then I got out of it when my Dad got sick and Ted and I had to take over farming."

~~~~~~~~

December 1935: Over breakfast the next morning, between mouthfuls of food, Jimmy chatted with his mother. "That onery white Ayrshire bull might not have horns, but he is always looking for some opportunity to chase Ted and me. Why Ted even took a pitchfork to him one time and Ted ended up on the fence with the pitchfork laying on the ground! Boy oh boy, I didn't know Ted could move that fast!"

~~~~~~~~

On the drive back to their home in Emblem, after Christmas shopping, Mary said, "John, did you know that Jimmy

Courtesy: Arnold Wamhoff

is joining another dance band? Helen's husband Merle, who is a band director, is putting it together. Jimmy will be on the drums, Chamberlain on the piano, Merle on the Saxophone, and another musician friend of Merle's from Greybull. Jimmy tells me they sound real good and are planning on charging ten cents for a night of dancing. He said they think they might make $15 a night if they play 3 – 4 hours. I can't quite believe the man he has grown into; why, he is even growing a mustache and I must say he looks quite dashing—like Robert Taylor the actor!"

Mary paused for a moment, staring out the window, then she added, "John, do you ever wonder what would have happened if we had let the Billings doctor put Arnold in a cast when he hurt his back and hip? Nevertheless, he came out of it pretty well. He is such a handsome young man with that devilish sense of humor, land sakes, he can make me laugh sometimes."

John said, "It is what it is Mary, we did what we thought was best for him at the time. Now, just where do they think they will have these dances—in our parlor?"

Mary replied, "Oh John, don't be silly. They are fixing up the old roadhouse building—he said the floor downstairs was so bad that they were going to have them upstairs. It's a good-sized room, about 60 feet long and 30 feet wide and they can rent it for next to nothing. They think they can draw a crowd from all around and maybe even a prom or two—who knows. He is so excited about being a part of something like that. He reminds me of you----always looking for ways to make a dollar or two."

<hr>

April 1936: Jimmy was roused from a sound sleep by the booming sound of his father's voice calling up the stairs. "Jimmy, get yourself out of bed, throw on some old clothes. I need help out in the barn with a couple of ewes who are having a hard time delivering!"

Jimmy put his feet on the floor and threw on some old pants and a shirt. He thought, "Oh brother, I hate this—I hope I don't throw up like the last time. Those ewes get in a bad way and I have to stick my hand up their 'yaw-yaw' to pull the lamb out. That has to hurt like hell plus it stinks to high heaven! Dad always makes me do it because my hands are smaller than his or Ted's or the sheepherders. I wish to hell my hands would grow!"

After two hours, Jimmy had helped birth four lambs and had only gagged once. He stood at the barnyard fence and watched the ewes, sniff, and clean their newborns. He had to admit it gave him a good feeling—those lambs could have died if he hadn't helped pull them out

~~~~~~~~~

Late September 1936: "The Band" had a good-sized dance gig up in Fromberg, Montana, just across the Wyoming border. Jimmy asked his father for permission to take the Hudson Terraplane for the evening drive, up there and back. "I suppose it will be plenty late when we get back, Dad. We usually play until after midnight and then, well—you know, folks want just one more song. I'll have Albert along with me to keep me awake."

John slapped Jimmy on the back and said, "Sure, that's fine. I'm glad to see you out there trying to make some extra money and I have to admit, I never knew you boys made so much on one dance night. $10-15 each is nothing to blow smoke at! Just be careful and stay awake!"

~~~~~~~~~

The dance in Fromberg was a great success. Jimmy was on the drums, and with his dark good looks attracted a lot of female attention. His brother-in-law and leader of the band, Merle Prugh, said, "Alright Lover Boy, just keep up the beat. Those girls will be waiting for you after the dance!"

Albert and Jimmy were the youngest guys in the band and the added female attention was a bonus both of them enjoyed. After the dance, they were loading up when a slim little blond cuddled up next to Jimmy. "Say, good lookin' you don't have to go back to Wyoming just yet, do you? Why don't you and your friend come on over to the café and we can get better acquainted?"

Jimmy looked at Albert and Albert looked at Jimmy. "Well, just for a half-hour. We have a long drive back and we're already tired." An hour later, the two fellas finally climbed into the Terraplane. Jimmy turned the ignition and the 'horses' under the hood, roared to life. He spun gravel as they hit the main road back to the Wyoming border.

Albert eased back in the passenger seat and loosen his tie, "Boy those dames were sure good lookin'. Too darn bad we had to be home tonight---we both might have got lucky! Say, how long does it take for you to stop tapping your foot to the music after you stop drumming? That was starting to get annoying---that tapping your foot and all when we was in that restaurant!" It wasn't a half-hour later, they were just about to the Wyoming/Montana border when Jimmy felt himself start to nod off. Albert had been asleep for the last twenty miles. *Darn good companion that guy is—suppose to keep me awake and all---and he falls asleep before we are out of the city limits! I have to stay awake—maybe, open the window, sing a little.*

Jimmy tried all the tricks, but the next thing he knew they were off the road and bouncing over the sagebrush-covered prairie. Jimmy woke up with a start and overcorrected the steering wheel which caused the Terraplane to roll.

When the dust settled, they were both wide awake. Neither man spoke for a few minutes. Finally, Jimmy stammered, "Al--Albert, you okay?"

Albert shook the sleep from his eyes and said, "By gosh Jim, they are going to have to do something with this road, it's getting pretty rough! I think I might upchuck—I got bounced around pretty darn good there!"

Luckily, the roads didn't have a deep drain ditch---it was fairly flat from road to the open prairie, but the problem was, the car wasn't on all four wheels. Albert and Jimmy climbed out of the passenger side of the car, the side that was facing upwards. Jimmy said, "Okay, Albert, you got to help me roll this thing back over or my Dad will kill us both."

The first couple of tries were not successful in putting the Terraplane back onto its wheels. Finally, in frustration, Jimmy gave Albert a sharp slap on the back and said, "Come on, Albert, wake up and push! On the count of three PUSH like you just spotted John Wamhoff walking down the road towards us!"

"One, Two, THREE!" The Terraplane paused, groaned, then flipped back onto its wheels. Jimmy gave a shout of triumph and said, "That-a-way—now let's get back inside and see if this old girl starts."

They climbed inside the Terraplane and Jimmy turned the ignition. The car belched and then began to purr. Jimmy shifted into first and climbed back onto the road. "Now, damn it, Albert, stay awake and talk to me, cause if you don't, I'm going to tell Dad it was your fault!"

~~~~~

Jimmy dropped Albert off at his lane, across the road from where the Wamhoffs lived. The Terraplane rolled quietly down the tree-covered lane and Jimmy drove it around by the machine shop and parked it. He got out and by the light of the moon, took off his shirt and dusted the car off, best he could. *Thank God, there aren't any dents that I can see, just pretty dusty!* Jimmy, grabbed his suit jacket and walked to the house. He let himself in as quietly as he could and began to tiptoe across the living room floor towards the stairway. He took the stairs two at a time, not stepping on the squeaky treads. Once upstairs, he undressed and slid into bed. *Thank you, dear God, for getting us home safe. That was a close one. Amen!*

~~~~~

The next morning Jimmy was eating breakfast before heading for the field. He had a forkful of pancakes and eggs on the way to his mouth when his father came in the back door. "Well now, that was a pretty short night for you, wasn't it? By the looks of that car, you came across the badlands and not on the road!"

Jimmy managed to swallow the fork full of food and then stammered, "Uhhh well, Dad---uhhh, Albert didn't do a very good job of keeping me awake and I ran off the road right there before the border, only once!"

John tried his best to hide a chuckle. "Well, you both probably learned a good lesson and the car looks just fine. It could do with a wash though!"

~~~~~~~~~

The Rural Electric Company was slowly making its way to the wilds of rural Wyoming, but for the present, the Wamhoffs still relied on their massive windmill and generator setup for their electric needs.

Note: From an interview with Arnold Wamhoff: *Dad had installed a large generating plant with a 2-cylinder motor that gave the house and the barns electric lights. Granted, our electricity in the house was a single light bulb hanging down from the center of each room, but it was a good deal better than light from a lantern. That windmill generated 210 watts and then ran the current through a battery bank to charge it up. When it had a total charge, it would automatically shut off. That worked well for years, then when I was out of high school, Dad got a new, bigger generator – it was almost 8 feet high with three sets of guide wires, one at 30' and another at 60', then another way up high on a steel tower. I volunteered to climb up the tower, with that generator tied to my back—it must have weighed between 60 and 70 pounds. Once up there, I had to assemble the whole thing. The only scare I had was when I first started to climb up there – the clouds were passing over and I looked up and I swear, it felt like the thing was falling over. I said to myself, 'Get ahold of yourself!'*

It looked very similar to the big wind turbines they have out in Palm Springs—like a big airplane propeller on a tower. It had this fan on the back that guided it in the wind and it also had an automatic clutch on it in case the wind would get too strong—it would slow it down.

Every once in a while when the wind was really blowing, you could hear the blades going swish, swish swish, faster and faster, and then all at once, that clutch would slow it down. The energy from that went down into the batteries; it generated electricity and kept the batteries charged up. We kept the batteries all down in the dugout cellar close to the house—where Mother kept her canning, potatoes, onions, things from the garden. That's what kind of electricity we had until the Rural Electric Association came in 1941, right before Mom and I were married.

~~~~~~~~

NOTE: Depression comparisons: *In 1930 the average income per year was $1,970 and by 1939 it was $1,730. In 1930 a new house cost $7,145 and by 1939 it cost $3,800. In 1930 a new car cost $640 and by 1939 it cost $700. Gasoline stayed at 10 cents a gallon, but in 1939 most folks didn't have 10 cents for gasoline. Shantytowns like in 'Grapes of Wrath', were found in every state, the larger the population, the more 'Hoovervilles' there were. They were nicknamed after President Herbert Hoover who couldn't seem to do anything to bring the country out of the Depression.*

November 1937: The harvest that year was good enough for John to send in the final payment on his Allis-Chalmers all-crop harvester. The [20]combine was pulled by a tractor and saved them time in and out of the field; there was no more expense to feed and/or keep draft horses. Upon delivery in 1936, John beamed, "I was fortunate that the Co-op agreed to let me have the combine for a down payment with the rest due next year." John put $385.00 down with the final payment of $305.00 to be paid on November 1st of 1937.

~~~~~~~~

It had been a long hot fall and John was ready for a nice drive somewhere. He stood outside in the back yard—stood looking at the Bighorn Mountains to the east. He turned and hurried back inside the house. "Mary, can you get somebody to watch the switchboard today? I think we need to get out of our rut and take a nice drive."

Mary looked up with surprise written all over her face. "What? Well, mercy me I don't know what has gotten into you all of a sudden? I suppose I can call Esther to take over for the afternoon. Can you give me an hour or so, I have to curl my hair and change my dress. You promise we will be gone only a few hours?"

John winked and grinning replied, "Well, it might be the entire afternoon!"

~~~~~~~~~

John and Mary climbed into the Chevrolet sedan and headed for the highway. John paused and said, "Which way do you want to go?"

Mary turned and looked at him. "Which way do I want to go? I thought you had some great idea in your head for a drive? Oh for heaven's sake—turn left!"

John turned the car left and they drove east toward Greybull, taking their time, looking at the fields. "It's good everybody had a fine harvest this year. The granaries are full and people are breathing easier now that it's over."

Mary said, "Yes, it was a long summer. I am almost through with my canning as well. We will have plenty to eat this winter!" She paused as they started down the hill into the Greybull valley. "So—we are going into Greybull? To do what?" John said, "Well, we are going through Greybull and will continue on our drive eastward!"

Mary threw her arms up in the air, "OH JOHN, for heaven's sake stop playing games. Where are we going---I know you have something up your sleeve. What is eastward except the Bighorn Mountains?"

John chuckled and said, "I have been wanting to see the road they've made up the Shell Canyon. I've heard it's beautiful and we can see the fall colors too!"

Mary's face blanched, "SHELL CANYON—you mean to drive up that oneway road that goes up along Shell Creek? Oh, John, I don't think---I don't think I want to do that. I have heard horror stories about that road—how narrow and steep the sides are. Let me off at the bottom and pick me up on your way back, I'm serious!"

John pinched her cheek and laughing, said, "Oh come on Mary, where is your sense of adventure? You have been over the Bighorn Mountains on a worse road and in a covered wagon. This will be a piece of cake!"

The next two hours were exciting and definitely 'something out of the everyday grind' on the farm. Mary screamed of fright more than once and John was fearful she might take his life!

The road was dry which was a blessing, but it lived up to every other frightening story about its steep grade, dropoffs to the canyon floor below, and hairpin turns.

Courtesy: Tom Davis

John found a place to turn around and they headed back down the way they had come up. Mary said, "I was hoping it would be better going down than it was coming up---I was wrong!" When they finally reached the bottom, they stopped at a gas station in Shell. John filled the car with gas and paid for two soda pops. John put his foot on the running board and leaned into the car. "Now Mrs. Wamhoff, THAT was an adventure, was it not?"

~~~~~~~

May 1938: Jimmy and Albert gassed up the Terraplane and gave her a good washing. There was a church social this evening at St. John's Lutheran Church in Lovell. The Lutheran churches in the Bighorn Basin participated in social occasions for their youth, and it was Lovell's turn to put on supper and a skit.

The narrow two-lane highway to Lovell wound through the badlands. Jimmy said, "Hey, Albert—did you know that until 1920 the road over to Lovell started in Greybull and followed the old stagecoach road?"

Albert remarked, "I'd say you're a regular encyclopedia. Where'd you learn all of that fascinating information? It looks to me like they just laid asphalt on top of the dirt, didn't take out too many of the hills and dips, did they? I could get sick to my stomach if I didn't watch the road."

Jimmy said, "Ahhh go shove it. I just thought you might want to add some factual education to your limited knowledge!"

~~~~~~~~~

The two dapper young men walked down the steps into the church basement where the youth gathering was to be held. Jimmy spotted 'her' before Albert and he nudged his friend in the ribs. "Say, get a load of that sweetheart over there, the one with the red ribbon in her hair. She is sure a cute one. I've got to see if she will pour me some of that lemonade."

Jimmy held his glass up so she could see it and that worked like a charm. Beata Korell walked over to the two fellows from Emblem. "I see you are fresh out of lemonade—I have plenty here. Let me fill your glasses." Jimmy took note of her sweet face with a few freckles sprinkled over her pert nose. She had sparkling blue eyes and soft brown hair rolled up in the latest style that reminded Jimmy of sausages. He said, "Thank you—uhh, do you have a name?"

Beata blushed and lowered her head, "Of course I have a name, it's Beata, what's yours?"

Jimmy said, "I'm Jimmy Wamhoff and this here guy is my buddy, Albert Blank. So, have you lived in Lovell long---and I don't mean to be rude, but I never heard the name 'Beata' before."

Beata blushed again and said, "Oh I get that a lot—actually, it's from the Bible---you know, the 'beatitudes'. I just graduated from Cowley High School and then we moved back to Lovell. I went to most of my high school years here. How about you?"

Jimmy said, "We're from Emblem. I lived on the farm my whole life except for the four years I lived in Greybull when I went to high school. Say, what are they serving for supper tonight, I sure am hungry?"

Beata glanced toward the kitchen, "I think it's meatloaf---it's really good, I tried some earlier. I'm sorry, they need me in the kitchen. Nice to meet both of you, let me know when you run out of lemonade."

~~~~~~~

On the way home, Jimmy had to stop the car at least twice so that he and Albert could take a leak. "Man, I musta drank a pitcher or two of lemonade. I just wanted to talk more to that Beata girl. She's a peach. I might try and ask her out."

Albert said, "Well, get in line because she was sure giving me the eye. You probably didn't notice that. I just might beat you to the draw on this one!"

~~~~~~~

Jimmy didn't waste any time--he found out that Beata worked as a fountain girl at the Lovell Drugstore and the next time he was in Lovell, he stopped in. He pushed open the drugstore's wooden door and the bell jingled, announcing his arrival. He took a moment to survey the store and then spotted Beata behind the soda counter. Jimmy made a beeline for one of the stools.

She turned around and stopped in her tracks. With her hands on her hips, she cocked her cute little face to the side and said, "Well now, who do we have here?"

Jimmy made several more trips to Lovell before he got up the nerve to ask Beata out. "I got a real feeling about you and me, I am falling pretty hard for you, Beata. Would you be my steady girl?"

She nudged him in the ribs and said, "Ahhh, I'll bet you say that to all the girls on the first date—is that your line or something?"

Jimmy slid over on the car seat and took her hand in his. "No Beata, I don't have a line. I am asking you to be my girl. What do you say?"

She said, "I like you a lot Jimmy, but I think you might be putting the rush on me. I am only 18. I think we can date now and then, but let's take it slow. By the way, Lovell high school is having their Prom next month—do you dance?"

Beata discovered at the Lovell Prom that the farmer from Emblem indeed knew how to dance and then some!

In his mind, Jimmy had found his girl. She was everything he had dreamed of and thought she would make a great wife. The trouble was, he was broke and he didn't have much to offer a wife, right now. He was determined that someday, Beata would be his!

He also knew he would have to watch Albert, who also had his eye on the sweet little thing from Lovell.

~~~~~~~~~

Mary watched John out of the corner of her eye, as he had been bent over his farm ledger for hours. "John, what in the world are you doing— you have been at that forever?"

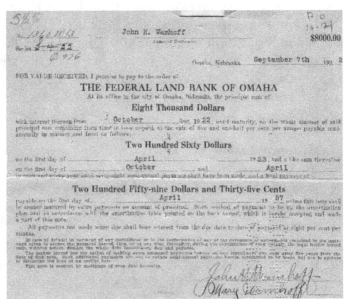

Courtesy: Arnold Wamhoff

John looked up, obviously frustrated. "I'm trying to figure out how I am going to pay the bills. I know I continue to buy machinery. We must have good machinery to maximize our time, we have to have it to keep up, to make a profit."

John rubbed his eyes and ran his hands back through his hair. "I feel like it all worked out until now and suddenly, I feel like I have my back up against a wall. Seriously, Mary, I think that my only way out of this tight spot is to mortgage the sheep before I send them up on the Bighorns. That will give us money to pay the Omaha bank and keep us going over the summer until I get the wool sold. I'll talk to Mr.Willams at the bank in Greybull, and see what he thinks."

Mary patted John's shoulder and said, "We'll get through this tight spot, just like we got through the rest of them. We just have to grit our teeth and dig in!"

~~~~~~~~

John stood on the back porch and watched as the clouds boiled up into thunderheads over the Bighorn Mountains; the sky turned to a threatening deep blue/black. Large raindrops smacked the dry earth as puffs of dust shot up then turned to mud. They hadn't had a good rainstorm in a month of Sundays, and they all prayed this much-needed rain would amount to more than a few sprinkles. The clouds hung low over the horizon as the rain increased and rivulets of water ran through the low spots in the farmyard. They needed a slow soaking rain, not a cloudburst.

Dry Creek and the other usually arid hill creeks turned dangerous, churning and rolling with chocolate-colored waves of runoff. They were filled with debris that was ripped from the banks as the raging water tore through the ravines and creekbeds.

John said, "Now, we get the rain? Now, when the pitiful crops are harvested and the growing season is over. We just can't seem to catch a break! Men are leaving their destitute families and riding the rails looking for work, any kind of work. President Roosevelt has put together a work program called the Civilian Conservation Corps to improve the national parks, build bridges, and hiking trails on the public lands. Why, I had a fellow walk down the lane the other day who just wanted a job, any job. I told him all I could pay him was a dollar to muck out the barn."

John ran his fingers through his hair, "I feel for these men, I'm just a footstep away from being in their situation too. My grain only grew to half the usual height last year. It's a hell of a time to be a farmer, but at least we can raise some food to eat. I hope the President's ideas work because this country is going to hell in a handbasket!"

John looked to the west as the sun was setting. The sky above the Rocky Mountains glowed red with the setting sun's fire. Every time he looked away for a moment then back again, it looked different—as if God was taking his paintbrush and swiping the sky with beautiful shades of mauve, red, orange, yellow—all swirled against the bird-egg blue sky.

~~~~~~~~

June 1938: John had been sitting at the kitchen table for two hours, going over and over his accounts and debts, trying to find some way to get through his financial crisis. He pushed back from the table; frustration and defeat crushing down on him. John walked out the back door and down the steps. With every step he took, it all came back to him---his plan for this land, for their future, every one of the struggles, every one of the defeats, along with every triumph and blessing the Lord had given them. He walked back by the machine shed, the shade of the giant cottonwood casting dark, long shadows as the day began to fade. He felt the need to be alone. John fell to his knees. "*Why Lord God, why did you bring us this far, put us through all---the trials, tribulations, defeats, and glorious prospering in this inhospitable land---to come to this point? I don't understand and I am losing heart. It seems that I work, I plan, I try my best to follow your word and, and---it's like trying to climb uphill in a landslide. Oh please, dear Lord, I feel like you have turned your face from me. Give me strength Lord. This I ask in your name. Amen*"

John rose on unsteady legs, feeling persistent nausea, dizziness, and ignoring the pressure in the middle of his chest, he pressed on, back toward the house. His breath came in short, gasping breathes, beads of sweat peppered his forehead, as he stumbled toward the back door. John barely made it to a chair in the kitchen where Mary was washing dishes. She took one look at him, dropped her dishcloth in the sink, and rushed to his side.

"John, what in the world? Are you ill, should I call the doctor?"

John Wamhoff put his head down between his knees and after a bit, he sat up. "No, I—uhhh—I just had a bit of a spell I think, nothing to worry about. I imagine that a cold beer and a cigar is just what I need! No need to worry, I'm strong as a bull!"

Alarm filled Mary as she urged him to lie down for a bit. "John, it's obvious you are not well, I don't recall ever seeing you like this. If you don't lay down on the couch right this minute, I am going to call the doctor!"

John grabbed Mary's arm, "No, no—don't go doing something as foolish as that. Like I said, I'm fine, just a little stressed and tired. I'll be fine, just fine."

Chapter Seventeen

THE LAST FULL MEASURE

"The Lord giveth and the Lord taketh away…."
                     Job 1:20 KJV

September 8, 1938: John finished supper and pushed his chair back from the kitchen table as Mary stacked the dirty dishes. He put a light to his cigar then went to stand at the front window and for the tenth time, he looked out towards the mountains.

Mary remarked, "John, what in the world is the matter with you? You've been as jumpy as a cat on a hot tin roof the entire day."

John turned from the window, "Well now, Mary—it's raining down here, but those clouds are laying low on the mountains and I have a bad feeling that it's putting down early snow up there. We all know what early snows can be like in this country and up on the mountain, they could be in an all-out blizzard. Fernando was supposed to start the sheep down off of the summer range yesterday. I can't even consider that they might all get caught in a blizzard."

The ring of the telephone in the outer room shattered the din of apprehension that enveloped John and Mary. Mary hurried to answer the telephone. "Hello---Yes, this is the Wamhoff residence, this is Mary. Can I help you?" There was silence as the voice on the other end spoke. Mary's face turned pale, her eyes opened wide as her left hand gripped the receiver. "Oh Mercy me, what did you say? Oh, that can't be, it just can't be. Here, wait a moment, I'll put my husband on the phone."

"John, John, come quick. Its, it's the doctor at the Greybull hospital on the other end. Brace yourself John—it isn't good news."

John picked up the phone, his hands were shaking. "Hello, this is John Wamhoff." He listened—and as he continued to listen, his hand grew white from gripping the phone as beads of sweat glistened on his forehead. He slumped onto the nearby chair. "Yes, yes, I understand. I appreciate the call doctor and of course, everything you did for Fernando—and you, you are sure about the herd of sheep, absolutely sure?"

With shaking hands, John reached up to hang the receiving end of the telephone in the cradle. He fell to his knees. Mary knelt beside him, holding him in her arms—and they wept.

"Oh, Mary, Mary---Fernando is dead—the doctors couldn't save him. He told me Fernando managed to tell him that the entire herd went off a cliff in the blizzard, including two dogs. He said he couldn't see his hand in front of his face. They were on their way down the mountain when the blizzard struck with subzero temperatures and gale winds. He couldn't tell the sky from the ground. Fernando tried to gather the sheep best he could, but they got spooked somehow and stampeded----1,500 sheep went off a sheer cliff, hundreds of feet to the canyon floor There is no way to reach them. Fernando barely made it off the mountain—he finally gave his horse the reins—that was the only way he made it. The doctor said Fernando was half-frozen, and his lungs were frostbitten so bad—he died."

Tears streamed down John's face as he managed to stand. He began to rant. "WHY? What am I going to do now? Those sheep were my last chance to make it through this year. We are broke now, Mary. I mortgaged every one of those sheep—the bank will take the farm!" John ran his hands through his thinning head of hair; his face was beet red as Mary tried to calm him.

"John, please calm yourself. We will find some way, we always do, always have. We can talk to the bank, perhaps sell the other farm to pay the mortgage. We will find a way to get through this. Let me fix you some tea, perhaps that will calm you down."

John turned on her, "TEA? Do you think a damned cup of tea is going to fix this? We are dead broke woman. How hard is that to understand? We have just lost everything, ev-ery-thing we have ever worked for---forty years of work and planning and now-----It's GONE!" He stomped out the back door and slammed it hard. Mary watched as he staggered down the path, kicked open the picket fence gate, and stumbled out into the farmyard. John reached the corral fence and leaned against it, his back heaving with gut-wrenching sobs. Mary stood alone, watching. *I can't help him, can't go to him---he needs to be alone.*

Eventually, John regained his composure and turned to walk back toward the white farmhouse. He pushed open the white picket gate and lifted his leg to kick it shut. As he started up the path toward the house, the pain exploded in his chest. He never made it.

~~~~~~~~~

Mary looked out the kitchen window to see if John was still down by the barn. In the waning light of the evening, her gaze was drawn to a figure on the ground between the white picket fence and the back door. It was John.

Mary dropped her cup in the kitchen sink. She didn't even hear it shatter as she ran for the back door, screaming for Arnold as she ran. Her feet flew down the steps and out onto the path where John lay. She rolled him over. His eyes fluttered and beads of perspiration peppered his forehead. Arnold was suddenly at her side, holding his father's head up in his hands. "Dad, Dad---can you hear me?"

John's eyes fluttered again and his lips tried to move, but no sound came out. "Mother, call Ted to come over here fast. I can't move Dad by myself, he's too big. We need to get him inside. After you call Ted, call the doctor from Greybull to come out. Explain what has happened. I don't know for sure, but I think Dad has had either a stroke or a heart attack!"

Ted lived just across the orchard. When he got the word, he ran out the back door and across the orchard as fast as he could run. He was at the house in a matter of minutes. Together, Arnold and Ted gently lifted their father and carried him into the house. They laid him on his bed as Mary adjust his clothing, took his shoes off as well as his belt. She opened his shirt and brought a cool washcloth to sponge off his face.

Mary put one hand under John's head as she wiped his face. "John, John—can you hear me?"

John's eyes fluttered again and his hand went to his chest— "Hur—hu—hurt, baa-bad."

Arnold and Ted looked at each other. "I think he's had a heart attack. You don't know this Ted, but he just got a call—all of the sheep and Fernando are dead. There was a whiteout blizzard in the Bighorns and the sheep—all of them went off a cliff. He got a call from the doctor in Greybull. We are broke now because he mortgaged those sheep, so we'd have money to get us through the year until the wool sales come in. He's sure the bank will have no recourse but to foreclose on the farm!"

Ted's face was ashen as the depth of the situation sank in. "What are we going to do?"

Arnold said, "First, we are going to get a doctor out here for Dad. We need him, he's got to pull through."

~~~~~~~~~

After calling their daughter Esther, who was a trained nurse, Mary waited for the doctor to make the eighteen-mile drive out to the farm. She did what she could to keep John comfortable and calm as she tried to focus on the glittering snow that covered the ground. Outside their bedroom window, the sky hung low like a piece of gray sheet metal. The last of the cottonwood leaves had fallen to the ground, leaving the twisted, naked branches clawing for the night sky.

After the doctor checked John over thoroughly he asked to speak to Mary and her sons in the next room. He shook his head as he took Mary's hand in his. "I don't have good news and I want to make it as easy on you as I can. Frankly, John has had a massive heart attack. The next few days will tell us if he is going to make it or not. It's not wise to try and move him into the hospital at this time. He needs complete bed rest and around the clock nursing. I've medicated him heavily and want him to stay in bed, in this semi-coma for several days."

Turning to her daughter, Mary said, "Our daughter Esther is a qualified nurse and she lives right here in Emblem. She will stay with him, and take care of him. Just leave her instructions if you will—what you think is needed. We'll just take it a day at a time and see what happens—that, and pray!"

Arnold and Ted walked the doctor out to his car. "We can't pay you right now, Doc, but send us a bill and it will be paid. Thank you for coming out here, it means a lot to us."

The doctor put his hand on the Wamhoff boy's shoulders. "He is a good man, a great man. I have seen the things he has done for other people and this community, he was always first in line to help out. You boys can be very proud of him. I don't want you to worry about paying me---it's on the house!"

As the doctor's car pulled away, Arnold and Ted looked at each other. Jimmy said, "Now, what do we do Ted?" The young brothers wrapped their arms around each other as their emotion and fear filled them. Ted pushed Jimmy back and with his hands resting on his brother's shoulders, said, "The fact of the matter is, the future of the farm is up to us now, we are in the driver's seat!"

Farming was all they knew and it was all they wanted to do---farm the land and keep the Wamhoff farm in the family. Finally, Arnold said, "Ted, I don't know right now, what we are going to do. I think maybe we wait and see if he pulls through. We have time to figure it out. I do know this, we have to concentrate on bringing the rest of this harvest in. We need the money from the crops in the worst way."

Ted said, "I know we can do that, we've done it a hundred times! I think we should get the legal papers together, go into the bank, and talk to Gerald Williams about our options. We need to know what he is can do for us now—so we know what he wants from us, and find out how, how.... in the hell, we hang onto this farm."

Ted started toward the pasture that separated their homes. He turned and said, "My gosh Jim, what else do we know how to do, but farm? I've got a wife and two kids to take care of too." Jimmy waved goodbye and walked back inside the house where his mother sat beside John's bed.

Jimmy laid his work-worn hand on her shoulder, and said, "How are you doing Mother? Do you want me to call the others, so they at least know about his heart attack? We're not going to know much for several days according to the doctor."

Mary nodded her head in agreement, "Yes, son, that would be a good idea. Let's wait until morning, to see how he does through the night. I'm just not up to seeing everyone right now. I'd probably burst into tears and I don't want that. Oh, and call the pastor, I'd like him to come over and say some prayers over your father tomorrow."

Arnold walked toward the telephone room. His boots felt like they had cement in them. He dreaded making these phone calls to his siblings and the pastor. After he finished making the necessary calls, he went out on the porch. The sun had just set, the fall air had a crispness to it and the grass was frosted with the first snow of the season. Arnold sat down on the wooden bench, put his head into his hands, and wept. As the tears subsided, he sat up and wiped his eyes. The black night sky to the north was a wash of pulsing Northern Lights, green, white, pink. He thought *it's a sign, a sign that Dad is going to pull through this!*

The young man rose to his feet and ran his fingers back through his thick head of hair. *I can't believe this has happened. Dad is built like a bull, he always seemed so strong, to have all the right answers—this all seems like a nightmare. Ted and I have to take control right now because I don't think Dad is ever going to be himself again. We can do it, I know we can. We still have Jack and Obie—they are good 'farm help' and they know this farm as well as we do. I just hope we will be able to keep them on. Maybe they will work for less this year until we get back on our feet. But, without the sheep, I don't know---it's not going to be easy. 'Please Dear, Lord Jesus, be with us, help us do what we have to do, and if it is your will, heal our father! Amen.'*

<p style="text-align:center">~~~~~~~~</p>

Four days later, the doctor made another visit to the Wamhoff farm. Esther had been at her father's side from that terrible night, only going back to her own family during the nights. The doctor suggested that they go to Billings and purchase a good wheelchair—"I think if you could find a sturdy wheelchair, one like President Roosevelt has—it reclines, John would be comfortable in it once he feels well enough to get out of bed." Jimmy got the name of the store that carried items for invalid patients—including a urinal, a bedpan, and the [21]wheelchair. He made a special trip to Billings to get the things that would make his father's life more comfortable. He sold his father's favorite horse to get enough money for the items—he never told his dad what he did, he never had to.

As the weeks, then months went by, daily tasks evolved into a system. They moved John into what had been the parlor—a large west-facing room, big enough for a bed for Esther when she needed to spend the night. If she didn't spend the night, somebody else slept near John. She usually came over in the morning to give John a sponge bath and his medications. Esther had been an assistant to Dr. Gorder and he taught her how to nurse. Ruth would come in the afternoons for an hour or so; Marie came out from Greybull, Ruth from Emblem, and Helen came from Casper----they all did what they could when they could.

NOTE: **Actual Wheelchair** discovered in the Wamhoff   granary   and refurbished by the author.

~~~~~~~~

Esther confided in her mother, "I don't see much improvement in Dad. He should be able to do more than he can. But we will wait and see."

Mary changed into her nightdress and combed her hair. After locking the doors and checking her kitchen for the last time, she turned and looked out the kitchen window. The house was eerily quiet, which seemed strange to her after everything the walls of their house had seen and heard over the past twenty years. *Now, it's as though this house and those of us living here are patiently and respectfully, waiting for what comes next!* She pulled back the covers of the bed which they had shared for so many years and crawled under the cool sheets. Mary pulled the blankets up to her chin as a shiver ran through her body, partly because of the cool sheets and partly because of the premonition which would not leave her be.

I always loved that kitchen window, to look out on our farm—everything we built here, on what was a vast parcel of the sage-brush-covered prairie. Now, I look out and all I feel is fear of the unknown, of a future without John. The doctors have been frank with us-- they don't expect he will live long and that he will never walk again. What is going to happen to the farm, to Ted and Arnold, *to me? We had $200 in the checking account and this farm is mortgaged to the hilt as the banker put it. I have the airport hill land but that's all I have. I pray for the strength to get through all this and to remain strong for my boys. I know Ted and Arnold can take over the farm if they are given a chance. It bothers me greatly that the neighbors and people who owe John money, refuse to acknowledge it. John worked to harvest their crops and being a good man he let them slide, waited for payment, and now they have turned their backs on us in our time of need. I never suspected they would do something so like this.*

Mary turned and walked through the quiet house. Arnold was upstairs sleeping in his room, the only sibling left at home. She paused outside the door to the large bedroom where John now slept. She pushed open the door. She stood at the foot of the narrow bed and looked at him. *He is still such a handsome man, even after the heart attack. He looks so peaceful, lying there. None of us know if John will ever come out of this heart attack, not even the doctors.*

Two days later John emerged from his coma-like state. He was very weak, but he knew what he wanted. His first words were to ask for his sons.

'Boys, it's all over with. I borrowed---- I mortgaged those sheep and now--- they are dead. The bank's President Gerald Williams has every right to take this farm. The only thing you can do is to go to town and walk in the bank with every confidence and convince them that you know this business, you know this farm, and you know you can make it work. I got a feeling there is another war coming and if I'm right, there will be good prices for crops again. If the bank will make it easy on you to repay the mortgage, then I know you can do it---you are smart boys, good farmers!'

~~~~~~~~~

Jimmy walked across the yard to where Obie and Jack shared the small bunkhouse. He knocked once and pushed open the door. A medley of odors hit him in the face---those particular odors of two bachelors living in close quarters. He noticed that the spittoon hadn't been emptied in a while. Jimmy envisioned bodies that hadn't met up with a bath in a while either; and clothes that just might be able to stand on their own.

Jack said, "Have a chair---just throw that thar shirt over there!" Jimmy pulled up a chair and sat down. "I wanted to come on down and have a talk with you men. It looks like it is going to be Ted and me running this farm, but we need you to stay on with us. Dad might not ever pull out of this thing and we have to pitch in to save the farm from the bank. Can we count on you? It might be just room and board for a while until we get our feet underneath us."

~~~~~~~~

John's recovery was slow going, but as soon as the boys and Mary thought John was up to it, the two young men sat down with their father and laid out a plan to run the farm. Ted and his family lived in a small house over on the corner of the orchard, about two city blocks from the home place. The brothers had a mutual agreement to share the outbuildings, stock, machinery, but would live in different homes. Ted would milk the cows one night and Jimmy, the next night. Mary said, "I still have the telephone switchboard money and I can certainly gather the eggs and take care of the chickens and turkeys. I won't have to plant big gardens. If Alleen wants to share the garden and help with the planting and all, that's fine with me too. The orchard is there for both of you as well."

John gave his sons his blessing and the first thing they did was to make an appointment with the bank president, Gerald Williams. The two young men washed up, put clean shirts and pants on along with their best hats. They got in the car and headed to town. Arnold had assembled the necessary legal documents to take to their banker to plead their case, including the outstanding debts owed by local farmers to John Wamhoff for harvesting. On the way into Greybull, Ted and Arnold discussed how they would present their long-range plan to Gerald Williams at the First National Bank.

The Wamhoff brothers were nervous when they climbed the steps to the bank and pushed open the double doors. Jimmy said, "Well brother, here we go—let's give it our best!" They were ushered into Mr. William's office and took their seats in front of his mahogany desk. Gerald Williams walked in and sat in his leather chair facing the two men. "First, I want to say how very sorry I am to hear about your father's health. I know these are difficult times. Your father was a master at managing his money and extremely generous to his neighbors. I wish you luck in collecting those harvesting debts from your neighbors—it's a hell of a thing!"

Gerald Williams moved forward in his chair, "I appreciate you coming in to see me today to talk about the situation. I want to tell you both that the secret to getting through these tough times, the secret to rebuilding is care and commitment and I can see you have those two attributes in spades. I realize you are taking on this debt for your father's sake, and secondly for your personal futures. As your bank, we want you to succeed and we will do everything we can to see that happen. We are not going to call the mortgage on the sheep. That was a terrible act of fate and we will extend your credit for another year. There will be money coming in from wool sales from the shearing last spring, of course. You will need that for operating expenses, I understand how that has worked for you in the past. Do you intend to restart the sheep business?"

Arnold spoke up, "No, Mr. Williams, we are going to stay out of the sheep business! We are sticking to row crops and once we get the bank paid off, we may look into registered cattle as a backup source of income. We are also going to sell the rest of the draft horses that Dad has hated to part with. The army is buying them and what they don't want, we're sure that the slaughterhouses will take them. Those horses aren't earning their keep anymore and it's time to part ways as we farm with tractors now. We have also discussed selling the Baxter farm. We certainly don't have the facilities to farm all that land and we don't need it for the sheep anymore. The problem is who has the money to buy a farm?"

"As we said, we now use tractors to farm with. They indeed have their costs, like gasoline, but the government sees to it we have our allotted share. They need tires, batteries, oil, and grease---and we are both pretty good when it comes to doing the repairs ourselves. We have two tractors, an Allis-Chalmers and a Case; and not to forget the Minneapolis Moline that we use only when one of the other tractors gets in a bind. Our machinery is sound and on the newer side, so we won't need to make any large purchases there."

Ted added, "We are committed! We work well together, always have and we know what we have to do to get the farm back on its feet—with your help of course. We have threshed two fields of beans and grain, the sugar beets look good and we plan to dig them, starting the first week in October. Prices are steady right now and if all goes well, we won't have any trouble making that first payment. We have done our homework Mr. Williams and think we have this farm where it should be."

Gerald Williams stood and extended his hand to both of the young men. "I will see to it that a significant amount of money is put into your operating account for spring planting and operations throughout next summer as you need it. The clerk out front will have the necessary papers ready for you to sign. I wish you the best of luck and I am betting you two will pull this out of the fire! Give my best to your father and mother!"

Ted and Arnold thanked the banker, signed the papers, and walked to their car. Ted slid behind the wheel as Arnold climbed in the passenger side. "Boy oh boy, I am shaking like a leaf! That went much better than I had even hoped. Ted, I know we can make this work—we're a good team and we're going to save the Wamhoff farm and our father's good name! I don't know about you---and, it is the middle of the day, but I could use a stiff drink, how about you?"

~~~~~~~~~

That afternoon when they returned to the farm, Ted and Arnold couldn't wait to tell their father about the meeting at the bank. Arnold said, "Dad, Mr. Williams said he believed in you. He believes Ted and I have what it takes to bring this farm back from the brink. He is not going to foreclose! We are going to go after those people up here who can afford to pay what they owe you from harvesting their crops. I have an appointment with the lawyer, Goppert in Cody to see if we can get some of the money back."

They didn't mention the plan to eventually sell the draft horses as some things were better left unsaid.

Ted reached over and touched his father's shoulder. "Dad, we won't let you down, we are going to keep the Wamhoff farm afloat. We have a plan and Mr. Williams liked what we told him."

John looked up at his two sons and replied in a weakened voice, "I-I am, glad—you went to town—to the bank. Williams is a- a fair banker---I know you two will do the job, God willing!"

~~~~~~~~~

Arnold and Ted concentrated on getting the crops out of the ground and to market. They got better than expected prices, which left a little extra money for emergencies. They had the whole winter to make their crop plan for the following spring. They tried and tried again to collect the long-overdue harvest money those folks owed their father. When attorney, Goppert told them they didn't have a legal leg to stand on, Jimmy blew his top. "Well, I think I'll take out a page in the Greybull Standard and post their names!"

Goppert said, "That won't get you anywhere but in court— you can't win because you don't have the paper to back it up, pure and simple!"

Jimmy said, "I guess we have learned another lesson, Ted. From now on if we harvest like that for others, we get the money upfront---or we don't harvest their crops. They know Dad is sick and we're in a tough spot, and still, they won't pay."

Ted said, "I guess you can't get blood out of a turnip—isn't that how the saying goes? Well, then, I say we plow those turnips under! Lesson learned!"

~~~~~~~~~

February 16, 1939: Mary looked out the kitchen window and couldn't spot the big horse barn because of swirling snow. A major snowstorm had been forecast, but this was a bit more than a snowstorm—it was a nasty blizzard and it was socked in! She thought to herself, *I am glad the boys milked the cows early, they were smart to get their chores done. Arnold has a long rope that he can still use from the house to the dings if worse comes to worst and Ted knows better than to try and walk across that pasture in this whiteout.* They listened to the radio that evening and the announcer predicted the most ferocious blizzard to hit the region in years. There were reports of moisture getting into car motors and shorting the ignitions. The county sent out warnings to all garages and filling stations to warn drivers not to venture out onto the roads. There were reports of roads being drifted over by large drifts of snow, six feet deep in places.

Mary said, "I'm certainly glad we are snug and safe right here at home. It looks bad out there. I'm going to leave lights on in windows, just in case some folks get in a jam." As the telephone operator, she received several calls regarding the storm over the next several hours. She helped out when she could.

~~~~~~~~~

May 1939: The Wamhoff brothers planted three fields in Great Northern Beans, one in sugar beets, and the rest in grain. The spring rains came when they were needed; the brothers didn't have to deal with mud or drought. So far so good!

When it was time to plant the garden, Mary looked at it as a blessing. A few days when she had her mind on something other than her husband's future and his suffering. Mary would be the first to admit that she didn't know what to do for John---it was beyond her. When not in her garden or gathering eggs, or separating milk, or cooking, she remained at the switchboard, a familiar, calming place in the big picture of what her daily life had become since John fell ill. She relied on Esther to care for John---she was a natural nurse and John responded to her more than to Mary.

For nine months, Esther came almost every day and administered to her father's needs. There was nothing wrong with his mind—it was clear as a bell and he had plenty of time, lying in bed, to think about his life and the error of his ways. *"Lord, I see it all so clearly now—you took what you gave so that I could see you. It wasn't me that accomplished all this, it wasn't by my abilities or insight that we prospered and rose above travesty. The more you gave, the more I took the credit for the success. It was through your grace that Mary and I have made it so far through this life. We have had some hard times---the loss of our first child, traveling to this far place. The recent years of struggle have taken their toll on us. I believe I have never been the husband Mary needed or deserve—I gave her this hard life and expected so much from her. She is such a gentle, giving soul and I think perhaps I took advantage of that. I thought of myself first and what I wanted. She has been a wonderful wife, giving everything she has and more, and rarely receiving the credit or admiration she deserves. I was the worst in taking her for granted. She deserved better than me.*

Through the good years, I began to think our success was because of my wisdom, of my choices, but I was wrong. I see it all so clearly now. I am ashamed that I did not see it before, I was blinded by earthly possessions, by success. Bless the life my wonderful Mary has left. I am ready whenever you give me the final call if you will have me.

~~~~~~~~~~

June 1939*:* John called Jimmy and Ted in to talk to them about the farm. They stood at the foot of his bed. Jimmy spoke first, "Dad, we want you to know the crops are planted, everything is going fine, just fine. Water is in the ditches and we are paying the bills. We sold the grain and beans—got top dollar for them. Prices for the crops are better than last year—starting to go up again, just like you predicted. We received one payment for the sugar beets, and another one will come in August or thereabouts."

John smiled faintly and said, "That's good news. Now, what about those folks who owe us money for harvesting?'

Ted said, "We are working on it Dad." They had agreed not to tell their father that according to the law, they would never recoup the money loaned.

John became agitated, "I loan them money, harvest crops, help them—now, I need help and---they, they act--like I----I arggghh!"

He grabbed his chest and his mouth opened but no words came out. Ted yelled for Esther and she came running. She put one hand behind John's head and eased him back onto the bed. She reached for her stethoscope to listen to his heart. His breath was coming in rapid gasps, sweat beaded on his forehead as he thrashed about. They couldn't understand a word he was saying, he was incoherent. Esther turned and shouted, "Call the doctor---he is having another heart attack! HURRY!"

Chapter Eighteen

MY COURSE IS RUN

**"I Have fought the good fight, I have finished the course,
I have kept the faith."**
2 Timothy 4:17 KJV

June 1939: Mary, Ted, and Arnold gathered at the foot of John's bed as Esther continued to work on her father, trying to keep him calm until the doctor arrived.

Dr. Myre asked everyone to wait in the living room while he administered to John. Esther stood nearby if he needed her. After what seemed an eternity, the door to the bedroom opened and the doctor walked out. He stood for a moment, looking at the floor, then he looked up and said, "That was a bad one. He is a strong man, with a stronger will, but I must advise you to prepare yourselves because he will not survive another attack if he gets through this one."

Jimmy and Ted thanked the doctor and walked him out to his car. "I want to thank you for coming out. I assume you will send us your bill? As you know, we will pay as much on what we owe every month as we can."

Dr. Myre said, "I told you before, it's on the house. I don't want you folks to worry about paying me. Spend as much time with your father as you can—that's all I can tell you." He shook hands with the Wamhoff brothers then climbed into his car.

Jimmy said, "Ted, I—ahh, I need some time. You might as well go on home for now." Jimmy walked down to the barn, he knew he needed to come to grips with his emotions, thoughts, and fears. His steps slowed as he entered the dank, familiar walls of the musty barn where he had spent so many hours, milking cows, helping with an animal birth, pitching hay. Everything came down on him at once and he punched the unpainted barn wood wall, then leaned against it as the pent-up emotion consumed him---the fear, the anguish, the blame.

Ted realized Jimmy was in a bad way as he too, turned and walked toward the barn. This was no time for his younger brother to be alone. He pushed the weathered barn door open and saw his younger brother, crumped on the floor. He walked over to Jimmy and put his hand on his shoulder. "Hey there—Dad is still alive, Jim—we still have him—even after he goes, he'll always be with us, everything he taught us, we'll remember it all. We have been blessed with a wonderful, talented, giving father."

Jimmy stood and looked at his brother, tears streaming down his face. "I---I just can't look at Dad like this. He was always so strong, like a bull—in control, so wise, so generous. We always went to Dad when things didn't go right, no matter what happened and now he can hardly lift his head. Who are we going to go to now, Ted, who? I just can't imagine life without our father, Ted---I can't!"

Ted looked out the barn door for a moment, gathering his own emotions and thoughts. "Jim, we've been through a lot, you and me. Dad is depending on us to bring this farm back, the Wamhoff farm. We have to be strong like he would expect us to be. He taught us well, we know what we have to do. He'll always be there in spirit whether or not he is there physically. I know, I've shed my tears too—I'm just as scared as you are, but together, brother, we will do what we have to. From now on we will count on each other, okay? I love you and I know, together we can do what Dad would want us to do!"

Jimmy wiped the tears from his face and ran his hands through his thick hair. He took a deep breath, and vowed, "I've got to figure out a way to get past what those farmers did to Dad, taking advantage of his generosity and all. It really sticks in my craw! The men who did this will know we remember when they look into our eyes—they will know! I hope they go to hell!"

~~~~~~~~

Four days later: Mary took solace as she stood at the kitchen sink and watched as the first light of the new day spread its warmth and light across the ancient valley. Mary blinked back the tears. *I am so tired, I barely slept last night, listening for John in the other room. How long can he hang on? Please, dear Lord, don't let*

John suffer. He is your lamb, your faithful servant and I know with
all my heart he believes as do I.

Mary heard Jimmy's familiar footsteps on the stairway and
she turned toward the stove. He cracked open the door to his father's
room first and found him sleeping peacefully. The youngest son of
John and Mary Wamhoff walked toward the kitchen—always
conscious of his hip—trying not to limp. "Good morning Mother,
how did you sleep?"

Mary reached up and kissed his scruffy cheek. "Not very
well, but I am used to that, how about you? What is on your agenda
today?"

Jimmy looked over Mary's shoulder as she cracked three
eggs into the frying pan. "Got any of that ham left?" She smiled as
she walked to the icebox and retrieved a couple of slices of ham and
laid them in the hot frying pan. "Do you want any toast this morning
or flapjacks?"

Jimmy smiled up at his mother, "No, I don't think so; just
some coffee with cream will do me fine along with what you are
cooking there." I think Ted and I are going to take a look at the
beans—it might be time to cultivate them and make sure the ditches
between the rows are deep enough. The water is ready to order as
soon as we need it, but with the recent rain, the plants are still green
and growing. We're not going to spend money on ditch water unless
we have to."

"The crops are growing fast now that the days are warmer. I
don't think we are going to even mess with sugar beets this year—
they are a lot of work. For now, Ted and I think we'll stick to what
we know best. I've decided to sell all those chickens to a butcher
shop or grocery stores. I still have almost 800 chickens—it was a
good business for a while, but now the picture has changed and I
don't have time for them."

Mary nodded in agreement. "We can butcher maybe 40-50
and I will preserve the meat in Mason jars. I know your sisters will
pay you for some too. I think that's a good plan to get rid of that
extra burden. We can keep about 30 for their eggs and a rooster so
we have little ones for fryers."

Jimmy grinned as Mary sat his plate in front of him. "Sounds
like a good plan. Ahhhh, Mother---you sure can whip up a good

breakfast. This is superb, as usual. Are you going to join me? I'm sure you need to eat something too."

Mary kissed her youngest son on the cheek and said, "I don't have much of an appetite. I'm going to check on your father. Esther should be here soon to take care of him. Sometimes I feel guilty, that I'm not the one caring for him, but I don't know what to do and he is so big, I can't lift him!"

Jimmy paused and looked up at her, "Mother, Ted, and I decided that we are going to sell the rest of the [22]Percheron draft horses, we have buyers. We have to tighten our belt."

Mary nodded in agreement and walked toward the bedroom where John slept. She opened the door just a crack and saw that he was awake. "Good morning John, did you have a good night?" She walked over to the bed to straighten the bedclothes and bent down to kiss his cheek.

John looked up at her, followed her every movement, he didn't need to speak, Mary could see what he was thinking—see it in his eyes. "Oh John, this is so hard on you, on all of us. I never wanted something like this to happen---I just wish there was something I could do to ease your discomfort. I do want you to know that Ted and Jimmy are doing so well with the farm---you'd be proud of them!"

Esther walked into the room and over to her father's bed. "How is my favorite patient this morning?"

John's face broke into a slight smile as he nodded and in a faint voice said, "I- I'm fine. Good sleep, ha-have to, use damn ur-urinal!"

~~~~~~~~

September 1939: Ted and Jimmy harvested the three fields of Great Northern Beans and they were happy with the better than expected yield. The price for beans had risen over the summer and this was a welcome surprise.

After a day in the fields, the two brothers were walking together, up to the house to tell their father about the good price for beans. Arnold said, "Do you remember when Dad predicted we would have another war? Both France and England have declared war on Germany. That's why the prices for our beans went up and we can also expect higher prices for our grain, just when we need it the most."

Ted grinned and said, "War is awful, I remember some stories Brother Bill told me, but it sure helps us farmers and the good Lord knows we need a bunch of help right now to make ends meet and get out of debt."

Arnold said, "I was going over Dad's ledgers the other night and if we tighten things up, our two farmhands stay on for fewer wages, and the prices for farm products continue to rise, we could be out of debt in five years. We can't buy any new machinery---anything. I'm glad Brother Bill taught us how to fix machinery and keep it moving; that puts money right back in our pockets. We can appreciate Dad buying that Allis Chalmers combine a few years back---that machine's worth its weight in gold! And, we are picking up a few other harvesting jobs—money upfront!"

Jimmy kicked the dirt as they walked, making Ted said, "Okay, what's up with you? It looks like we are going to be able to save the farm and all, but you have a hang-dog look on your face."

Jimmy said, "I think I am in love---and don't laugh—if you do, I'll sock you!"

Ted said, "It's that little Korell gal from Lovell isn't it? She's a cute one and a Lutheran as well."

Jimmy said, "But Ted, what do I have to offer her—a house with peeling paint, a farm that's in debt—and we don't know what is going to happen to Dad. I feel like I am corraled in and I don't have the answers."

Ted slapped his brother on the back, "Jim, perk up. I don't think she is used to a lot---her folks don't have a lot of money either. I would like to give Alleen more things too, but she understands we are in this together. Beata will understand, it'll be good for you to settle down and have a wife."

Jimmy replied, "What about Mother? I don't know what she would do if I brought another woman into the house?"

Ted laughed and said, "She'd put her to work! Now, seriously, we need to get this harvest over with and see what happens with Dad. Everything will work out like it is supposed to, you'll see."

~~~~~~~~

Friday, September 22, 1939: John had a restless night, he was haunted by the way he and Mary had grown apart over the past years He knew he hadn't given her the attention she needed and deserved. *I need to go to Mary, to tell her that I am sorry for not always thinking of her, of not always giving her what she needed. I have to get out of bed-----Mary---.*"

Motivated by sheer will, John slid one leg out of bed and pulled himself to a sitting position. He swung his legs over the edge of the bed and pushed himself up. His whole body shook with the trama of standing. A smile slid over his face as he looked down, his legs were holding him up. He stared at the bedroom door. *One foot out, then slide the other one up next to it. If I can reach the wheelchair, I can go to her.* He lunged for the wheelchair, clinging to the safety of the arms. John swung his body around and collapsed into the safety of the wooden wheelchair. Reaching down and with a supreme effort, he began to push the wheels forward, towards the door. He was sweating profusely from the effort it took to roll the wheelchair. He was ten feet from the door when his world exploded. He fell forward out of the wheelchair and onto the floor of the bedroom. His right arm was extended, reaching for the bedroom door, reaching for his Mary.

~~~~~~~~

Mary rose at dawn to begin her day. She went into the bathroom and closed the door quietly, not to wake John. She went through her familiar morning routine. Lastly, she took the scented powder puff from the amber-colored glass container John had given her for Christmas two years ago and puffed the lovely scent on her neck and bosom.

Looking in the mirror at her reflection, she thought—*The years have not been kind to me—I am as weathered as an old barn. But I would do it all again. It was so difficult, much more than I expected. On the other hand, taking the chance to come to this far place to build our lives together was well worth it, we persevered.* She slid a hairpin into her hair to hold it in place and walked out into the connecting hallway. Mary hesitated at John's door, not wanting to wake him. *I'll just open the door a crack and see if he is awake.* Much to her horror, John was not in bed but was lying on the floor, only feet from the door, in front of his empty wheelchair---his arm outstretched toward the door.

Mary screamed and bent to check John for a pulse. There was none. In a total state of shock, she ran to the bottom of the stairway and screamed, "Arnold, ohhh Arnold, come quick—it's your father!"

Jimmy leaped from bed, pulled on his pants, and flew down the stairs. Mary stood at the bottom of the stairs, her face ashen, and all she could do was—to point at the bedroom floor and the body of John Wamhoff. Arnold bent over his father and rolled him over onto his back. His face was gray and frozen into a grimace from the massive pain which had sucked the life from his body. Jimmy buried his face in his father's chest and sobbed. "Ahhh Dad, Dadddddd!!!" After a few moments, he felt hands pulling him away from his father's body. Ted said, "Jim---come on now. It's over for him, he doesn't hurt anymore. Let's go outside and sit for a bit."

Esther covered her father's body with a sheet then went to her mother's side, taking her pulse and administering a sedative for her. She went into the telephone office to call their Pastor, and then the mortuary in Greybull. She went back into the kitchen where Mary sat alone on a straight-back kitchen chair, staring out of the east window where the morning sun spilled through. Esther put her arms around her mother,

"Mother, I have called Pastor and the mortuary in Greybull. They will be out later this morning to pick Dad up. I'm going to ask Jimmy to call the cemetery, so they can get his plot ready. We need to sit down as a family and decide when to have Dad's funeral. But for now, you rest. It's over Mother, it's over." Esther reached down and gently kissed Mary's forehead and lovingly smoothed her white hair.

~~~~~~~~~

The funeral arrangements were made, the immediate and extended family had been notified, the local newspaper was given the information for the obituary—it was all taken care of. Marie Grabbert came over to ask if she could be of help, as she had done so often in the past. She was like a part of the Wamhoff family. Without being asked or told, she began to clean and clear the

RSDAY SEPTEMBER 28, 19:

WAMHMOFF OF EMBLEM DIES FRIDAY

Pioneer Resident of Tl Section Succumbs Aft Heart Attack.

J. H. Wamhoff, 73, a fine and r spected citizen of the Emblem cor munity, passed away Friday follov ing an heart attack. This well-lov pioneer of this community had bec in ailing health since his first hea attack September 8 of last year. I was stricken again in June of th year. The third attack Frid proved fatal. He had attained tl age of 73 years, seven months ar 28 days at the time of his deat

In 1901 Mr. Wamhoff came Emblem and settled on a farm. I lived on the home place for 39 yea and was a familiar and highly r spected figure in this section.

Thruout his life, Mr. Wamho had interested himself in religio work. In early youth he receiv religious instruction and was co firmed at Fort Wayne, Ind. Wh he was engaged in business in Ge mantown, Nebr. he was elevated position of deacon of the Luther church. When he came to Embl he affiliated with the Luther church, and for many years serv as secretary-treasurer of th church. It was at this church, which he had given generously his time and effort, that fune services were held Monday, wl the Rev. H. A. Bode performing t service.

Martin Oleson, Herman Ahlgri Carsten Jensen, Ernest Moell Herman Werbelow, Herbert Pet son, Adam Pries Sr. and Fred Ma and, long intimate friends of I Wamhoff, were pallbearers. Int ment was made at the Embl church cemetery.

John H. Wamhoff was born Fort Wayne, Ind. January 25, 18 He was the son of Mr. and M Wm. Wamhoff. At 17 years of a he moved to Germantown, Ne where he made his home for tl years. Later he moved to Sewa Nebr. where he was engaged in t furniture and undertaking busine until he moved to Emblem in 19 He was married June 22, 1894. Miss Mary Westerhoff. To them w born nine children. The seco child, a daughter, died in infanc

He leaves to mourn him, his w and eight children—William of S attle, Wash.; Mrs. Wm. Werbelow Emblem, Mrs. Walter Blank Greybull, Mrs. Richard Smith Pratt, Kan., Mrs. James Yates Greybull, Mrs. Merle Prugh of Co Theodore and Arnold of Emble He is also survived by 17 gra children and a half sister at Fr Wayne, Ind.

Mr. Wamhoff had lived a full a interesting life. He made frien easily and kept them. Those w knew him best loved him most. ! was a fine husband and father.

bedroom of the 'hospital' equipment which John Wamhoff had used for almost a year to the day.

Mary directed Jimmy and Ted to put all of the 'hospital' equipment out in the granary—the wheelchair—all of it! *I don't want to ever look at those things again in my life. If I could, I would bury them as well.*

~~~~~~~~~

John Wamhoff's obituary appeared in the next issue of the Greybull Standard on Thursday, September 28th. It was a worthy tribute to a giant of a man. The funeral was held in the Zion Lutheran Church in Emblem where he had faithfully served as secretary-treasurer for many years. Mary was surrounded by her eight children; William (Anna), Seattle, WA.; Ruth (Bill) Werbelow, Emblem; Esther (Walt) Blank, Emblem; Adella Smith (Richard) Pratt, KS.; Marie Yates (James) Greybull; Helen Prugh (Merle) Casper, Wy. ; Theodore (Alleen) Emblem, and Arnold of Emblem.

John Henry Wamhoff's funeral was the largest the community could remember. Cars were parked up and down the road and there was standing room only in the church. The pastor gave a comforting sermon and closed with John's favorite song --- 'Just As I Am Without One Plea'.

After the service, the family gathered in a receiving line, to thank the many people who had taken the time to attend the funeral. Jimmy spotted Beata and her mother. She took his hand as she and her mother walked through the receiving line. "I am so very sorry Jimmy. I do know how hard this has been on you. I only wish I could have met your father before he passed away. We are going to go on home now---you and your family have guests to attend to." Jimmy gave a little grin and said, "I appreciate you coming all this way to the funeral, it means a lot to me, Beata. I will call you, sometime in the next couple of weeks when things settle down. Thanks again."

~~~~~~~~~

The folks gathered in their cars, turning their lights on for the journey to the cemetery. One by one, they followed the hearse over the dusty dirt road, to the Emblem cemetery, the cemetery John had helped plan and establish. It was still prairie dirt, cactus, and sagebrush, but there were plans to fence it and plant grass, someday when there was extra money. The family stood close around the

Courtesy: Arnold Wamhoff

grave as the Pastor spoke the final words. Then, it was over for Mary Wamhoff and her family, as a new chapter in their life began.

~~~~~~~~~~

It took several days for Jimmy to get up the courage or will to visit his father's grave by himself. He had idolized his father---to him he had been a giant of a man, a true Christian, a man who would give his neighbor the shirt off his back; Jimmy had seen him do just that, time and time again. It was no secret John Wamhoff lived life large, he enjoyed a good pint of beer and a fine Cuban cigar. He had been eternally proud and grateful for his family---they were the reason he worked so hard. He wanted to leave a legacy, wanted his life to stand for good things, wanted to leave his mark, and this---- he accomplished.

Jimmy knelt, alone, beside the grave as the dam holding back his grief broke and the tears rolled down his face. *My father's body lies beneath that mound of dirt, he is gone from this earth! Ahhhh, Dad—Dad, I loved you so much, learned so much from you. My life was blessed having had you for my father and I know if it hadn't been for you and Mother, I would never have walked again after that accident. I'm sorry I didn't want to be an accountant or banker like you thought best---I wanted to be like you—a farmer, a businessman. I'm going to miss you every day and I vow that we will bring the Wamhoff place back! Ted and I have a mountain to climb to keep the farm, but then, you had taught us how to climb mountains!* Jimmy put his finger to his lips and touched the headstone.

John Henry Wamhoff, 1866 - 1939

Epilogue

THE REST OF THE STORY

NOTE: 1940: *Wamhoff Brothers Partnership* was legally established between Ted and Arnold Wamhoff after the death of their father. They took responsibility for all farm operations and the debt associated with the Wamhoff farm. Arnold took possession of the home on the original farm where he and his mother lived. Ted and Alleen and their two children lived across the orchard from the main farm. Their work was cut out for them and they dove in, headfirst!

During the next two years, they were able to make the first two payments on the debt owed the bank, with a little leftover, enough for Jimmy to make a downpayment on an engagement ring. Mary earned her own money from running the telephone switchboard and kept plenty busy with her garden and canning. Everything and everyone had settled into a routine—a new lifestyle.

~~~~~~~~~~

Over breakfast one morning, Mary said, "Arnold, I think I would like to convert what was once the post office storage room, there behind the switchboard room, into a small bedroom for myself. That way you could move downstairs into the back bedroom. No sense you sleeping upstairs all by yourself like that. We've moved all the furniture back into the parlor like it was before your father passed away. It's just you and me in the house. We can close those upper bedrooms off and save heat. I'd be near to the kitchen and telephone---what do you think about the change?"

Jimmy thought for a minute, then said, "I think that sounds very sensible, Mother—good thinking. We all want to save any place we can."

Mary added, "Oh, I also talked to the banker the other day when we were in town. I've decided to sell a few acres of land down by the airport that your father deeded to me. I will use the money to buy a modest house in Greybull. I saw a gyp-block two-bedroom house on the corner of 4th and Greybull Avenue—they have lowered the price and I like the location, right there on the main highway. I am going to rent it to Esther and Walt for now; but when I move into Greybull, after I retire from the telephone business, I will have a place to live. It has an apartment upstairs that I can rent as well. I have had some ideas about starting up a tourist 'rooms to rent' business. That house would be perfect, nice location on the corner of the main highway. I won't live out on the farm forever, especially after you marry. It's simply not my life anymore."

Arnold blushed at the thought of his girl, "Well, Mother, it sounds like you have been thinking of the future. It sounds like a fine idea, I'm sure Dad would have approved. We'll have to wait to see what the future holds for all of us. I have been thinking of asking Beata to marry me, but I can't afford a wife yet. How would you feel with me bringing my wife to live in this house?"

Mary smiled and threw her arms around her youngest son. "Well now, I 'spect that will mean I don't have to cook or clean anymore ---it will be Beata's house! She is a lovely girl and I would welcome her with open arms. And, I might add, it's about time you marry and settle down!"

~~~~~~~

Spring 1941: On Good Friday, Jimmy took extra pains getting ready. He took a bath and washed his hair. He had such thick wavy hair that it was uncontrollable after he washed it and he usually wore one of his sister's hairnets to settle it into place while it dried. This was going to be a big day---he had special plans after church that nobody knew about.

Driving across the winding road over to Lovell, Jimmy was distracted. He kept thinking about how he was going to pop the question and when he would give Beata the ring he had in his pocket. He pulled up outside their small house on Shoshone Avenue and parked the car. Jimmy climbed out, slammed the car door, and walked up to the front door. He knocked on the door and stood waiting. He had this nervous habit where he would run his fingers up through his hair. At that moment--- to his horror, he felt the hairnet still on his head!! Just in time he pulled the hairnet off and shoved it into his pocket.

Beata opened the door and gave him a quick kiss. She had been looking out the window, waiting for him to drive up, and had seen the hairnet when he walked up to the door. It was all she could do, not to burst out laughing.

All through the church service, Jimmy was fidgeting until Beata gave him an elbow in the ribs. Finally, the service was over and they were back in the car. Jimmy drove back down Shoshone Drive, but he didn't stop at her house, instead, he drove up on the hilltop and parked the car.

Beata said, "Mom is expecting us for supper—we should be getting back."

Jimmy reached into his pocket, "Well, I thought you might want to be wearing this engagement ring when we go back to the house. Will you marry me, Beata?"

~~~~~~~~~~

Jimmy and Beata agreed on an early fall wedding, at St. John's Lutheran Church in Lovell. "Ted and I will be working all summer making sure we have a good crop and I need time to harvest the beans and grain in the fall. I think the end of September will be just fine."

Beata smiled up at her fiancée, "I think that will be perfect and I'd love a fall wedding—the trees and everything are so pretty then. It also gives Mom and me time to make my dress and the bridesmaid's dresses. There is so much to do, but you leave it all up to me—I will handle the wedding plans while you are busy making a living. You know that my parents like you—I think Mom's got a crush on you. She says you look like Robert Taylor the movie star."

Jimmy laughed and said, "I think your mother is a very smart woman!"

Jimmy said, "You make me so happy. We are going to have a good life, you and me!"

~~~~~~~~~~

Arnold/Jimmy Wamhoff and Beata Korell were married on the 28th of September 1941, on a beautiful fall day. Beata's dress was simple, a 'V' neck, white net formal with lace appliques, and short lace sleeves with a wide satin belted bow. Her headdress was a crown of seed pearls and she carried ivory and peach roses. Following a short honeymoon in Billings, Montana, they drove back to the farm to begin their life together.

Jimmy and his bride drove down the lane of cottonwood trees to the Wamhoff farm where they would spend most of their married life. Beata said, "Oh, I can't believe that we are married—I have dreamed of this day, of driving up to this big white house—our house. I am so happy and I will try very hard not to poison you with my cooking!"

They walked up to the back door together and he held the door open for her. Inside the house, Beata turned a complete circle, "Oh my word—it's all been painted, it's beautiful, so fresh and pretty!"

Jimmy smiled and said, "My mother and sisters wanted to do that for you. A bride should have at least newly painted walls. We will get to the outside next year!"

~~~~~~~~~

December 7, 1941: It was a Sunday morning and the second generation of Wamhoff's were having a leisurely breakfast before church services. They had gotten into the habit of having the little countertop Philco radio turned on while they were eating--- especially at noon, so Jimmy could listen to the farm news. But this morning, they heard something entirely different, and unexpected. The Japanese had bombed Pearl Harbor, Hawaii! The first count noted thousands of dead Americans, but several destroyers escaped the harbor and had made it out to the safety of the open sea.

Mary, Jimmy, and Beata were all in shock as they listened to the newscaster. Mary said, "Arnold, isn't Sister Ruth's son, Louis on a destroyer---I think he said it was the Monaghan or something like that?"

Jimmy's face grew pale, "I think you are right Mother, we need to call Ruth and Bill. I am sure they will know. I bet you a bottom's dollar President Roosevelt will declare war. This is the last straw—I didn't think we even considered the Japanese as an enemy—not like we do Germany. That will be next, mark my words. We are just another bomb away from declaring war on Germany too and then folks, we will be in another world war!"

Mary called her daughter Ruth, who confirmed that indeed their son Louis was on the Monaghan destroyer in the Pacific. Minutes later, Mary walked back into the kitchen. "They have had word from Louis, and yes—he is on that ship, one of those that escaped. As far as they know he is safe, somewhere out in the Pacific Ocean."

~~~~~~~

August 10, 1942: Beata and Arnold became parents to their first daughter, Karen. After the birth of her first child, Beata stayed at her parent's home in Lovell for three weeks, then she and her new-born daughter went home to the farm in Emblem. Mary was thrilled to have a new baby in the house again and was a great help to Beata, who knew little to nothing about caring for a newborn.

The Wamhoff Brothers were doing well---with the war on they got top dollar for their crops and paid off their father's debt faster than expected. That fall they had enough money left over to buy a new Chevrolet truck—their old 1935 truck was on its last leg and falling apart!

~~~~~~~

January 5, 1944: Mary sorted through the mail sack which the 'stage' had just delivered from the Greybull post office. She picked up a postcard and looked at the address. It was addressed to

Mr. and Mrs. William Werbelow and was from their son Louis who was still on the Monoghan destroyer in the Pacific Ocean. Mary couldn't help herself and read it. It was a 'standard form' postcard, simply stating that 'I have received your letter. I am well' and signed by Louis Carl Werbelow. 2/8/44. Mary shook her head and thought—*I don't know what it is—a feeling that Louis isn't coming home.*

~~~~~~~

January 9, 1945: WESTERN UNION: *TO MR AND MRS AND WILLIAM FRED WERBELOW ---EMBLEM WYO*

THE NAVY DEPARTMENT DEEPLY REGRETS TO INFORM YOU THAT YOUR SON LOUIS CARL WERBELOW SECOND CLASS USN IS MISSING WHILE IN THE SERVICE OF HIS COUNTRY. THE DEPARTMENT APPRECIATES YOUR GREAT ANXIETY BUT DETAILS NOT NOW AVAILABLE AND DELAY IN RECEIPT THEREOF MUST OF NECESSITY BE EXPECTED TO PREVENT POSSIBLE AID TO OUR ENEMIES/ PLEASE DO NOT DIVULGE THE NAME OF HIS SHIP OR STATION/

VICE ADMIRAL RANDAL JACOBS
CHIEF OF NAVAL PERSONNEL, 315.AM

Bill and Ruth were beside themselves with worry, waiting for word of any kind was excruciating. Weeks, then months went by without any word from the Navy. THEN – another telegram came:

WASHINGTON DC 1233AM FEB 22^{ND,} 1945
MR. AND MRS WILLIAM FRED WERBELOW - EMBLEM WYO.

THE NAVY DEPARTMENT DEEPLY REGRETS TO INFORM YOU THAT A CAREFUL REVIEW OF ALL THE FACTS AVAILABLE TO THE DISAPPEARANCE OF YOUR SON LOUIS CARL WERBELOW YEOMAN SECOND CLASS USN PREVIOUSLY REPORTED MISSING LEADS TO THE CONCLUSION THAT THERE IS NO HOPE FOR HIS

SURVIVAL AND THAT HE LOST HIS LIFE AS A RESULT OF SHIP DISASTER DURING TYPHOON 18 DEC 1944 WHILE IN THE SERVICE OF HIS COUNTRY IF ADDITIONAL INFORMATION IS RECEIVED IT WILL BE FORWARDED TO YOU PROMPTLY SINCERE SYMPATHY IS EXTENDED TO YOU IN YOUR GREAT SORROW
> *VICE ADMIRAL RANDALL JACOBS*
> *CHIEF OF NAVAL PERSONNEL 627AM*

April 12, 1945: *Franklin D. Roosevelt, President of the United States for the last 12 years, died at 1:05 p.m. today at Warm Springs, Georgia.*

May 8, 1945: World War II officially ended in Europe. The Japanese refused to surrender until August 15th after the United States dropped toxic bombs on two major cities; then, IT WAS OVER.

Louis Carl Werbelow U.S. Navy
Dec. 11, 1920 - Dec. 18, 1944
Age: 24

Memorial Services were held for Louis Werbelow at the Zion Lutheran Church in Emblem in May 1945. Rev. Ralph Temme delivered a moving message. The American Legion of Greybull presented Ruth and Bill with the American flag.

July 27, 1945: After thirty-one years of operating the telephone switchboard at Emblem, Mary felt that it was time she moved on. It was becoming difficult for her to keep the hours that the switchboard demanded; and besides that, Arnold and Beata needed their own space with their growing family. *I have never lived in a real town with sidewalks except for Germantown and those were wooden. I have some good ideas of just how I am going to support myself. I can't depend on Arnold and Ted for the rest of my life. I have land I can sell if I need to and I have given it a lot of thought. Philippians' chapter four, verse eleven keeps popping into my head:' For I have learned, in whatsoever state I am, therewith to be content.'*

Telephone pioneer retires after 31 years of service

EMBLEM, July 27, 1945 — After 31 years of faithful service, Mrs. Mary Wamhoff has retired from her duties as Emblem telephone operator..

Mrs. Wamhoff took over the management of the Emblem office in 1914 at which time it was moved from the Germania Store, run by H.D. Beuhner and the late Henry Wagner, to the Wamhoff ranch. From that time it has been run under her constant care, always ready and willing to give her community 24-hour service on long distance and local calls alike.

Many sheep and cattle men and farmers have placed thousands of long distance calls to all parts of the United States. Anxious fathers and mothers have depended on her getting the doctor at all times of day or night. Mrs. Wamhoff has the reputation of always being there with a willing, cheerful voice to place calls for everyone.

During any emergency, as when a house or barn caught fire, she never grumbled at the extra work it entailed, but was always there to do all she could to help in an emergency.

Much credit and appreciation are due her for her years of service to the community.

Mrs. Wamhoff has recently purchased a home in Greybull where she plans to make her future home.

Mary packed up her few belongings and said goodbye to the large white farmhouse in which she and John had raised their family for so many years. It was time to go and she looked forward to a new life, new opportunities, new challenges.

On the morning of her big move into town, Mary walked into the kitchen where breakfast was on the table. "Good morning, it looks like another beautiful day." She pulled out a chair and took her place at the table. "I can stay until the canning is done if you need me, Beata, but I went to the bank the other day and sold a few more acres of the land I own on Airport Bench. I am going to continue to rent the house on the corner of North 4th and Greybull Avenue to Esther and Walt. I have that as well as rent money from the upstairs apartment. That gives me a good income right there. When Esther is ready to move, I will sell the new house I am moving into and move into that house on the corner so I can start my 'tourist rooms' business.

Jimmy looked with amazement at his mother, "Well look at you, the wheeling-dealing businesswoman. That was a very smart decision and move on your part Mother. We have loved having you live with us, but we understand that you certainly need your privacy and deserve to move on with your life as you want."

Grandma Mary and Karen
Courtesy: Karen Schutte

~~~~~~~~~

NOTE: *Mary Wamhoff lived in the house on the east end of North 4th street for about two years then sold it. She moved into her two-bedroom gyp blockhouse at 544 4th Avenue North, where she ran her successful 'tourist rooms to rent' business for many years until a new business called motels, began to spring up in Greybull.*

When she had some spare time, she enjoyed visits from her many grandchildren and sitting in her rocking chair on the front porch, watching cars go by as she crocheted yet another doily for her grandchildren. She commented that her rocking chair was like a comfortable, familiar, old friend. It was where she could relax and bask in the rhythm of her new life leaving the familiar hectic rhythms of her former life behind. After 1954, her health took a turn for the worse and she couldn't get around without a wheelchair. Mary Elizabeth Wamhoff died at her daughter, Marie's breakfast table in September of 1963. She was 87 years old and had lived an amazing, full life. She was proud to be one of the founding members of the Zion Lutheran Church and the settlement they called GERMANIA. She was greatly loved and respected by her family. Mary was laid to rest beside her husband John, in the Emblem Cemetery.

In 1963, when Mary passed away, John and Mary Wamhoff's legacy counted twenty-six grandchildren and seventy-three great-grandchildren.

~~~~~~~~

1946 to 1958: The Wamhoff Brothers partnership decided to raise registered Black Angus cattle as a supplement to their row crops. Arnold recalled: *We were young guys and that was big business in those days. We thought that we were real big shots the first time we went to Billings and bought eight head of registered black Angus cows and one bull. I think we paid $150 apiece for them. That was a lot of money for us then.*

~~~~~~~~

It was Ted's night to milk the cows and he had almost finished when Jimmy walked into the barn. "You better get a move on, it's getting dark outside and you have to walk across that pasture, but I guess you have a path across it, and at your age, aren't afraid of the Boogie Man!"

Ted set his milk buckets aside, careful not to spill any as he released the cows into the corral for the night. "Say, Jim, I was thinking, why don't we load that ornery Ayrshire bull in the truck next time we go up to Billings to the stockyards and sell that critter.

He about got me again tonight and I hate that 'Beller' he has—I never heard a bull moo that loud and so high pitched, it sends chills up my back! "

Jimmy scratched his head and said, "Well, I suppose we can, that or the slaughter yard. But, it's up to you to get him in the back of that truck!"

Ted said, "Okay then, I better get this milk home to Alleen before it gets too dark. Have a good night, see you tomorrow—we have to get that east forty plowed."

Jim watched Ted open and close the fence/gate to the pasture and pick up the buckets of milk then start across. It was pitch black when Jimmy slipped under the fence and followed the path that Ted took across the pasture to his house. He picked his steps carefully and silently. Ted was strolling through the pasture, singing softly to himself, when Jimmy snuck right up behind his brother and let out the most God awful, high-pitched beller he could muster.

Ted jumped three feet into the air and the buckets of milk went with him, at least some of the milk did. When his feet hit the ground, he was running as fast and hard as he could with visions of that white Ayrshire bull fast on his tail. THEN, he heard Jimmy laughing his head off, somewhere in the dark. "It wasn't the Boogie Man, but the thought of that bull coming after you in the dark put the fear in you for sure! That WAS the funniest thing I have ever seen. Now, we are even for all the mean 'Boogie Man' tricks you used to play on me! Have a good night, Brother!"

Ted kicked one of the empty milk buckets and wiping milk off his face shouted into the darkness, "Go ahead and think what you want to think—you never know when that Boogie Man is lurking in the dark!"

~~~~~~~~~

In 1950 Arnold and Beata remodeled the old farmhouse adding a newly renovated kitchen and modernizing the lower level with large picture windows. They tore off the old post office/ telephone rooms and made a covered front patio with brick flower planters and a brick fishpond. In 1954 they doubled their family of two daughters with the birth of twin daughters, this meant remodeling the two upstairs bedrooms and adding another bathroom. In 1958 Wamhoff Brothers Partnership was dissolved. Arnold kept the home place/house and 160 acres and Ted took sole possession of the original farm (160) acres across the highway. There he built a spacious brick home for his growing family. Shortly after Ted's death, his youngest daughter Sue Carole, and her husband Bob Coguill, bought that farm. She lives on the farm to this day, the 'last Wamhoff in Emblem.'

In 1999, Arnold and Beata sold out and moved to their retirement home in Powell. Arnold died in 2003, and to date, Beata is alive and thriving in a Powell nursing home, she celebrated her 100th birthday, on November 28, 2020.

IT WAS, A FAR PLACE.........BUT A GOOD PLACE!

CREDITS/ACKNOWLEDGEMENTS:

<u>Lylas Skovgard</u> --- **BASIN CITY,** The First Country Seat in the Bighorn Basin.

<u>Bill Sniffin</u> –**WYOMING AT 125 – Our Place in the West.**

<u>Tom Davis</u> – **GLIMPSES OF GREYBULL & THEY CALLED IT GERMANIA.**

<u>Greybull Standard</u> – Many thanks for the photos and news articles over the years.

<u>Jeannie Edwards Cook</u> - **WILEY'S DREAM OF EMPIRE – The Wiley Irrigation Project.**

<u>100 YEARS OF GOD'S BLESSINGS</u> – **Zion Lutheran Church—Emblem, Wyoming 1899-1999 - compiled** by the Centennial Book Committee.

<u>HOME IN THE VALLEY</u> – **Powell's 1st Century by Bonner and Churchill.**

<u>Sue Wamhoff Coguill (Ted):</u> The favorite cousin I grew up with—was instrumental in collaborating on my memories and the part her family played in this story.

<u>Robert and Martha Werbelow (Ruth):</u> Martha and the late Bob Werbelow put together a wonderful history of the family of Ruth (Wamhoff) and Bill Werbelow.

<u>The Bill and Anna Wamhoff Family</u>: Permission was given to use the love letters.

ACKNOWLEDGMENTS
FOR EDITING

Todd W. Schutte: The second-born son of Mike and Karen Schutte, Todd is a graduate of the University of Wyoming with a Bachelor's degree in Finance. While in college, Todd served as president of Sigma Alpha Epsilon. Currently, he is the director of Global Learning for Bona AB(Sweden); he also serves as the event chair for the St. Jude Walk/Run – Denver, where they've helped raise hundreds of thousands of dollars for that heartfelt charity. He and his wife Julie are the parents of a daughter and three sons and reside in Parker, CO. (*As a child, my brothers and I were frequent visitors to the Wamhoff family farm where many adventures played out in the barns, fields, and riding the three-wheeler. The best was when we helped Papa Jimmy drive the tractors and set the irrigation pipes, we also loved Grandma Bea's cooking!*)

Nancy Hansford holds a degree from UC Davis and Colorado State University. She is a Fort Collins resident and a longtime freelance writer, publisher of a local magazine, **Business World**, and author of two titles, ***Fort Collins Highlights*** and ***Northern Colorado Ghost Stories***. As a local author's columnist for the Coloradoan, she has supported outstanding local authors for many years.

END NOTES

1 Union Pacific Railroad: Originated in Council Bluffs, Iowa running to Omaha, Nebraska. In 1900, Nebraska was covered with an ample network of independent railroads, all linking up to the Union Pacific. The B & M Railroad from Lincoln was the first loop link that ran through Germantown, NE.

2 Lutheran Missionary August Wunderlich: Pastor Wunderlich served the state of Nebraska from his main office, in Omaha. In 1899 he met a man by the name of **Solon Wiley** on the train from Billings, MT, to Hemingford, Nebraska (north of Scottsbluff). Wiley lost no time in convincing Pastor Wunderlich of the wonderful opportunity/project to be had in the Bighorn Basin of Wyoming.

3 1862 Homestead Act: This law encouraged settlement of the land west of the Mississippi River. It permitted any citizen, 21 or older to lay claim to 160 acres. Requirements: live on the land for five years, improve it, build a house and outbuildings and the land would be theirs for a standard fee.

NOTE: Lands to be irrigated were segregated out of the homestead lands---title to them was gained through the "Carey Act" which provided for a certain portion of the acreage to be irrigated---and payment made to the canal developer---Solon Wiley. Landholders had the option to buy shares in the canal--$640 for each 40-acre share. Those who couldn't come up with the money signed a mortgage with Wiley. Many of the German settlers paid for their stock by actually working on the canal. From the date of filing, the homesteader had six months to establish a residence. They had to live on the land for five years before getting a free title. Civil War veterans were given a better incentive of one year. (In 1912 Congress reduced the amount of time homesteaders had to live on their farm and prove it up, from five to three years. The maximum homesteading claim was increased to 640 acres of grazing land in areas not suitable for irrigation.)

4 North Platte River: a major tributary of the Platte River it is about 717 miles long and traveling over 550 miles. It winds its course through Colorado, Wyoming, and Nebraska to join the South Platte River near North Platte, Nebraska. The Platte River flows into

Missouri and then the Mississippi River. It was widely used during the emigration trails to the west as well as by early trappers.

5 Bighorn Basin: This scenic and geologically diverse basin lies directly to the east of Yellowstone National Park. The rolling hills, badland buttes, and ravines are covered with sagebrush and buffalo grass. The 125-mile wide geologic basin is surrounded by mountains---the Bighorns to the east, Pryors to the northeast, Absarokas to the west (Rocky Mountains), Beartooths to the northwest, Owl and Copper mountains to the south. For over 10,000 years, Indian tribes had lived and hunted in the valleys and mountains of this region. A treaty with the Indians in 1868 established this entire region as strictly Indian land. In 1878, the Bighorn Basin officially opened for settlement. Buffalo hunters & trappers came first, followed by cattle and sheepmen as ranches and frontier towns sprang up. In 1896, Bighorn County separated from Fremont County, and Basin City became the first county seat.

6 Ferry Crossings, 1901: Earlier emigrants took note of the excessive number of expensive and excessive ferry crossings of the North Plate River. Drownings were common with horses and cattle attempting to swim across in the swift current. Child's Crossing Cutoff eliminated many of these crossings. After crossing the North Platte River at Ft. Laramie, they didn't cross again until they reach Ft. Casper, Wyoming. It was common to see 50 – 100 wagons waiting their turn to cross via ferry, which could take fifty wagons across in a day.

7 Wolton: In 1901, Wolton was a bustling sheep station with a hotel, post office, and railroad station. Local sheep ranchers drove their sheep to Wolton to have them dipped at the Cooper Dipping Plant, sheared, and shipped back east to sell. The wool was taken by freighter wagons to Casper for sale. In 1914, the new Burlington Railroad line from Billings to Casper bypassed Wolton, cutting through the treacherous Wind River Canyon. The town was moved to a new location called Arminto. In 1925, the Wolton post office was renamed---Hiland!

8 Sheep----in Wyoming: The Dingley Act of 1897 created a boom in sheep production compared to cattle. By 1900, there were over 712,500 sheep in Wyoming; and, by 1908, six million sheep covered the hills as the state led the nation in wool production at a value of $32 million—topping the beef industry. Due to a new tariff law—the Payne-Aldrich Tariff Act of 1914, the number of sheep dropped by forty percent. Wyoming had more trouble between cattlemen and sheepmen than any other state.

9 Bighorn River: This main river artery flows north from the Wind River Canyon in the southern part of Wyoming, across the Bighorn Basin - a major tributary feeding into the Missouri River in Montana. The Greybull and Shoshone Rivers originate in the Absaroka Range, to the west, and flow east through the Basin to drain into the Bighorn River.

10 Wiley Project: Solon Wiley was an educated, hydraulic engineer, an ambitious visionary, and a risk-taker. He invested heavily in his vision of the immense possibilities of the Bighorn Basin and its development. In the end, he lost over $600,000 of his personal fortune on the Wiley Project. The Germania section of the Wiley Project was the only portion to survive.

11 Wether: A neutered, mature male sheep, kept in the flock for their wool **11**

12 Two-Span Howe Truss Bridge: These bridges were owned and used by the CB&Q Railroad. They were easily converted for use as a vehicular bridge. The truss bridges were built using a combination of timber and iron. The bridge's biggest advantage was that it could be moved wherever it was needed.

13 Black Fritz Moeller: There were two farmers living on the Germania Bench by the name of Fritz Moeller. One was blond and kindly—White Fritz, while the other had wild black hair, a large black handlebar mustache, and piercing dark eyes—he was called 'Black Fritz'---and he was more than a bit strange.

14 Pitchers: This term refers to men who used pitchforks to pitch or throw the straw/ hay up onto a hayrack or a haystack. At first, they used wooden pitchforks; later switching to more efficient metal forks with a wooden handle and sharp metal prongs.

15 Bay City Dredge: In 1914, the Bench Canal Drainage District used this massive machine to dig ditches up and down the benchland, to drain the boggy land. Digging drain ditches over Germania was a phenomenal, but necessary feat. The Dredge was an odd-looking machine—something like a dinosaur; originally used in the mining industry to dig upriver beds.

16 Lycoming Engine: The engine was developed for automobile engines in a market-driven by a nation at war. The first Lycoming R-680, 9 cylinders, 200 hp piston-driven radial engine was developed for general aviation. The Dort automobile used a Lycoming aircraft engine. It was founded by William C. Durant and J. Dallas Dort in 1886. In 1926, Dort was the country's 13th largest automobile producer and was based in Flint, Michigan. The company ceased manufacturing in the recession that followed.

17 World War I: The United States entered this 'war to end all wars, originating in Europe, July 28, 1914. On June 26, 1917, over 14,000 American men went to France to train with the French in the art of trench warfare. When the war ended on November 11, 1918, more than two million American soldiers had served on the Western Front battlefields. It was estimated that some 50,000 Americans lost their lives in the war.

18 1930 Drought or Dust Bowl: The worst-hit area was the Great Plains (1917-1940), where the homesteaders had plowed up the prairie grass that previously held the soil—leaving it barren and vulnerable to the wind. The wind picked up the soil, tumbleweeds, and people's livelihood in gigantic clouds of rolling soil. It ruined thousands of farms, ending their existence in bankruptcy. Thousands of displaced Americans packed the Model T and moved off the farms to sharecrop, pick fruit, any odd jobs they could find. Their land was worth nothing.

19 1931 Chevrolet: In 1927, Chevrolet took over the spot in U.S. car sales when Ford shut down its lines early to convert to the Model A. That was also a milestone year for Chevrolet with its first annual output of more than one million vehicles. Ford took the sales lead again in 1929 and 1930; and then Chevrolet bounded back to first place in the depression year of 1931, with the Chevrolet Independence Series AE.

20 Combine/harvester: In 1937, the major combine producers were: Allis-Chalmers, Massey-Harris, International Harvester, Gleaner Manufacturing, Minneapolis Moline, and John Deere.

21 1938 Three-wheel wheelchair: Around 2001, John Wamhoff's wheelchair was spotted in the corner of Wamhoff's granary (by the author). President Franklin Roosevelt used this same style of the wheelchair during his time in the Whitehouse. By design, it can recline with a third wheel in the back.

22 Percheron draft horses: This French-bred draft horse is usually gray dapple or black. These powerful workhorses have chests that are wide and deep with a short and straight back, powerful front legs, and wide, muscular haunches. The buttocks are low—tail high, with a supple and light gait. The head has a square, wide forehead; long, thin ears; a fine straight nose, and wide nostrils. The average height is between 14.3 to 16 hands. They are a massive, well-behaved workhorse. Most are not ridden because their backs are so wide.

READER QUOTES CRITIQUE:

Nancy Hansford: Y*ou have compiled an amazing volume of research and family stories to produce a very interesting manuscript. Your characters are well developed and interesting, and ones the reader can become involved with. Good work. Your epilogue or wrapup of the loose ends is good.*

Todd Schutte: *Well Done! Personally, I learned so much more about my grandparents and great-grandparents and the vast history of the family farm and of Wyoming. The story was easy to get caught up in, the characters are complex and interesting. It's sad that today, there is just a footprint of what was.*

ABOUT THE AUTHOR

Karen Wamhoff Schutte was raised on the Wamhoff family farm, homesteaded by her paternal grandparents, John and Mary Wamhoff in Emblem, Wyoming. She was the first-born daughter of Arnold and Beata Wamhoff, and oldest of their four daughters. For the first eight years of her elementary education, she attended the two-room schoolhouse in Emblem, built by her grandfather John. She attended Greybull High School, graduating in 1960, then on to the University of Wyoming for two years. She dropped out of college to marry Michael Schutte of Greybull, over the next ten years, they had four sons. In 1984, she re-enrolled in the University, graduating in 1987 with a bachelor's degree in Design/Marketing. Karen was a professional A.S.I.D Interior Designer for the next twenty-five years in both commercial and residential design. In 2004, after retirement, she reinvented herself and became a successful historical author, writing six books based on her maternal and paternal German background. Her work has received numerous, prestigious awards over the years including The PEN Award and a three-time winner of Wyoming Historical Societies' *Best Historical Fiction of the year*.

~~~~~~~~~

My books are classified as Historical Fiction but are based on true stories. None of us could possibly know everything thing a character said or did. I take what I know from family stories and combined with what I have learned from extensive historical research, I blend it with my imagination. When I sit down to write, I am 'in' the story—I feel it happening to me, which gives me great insight as to the rhythm and emotion of the story. I feel a profound responsibility and honor to be able to tell the stories of sacrifice, of dedicated determination and faith, of unbelievable life experiences, even persecution during war time with Germamy, which my family experienced in order to live in this country. I am a second generation German American and am most grateful to my ancestors for everything they did so we might live in this great country. I grew up knowing Mary Westerhoff Wamhoff and spending many memorable days with her. She was a wonderful grandmother and I cherish the time I had with her. My grandfather, John Wamhoff died four years before I was born; I remember hearing the many stories about this remarkable man.

*If you want to learn more about Germania/Emblem, Wyoming, read Tom Davis' book—(**They Called it Germania**) as well as Jeannie Cook's book—(**The Wiley's Dream of Empire**).*

Emblem, Wyoming was such a special place to grow up—there were about 50-60 farms scattered over the Bench. Now there are four! The mechanics and markets of farming have changed dramatically as a result of the evolution of farming and the machinery. This is what has compelled me to consider writing one more novel—BAREFOOT UNDER THE COTTONWOODS. I plan to write it in first person—it will be 'my' story of growing up in '2nd generation Emblem community'---all of the ways we found to have fun, the long days in the fields, swimming in the canals, riding horses in the hills, ice skating on natural sping flows out in the hills. It was a life so foreign to what most children know today. It was a life of innocence centered around family and the church—a fading lifestyle.

Thank you for reading my books, and for those who have taken the time to write, call, and message me with your amazing insights and compliments regarding my stories. As long as you want to read what I write, I will keep on.